GREAT BIBLE TRUTHS

A Bible Reader

English Edition
THE WORLD ENGLISH BIBLE

Published by Ephesians 3:20 Publishing
4180 44th Street Suite A
Grand Rapids, Michigan 49512

Copyright ©2018 Ephesians 3:20 Publishing
General Editors:
John DeVries, Bert Block
Bert Block (Spanish Version)
Terry Slachter

Cover and Interior Design:
JR Underhill Communications, Kalamazoo, MI
Cover illustration based on a photo of Earth sunrise as seen from outer space

We acknowledge with gratitude the use of the
The World English Bible (WEB) which is a Public Domain,
Modern English translation of the Holy Bible.
The World English Bible is based upon the American Standard
Version of the Holy Bible first published in 1901.

GREAT BIBLE TRUTHS
Table of Contents

PART ONE: SELECTIONS FROM THE OLD TESTAMENT
I GOD CREATES THE WORLD

		Page No.
1. The Creation of Man	Genesis 1 and 2:1-9, 15-25	11
2. The Rebellion	Genesis 3	14
3. The First Murder	Genesis 4:1-16	15
4. The Worldwide Flood	Genesis 6:5-22 and 7	16
5. The First Rainbow	Genesis 8 and 9:8-19	18
6. The First Metropolis	Genesis 11:1-9	20

II GOD FORMS A NATION
A. THE PROMISE OF GOD

7. The Miracle Baby	Genesis 12:1-7; 15:1-6; 17:1-5; 18:1-15; 21:1-7	22
8. A Man of Faith	Genesis 22:1-18	24
9. The Chosen Bride	Genesis 24:1-38, 49-52, 57-67	25
10. The Stolen Blessing	Genesis 25:19-34 ; 27:1-37, 41-45	28
11. The Ladder to Heaven	Genesis 28:10-22	30

B. THE FAVOR OF GOD

12. The Evil Deed	Genesis 37:1-14, 17-36	31
13. A Good Man	Genesis 39 and 40	33
14. The King's Dreams	Genesis 41:14-41	36
15. Joseph Is Vindicated	Genesis 42:1-29	37
16. The Happy Ending	Genesis 45:1-28	39

C. THE DELIVERANCE OF GOD

17. Egypt Enslaves Israel	Exodus 1:1-22	41
18. God Calls Israel's First Leader	Exodus 2:1-25	42
19. Holy Ground	Exodus 3:1-22 and 4:1-17	43
20. The Death Plague	Exodus 12:1-13, 21-42	46
21. Free at Last	Exodus 14:5-31	48

D. ISRAEL AND THE WILDERNESS EXPERIENCE

22. Bread from Heaven	Exodus 15:22-27; 16:1-35	50
23. The Laws of God	Deuteronomy 5:1-33	53

E. THE BLESSINGS OF GOD

24. Blessing and Curse	Deuteronomy 6:1-19, 28:1-6, 15-19	55
25. Plan for Prosperity	Deuteronomy 30:1-20	56
26. The Dry River	Joshua 1:1-11; 3:1-17	58
27. The March of Victory	Joshua 6:1-21	59
28. Joshua's Challenge to Israel	Joshua 23:1-16; 24:14-28	61

F. THE MEN OF GOD		Page No.
29. The Judges	Judges 2:6-23	63
30. The Boy Prophet	1 Samuel 1:1-28; 2:18-26; 3:1-21	65
31. The Shepherd King	1 Samuel 15:17-29; 16:1-13	68
32. Killing a Giant	1 Samuel 17:1-54	69
33. The Coming King	2 Samuel 5:1-10 and 7:8-29	72

III. GOD REVEALS HIS WAYS

A. THE GREATNESS OF GOD		
34. God Forgives	Psalm 51:1-17	75
35. God Guides	Psalm 32, 63 and 25	76
36. God Knows	Psalm 1 and 139	79
37. God's Glory	Psalm 8, 19 and 24	81
38. The God Who Loves	Psalm 23 and 46	83
39. God Is Good	Psalm 100 and 103	84
40. God Is Praised	Psalm 148 and 150	86

B. THE WISDOM OF GOD		
41. Wisdom Is Given	1 Kings 3:5-14; 4:29-34	87
42. True Wisdom	Proverbs 2:1-11; 3:1-35	89
43. The Good and the Wicked	Proverbs 12:1-25	91
44. Wisdom to Live By	Proverbs 21 and 22:1-9	93

C. THE JUDGMENT OF GOD		
45. A Divided Nation	1 Kings 11:1-13; 12:1-17	95
46. God's Prophets Warn Israel	1 Kings 12:25-33; 13:1-6, 33-34; 1 Kings 16:29-33; Jeremiah 5:11-19; 7:1-15	97
47. The Living God	1 Kings 17 and 18:1-45	100
48. God's Warning	Amos 5:4-15 and 21-27	104
49. Taken Captive	2 Kings 17:7-23	106
50. Turn from Evil	Isaiah 1:1-20	107
51. A Fallen Nation	2 Chronicles 36:11-21	109

D. THE MERCY OF GOD		
52. A Nation in Captivity	Jeremiah 29:4-14 and Daniel 1	110
53. The Fire Walkers	Daniel 3	112
54. A Man of Principle	Daniel 6	115
55. A Leper Is Healed	2 Kings 5:1-27	117
56. A Spy in the Enemy's Camp	2 Kings 6:8-23	119
57. Miracles in Ordinary Life	2 Kings 2:19-22; 4:1-44; 6:1-7; 8:1-6	120
58. A Nation Repents	Jonah 1:1-17; 2:1-2, 9-10; 3:1-10	124
59. The Happy Homecoming	Ezra 1:1-11; 3:1-3, 10-13 Nehemiah 1:1-4; 2:4-18; 6:15-16	126

E. THE PLAN OF GOD		
60. Signs of His Coming	Isaiah 7:14; 9:2-7; 11:1-5; 61:1-3 and Malachi 3:1-5	129

61. The Suffering Servant	Isaiah 53	131
62. The Suffering Savior	Psalm 22	132
63. God's Invitation to Man	Isaiah 55	134
64. A New Heart and Spirit	Jeremiah 17:5-10; 24:7; 31:31-34; 32:39-41; Ezekiel 11:19-20; 36:25-28	135
65. God Is Great	Isaiah 40	138

PART TWO: SELECTIONS FROM THE NEW TESTAMENT
IV. GOD FULFILLS HIS PROMISE

A. THE SON OF GOD

66. The Greatest Prophet	Luke 1:5-45 and 57-80	145
67. The Savior Is Born	Matthew 1:18-25; Luke 2:1-20	148
68. Visit of the Wise Men	Matthew 2:1-23	149
69. The Son of Man	John 1:1-18; Matthew 1:1-17; Luke 2:40-52	151

B. The Power of God

70. The Spirit of Power	Luke 3:1-18; Matthew 3:13-17; Luke 4:1-15; Matthew 4:12-17	154
71. Power over Sin and Evil	Luke 4:14-37 and 5:12-26	157
72. Power over Nature	John 2:1-11 and 6:1-21; Luke 8:22-25	159
73. Power over Demons and Disease	Luke 8:26-39; Matthew 8:5-17	161
74. Power over Death	John 11:17-45; Luke 8:40-56	162

C. THE NAMES OF CHRIST

75. The Son of God	John 5:16-47	165
76. The Bread of Life	John 6:25-59	167
77. The Light of the World	John 8:12-59	168
78. The Good Shepherd	John 10: 1-42	171

D. THE FOLLOWERS OF JESUS

79. The Chosen Twelve	Luke 5:1-11, 27-32; 6:12-16; 9:1-6	173
80. A Religious Man Seeks the Truth	John 3:1-21	174
81. The Woman at the Well	John 4:1-42	176
82. Blind Eyes See	John 9:1-41	178
83. Changed Lives	John 8:1-11; Luke 7:36-50; Luke 18:35-43; 19:1-10	180

E. THE MESSAGE OF CHRIST

84. Lost and Found	Luke 15	182
85. Secrets of the Kingdom	Matthew 13:1-23, 44-52; Luke 17:20-21	184
86. The Rich and the Poor	Mark 12:41-44; Luke 12:13-21, 32-34 and Luke 18:18-30	186
87. Heaven or Hell	Matthew 13:24-30, 36-43 and Luke 14:15-24; 16:19-31	188

		Page No.
F. THE TEACHINGS OF JESUS		
88. Words to Live By	Matthew 5:1-26	190
89. The Issues of Life	Matthew 5:27-48	192
90. Treasure and Rewards	Matthew 6	193
91. The Narrow Road	Matthew 7	195
92. The Clean and the Unclean	Mark 7:1-23	197
93. The Place of Honor	Luke 14:7-14; Matthew 20:20-28 and Mark 9:33-37	198
94. The Importance of Forgiveness	Matthew 18:15-35	200
G. THE PROMISES OF JESUS		
95. Words from the Father	Matthew 16:13-28; 17:1-13	201
96. The Way to God	John 14:1-14; 15:1-17	203
97. The Spirit of Truth	John 14:15-31; 16:5-16	205
98. The Prayer of Jesus	John 17	206
99. The Second Coming	Matthew 24	208
100. The Coming Judgment	Matthew 25	210
H. THE DEATH AND RESURRECTION OF JESUS CHRIST		
101. Friends and Enemies	Matthew 26:1-16; John 13:1-30	212
102. The Arrest of Jesus	Matthew 26:26-56	215
103. Sentenced to Die	Luke 22:54-71; 23:1-25	217
104. Death of the King	Luke 23:26-43; John 19:23-27 Luke 23:44-45; Mark 15:33-36; John 19:30a; Luke 23:46-56	219
105. Alive Again!	Matthew 27:62-66; 28:1-15; and John 20:3-18	221
106. Walking with Jesus	Luke 24:13-49; John 20:24-31	223
107. The Return to Heaven	John 21:1-19; Matthew 28:16-20 and Luke 24:50-53	225

V. CHRIST BUILDS HIS CHURCH

A. THE GROWTH OF THE CHURCH

108. The Coming of the Holy Spirit	Acts 1:1-14 and 2:1-41	228
109. The Name of Jesus	Acts 2:42-47 and 3:1-26	231
110. Boldness to Speak	Acts 4:1-31	232
111. Spreading the Good News	Acts 5:12-42 and 6:7	234
112. The First Christian Martyr	Acts 6:8-15; 7:1-60; 8:1-3	236
113. Christianity Expands	Acts 8:4-40	240
114. Changed by Jesus	Acts 9:1-43	242
115. No Longer Unclean	Acts 10:1-48	244

B. EXPANSION OF CHRISTIANITY INTO THE WORLD

116. Into All the World	Acts 13	247
117. Open Doors	Acts 15:36-41 and 16	250
118. The Unknown God	Acts 17	253
119. The Only Way	Acts 18:1-17; 19:1-41 and 20:1	255
120. Sad Farewells	Acts 20:7-38; 21:1-36; 22:23-29	259

121. Bound by Love	Acts 24:1-9, 22-27; 25:1-22; 26:1-32; 27:1-2; 28:14b-31	262

VI. CHRIST TEACHES HIS CHURCH

A. NEW LIFE IN CHRIST

122. The Word of God	Psalm 119:105, 129-130, 160, 162-163, 165; Psalm 119:9-11; Romans 15:4; Matthew 4:4; Psalm 19:7-11; Proverbs 30:5; Isaiah 34:16; Isaiah 40:8; 2 Timothy 3:16-17; 2 Peter 1:16-21; 1 Corinthians 2:6-16; Isaiah 55:10-11; Hebrews 4:12-13	268
123. God Confronts Sin and Evil	Romans 1	271
124. Everyman's Need for Salvation	Romans 2:1-11; 3:9-31; 4:13-25	273
125. Peace with God	Romans 5:1-14; Hebrews 9:22-28 Hebrews 10:1-18	276
126. A New Life with God	Gal. 2:19-20; Romans 6:1-23; 2 Corinthians 5:14-21	278
127. Alive in Christ	Ephesians 2:1-22; Titus 3:1-8	280
128. The Struggle Within Us	Romans 7:14-25; 1 John 1:5-10; 2:1-11	282
129. Eternal Life in the Son	1 John 5:1-21	283

B. LIFE THROUGH THE HOLY SPIRIT

130. The Spirit of Sonship	Romans 8:1-17	285
131. Life by the Spirit	Galatians 2:20; Romans 12:1-2; Galatians 5:13-26; 6:1-10	286
132. Filled with the Spirit	Ephesians 1:1-23; 4:17-32 and 5:1-21	288
133. Pressing On	Philippians 3:7-21; 4:1; Ephesians 3:14-21; 2 Peter 1:3-11	290
134. Trials and Temptations	1 Peter 5:6-11; James 1:2-18; 1 John 2:18-27; Ephesians 6:10-18; Philippians 4:4-8	292
135. The Benefits of Suffering	1 Peter 4:1-19; Romans 8:18-39	295
136. Faith in God	Hebrews 11:1-40; 12:1-3; James 5:13-18	297
137. Life After Death	Hebrews 9:27-28; John 14:1-4; 1 Corinthians 15:1-26, 35-58 2 Corinthians 4:7-18; 5:1-10 1 Thessalonians 4:13-18; 5:1-11; 2 Peter 3:1-14	300
138. Proclaiming the Truth	Romans 10:8-15; Colossians 2:6-10, 16-23 1 Timothy 4:1-16; 2 Timothy 3:10-17 2 Timothy 4:1-5	306

C. THE CHRISTIAN LIFE OF LOVE

139. God Is Love	1 John 4:7-21; Mark 12:28-34; Philippians 2:1-11	309
140. Love One Another	Galatians 5:13-15; Colossians 3:12-17; Romans 12:9-21;1 John 3:11-24	311
141. The Body of Christ	Romans 12:3-8; 1 Corinthians 12:1-31a 1 Peter 4:7-11	312
142. The Gift of Unity and Love	Romans 13:8-10; Ephesians 4:1-16; 1 Corinthians 12:31b and 13:1-13	314

143. The Care of the Church	James 2:1-19; 1 Timothy 3:1-13; 1 Peter 5:1-5	316
144. The Secret of Giving	2 Corinthians 9:6-15 1 Timothy 5:17-18; 6:3-10, 17-19 Philippians 4:10-20	318
145. The Christian Family	Ephesians 5:22-33; 1 Peter 3:1-7 Ephesians 6:1-9; Colossians 3:18-25; 4:1	320
146. Christian Conduct	1 Corinthians 6:1-20; 2 Thessalonians 3:6-13; 2 Corinthians 6:14-18; 7:1; 1 Corinthians 10:23-24	322
147. The Christian and Government	1 Peter 2:13-17; Romans 13:1-10; 1 Timothy 2:1-6	324

D. ETERNAL LIFE TO COME

148. The Living One	Revelation 1:1-20	326
149. The Churches in Asia	Revelation 2:1-29; 3:1-22	328
150. The Throne of God	Revelation 4:1-11; 5:1-14 and 7:9-17	331
151. The Book of Life	Revelation 19:1-16; 20:11-15	334
152. The New Heaven and Earth	Revelation 21:1-14, 22-27 and 22:1-21	336

Read This First!

We believe the Bible is the most treasured book in the entire world because it is the word of God, containing the message of Truth for which all people are searching. Although we believe all of the Bible was inspired by God, *Great Bible Truths* contains selected portions that will give the reader a clear understanding of the total message of the Bible.

The Bible is a collection of many separate books contained in one volume. They were written by 40 different authors who wrote in three different languages on three different continents. They were separated in time by a span of over 1600 years. Although the Bible is divided into two parts, the Old Testament and the New Testament, all the books reveal one great Truth: Jesus Christ is Savior of the world.

The first part of *Great Bible Truths* contains selections taken from the Old Testament. These passages describe God's creation of the world and man's fall into sin. God's message in the Old Testament is His promise to send a Savior to cleanse man of his sin. God's promise is worked out through the lives of the nation of Israel.

The second part of *Great Bible Truths* contains selections from the New Testament. These passages record the life and teachings of Jesus Christ. He is the fulfillment of God's promise that was given in the Old Testament. The message of the New Testament is the new heart and life that Jesus Christ brings to those who believe in Him as their Savior. We read of the change this new life brought in the lives of the people of the early Christian church.

The following selections were chosen to familiarize you with the Bible and its Truth. It begins with the creation of all things and ends with the end of the world. If you read this book completely, you will learn about God, his creation of the universe and mankind, the entrance of evil into a perfect world, man's estrangement from the God who had created him, and God's remedy for sin, Jesus Christ. The Bible is the story of how God has reached out to man through the ages. It is a fascinating story worked out through many generations of different peoples all around the world.

To help guide you in your reading, each selection is titled, and a Bible reference is given for the portion of Scripture used. At the beginning of each selection there are paragraphs containing important background information on the Scripture passage. Following the Scripture passage, there are questions for reflection upon the important teachings of that selection. For more concentrated growth, we recommend that you study this book with a group of other people. After completion of *Great Bible Truths*, you will want to obtain a copy of the complete Bible from a local bookstore.

May God richly bless you and reveal His perfect truth to you as you read and study His Holy Word.

The Publishers of Great Bible Truths

Bible Time Line
The Old Testament Period

2094 B.C.   The call of Abraham

1879 B.C.   Jacob and his family move to Egypt under the direction of Joseph who became prime minister over Egypt during the great famine.

1449 B.C.   Moses leads the exodus out of Egypt.

1388 B.C.   The 12 tribes of Israel occupy the land of Canaan.

1012 B.C.   David becomes the second king of Israel.

932 B.C.   The death of King Solomon and the division of the 12 tribes into two separate kingdoms (Israel/ Judah) with two different kings ruling in their respective capitals (Samaria/Jerusalem).

722 B.C.   The capital city of Samaria falls under the Assyrian Empire.

586 B.C.   The capital city of Jerusalem falls under the Babylonian Empire.

516 B.C.   The first group of exiles returns and rebuilds the temple in Jerusalem.

458-445 B.C   Ezra and Nehemiah return with more exiles to rebuild the walls of Jerusalem.

336 B.C.   The books of Ezra and Nehemiah were added to the Old Testament, completing the Aramaic version.

150 B.C.   The Old Testament was translated into the Greek language.

63 B.C.   Roman troops occupy the city of Jerusalem.

PART ONE

Selections from the Old Testament

Beginning with the writings of Moses, the Old Testament describes the creation of the world and the first generations of people, leading up to the worldwide flood. Then the formation of the nation of Israel through Abraham and his descendants follows. The important events in Israel's history are recorded through the lives of the different kings and prophets. The writings of two famous kings of Israel reveal the wisdom and goodness of God to man. Through His dealings with the people of Israel, God's character and ways are made known to us. We are able to see God's mercy and love as He sets forth His plan to bring about a way of salvation for the world through a Savior. At the same time, we understand God's hatred for sin and the judgment that must come to those who refuse to acknowledge and worship the true and living God.

I. GOD CREATES THE WORLD

These first five selections from the Bible tell about the creation and man's fall into sin. Although God's judgment comes on man and creation, we read of God's promise to send a Savior who will rescue man from sin and death.

1. THE CREATION OF MAN
Genesis 1 and 2:1-9, and 15-25

The universe that God created reveals His great love and power. God simply spoke and everything came into being. The fact that God created human beings to be like Himself shows that God is alive.

The Account of Creation

1 In the beginning, God created the heavens and the earth. ²The earth was formless and empty. Darkness was on the surface of the deep and God's Spirit was hovering over the surface of the waters.

³God said, "Let there be light," and there was light.⁴ God saw the light, and saw that it was good. God divided the light from the darkness. ⁵ God called the light "day", and the darkness he called "night". There was evening and there was morning, the first day. ⁶ God said, "Let there be an expanse in the middle of the waters, and let it divide the waters from the waters." ⁷ God made the expanse, and divided the waters which were under the expanse

from the waters which were above the expanse; and it was so. ⁸ God called the expanse "sky". There was evening and there was morning, a second day.

⁹ God said, "Let the waters under the sky be gathered together to one place, and let the dry land appear"; and it was so. ¹⁰ God called the dry land "earth", and the gathering together of the waters he called "seas". God saw that it was good. ¹¹ God said, "Let the earth yield grass, herbs yielding seeds, and fruit trees bearing fruit after their kind, with their seeds in it, on the earth"; and it was so. ¹² The earth yielded grass, herbs yielding seed after their kind, and trees bearing fruit, with their seeds in it, after their kind; and God saw that it was good. ¹³ There was evening and there was morning, a third day. ¹⁴ God said, "Let there be lights in the expanse of sky to divide the day from the night; and let them be for signs to mark seasons, days, and years; ¹⁵ and let them be for lights in the expanse of sky to give light on the earth"; and it was so. ¹⁶ God made the two great lights: the greater light to rule the day, and the lesser light to rule the night. He also made the stars. ¹⁷ God set them in the expanse of sky to give light to the earth,¹⁸ and to rule over the day and over the night, and to divide the light from the darkness. God saw that it was good. ¹⁹ There was evening and there was morning, a fourth day.

²⁰ God said, "Let the waters abound with living creatures, and let birds fly above the earth in the open expanse of sky." ²¹ God created the large sea creatures and every living creature that moves, with which the waters swarmed, after their kind, and every winged bird after its kind. God saw that it was good. ²² God blessed them, saying, "Be fruitful, and multiply, and fill the waters in the seas, and let birds multiply on the earth." ²³ There was evening and there was morning, a fifth day.

²⁴ God said, "Let the earth produce living creatures after their kind, livestock, creeping things, and animals of the earth after their kind"; and it was so. ²⁵ God made the animals of the earth after their kind, and the livestock after their kind, and everything that creeps on the ground after its kind. God saw that it was good.

²⁶ God said, "Let us make man in our image, after our likeness: and let them have dominion over the fish of the sea, and over the birds of the sky, and over the livestock, and over all the earth, and over every creeping thing that creeps on the earth." ²⁷ God created man in his own image. In God's image he created him; male and female he created them. ²⁸ God blessed them. God said to them, "Be fruitful, multiply, fill the earth, and subdue it. Have dominion over the fish of the sea, over the birds of the sky, and over every living thing that moves on the earth." ²⁹ God said, "Behold, I have given you every herb yielding seed, which is on the surface of all the earth, and every tree, which bears fruit yielding seed. It will be your food. ³⁰ To every animal of the earth, and to every bird of the sky, and to everything that

creeps on the earth, in which there is life, I have given every green herb for food;" and it was so.

 ³¹ God saw everything that he had made, and, behold, it was very good. There was evening and there was morning, a sixth day.

2 The heavens, the earth, and all their vast array were finished. ² On the seventh day God finished his work which he had done; and he rested on the seventh day from all his work which he had done. ³ God blessed the seventh day, and made it holy, because he rested in it from all his work of creation which he had done.

Adam and Eve
⁴ This is the history of the generations of the heavens and of the earth when they were created, in the day that Yahweh the Lord God made the earth and the heavens. ⁵ No plant of the field was yet in the earth, and no herb of the field had yet sprung up; for Yahweh God had not caused it to rain on the earth. There was not a man to till the ground, ⁶ but a mist went up from the earth, and watered the whole surface of the ground. ⁷ Yahweh God formed man from the dust of the ground, and breathed into his nostrils the breath of life; and man became a living soul. ⁸ Yahweh God planted a garden eastward, in Eden, and there he put the man whom he had formed. ⁹ Out of the ground Yahweh God made every tree to grow that is pleasant to the sight, and good for food, including the tree of life in the middle of the garden and the tree of the knowledge of good and evil. ¹⁵ Yahweh God took the man, and put him into the Garden of Eden to cultivate and keep it. ¹⁶ Yahweh God commanded the man, saying, "You may freely eat of every tree of the garden; ¹⁷ but you shall not eat of the tree of the knowledge of good and evil; for in the day that you eat of it, you will surely die."

 ¹⁸ Yahweh God said, "It is not good for the man to be alone. I will make him a helper comparable to him." ¹⁹Out of the ground Yahweh God formed every animal of the field, and every bird of the sky, and brought them to the man to see what he would call them. Whatever the man called every living creature became its name. ²⁰ The man gave names to all livestock, and to the birds of the sky, and to every animal of the field; but for man there was not found a helper comparable [suitable] to him. ²¹ Yahweh God caused the man to fall into a deep sleep. As the man slept, he took one of his ribs, and closed up the flesh in its place. ²² Yahweh God made a woman from the rib which had taken from the man, and brought her to the man. ²³ The man said, "This is now bone of my bones, and flesh of my flesh. She will be called 'woman,' because she was taken out of Man." ²⁴ Therefore a man will leave his father and his mother, and will join with his wife, and they will be one flesh.²⁵ The man and his wife were both naked, and they were not ashamed.

Great Bible Truths

1. *What is the difference between human beings and other creatures?*
2. *What do you think life was like in the Garden for Adam and Eve?*
3. *What were they told not to do in the Garden?*

2. THE REBELLION
Genesis 3

Satan, a fallen angel and chief of the powers of evil, came to Eve and Adam and tempted them to disobey God. They believed Satan's lies and rebelled against God, plunging the whole human race into sin. Although the result of sin is spiritual death, God promised to send a Savior to save mankind and restore his spiritual life.

The Fall of Man into Sin

3 Now the serpent was more subtle than any animal of the field which Yahweh God had made. He said to the woman, "Has God really said, 'You shall not eat of any tree of the garden?'"

² The woman said to the serpent, "We may eat fruit from the trees of the garden, ³ but not the fruit of the tree which is in the middle of the garden. God has said, 'You shall not eat of it. You shall not touch it, lest you die.'"

⁴ The serpent said to the woman, "You won't surely die, ⁵ for God knows that in the day you eat it, your eyes will be opened, and you will be like God, knowing good and evil."

⁶ When the woman saw that the tree was good for food, and that it was a delight to the eyes, and that the tree was to be desired to make one wise, she took some of its fruit, and ate; and she gave some to her husband with her, and he ate it, too. ⁷ Their eyes were opened, and they both knew that they were naked. They sewed fig leaves together, and made coverings for themselves. ⁸ They heard Yahweh God's voice walking in the garden in the cool of the day, and the man and his wife hid themselves from the presence of Yahweh God among the trees of the garden.

⁹Yahweh God called to the man, and said to him, "Where are you?"

¹⁰The man said, "I heard your voice in the garden, and I was afraid, because I was naked; and I hid myself."

¹¹God said, "Who told you that you were naked? Have you eaten from the tree that I commanded you not to eat from?"

¹²The man said, "The woman whom you gave to be with me, she gave me fruit from the tree, and I ate it."

¹³Yahweh God said to the woman, "What have you done?"
The woman said, "The serpent deceived me, and I ate."

¹⁴Yahweh God said to the serpent,
"Because you have done this, you are cursed above all livestock, and above every animal of the field. You shall go on your belly and you shall eat dust all the days of your life. ¹⁵ I will put hostility between you and

the woman, and between your offspring and her offspring. He will bruise your head, and you will bruise his heel." [16] To the woman he said "I will greatly multiply your pain in childbirth. In pain you will bear children. Your desire will be for your husband, and he will rule over you." [17] To Adam he said, "Because you have listened to your wife's voice, and ate from the tree, about which I commanded you, saying, 'You shall not eat of it,' the ground is cursed for your sake. You will eat from it with much labor all the days of your life. [18]It will yield thorns and thistles to you; and you will eat the herb of the field. [19] By the sweat of your face will you eat bread until you return to the ground, for out of it you were taken. For you are dust, and to dust you shall return."

Paradise Lost, God's Judgment
[20] The man called his wife Eve because she would be the mother of all the living. [21]Yahweh God made coats of animal skins for Adam and for his wife, and clothed them. [22] Yahweh God said, "Behold, the man has become like one of us, knowing good and evil. Now, lest he reach out his hand, and also take of the tree of life, and eat, and live forever..." [23] Therefore Yahweh God sent him out from the garden of Eden, to till the ground from which he was taken. [24] So he drove out the man; and he placed cherubim [angels] at the east of the garden of Eden, and a flaming sword which turned every way, to guard the way to the tree of life.

1. What did Eve fail to do when tempted by the serpent?
2. As God pronounced judgment, what word of hope and promise did God give to them and to the entire human race?
3. God's promise that "He will crush your head" refers to the coming Savior. Whose head will the Savior crush?
4. Can you see how the introduction of sin into the world profoundly changed the earth's environment and living conditions for the entire human race from that time on?

3. THE FIRST MURDER!
Genesis 4:1-16

Life became very difficult for Adam and Eve after they were made to leave the Garden and work for their own food. The sin that had entered them was now passed on to their children. This passage shows how the sin of jealousy led to the first murder and brought punishment to the killer. Sin always removes man from God's presence, but God still shows His love and mercy, even to the worst sinner.

Cain and Abel
4 The man knew Eve his wife. She conceived, and gave birth to Cain, and said, "I have gotten a man with Yahweh's help." [2] Again she gave birth, to

Cain's brother Abel. Abel was a keeper of sheep, but Cain was a tiller of the ground. ³ As time passed, Cain brought an offering to Yahweh from the fruit of the ground. ⁴ Abel also brought some of the firstborn of his flock and of its fat. Yahweh respected Abel and his offering, ⁵ but he didn't respect Cain and his offering. Cain was very angry, and the expression on his face fell. ⁶ Yahweh said to Cain, "Why are you angry? Why has the expression of your face fallen? ⁷ If you do well, won't it be lifted up? If you don't do well, sin crouches at the door. Its desire is for you, but you are to rule over it." ⁸ Cain said to Abel, his brother, "Let's go into the field." While they were in the field, Cain rose up against Abel, his brother, and killed him. ⁹ Yahweh said to Cain, "Where is Abel, your brother?" He said, "I don't know. Am I my brother's keeper?" ¹⁰ Yahweh said, "What have you done? The voice of your brother's blood cries to me from the ground. ¹¹ Now you are cursed because of the ground, which has opened its mouth to receive your brother's blood from your hand. ¹² From now on, when you till the ground, it won't yield its strength to you. You will be a fugitive and a wanderer in the earth."

¹³ Cain said to Yahweh, "My punishment is greater than I can bear. ¹⁴ Behold, you have driven me out today from the surface of the ground. I will be hidden from your face, and I will be a fugitive and a wanderer in the earth. Whoever finds me will kill me."

¹⁵Yahweh said to him, "Therefore whoever slays Cain, vengeance will be taken on him sevenfold." Yahweh appointed a sign for Cain, so that anyone finding him would not strike him.

¹⁶Cain left Yahweh's presence, and lived in the land of Nod, east of Eden.

1. *Why did Cain kill Abel?*

2. *What was Cain's punishment?*

3. *How did God show mercy, even to Cain?*

4. THE WORLDWIDE FLOOD
Genesis 6:5-22 and 7

As people began to populate the earth, the evil within them grew, bringing misery and death to God's beautiful creation. God, who is holy and without sin, painfully decided to destroy mankind because of its great wickedness. God saved one good and righteous man named Noah, along with his family, so that His promise to send a Savior might be fulfilled.

The Flood

6 ⁵Yahweh saw that the wickedness of man was great in the earth, and that every imagination of the thoughts of man's heart was continually only evil. ⁶ Yahweh was sorry that he had made man on the earth, and it grieved him in his heart. ⁷ Yahweh said, "I will destroy man whom I have created from the surface of the ground—man, along with animals, creeping things, and birds of the sky—for I am sorry that I have made them."⁸ But Noah found favor in Yahweh's eyes.

The Story of Noah
⁹This is the history of the generations of Noah: Noah was a righteous man, blameless among the people of his time. Noah walked with God. ¹⁰ Noah became the father of three sons: Shem, Ham, and Japheth. ¹¹ The earth was corrupt before God, and the earth was filled with violence. ¹² God saw the earth, and saw that it was corrupt, for all flesh had corrupted their way on the earth. ¹³ God said to Noah, "I will bring an end to all flesh, for the earth is filled with violence through them. Behold, I will destroy them and the earth. ¹⁴ Make a ship of gopher wood. You shall make rooms in the ship, and shall seal it inside and outside with pitch. ¹⁵ This is how you shall make it. The length of the ship shall be three hundred cubits [450 feet], its width fifty cubits [75 feet], and its height thirty cubits [45 feet].¹⁶ You shall make a roof in the ship, and you shall finish it to a cubit upward. You shall set the door of the ship in its side. You shall make it with lower, second, and third levels. ¹⁷ I, even I, do bring the flood of waters on this earth, to destroy all flesh having the breath of life from under the sky. Everything that is in the earth will die. ¹⁸ But I will establish my covenant with you. You shall come into the ship, you, your sons, your wife, and your sons' wives with you. ¹⁹ Of every living thing of all flesh, you shall bring two of every sort into the ship, to keep them alive with you. They shall be male and female. ²⁰ Of the birds after their kind, of the livestock after their kind, of every creeping thing of the ground after its kind, two of every sort will come to you, to keep them alive. ²¹ Take with you of all food that is eaten, and gather it to yourself; and it will be for food for you, and for them." ²² Thus Noah did. He did all that God commanded him.

The Flood Covers the Earth
7 Yahweh said to Noah, "Come with all of your household into the ship, for I have seen your righteousness before me in this generation. ² You shall take seven pairs of every clean animal with you, the male and his female. Of the animals that are not clean, take two, the male and his female. ³ Also of the birds of the sky, seven and seven, male and female, to keep seed alive on the surface of all the earth. ⁴ In seven days, I will cause it to rain on the earth for forty days and forty nights. Every living thing that I have made, I will destroy from the surface of the ground." ⁵Noah did everything that Yahweh commanded him. ⁶Noah was six hundred years old when the flood of waters came on the earth. ⁷Noah went into the ship with his sons, his wife, and his son's wives because of the flood waters. ⁸Clean animals, unclean animals, birds, and everything that creeps on the ground went by pairs to Noah into the ship, ⁹male and female, as God commanded Noah. ¹⁰ After the seven days, the floodwaters came on the earth. ¹¹ In the six hundredth year of Noah's life,

in the second month, on the seventeenth day of the month, on the same day all the fountains of the great deep were burst open, and the sky's windows were opened. [12] It rained on the earth forty days and forty nights.

[13] In the same day Noah, and Shem, Ham, and Japheth—the sons of Noah—and Noah's wife and the three wives of his sons with them, entered into the ship— [14] they, and every animal after its kind, all the livestock after their kind, every creeping thing that creeps on the earth after its kind, and every bird after its kind, every bird of every sort. [15] Pairs from all flesh with the breath of life in them went to Noah into the ship. [16] Those who went in, went in male and female of all flesh, as God commanded him; then Yahweh shut him in. [17] The flood was forty days on the earth. The waters increased, and lifted up the ship, and it was lifted up above the earth. [18] The waters rose, and increased greatly on the earth; and the ship floated on the surface of the waters. [19] The waters rose very high on the earth. All the high mountains that were under the whole sky were covered. [20] The waters rose fifteen cubits [23 feet] higher, and the mountains were covered. [21] All flesh died that moved on the earth, including birds, livestock, animals, every creeping thing that creeps on the earth, and every man. [22] All on the dry land, in whose nostrils was the breath of the spirit of life, died. [23] Every living thing was destroyed that was on the surface of the ground, including man, livestock, creeping things, and birds of the sky. They were destroyed from the earth. Only Noah was left, and those who were with him in the ship. [24] The waters flooded the earth one hundred fifty days.

1. How evil had people become?
2. Why did God choose Noah and spare him? Why was this important?
3. How much of the world did God destroy through the flood?
4. What did God tell Noah to take into the ark and why?

5. THE FIRST RAINBOW
Genesis 8 and 9:8-19

After the waters receded, Noah, his family and the animals left the ark. The earth would be repopulated from these survivors. God made a promise to never again destroy the world with a flood, and He sealed His promise with the appearance of the first rainbow.

The Flood Recedes

8 God remembered Noah, all the animals, and all the livestock that were with him in the ship; and God made a wind to pass over the earth. The waters subsided. [2] The deep's fountains and the sky's windows were also stopped, and the rain from the sky was restrained. [3] The waters continually receded from the earth. After the end of one hundred fifty days the waters decreased. ⁴ The ship rested in the seventh month, on the seventeenth day of the month, on Ararat's mountains. ⁵ The waters receded continually until the tenth month. In the tenth month, on the first day of the month, the tops of the mountains were visible.

⁶ At the end of forty days, Noah opened the window of the ship which he had made, ⁷ and he sent out a raven. It went back and forth, until the waters were dried up from the earth. ⁸ He himself sent out a dove to see if the waters were abated from the surface of the ground, ⁹ but the dove found no place to rest her foot, and she returned to him into the ship, for the waters were on the surface of the whole earth. He put out his hand, and took her, and brought her to him into the ship. ¹⁰ He waited yet another seven days; and again he sent the dove out of the ship. ¹¹ The dove came back to him at evening and, behold, in her mouth was a freshly plucked olive leaf. So Noah knew that the waters were abated from the earth. ¹² He waited yet another seven days, and sent out the dove; and she didn't return to him anymore.

¹³ In the six hundred first year, in the first month, the first day of the month, the waters were dried up from the earth. Noah removed the covering of the ship, and looked. He saw that the surface of the ground was dried. ¹⁴ In the second month, on the twenty-seventh day of the month, the earth was dry.

The New Beginning

¹⁵ God spoke to Noah, saying, ¹⁶ "Go out of the ship, you, and your wife, and your sons, and your sons' wives with you. ¹⁷ Bring out with you every living thing that is with you of all flesh, including birds, livestock, and every creeping thing that creeps on the earth, that they may breed abundantly in the earth, and be fruitful, and multiply on the earth."

¹⁸ Noah went out, with his sons, his wife, and his sons' wives with him. ¹⁹ Every animal, every creeping thing, and every bird, whatever moves on the earth, after their families, went out of the ship.

²⁰ Noah built an altar to Yahweh, and took of every clean animal, and of every clean bird, and offered burnt offerings on the altar. ²¹ Yahweh smelled the pleasant aroma. Yahweh said in his heart, "I will not again curse the ground any more for man's sake because [even though] the imagination of man's heart is evil from his youth. I will never again strike every living thing, as I have done.

> ²² While the earth remains,
> seed time and harvest
> and cold and heat,
> and summer and winter,
> and day and night
> will not cease."

Great Bible Truths

God's Covenant with Mankind

9 God spoke to Noah and to his sons with him, saying, [9] "As for me, behold, I establish my covenant with you, and with your offspring after you, [10] and with every living creature that is with you: the birds, the livestock, and every animal of the earth with you, of all that go out of the ship, even every animal of the earth. [11] I will establish my covenant with you: All flesh will not be cut off any more by the waters of the flood. There will never again be a flood to destroy the earth."

The Rainbow, Sign of the Covenant

[12] God said, "This is the token of the covenant which I make between me and you and every living creature that is with you, for perpetual generations: [13] I set my rainbow in the cloud, and it will be a sign of a covenant between me and the earth. [14] When I bring a cloud over the earth, that the rainbow will be seen in the cloud, [15] and I will remember my covenant, which is between me and you and every living creature of all flesh, and the waters will no more become a flood to destroy all flesh. [16] The rainbow will be in the cloud. I will look at it that I may remember the everlasting covenant between God and every living creature of all flesh that is on the earth." [17] God said to Noah, "This is the token of the covenant which I have established between me and all flesh that is on the earth."

[18] The sons of Noah who went out from the ship were Shem, Ham, and Japheth. Ham is the father of Canaan. [19] These three were the sons of Noah, and from these, the whole earth was populated.

1. *How did Noah know when to come out of the ark?*
2. *What was the first thing Noah did after he released all the animals from the ark?*
3. *What divine promise did God give to Noah, and what was the sign of that forever promise?*
4. *Will you remember that promise when you see a rainbow?*

6. THE FIRST METROPOLIS
Genesis 11:1-9

After the waters of the worldwide flood disappeared, Noah's descendants multiplied, established new settlements and developed a new civilization. Although God had told them to disperse over the earth, they decided instead to unite together and build a huge new city with a prominent religious tower. This work demonstrated the unique abilities of human beings who are made in the image of God. However, at Babel these extraordinary abilities were used as an act of pride and rebellion against God. God stopped this rebellion. He confounded the people by giving them different languages, causing total confusion. The end result was that people were dispersed all over the earth, just as God had intended.

The Tower of Babel

11 The whole earth was of one language and of one speech. ² As they traveled east, they found a plain in the land of Shinar, and they lived there. ³ They said to one another, "Come, let's make bricks, and burn them thoroughly." They had brick for stone, and they used tar for mortar. ⁴ They said, "Come, let's build ourselves a city, and a tower whose top reaches to the sky, and let's make a name for ourselves, lest we be scattered abroad on the surface of the whole earth."

⁵ Yahweh came down to see the city and the tower, which the children of men built.⁶ Yahweh said, "Behold, they are one people, and they have all one language, and this is what they begin to do. Now nothing will be withheld from them, which they intend to do.⁷ Come, let's go down, and there confuse their language, that they may not understand one another's speech." ⁸ So Yahweh scattered them abroad from there on the surface of all the earth. They stopped building the city. ⁹ Therefore its name was called Babel, because there Yahweh confused the language of all the earth. From there, Yahweh scattered them abroad on the surface of all the earth.

1. Why did everyone want to build this huge city?
2. Their motive was to glorify man, to "make a name for ourselves." Why was this a bad idea?
3. Think of their motive and mindset to build this project. Do we see anything like this in today's world?
4. Why do you suppose God wanted the people to scatter all over the world?
5. Given the resourcefulness of man, what do you suppose could have happened if God had not stopped this project?
6. Do you understand now why the world is filled with all kinds of people who speak different languages and have different cultures, and how that came to be?

II. GOD FORMS A NATION

After the tower of Babel, the people multiplied and populated the earth. However, because the people did not know much about the God of creation, they began to worship the created things around them. Thinking that these things had divine powers, they named them gods, but they were false gods. God wanted to fulfill His promise to send a Savior to deliver man from the misery that sin had brought into the world. However, before a Savior could come, God needed a people who would worship only Him as the true and living God. These people would reveal God's way to all mankind, and they would produce a Savior.

Looking for a man of faith, God chose Abraham and began to form a nation of people who would worship and obey Him. Through Abraham's descendants, the twelve tribes of Israel were formed. We read of Israel's slavery and their deliverance from Egypt. After many years of travelling in the wilderness, they finally settled in the land that God had promised to give them. During this time, the people turned away from God time after time and worshiped false gods. They rejected God's many warnings, and He finally brought judgment on the people. In order to fulfill His promise to Abraham, God preserved a small group of Israelites through whom He brought the Savior.

A. THE PROMISE OF GOD

These next five selections lay the foundation for the formation of the nation of Israel. We read of God's promise to Abraham and the testing of his faith. The faithfulness of God is shown as He hears and answers the prayers of Abraham, Isaac and Jacob.

7. THE MIRACLE BABY
Genesis 12:1-7 and 15:1-6 and 17:1-5 and 18:1-15 and 21:1-7

God chose to build a nation of people who would be a light to the nations. He chose the most unlikely of couples to be the progenitors. Abraham and Sarah could not have children, and yet God gave them a two-fold promise: an actual son and the land of Canaan. God fulfilled His promises and established a nation that would actually settle on the land God gave to Abraham. God also promised Abraham that through his descendants all families of the earth would be blessed. God has always had His eye on bringing salvation to the world. He would use Abraham and the Hebrews to accomplish this work. Abraham believed God and was rewarded for his faith.

The Call of Abraham

12 Now Yahweh said to Abram, "Leave your country, and your relatives, and your father's house, and go to the land that I will show you.

> ² I will make of you a great nation. I will bless you and make your name great. You will be a blessing.
> ³ I will bless those who bless you,
> and I will curse him who curses you.
> All the families of the earth will be blessed through you."

⁴ So Abram went, as Yahweh had told him. Lot went with him. Abram was seventy-five years old when he departed from Haran. ⁵ Abram took Sarai his wife, Lot his brother's son, all their possessions that they had gathered, and the people whom they had acquired in Haran, and they went to go into the land of Canaan. They entered into the land of Canaan. ⁶ Abram passed through the land to the place of Shechem, to the oak of Moreh. The Canaanites were in the land, then.

⁷ Yahweh appeared to Abram and said, "I will give this land to your offspring." He built an altar there to Yahweh, who had appeared to him.

Great Bible Truths

God's Covenant with Abraham

15 After these things Yahweh's word came to Abram in a vision, saying, "Don't be afraid, Abram. I am your shield, your exceedingly great reward."

² Abram said, "Lord Yahweh, what will you give me, since I go childless, and he who will inherit my estate is Eliezer of Damascus?" ³ Abram said, "Behold, to me you have given no children: and, behold, one born in my house is my heir." ⁴ Behold, Yahweh's word came to him, saying, "This man will not be your heir, but he who will come out of your own body will be your heir." ⁵ Yahweh brought him outside, and said, "Look now toward the sky, and count the stars, if you are able to count them." He said to Abram, "So will your offspring be." ⁶ He believed in Yahweh, who credited it to him for righteousness.

The Covenant

17 When Abram was ninety-nine years old, Yahweh appeared to Abram, and said to him, "I am God almighty. Walk before me, and be blameless. ² I will make my covenant between me and you, and will multiply you exceedingly."

³ Abram fell on his face. God talked with him, saying, ⁴As for me, behold, my covenant is with you. You will be the father of a multitude of nations. ⁵ Your name will no more be called Abram, but your name will be Abraham; for I have made you the father of a multitude of nations.

The Three Visitors

18 Yahweh appeared to him by the oaks of Mamre, as he sat in the tent door in the heat of the day. ² He lifted up his eyes and looked, and saw that three men stood opposite him. When he saw them, he ran to meet them from the tent door, and bowed himself to the earth, ³ and said, "My lord, if now I have found favor in your sight, please don't go away from your servant. ⁴ Now let a little water be fetched, wash your feet, and rest yourselves under the tree. ⁵ I will get a morsel of bread so you can refresh your heart. After that you may go your way, now that you have come to your servant."
They said, "Very well, do as you have said."

⁶ Abraham hurried into the tent to Sarah, and said, "Quickly prepare three seahs of fine meal, knead it, and make cakes." ⁷ Abraham ran to the herd, and fetched a tender and good calf, and gave it to the servant. He hurried to dress it. ⁸ He took butter, milk, and the calf which he had dressed, and set it before them. He stood by them under the tree, and they ate.

⁹ They asked him, "Where is Sarah, your wife?"
He said, "See, in the tent."

¹⁰ He said, "I will certainly return to you when the season comes round. Behold, Sarah your wife will have a son."

Sarah heard in the tent door, which was behind him. ¹¹ Now Abraham and Sarah were old, well advanced in age. Sarah had passed the age of childbearing. ¹² Sarah laughed within herself, saying, "After I have grown old will I have pleasure, my lord being old also?"

¹³ Yahweh said to Abraham, "Why did Sarah laugh, saying, 'Will I really bear a child, yet I am old?' ¹⁴ Is anything too hard for Yahweh? At the set time I will return to you, when the season comes round, and Sarah will have a son."

¹⁵ Then Sarah denied it, saying, "I didn't laugh," for she was afraid.
He said, "No, but you did laugh."

The Birth of Isaac

21 Yahweh visited Sarah as he had said, and Yahweh did to Sarah as he had spoken. ² Sarah conceived, and bore Abraham a son in his old age, at the set time of which God had spoken to him. ³ Abraham called his son who was born to him, whom Sarah bore to him, Isaac. Abraham circumcised his son, Isaac, when he was eight days old, as God had commanded him. ⁵ Abraham was one hundred years old when his son, Isaac, was born to him. ⁶ Sarah said, "God has made me laugh. Everyone who hears will laugh with me." ⁷ She said, "Who would have said to Abraham, that Sarah would nurse children? For I have borne him a son in his old age."

> 1. What great promise did God give to Abraham?
> 2. What conditions in Abraham's life would make it difficult for him to believe that he could be a father and founder of a great nation?
> 3. What quality of Abraham's life was pleasing to God?
> 4. How did Sarah's attitude change after the birth of Isaac?

8. A MAN OF FAITH
Genesis 22:1-18

God tested the faith of Abraham by asking for his son Isaac to be sacrificed. Abraham was confident that God could give life to Isaac again if he died, so he proceeded to obey God. God was pleased with Abraham's faith and provided an animal for the sacrifice. This incident pointed forward to the time when the only Son of God, the Savior, would sacrifice His life for the sins of the world.

Abraham Tested

22 After these things, God tested Abraham, and said to him, "Abraham!" He said, "Here I am."

² He said, "Now take your son, your only son, whom you love, even Isaac, and go into the land of Moriah. Offer him there as a burnt offering on one of the mountains which I will tell you of."

³ Abraham rose early in the morning, and saddled his donkey, and took two of his young men with him, and Isaac his son. He split the wood for the burnt offering, and rose up, and went to the place of which God had told him. ⁴ On the third day Abraham lifted up his eyes, and saw the place far off.
⁵ Abraham said to his young men, "Stay here with the donkey. The boy and I

will go yonder. We will worship, and come back to you." ⁶ Abraham took the wood of the burnt offering and laid it on Isaac his son. He took in his hand the fire and the knife. They both went together. ⁷ Isaac spoke to Abraham his father, and said, "My father?"

He said, "Here I am, my son."

He said, "Here is the fire and the wood, but where is the lamb for a burnt offering?"

⁸ Abraham said, "God will provide himself the lamb for a burnt offering, my son." So they both went together. ⁹ They came to the place which God had told him of. Abraham built the altar there, and laid the wood in order, bound Isaac his son, and laid him on the altar, on the wood. ¹⁰Abraham stretched out his hand, and took the knife to kill his son.

¹¹ Yahweh's angel called to him out of the sky, and said, "Abraham, Abraham!"

He said, "Here I am."

¹² He said, "Don't lay your hand on the boy or do anything to him. For now I know that you fear God, since you have not withheld your son, your only son, from me."

¹³ Abraham lifted up his eyes, and looked, and saw that behind him was a ram caught in the thicket by his horns. Abraham went and took the ram, and offered him up for a burnt offering instead of his son. ¹⁴ Abraham called the name of that place Yahweh Will Provide. As it is said to this day, "On Yahweh's mountain, it will be provided."

¹⁵ Yahweh's angel called to Abraham a second time out of the sky, ¹⁶ and said, "I have sworn by myself, says Yahweh, because you have done this thing, and have not withheld your son, your only son, ¹⁷ that I will bless you greatly, and I will multiply your offspring greatly like the stars of the heavens, and like the sand which is on the seashore. Your offspring will possess the gate of his enemies. ¹⁸ All the nations of the earth will be blessed by your offspring, because you have obeyed my voice."

> 1. Why did God ask Abraham to sacrifice Isaac, the miracle child?
>
> 2. How do we know that Abraham trusted God?
>
> 3. How would "all the nations of the earth be blessed" through the offspring of Abraham?

9. THE CHOSEN BRIDE
Genesis 24:1-38, 49-52, 57-67

Abraham's servant was given the task of finding a wife for Isaac. We see God's concern for the practical needs of His people as He guided the servant and answered his prayer.

Isaac and Rebecca

24 Abraham was old, and well stricken in age. Yahweh had blessed Abraham in all things. ² Abraham said to his servant, the elder of his house, who ruled over all that he had, "Please put your hand under my thigh. ³ I will make you swear by Yahweh, the God of heaven and the God of the earth, that you shall not take a wife for my son of the daughters of the Canaanites, among whom I live. ⁴ But you shall go to my country, and to my relatives, and take a wife for my son Isaac." ⁵ The servant said to him, "What if the woman isn't willing to follow me to this land? Must I bring your son again to the land you came from?"

⁶ Abraham said to him, "Beware that you don't bring my son there again. ⁷ Yahweh, the God of heaven, who took me from my father's house, and from the land of my birth, who spoke to me, and who swore to me, saying, 'I will give this land to your offspring. He will send his angel before you, and you shall take a wife for my son from there. ⁸ If the woman isn't willing to follow you, then you shall be clear from this oath to me. Only you shall not bring my son there again."

⁹ The servant put his hand under the thigh of Abraham his master, and swore to him concerning this matter. ¹⁰ The servant took ten camels, of his master's camels, and departed, having a variety of good things of his master's with him. He arose, and went to Mesopotamia, to the city of Nahor. ¹¹ He made the camels kneel down outside the city by the well of water at the time of evening, the time that women go out to draw water. ¹² He said, "Yahweh, the God of my master Abraham, please give me success today, and show kindness to my master Abraham. ¹³ Behold, I am standing by the spring of water. The daughters of the men of the city are coming out to draw water. ¹⁴ Let it happen, that the young lady to whom I will say, 'Please let down your pitcher, that I may drink,' and she will say, 'Drink, and I will also give your camels a drink,' let her be the one you have appointed for your servant Isaac. By this I will know that you have shown kindness to my master."

¹⁵ Before he had finished speaking, behold, Rebekah came out, who was born to Bethuel the son of Milcah, the wife of Nahor, Abraham's brother, with her pitcher on her shoulder.¹⁶ The young lady was very beautiful to look at, a virgin. No man had known her. She went down to the spring, filled her pitcher, and came up. ¹⁷ The servant ran to meet her, and said, "Please give me a drink, a little water from your pitcher."

¹⁸ She said, "Drink, my lord." She hurried, and let down her pitcher on her hand, and gave him drink. ¹⁹ When she had done giving him drink, she said, "I will also draw for your camels, until they have done drinking." ²⁰ She hurried, and emptied her pitcher into the trough, and ran again to the well to draw, and drew for all his camels.

²¹ The man looked steadfastly at her, remaining silent, to know whether Yahweh had made his journey prosperous or not. ²² As the camels had done drinking, the man took a golden ring of half a shekel weight, and two bracelets for her hands of ten shekels weight of gold, ²³ and said, "Whose daughter are you? Please tell me. Is there room in your father's house for us to lodge in?"

²⁴ She said to him, "I am the daughter of Bethuel the son of Milcah, whom she bore to Nahor." ²⁵ She said moreover to him, "We have both straw and feed enough, and room to lodge in."

²⁶ The man bowed his head, and worshiped Yahweh. ²⁷ He said, "Blessed be Yahweh, the God of my master Abraham, who has not forsaken his loving kindness and his truth toward my master. As for me, Yahweh has led me on the way to the house of my master's relatives."

²⁸ The young lady ran, and told her mother's house about these words. ²⁹ Rebekah had a brother, and his name was Laban. Laban ran out to the man, to the spring. ³⁰ When he saw the ring, and the bracelets on his sister's hands, and when he heard the words of Rebekah his sister, saying, "This is what the man said to me," he came to the man. Behold, he was standing by the camels at the spring. ³¹ He said, "Come in, you blessed of Yahweh. Why do you stand outside? For I have prepared the house, and room for the camels."

³² The man came into the house, and he unloaded the camels. He gave straw and feed for the camels, and water to wash his feet and the feet of the men who were with him. ³³ Food was set before him to eat, but he said, "I will not eat until I have told my message."

He said, "Speak on."

³⁴ He said, "I am Abraham's servant. ³⁵ Yahweh has blessed my master greatly. He has become great. He has given him flocks and herds, silver and gold, male servants and female servants, and camels and donkeys. ³⁶ Sarah, my master's wife, bore a son to my master when she was old. He has given all that he has to him. ³⁷ My master made me swear, saying, 'You shall not take a wife for my son from the daughters of the Canaanites, in whose land I live, ³⁸ but you shall go to my father's house, and to my relatives, and take a wife for my son.'

⁴⁹ Now if you will deal kindly and truly with my master, tell me. If not, tell me, that I may turn to the right hand, or to the left."

⁵⁰ Then Laban and Bethuel answered, "The thing proceeds from Yahweh. We can't speak to you bad or good. ⁵¹ Behold, Rebekah is before you. Take her, and go, and let her be your master's son's wife, as Yahweh has spoken."

When Abraham's servant heard their words, he bowed himself down to the earth to Yahweh. ⁵⁷ They said, "We will call the young lady, and ask her."

⁵⁸ They called Rebekah, and said to her, "Will you go with this man?" She said, "I will go."

⁵⁹ They sent away Rebekah, their sister, with her nurse, Abraham's servant, and his men. ⁶⁰ They blessed Rebekah, and said to her, "Our sister, may you be the mother of thousands of ten thousands, and let your offspring possess the gate of those who hate them."

⁶¹ Rebekah arose with her ladies. They rode on the camels, and followed the man. The servant took Rebekah, and went his way. ⁶² Isaac came from the way of Beer Lahai Roi, for he lived in the land of the South. ⁶³ Isaac went out to meditate in the field at the evening. He lifted up his eyes, and saw, and, behold, there were camels coming. ⁶⁴ Rebekah lifted up her eyes, and when she saw Isaac, she dismounted from the camel. ⁶⁵ She said to the servant, "Who is the man who is walking in the field to meet us?" The servant said, "It is my master." She took her veil, and covered herself. ⁶⁶ The servant told Isaac all the things that he had done. ⁶⁷ Isaac brought her into his mother Sarah's tent, and took Rebekah, and she became his wife. He loved her. Isaac was comforted after his mother's death.

1. *Tell of the specific requests made by the servant and how God answered them.*
2. *What quality was the servant looking for in a wife for Isaac?*

10. THE STOLEN BLESSING
Genesis 25:19-34, 27:1-37, 41-45

God continued to develop the new nation of Israel by giving two sons to Isaac, Jacob and Esau. Jacob was a liar, who tricked his brother Esau into giving him his inheritance. Although God does not approve of deceit, He is able to overcome man's evil and still accomplish His purposes.

The Birth of Jacob and Esau

25 ¹⁹ This is the history of the generations of Isaac, Abraham's son. Abraham became the father of Isaac. ²⁰ Isaac was forty years old when he took Rebekah, the daughter of Bethuel the Syrian of Paddan Aram, the sister of Laban the Syrian, to be his wife. ²¹ Isaac entreated Yahweh for his wife, because she was barren. Yahweh was entreated by him, and Rebekah his wife conceived. ²² The children struggled together within her. She said, "If it is like this, why do I live?" She went to inquire of Yahweh. ²³ Yahweh said to her,

"Two nations are in your womb.
Two peoples will be separated from your body.
The one people will be stronger than the other people.
The elder will serve the younger."

²⁴ When her days to be delivered were fulfilled, behold, there were twins in her womb. ²⁵ The first came out red all over, like a hairy garment.

They named him Esau. ²⁶ After that, his brother came out, and his hand had hold on Esau's heel. He was named Jacob. Isaac was sixty years old when she bore them.

²⁷ The boys grew. Esau was a skillful hunter, a man of the field. Jacob was a quiet man, living in tents. ²⁸ Now Isaac loved Esau, because he ate his venison. Rebekah loved Jacob. ²⁹ Jacob boiled stew. Esau came in from the field, and he was famished. ³⁰ Esau said to Jacob, "Please feed me with some of that red stew, for I am famished." Therefore his name was called Edom. ³¹ Jacob said, "First, sell me your birthright." ³² Esau said, "Behold, I am about to die. What good is the birthright to me?" ³³ Jacob said, "Swear to me first." He swore to him. He sold his birthright to Jacob. ³⁴ Jacob gave Esau bread and lentil stew. He ate and drank, rose up, and went his way. So Esau despised his birthright.

Jacob Gets Esau's Blessing
27 When Isaac was old, and his eyes were dim, so that he could not see, he called Esau his elder son, and said to him, "My son?"

He said to him, "Here I am." ² He said, "See now, I am old. I don't know the day of my death. ³ Now therefore, please take your weapons, your quiver and your bow, and go out to the field, and take me venison. ⁴ Make me savory food, such as I love, and bring it to me, that I may eat, and that my soul may bless you before I die."

⁵ Rebekah heard when Isaac spoke to Esau his son. Esau went to the field to hunt for venison, and to bring it. ⁶ Rebekah spoke to Jacob her son, saying, "Behold, I heard your father speak to Esau your brother, saying, ⁷ 'Bring me venison, and make me savory food, that I may eat, and bless you before Yahweh before my death.' ⁸ Now therefore, my son, obey my voice according to that which I command you. ⁹ Go now to the flock, and get me from there two good young goats. I will make them savory food for your father, such as he loves. ¹⁰ You shall bring it to your father, that he may eat, so that he may bless you before his death."

¹¹ Jacob said to Rebekah his mother, "Behold, Esau my brother is a hairy man, and I am a smooth man. ¹² What if my father touches me? I will seem to him as a deceiver, and I would bring a curse on myself, and not a blessing."

¹³ His mother said to him, "Let your curse be on me, my son. Only obey my voice, and go get them for me."

¹⁴ He went, and got them, and brought them to his mother. His mother made savory food, such as his father loved. ¹⁵ Rebekah took the good clothes of Esau, her elder son, which were with her in the house, and put them on Jacob, her younger son. ¹⁶ She put the skins of the young goats on his hands, and on the smooth of his neck. ¹⁷ She gave the savory food and the bread, which she had prepared, into the hand of her son Jacob.

¹⁸ He came to his father, and said, "My father?"

He said, "Here I am. Who are you, my son?"

¹⁹ Jacob said to his father, "I am Esau your firstborn. I have done what you asked me to do. Please arise, sit and eat of my venison, that your soul may bless me."

²⁰ Isaac said to his son, "How is it that you have found it so quickly, my son?"

He said, "Because Yahweh your God gave me success."

²¹ Isaac said to Jacob, "Please come near, that I may feel you, my son, whether you are really my son Esau or not."

²² Jacob went near to Isaac his father. He felt him, and said, "The voice is Jacob's voice, but the hands are the hands of Esau." ²³ He didn't recognize him, because his hands were hairy, like his brother, Esau's hands. So he blessed him. ²⁴ He said, "Are you really my son Esau?"

He said, "I am."

²⁵ He said, "Bring it near to me, and I will eat of my son's venison, that my soul may bless you."

He brought it near to him, and he ate. He brought him wine, and he drank. ²⁶ His father Isaac said to him, "Come near now, and kiss me, my son." ²⁷ He came near, and kissed him. He smelled the smell of his clothing, and blessed him, and said,

> "Behold, the smell of my son is as the smell of a field which Yahweh has blessed.
> ²⁸ God give you of the dew of the sky,
> of the fatness of the earth,
> and plenty of grain and new wine.
> ²⁹ Let peoples serve you,
> and nations bow down to you.
> Be lord over your brothers.
> Let your mother's sons bow down to you.
> Cursed be everyone who curses you.
> Blessed be everyone who blesses you."

³⁰ As soon as Isaac had finished blessing Jacob, and Jacob had just gone out from the presence of Isaac his father, Esau his brother came in from his hunting. ³¹ He also made savory food, and brought it to his father. He said to his father, "Let my father arise, and eat of his son's venison, that your soul may bless me."

³³ Isaac his father said to him, "Who are you?"

He said, "I am your son, your firstborn, Esau."

³³ Isaac trembled violently, and said, "Who, then, is he who has taken venison, and brought it me, and I have eaten of all before you came, and have blessed him? Yes, he will be blessed."

³⁴ When Esau heard the words of his father, he cried with an exceeding

great and bitter cry, and said to his father, "Bless me, even me also, my father."

³⁵ He said, "Your brother came with deceit, and has taken away your blessing."

³⁶ He said, "Isn't he rightly named Jacob? For he has supplanted me these two times. He took away my birthright. See, now he has taken away my blessing." He said, "Haven't you reserved a blessing for me?"

³⁷ Isaac answered Esau, "Behold, I have made him your lord, and all his brothers have I given to him for servants. With grain and new wine have I sustained him. What then will I do for you, my son?"

Jacob Flees to Laban

⁴¹ Esau hated Jacob because of the blessing with which his father blessed him. Esau said in his heart, "The days of mourning for my father are at hand. Then I will kill my brother Jacob."

⁴² The words of Esau, her elder son, were told to Rebekah. She sent and called Jacob, her younger son, and said to him, "Behold, your brother Esau comforts himself about you by planning to kill you. ⁴³ Now therefore, my son, obey my voice. Arise, flee to Laban, my brother, in Haran. ⁴⁴ Stay with him a few days, until your brother's fury turns away;⁴⁵ until your brother's anger turn away from you, and he forgets what you have done to him. Then I will send, and get you from there. Why should I be bereaved of you both in one day?"

    1. How did Jacob trick Esau and deceive Isaac?

    2. What promise was given to Jacob?

    3. What suffering did Jacob bring upon himself and his mother?

11. THE LADDER TO HEAVEN
Genesis 28:10-22

Although Jacob went about it in the wrong way, he did sincerely want the blessing that belonged to the family of Abraham. In a vision, God revealed to Jacob His plan for the future. God later changed Jacob's name to Israel and it was his sons whose families became the twelve tribes of the nation of Israel. It was God's plan that the Savior of the world would be born in Israel and be the ladder to heaven for all people.

Jacob's Dream at Bethel

28 ¹⁰Jacob went out from Beersheba, and went toward Haran. ¹¹ He came to a certain place, and stayed there all night, because the sun had set. He took one of the stones of the place, and put it under his head, and lay down in that place to sleep. ¹² He dreamed. Behold, a stairway set upon the earth, and its top reached to heaven. Behold, the angels of God ascending and descending on it. ¹³ Behold, Yahweh stood above it, and said, "I am Yahweh, the God of

Abraham your father, and the God of Isaac. The land whereon you lie, to you will I give it, and to your offspring. [14] Your offspring will be as the dust of the earth, and you will spread abroad to the west, and to the east, and to the north, and to the south. In you and in your offspring will all the families of the earth be blessed. [15] Behold, I am with you, and will keep you, wherever you go, and will bring you again into this land. For I will not leave you, until I have done that which I have spoken of to you."

[16] Jacob awakened out of his sleep, and he said, "Surely Yahweh is in this place, and I didn't know it." [17] He was afraid, and said, "How dreadful is this place! This is none other than God's house, and this is the gate of heaven."

[18] Jacob rose up early in the morning, and took the stone that he had put under his head, and set it up for a pillar, and poured oil on its top. [19] He called the name of that place Bethel, but the name of the city was Luz at the first. [20] Jacob vowed a vow, saying, "If God will be with me, and will keep me in this way that I go, and will give me bread to eat, and clothing to put on, [21] so that I come again to my father's house in peace, and Yahweh will be my God, [22] then this stone, which I have set up for a pillar, will be God's house. Of all that you will give me I will surely give a tenth to you."

  1. *What promises did God make to Jacob?*

  2. *How did Jacob react to the dream?*

  3. *What vow did Jacob make to God?*

B. THE FAVOR OF GOD

The story of the life of Joseph is one of the most exciting accounts in the Old Testament. These next five selections record how God took an act meant for evil and turned it around for the good of all concerned.

12. THE EVIL DEED
Genesis 37:1-14, 17-36

Jacob, who was now called Israel, had twelve sons. He favored one son; and because of that, the other sons sought revenge. Evil deeds always begin with a seed of sin that grows within the heart of man.

Joseph's Dreams

37 [1]Jacob lived in the land of his father's travels, in the land of Canaan. [2] This is the history of the generations of Jacob. Joseph, being seventeen years old, was feeding the flock with his brothers. He was a boy with the sons of Bilhah and Zilpah, his father's wives. Joseph brought an evil report of them to their father. [3]Now Israel loved Joseph more than all his children, because he was the son of his old age, and he made him a coat of many colors. [4] His brothers saw that their father loved him more than all his brothers, and they hated him, and couldn't speak peaceably to him.

⁵ Joseph dreamed a dream, and he told it to his brothers, and they hated him all the more. ⁶ He said to them, "Please hear this dream which I have dreamed: ⁷ for behold, we were binding sheaves in the field, and behold, my sheaf arose and also stood upright; and behold, your sheaves came around, and bowed down to my sheaf."

⁸ His brothers said to him, "Will you indeed reign over us? Or will you indeed have dominion over us?" They hated him all the more for his dreams and for his words. ⁹ He dreamed yet another dream, and told it to his brothers, and said, "Behold, I have dreamed yet another dream: and behold, the sun and the moon and eleven stars bowed down to me." ¹⁰ He told it to his father and to his brothers. His father rebuked him, and said to him, "What is this dream that you have dreamed? Will I and your mother and your brothers indeed come to bow ourselves down to you to the earth?" ¹¹ His brothers envied him, but his father kept this saying in mind.

Joseph Sold by His Brothers

¹² His brothers went to feed their father's flock in Shechem. ¹³ Israel said to Joseph, "Aren't your brothers feeding the flock in Shechem? Come, and I will send you to them." He said to him, "Here I am."

¹⁴ He said to him, "Go now, see whether it is well with your brothers, and well with the flock; and bring me word again." So he sent him out of the valley of Hebron, and he came to Shechem.

¹⁷ The man said, "They have left here, for I heard them say, 'Let us go to Dothan.'"

Joseph went after his brothers, and found them in Dothan. ¹⁸ They saw him afar off, and before he came near to them, they conspired against him to kill him. ¹⁹ They said to one another, "Behold, this dreamer comes. ²⁰ Come now therefore, and let's kill him, and cast him into one of the pits, and we will say, 'An evil animal has devoured him.' We will see what will become of his dreams."

²¹ Reuben heard it, and delivered him out of their hand, and said, "Let's not take his life." ²² Reuben said to them, "Shed no blood. Throw him into this pit that is in the wilderness, but lay no hand on him"—that he might deliver him out of their hand, to restore him to his father. ²³ When Joseph came to his brothers, they stripped Joseph of his coat, the coat of many colors that was on him; ²⁴ and they took him, and threw him into the pit. The pit was empty. There was no water in it.

²⁵ They sat down to eat bread, and they lifted up their eyes and looked, and saw a caravan of Ishmaelites was coming from Gilead, with their camels bearing spices and balm and myrrh, going to carry it down to Egypt. ²⁶ Judah said to his brothers, "What profit is it if we kill our brother and conceal his

blood? ²⁷ Come, and let's sell him to the Ishmaelites, and not let our hand be on him; for he is our brother, our flesh." His brothers listened to him. ²⁸ Midianites who were merchants passed by, and they drew and lifted up Joseph out of the pit, and sold Joseph to the Ishmaelites for twenty pieces of silver. They brought Joseph into Egypt.

²⁹ Reuben returned to the pit; and saw that Joseph wasn't in the pit; and he tore his clothes. ³⁰ He returned to his brothers, and said, "The child is no more; and I, where will I go?" ³¹ They took Joseph's coat, and killed a male goat, and dipped the coat in the blood.³² They took the coat of many colors, and they brought it to their father, and said, "We have found this. Examine it, now, whether it is your son's coat or not."

³³ He recognized it, and said, "It is my son's coat. An evil animal has devoured him. Joseph is without doubt torn in pieces." ³⁴ Jacob tore his clothes, and put sackcloth on his waist, and mourned for his son many days. ³⁵ All his sons and all his daughters rose up to comfort him, but he refused to be comforted. He said, "For I will go down to Sheol[the place of the dead] to my son mourning." His father wept for him. ³⁶ The Midianites sold him into Egypt to Potiphar, an officer of Pharaoh's, the captain of the guard.

1. *Describe Joseph's dreams and tell why they made his brothers angry.*
2. *How did God thwart the plan to kill Joseph?*
3. *Do you see how jealousy breeds hatred and can lead men to commit evil acts that they later regret?*
4. *Note how the news about Joseph affected his father, Jacob. Can you see how evil can affect innocent people?*
5. *We see that deceit followed the family line of Abraham, Isaac and Jacob. Jacob himself was deceived by his own sons, and suffered because of it.*

13. A GOOD MAN
Genesis 39 and 40

God was with Joseph in Egypt, helping him and blessing him in spite of all the difficulties he faced. We read that Joseph refused to sin even though his action resulted in much personal suffering. Because of his sincere desire to please God, Joseph continued to be successful in all situations. God's favor and blessing always follow those who love and obey Him.

Joseph and Potiphar's Wife

39 Joseph was brought down to Egypt. Potiphar, an officer of Pharaoh's, the captain of the guard, an Egyptian, bought him from the hand of the Ishmaelites that had brought him down there. ² Yahweh was with Joseph, and he was a prosperous man. He was in the house of his master the Egyptian. ³ His master saw that Yahweh was with him, and that Yahweh made all that he did prosper in his hand. ⁴ Joseph found favor in his sight. He ministered to him, and he made him overseer over his house, and all that he had he put into his hand. ⁵ From the time that he made him overseer in his house, and over all that he had, Yahweh blessed the Egyptian's house for

Joseph's sake. Yahweh's blessing was on all that he had, in the house and in the field. ⁶ He left all that he had in Joseph's hand. He didn't concern himself with anything, except for the food which he ate.

Joseph was well-built and handsome. ⁷ After these things, his master's wife set her eyes on Joseph; and she said, "Lie with me."

⁸ But he refused, and said to his master's wife, "Behold, my master doesn't know what is with me in the house, and he has put all that he has into my hand. ⁹ No one is greater in this house than I am, and he has not kept back anything from me but you, because you are his wife. How then can I do this great wickedness, and sin against God?"

¹⁰ As she spoke to Joseph day by day, he didn't listen to her, to lie by her, or to be with her. ¹¹ About this time, he went into the house to do his work, and there were none of the men of the house inside.¹² She caught him by his garment, saying, "Lie with me!"

He left his garment in her hand, and ran outside. ¹³ When she saw that he had left his garment in her hand, and had run outside, ¹⁴ she called to the men of her house, and spoke to them, saying, "Behold, he has brought in a Hebrew to us to mock us. He came in to me to lie with me, and I cried with a loud voice. ¹⁵ When he heard that I lifted up my voice and cried, he left his garment by me, and ran outside." ¹⁶ She laid up his garment by her, until his master came home. ¹⁷ She spoke to him according to these words, saying, "The Hebrew servant, whom you have brought to us, came in to me to mock me,¹⁸ and as I lifted up my voice and cried, he left his garment by me, and ran outside."

Joseph Put in Prison

¹⁹ When his master heard the words of his wife, which she spoke to him, saying, "This is what your servant did to me," his wrath was kindled. ²⁰ Joseph's master took him, and put him into the prison, the place where the king's prisoners were bound, and he was there in custody. ²¹ But Yahweh was with Joseph, and showed kindness to him, and gave him favor in the sight of the keeper of the prison. ²² The keeper of the prison committed to Joseph's hand all the prisoners who were in the prison. Whatever they did there, he was responsible for it. ²³ The keeper of the prison didn't look after anything that was under his hand, because Yahweh was with him; and that which he did, Yahweh made it prosper.

Joseph Interprets Two Dreams

40 After these things, the butler of the king of Egypt and his baker offended their lord, the king of Egypt. ²Pharaoh was angry with his two officers, the chief cup bearer and the chief baker. ³ He put them in custody in the house of the captain of the guard, into the prison, the place where Joseph was bound. ⁴ The captain of the guard assigned them to Joseph, and he took care of them. They stayed in prison many days. ⁵ They both dreamed a dream, each man his dream, in one night, each man according to the interpretation of his dream, the cup bearer and the baker of the king of Egypt, who were bound in the prison. ⁶ Joseph came in to them in the morning, and saw them, and saw that they were sad. ⁷ He asked Pharaoh's officers who were with him in custody in his master's house, saying, "Why do you look so sad today?"

⁸They said to him, "We have dreamed a dream, and there is no one who can interpret it."

Joseph said to them, "Don't interpretations belong to God? Please tell it to me."

⁹ The chief cup bearer told his dream to Joseph, and said to him, "In my dream, behold, a vine was in front of me, ¹⁰ and in the vine were three branches. It was as though it budded, it blossomed, and its clusters produced ripe grapes. ¹¹ Pharaoh's cup was in my hand; and I took the grapes, and pressed them into Pharaoh's cup, and I gave the cup into Pharaoh's hand."

¹² Joseph said to him, "This is its interpretation: the three branches are three days.¹³ Within three more days, Pharaoh will lift up your head, and restore you to your office. You will give Pharaoh's cup into his hand, the way you did when you were his cup bearer.¹⁴ But remember me when it will be well with you, and please show kindness to me, and make mention of me to Pharaoh, and bring me out of this house. ¹⁵ For indeed, I was stolen away out of the land of the Hebrews, and here also have I done nothing that they should put me into the dungeon."

¹⁶ When the chief baker saw that the interpretation was good, he said to Joseph, "I also was in my dream, and behold, three baskets of white bread were on my head. ¹⁷ In the uppermost basket there were all kinds of baked food for Pharaoh, and the birds ate them out of the basket on my head."

¹⁸ Joseph answered, "This is its interpretation. The three baskets are three days. ¹⁹ Within three more days, Pharaoh will lift up your head from off you, and will hang you on a tree; and the birds will eat your flesh from off you." ²⁰ On the third day, which was Pharaoh's birthday, he made a feast for all his servants, and he lifted up the head of the chief cup bearer and the head of the chief baker among his servants. ²¹ He restored the chief cup bearer to his position again, and he gave the cup into Pharaoh's hand; ²² but he hanged the chief baker, as Joseph had interpreted to them. ²³ Yet the chief cup bearer didn't remember Joseph, but forgot him.

1. Why was Joseph so successful when he first came to Egypt?
2. Notice Joseph's attitude toward sin. Could you also say NO to evil and YES to God as Joseph did?
3. Can you explain Joseph's rise to a positon of responsibility in prison?

14. THE KING'S DREAMS
Genesis 41:14-41

Although Joseph unfairly languished in prison for a long time, he decided to make the best of the situation. He had a positive attitude and a helpful spirit, knowing that God controlled his circumstances. Joseph interpreted the dreams of two other prisoners. When the king needed someone to interpret a dream for him, he was told about Joseph and sent for him. Again, we see God's hand guiding Joseph and bringing him to a place of honor because of his obedience.

Pharaoh's Dreams

41 [14]Then Pharaoh sent and called Joseph, and they brought him hastily out of the dungeon. He shaved himself, changed his clothing, and came in to Pharaoh. [15] Pharaoh said to Joseph, "I have dreamed a dream, and there is no one who can interpret it. I have heard it said of you, that when you hear a dream you can interpret it."

[16] Joseph answered Pharaoh, saying, "It isn't in me. God will give Pharaoh an answer of peace."

[17] Pharaoh spoke to Joseph, "In my dream, behold, I stood on the brink of the river: [18] and behold, there came up out of the river seven cattle, fat and sleek. They fed in the marsh grass, [19] and behold, seven other cattle came up after them, poor and very ugly and thin, such as I never saw in all the land of Egypt for ugliness. [20] The thin and ugly cattle ate up the first seven fat cattle, [21] and when they had eaten them up, it couldn't be known that they had eaten them, but they were still ugly, as at the beginning. So I awoke. [22] I saw in my dream, and behold, seven heads of grain came up on one stalk, full and good: [23] and behold, seven heads of grain, withered, thin, and blasted with the east wind, sprung up after them. [24] The thin heads of grain swallowed up the seven good heads of grain. I told it to the magicians, but there was no one who could explain it to me."

[25] Joseph said to Pharaoh, "The dream of Pharaoh is one. What God is about to do he has declared to Pharaoh. [26] The seven good cattle are seven years; and the seven good heads of grain are seven years. The dream is one. [27] The seven thin and ugly cattle that came up after them are seven years, and also the seven empty heads of grain blasted with the east wind; they will be seven years of famine. [28] That is the thing which I spoke to Pharaoh. What God is about to do he has shown to Pharaoh. [29] Behold, there come seven years of great plenty throughout all the land of Egypt. [30] There will arise after them seven years of famine, and all the plenty will be forgotten in the land of Egypt. The famine will consume the land, [31] and the plenty will not be known in the land by reason of that famine which follows; for it will be very grievous. [32] The dream was doubled to Pharaoh, because the thing is established by God, and God will shortly bring it to pass.

[33] "Now therefore let Pharaoh look for a discreet and wise man, and set him over the land of Egypt. [34] Let Pharaoh do this, and let him appoint overseers over the land, and take up the fifth part of the land of Egypt's produce in the seven plenteous years. [35] Let them gather all the food of these good years that come, and lay up grain under the hand of Pharaoh for food in the cities, and let them keep it. [36] The food will be for a store to the land against the seven years of famine, which will be in the land of Egypt; that the land not perish through the famine."

[37] The thing was good in the eyes of Pharaoh, and in the eyes of all his servants. [38] Pharaoh said to his servants, "Can we find such a one as this, a man in whom is the Spirit of God?" [39] Pharaoh said to Joseph, "Because God has shown you all of this, there is no one so discreet and wise as you. [40] You shall be over my house, and according to your word will all my people

be ruled. Only in the throne I will be greater than you." ⁴¹ Pharaoh said to Joseph, "Behold, I have set you over all the land of Egypt."

1. How do we know that Joseph was a humble man?
2. How does this story show that God controls future events?
3. Describe how Joseph's trust in God over the years led to his vindication and rise to a position of greatness.

15. JOSEPH IS VINDICATED
Genesis 42:1-29

Joseph went from being a prisoner slave to being a prime minister. As God had predicted, the famine came and was severe. All the countries of the world came to Egypt to buy food, including Joseph's brothers. God used the famine to rescue Joseph and vindicate him. The brothers' evil deed had followed them and they suffered for it. However, Joseph like God was merciful.

Joseph's Brothers Go to Egypt

42 Now Jacob saw that there was grain in Egypt, and Jacob said to his sons, "Why do you look at one another?" ² He said, "Behold, I have heard that there is grain in Egypt. Go down there, and buy for us from there, so that we may live, and not die." ³ Joseph's ten brothers went down to buy grain from Egypt. ⁴ But Jacob didn't send Benjamin, Joseph's brother, with his brothers; for he said, "Lest perhaps harm happen to him." ⁵ The sons of Israel came to buy among those who came, for the famine was in the land of Canaan. ⁶ Joseph was the governor over the land. It was he who sold to all the people of the land. Joseph's brothers came, and bowed themselves down to him with their faces to the earth. ⁷ Joseph saw his brothers, and he recognized them, but acted like a stranger to them, and spoke roughly with them. He said to them, "Where did you come from?"

They said, "From the land of Canaan to buy food."

⁸ Joseph recognized his brothers, but they didn't recognize him. ⁹ Joseph remembered the dreams which he dreamed about them, and said to them, "You are spies! You have come to see the nakedness of the land."

¹⁰ They said to him, "No, my lord, but your servants have come to buy food. ¹¹ We are all one man's sons; we are honest men. Your servants are not spies."

¹² He said to them, "No, but you have come to see the nakedness of the land!"

¹³ They said, "We, your servants, are twelve brothers, the sons of one man in the land of Canaan; and behold, the youngest is today with our father, and one is no more."

¹⁴ Joseph said to them, "It is like I told you, saying, 'You are spies!' ¹⁵ By this you shall be tested. By the life of Pharaoh, you shall not go out from here, unless your youngest brother comes here. ¹⁶ Send one of you, and let him get your brother, and you shall be bound, that your words may be tested, whether there is truth in you, or else by the life of Pharaoh surely you are spies." ¹⁷ He put them all together into custody for three days.

¹⁸ Joseph said to them the third day, "Do this, and live, for I fear God. ¹⁹ If

you are honest men, then let one of your brothers be bound in your prison; but you go, carry grain for the famine of your houses. ²⁰ Bring your youngest brother to me; so will your words be verified, and you won't die."

They did so. ²¹ They said to one another, "We are certainly guilty concerning our brother, in that we saw the distress of his soul, when he begged us, and we wouldn't listen. Therefore this distress has come upon us." ²² Reuben answered them, saying, "Didn't I tell you, saying, 'Don't sin against the child,' and you wouldn't listen? Therefore also, behold, his blood is required." ²³ They didn't know that Joseph understood them; for there was an interpreter between them. ²⁴ He turned himself away from them, and wept. Then he returned to them, and spoke to them, and took Simeon from among them, and bound him before their eyes. ²⁵ Then Joseph gave a command to fill their bags with grain, and to restore each man's money into his sack, and to give them food for the way. So it was done to them.

²⁶ They loaded their donkeys with their grain, and departed from there. ²⁷ As one of them opened his sack to give his donkey food in the lodging place, he saw his money. Behold, it was in the mouth of his sack. ²⁸ He said to his brothers, "My money is restored! Behold, it is in my sack!" Their hearts failed them, and they turned trembling to one another, saying, "What is this that God has done to us?" They came to Jacob their father, to the land of Canaan, and told him all that had happened to them.

1. How were the visions and promises given by God to Joseph as a boy fulfilled?
2. What does this passage teach us about the result of sin?
3. What does this passage tell you about the phrase, "You reap what you sow?"

16. THE HAPPY ENDING
Genesis 45

The brothers returned to their father Jacob and told him all that had happened. Although they were afraid to return to Egypt, the famine forced them to go for more food. This time they took Benjamin with them as Joseph had told them to do. When Joseph revealed himself to them, he told them how God turned the evil deed of his brothers into something good. By bringing them to Egypt to live, God again saved the descendants of Abraham.

Joseph Makes Himself Known

45 Then Joseph couldn't control himself before all those who stood before him, and he cried, "Cause everyone to go out from me!" No one else stood with him, while Joseph made himself known to his brothers. ² He wept aloud. The Egyptians heard, and the house of Pharaoh heard. ³ Joseph said to his brothers, "I am Joseph! Does my father still live?"

His brothers couldn't answer him; for they were terrified at his presence. ⁴ Joseph said to his brothers, "Come near to me, please."

They came near. "He said, I am Joseph, your brother, whom you sold into Egypt. ⁵ Now don't be grieved, nor angry with yourselves, that you sold me here, for God sent me before you to preserve life. ⁶ For these two years the famine has been in the land, and there are yet five years, in which there will be no plowing and no harvest. ⁷ God sent me before you to preserve for you a remnant in the earth, and to save you alive by a great deliverance. ⁸ So now it wasn't you who sent me here, but God, and he has made me a father to Pharaoh, lord of all his house, and ruler over all the land of Egypt. ⁹ Hurry, and go up to my father, and tell him, 'This is what your son Joseph says, "God has made me lord of all Egypt. Come down to me. Don't wait. ¹⁰ You shall dwell in the land of Goshen, and you will be near to me, you, your children, your children's children, your flocks, your herds, and all that you have. ¹¹ There I will nourish you; for there are yet five years of famine; lest you come to poverty, you, and your household, and all that you have."'¹² Behold, your eyes see, and the eyes of my brother Benjamin, that it is my mouth that speaks to you. ¹³ You shall tell my father of all my glory in Egypt, and of all that you have seen. You shall hurry and bring my father down here." ¹⁴ He fell on his brother Benjamin's neck, and wept, and Benjamin wept on his neck. ¹⁵ He kissed all his brothers, and wept on them. After that his brothers talked with him.

¹⁶ The report of it was heard in Pharaoh's house, saying, "Joseph's brothers have come." It pleased Pharaoh well, and his servants. ¹⁷ Pharaoh said to Joseph, "Tell your brothers, 'Do this. Load your animals, and go, travel to the land of Canaan. ¹⁸ Take your father and your households, and come to me, and I will give you the good of the land of Egypt, and you will eat the fat of the land.' ¹⁹ Now you are commanded: do this. Take wagons out of the land of Egypt for your little ones, and for your wives, and bring your father, and come. ²⁰ Also, don't concern yourselves about your belongings, for the good of all the land of Egypt is yours."

²¹ The sons of Israel did so. Joseph gave them wagons, according to the commandment of Pharaoh, and gave them provision for the way. ²² He gave each one of them changes of clothing, but to Benjamin he gave three hundred pieces of silver and five changes of clothing. ²³ He sent the following to his father: ten donkeys loaded with the good things of Egypt, and ten female donkeys loaded with grain and bread and provision for his father by the way. ²⁴ So he sent his brothers away, and they departed. He said to them, "See that you don't quarrel on the way."

²⁵ They went up out of Egypt, and came into the land of Canaan, to Jacob their father.²⁶ They told him, saying, "Joseph is still alive, and he is ruler over all the land of Egypt." His heart fainted, for he didn't believe them. ²⁷ They told him all the words of Joseph, which he had said to them. When he saw the wagons which Joseph had sent to carry him, the spirit of Jacob, their father, revived. ²⁸ Israel said, "It is enough. Joseph my son is still alive. I will go and see him before I die."

> 1. How did Joseph explain the purposes of God in all that had happened?
> 2. Can you see the favor of God upon Joseph as Pharaoh was moved to help Joseph's family move to Egypt?

3. How did Joseph show that he had forgiven his brothers, in spite of what they had done to him?
4. What does this story about Joseph and his family tell you about the importance God places on human relationships?
5. What outstanding characteristic of Joseph's life would you like to make part of your life?

C. THE DELIVERANCE OF GOD

In these next five selections we read of the deliverance of the Israelites from their slavery. God miraculously led the people out of Egypt and into freedom. This is God's desire for all people, that they would be free from their bondage to sin. God's deliverance is provided in the Savior, whose blood paid the price for man's sin.

17. EGYPT ENSLAVES ISRAEL
Exodus 1:1-22

During the 430 years that the children of Israel lived in Egypt, they grew into a very strong nation. After Joseph's death, the kings of Egypt oppressed the people of Israel and made them slaves.

The Israelites Oppressed

1 Now these are the names of the sons of Israel, who came into Egypt (every man and his household came with Jacob): ² Reuben, Simeon, Levi, and Judah, ³ Issachar, Zebulun, and Benjamin, ⁴ Dan and Naphtali, Gad and Asher. ⁵ All the souls who came out of Jacob's body were seventy souls, and Joseph was in Egypt already. ⁶ Joseph died, as did all his brothers, and all that generation. ⁷ The children of Israel were fruitful, and increased abundantly, and multiplied, and grew exceedingly mighty; and the land was filled with them. ⁸ Now there arose a new king over Egypt, who didn't know Joseph. ⁹ He said to his people, "Behold, the people of the children of Israel are more and mightier than we. ¹⁰ Come, let us deal wisely with them, lest they multiply, and it happen that when any war breaks out, they also join themselves to our enemies, and fight against us, and escape out of the land." ¹¹ Therefore they set taskmasters over them to afflict them with their burdens. They built storage cities for Pharaoh: Pithom and Raamses. ¹² But the more they afflicted them, the more they multiplied and the more they spread out. They were grieved [distressed] because of the children of Israel. ¹³ The Egyptians ruthlessly made the children of Israel serve, ¹⁴ and they made their lives bitter with hard service, in mortar and in brick, and in all kinds of service in the field, all their service, in which they ruthlessly made them serve.

¹⁵ The king of Egypt spoke to the Hebrew midwives, of whom the name of the one was Shiphrah, and the name of the other Puah, ¹⁶ and he said, "When you perform the duty of a midwife to the Hebrew women, and see them on the birth stool; if it is a son, then you shall kill him; but if it is a daughter, then she

shall live." ¹⁷ But the midwives feared God, and didn't do what the king of Egypt commanded them, but saved the baby boys alive. ¹⁸ The king of Egypt called for the midwives, and said to them, "Why have you done this thing, and have saved the boys alive?"

¹⁹ The midwives said to Pharaoh, "Because the Hebrew women aren't like the Egyptian women; for they are vigorous, and give birth before the midwife comes to them."

²⁰ God dealt well with the midwives, and the people multiplied, and grew very mighty. ²¹ Because the midwives feared God, he gave them families. ²² Pharaoh commanded all his people, saying, "You shall cast every son who is born into the river, and every daughter you shall save alive."

1. How large did Jacob's family become while living in Egypt?
2. Why did the king oppress the Israelites?
3. Why do you suppose the Lord allowed the Israelites to be oppressed by the Egyptians?
4. How did the Lord reward the midwives?

18. GOD CALLS ISRAEL'S FIRST LEADER
Exodus 2:1-25

The people cried out to God, and He heard them and remembered His promise to Abraham. God raised up Moses and prepared him to lead the Israelites out of Egypt. We read now of God's hand in the life of Moses, who was saved from death and prepared by God to lead the Israelites out of slavery.

The Birth of Moses

2 A man of the house of Levi went and took a daughter of Levi as his wife. ² The woman conceived, and bore a son. When she saw that he was a fine child, she hid him three months. ³ When she could no longer hide him, she took a papyrus basket for him, and coated it with tar and with pitch. She put the child in it, and laid it in the reeds by the river's bank. ⁴ His sister stood far off, to see what would be done to him. ⁵ Pharaoh's daughter came down to bathe at the river. Her maidens walked along by the riverside. She saw the basket among the reeds, and sent her servant to get it. ⁶ She opened it, and saw the child, and behold, the baby cried. She had compassion on him, and said, "This is one of the Hebrews' children."

⁷ Then his sister said to Pharaoh's daughter, "Should I go and call a nurse for you from the Hebrew women, that she may nurse the child for you?"

⁸ Pharaoh's daughter said to her, "Go."

The maiden went and called the child's mother. ⁹ Pharaoh's daughter said to her, "Take this child away, and nurse him for me, and I will give you your wages."

The woman took the child, and nursed it. ¹⁰ The child grew, and she brought him to Pharaoh's daughter, and he became her son. She named him Moses, and said, "Because I drew him out of the water."

Moses Flees to Midian

[11] In those days, when Moses had grown up, he went out to his brothers, and looked at their burdens. He saw an Egyptian striking a Hebrew, one of his brothers. [12] He looked this way and that way, and when he saw that there was no one, he killed the Egyptian, and hid him in the sand.

[13] He went out the second day, and behold, two men of the Hebrews were fighting with each other. He said to him who did the wrong, "Why do you strike your fellow?"

[14] He said, "Who made you a prince and a judge over us? Do you plan to kill me, as you killed the Egyptian?"

Moses was afraid, and said, "Surely this thing is known." [15] Now when Pharaoh heard this thing, he sought to kill Moses. But Moses fled from the face of Pharaoh, and lived in the land of Midian, and he sat down by a well.

[16] Now the priest of Midian had seven daughters. They came and drew water, and filled the troughs to water their father's flock. [17] The shepherds came and drove them away; but Moses stood up and helped them, and watered their flock. [18] When they came to Reuel, their father, he said, "How is it that you have returned so early today?"

[19] They said, "An Egyptian delivered us out of the hand of the shepherds, and moreover he drew water for us, and watered the flock."

[20] He said to his daughters, "Where is he? Why is it that you have left the man? Call him, that he may eat bread."

[21] Moses was content to dwell with the man. He gave Moses Zipporah, his daughter. [22] She bore a son, and he named him Gershom, for he said, "I have lived as a foreigner in a foreign land."

[23] In the course of those many days, the king of Egypt died, and the children of Israel sighed because of the bondage, and they cried, and their cry came up to God because of the bondage. [24] God heard their groaning, and God remembered his covenant with Abraham, with Isaac, and with Jacob. [25] God saw the children of Israel, and God was concerned about them.

1. *How did God protect Moses at birth and begin to train him as a leader?*
2. *Why did Moses identify with Israel and not with Egypt?*
3. *What serious mistake did Moses make? What was the result?*

19. HOLY GROUND
Exodus 3:1-22 and 4:1-17

After Moses fled from Egypt, he lived as a shepherd in the wilderness for forty years. Moses was an old man when God finally revealed Himself to Moses and spoke to him personally out of a burning bush. God called Moses to deliver the Israelites from the Egyptians. God promised to be with Moses and perform miraculous wonders before the Egyptians. Because God has always been and never changes, God calls Himself, "I AM WHO I AM."

Great Bible Truths

Moses and the Burning Bush

3 Now Moses was keeping the flock of Jethro, his father-in-law, the priest of Midian, and he led the flock to the back of the wilderness, and came to God's mountain, to Horeb. [2] Yahweh's angel appeared to him in a flame of fire out of the middle of a bush. He looked, and behold, the bush burned with fire, and the bush was not consumed. [3] Moses said, "I will turn aside now, and see this great sight, why the bush is not burnt."

[4] When Yahweh saw that he turned aside to see, God called to him out of the middle of the bush, and said, "Moses! Moses!"

He said, "Here I am."

[5] He said, "Don't come close. Take your sandals off of your feet, for the place you are standing on is holy ground." [6] Moreover he said, "I am the God of your father, the God of Abraham, the God of Isaac, and the God of Jacob."

Moses hid his face; for he was afraid to look at God.

[7] Yahweh said, "I have surely seen the affliction of my people who are in Egypt, and have heard their cry because of their taskmasters, for I know their sorrows. [8] I have come down to deliver them out of the hand of the Egyptians, and to bring them up out of that land to a good and large land, to a land flowing with milk and honey; to the place of the Canaanite, the Hittite, the Amorite, the Perizzite, the Hivite, and the Jebusite. [9] Now, behold, the cry of the children of Israel has come to me. Moreover I have seen the oppression with which the Egyptians oppress them. [10] Come now therefore, and I will send you to Pharaoh, that you may bring my people, the children of Israel, out of Egypt."

[11] Moses said to God, "Who am I, that I should go to Pharaoh, and that I should bring the children of Israel out of Egypt?"

[12] He said, "Certainly I will be with you. This will be the token to you, that I have sent you: when you have brought the people out of Egypt, you shall serve God on this mountain."

The Name of God

[13] Moses said to God, "Behold, when I come to the children of Israel, and tell them, 'The God of your fathers has sent me to you;' and they ask me, 'What is his name?' What should I tell them?"

[14] God said to Moses, "I AM WHO I AM," and he said, "You shall tell the children of Israel this: 'I AM has sent me to you.'" [15] God said moreover to Moses, "You shall tell the children of Israel this, 'Yahweh, the God of your fathers, the God of Abraham, the God of Isaac, and the God of Jacob, has sent me to you.' This is my name forever, and this is my memorial to all generations. [16] Go, and gather the elders of Israel together, and tell them, 'Yahweh, the God of your fathers, the God of Abraham, of Isaac, and of Jacob, has appeared to me, saying, "I have surely visited you, and seen that which is done to you in Egypt; [17] and I have said, I will bring you up out of the affliction of Egypt to the land of the Canaanite, the Hittite, the Amorite, the Perizzite, the Hivite, and

the Jebusite, to a land flowing with milk and honey.'" ¹⁸ They will listen to your voice, and you shall come, you and the elders of Israel, to the king of Egypt, and you shall tell him, 'Yahweh, the God of the Hebrews, has met with us. Now please let us go three days' journey into the wilderness, that we may sacrifice to Yahweh, our God.' ¹⁹ I know that the king of Egypt won't give you permission to go, no, [only] by a mighty hand [of power]. ²⁰ I will reach out my hand and strike Egypt with all my wonders which I will do among them, and after that he will let you go. ²¹ I will give this people favor in the sight of the Egyptians, and it will happen that when you go, you shall not go empty-handed. ²² But every woman shall ask of her neighbor, and of her who visits her house, jewels of silver, jewels of gold, and clothing; and you shall put them on your sons, and on your daughters. You shall plunder the Egyptians."

Signs for Moses

4 Moses answered, "But, behold, they will not believe me, nor listen to my voice; for they will say, 'Yahweh has not appeared to you.'"

² Yahweh said to him, "What is that in your hand?"

He said, "A rod."

³ He said, "Throw it on the ground."

He threw it on the ground, and it became a snake; and Moses ran away from it.

¹ Yahweh said to Moses, "Stretch out your hand, and take it by the tail."

He stretched out his hand, and took hold of it, and it became a rod in his hand.

² "That they may believe that Yahweh, the God of their fathers, the God of Abraham, the God of Isaac, and the God of Jacob, has appeared to you." ⁶ Yahweh said furthermore to him, "Now put your hand inside your cloak."

He put his hand inside his cloak, and when he took it out, behold, his hand was leprous, as white as snow.

⁷ He said, "Put your hand inside your cloak again."

He put his hand inside his cloak again, and when he took it out of his cloak, behold, it had turned again as his other flesh.

⁸ "It will happen, if they will not believe you or listen to the voice of the first sign, that they will believe the voice of the latter sign. ⁹ It will happen, if they will not believe even these two signs or listen to your voice, that you shall take of the water of the river, and pour it on the dry land. The water which you take out of the river will become blood on the dry land."

¹⁰ Moses said to Yahweh, "O Lord, I am not eloquent, neither before now, nor since you have spoken to your servant; for I am slow of speech, and of a slow tongue."

¹¹ Yahweh said to him, "Who made man's mouth? Or who makes one mute, or deaf, or seeing, or blind? Isn't it I, Yahweh? ¹² Now therefore go, and I will be with your mouth, and teach you what you shall speak."

¹³ He said, "Oh, Lord, please send someone else."

¹⁴ Yahweh's anger burned against Moses, and he said, "What about Aaron, your brother, the Levite? I know that he can speak well. Also, behold, he comes out to meet you. When he sees you, he will be glad in his heart. ¹⁵ You shall speak to him, and put the words in his mouth. I will be with your mouth, and with his mouth, and will teach you what you shall do. ¹⁶ He will be your spokesman to the people; and it will happen, that he will be to you a mouth, and you will be to him as God. ¹⁷ You shall take this rod in your hand, with which you shall do the signs."

1. What kind of a man do you think Moses was?
2. What does God's name tell us about Him?
3. What did God promise to do for the people of Israel?
4. What miraculous signs did God give Moses?

20. THE DEATH PLAGUE
Exodus 12:1-13, 21-42

After receiving God's instructions, Moses and his brother, Aaron, went to Pharaoh and asked him to release the people of Israel. Pharaoh stubbornly refused. Because of Pharaoh's refusal to release Israel, God caused ten terrible plagues to occur in Egypt. As each plague came, Pharaoh promised to let the people go but then he changed his mind once the plague stopped. The first of the ten plagues came when God turned all the water in Egypt into blood. Then, in one plague after another, God covered the land with frogs, lice, and flies and caused sickness to kill the cattle. Still, Pharaoh would not let the Israelites go free. Then God sent boils and sores, hail and fire, grasshoppers and locusts. He also sent three days of darkness, but still Pharaoh's heart was hardened against the people. Finally, God sent the tenth plague which would kill all of the first born of the Egyptians. In order to protect the Israelites from this death plague, God gave them a ritual, called the Passover, that they were to perform. In this account, the Passover lamb gives us a picture of the Savior whose blood was shed to save the world from spiritual death.

(You can read about these amazing events in Exodus 7-12.)

The Passover

12 Yahweh spoke to Moses and Aaron in the land of Egypt, saying, ² "This month shall be to you the beginning of months. It shall be the first month of the year to you. ³ Speak to all the congregation of Israel, saying, 'On the tenth day of this month, they shall take to them every man a lamb, according to their fathers' houses, a lamb for a household; ⁴ and if the household is too little for a lamb, then he and his neighbor next to his house shall take one according to the number of the souls; according to what everyone can eat you shall make your count for the lamb. ⁵ Your lamb shall be without defect, a male a year old. You shall take it from the sheep, or from the goats: ⁶ and you shall keep it until the fourteenth day of the same month; and the whole assembly of the congregation of Israel shall kill it at evening. ⁷ They shall take some of the blood, and put it on the two door posts and on the lintel, on the houses in which they shall eat it. ⁸ They shall eat the flesh in that night, roasted with fire, and unleavened bread. They shall eat it with bitter herbs.⁹ Don't eat it raw, nor boiled at all with water, but roasted with fire; with its head, its legs and its inner parts. ¹⁰ You shall let nothing of it remain until the morning; but that which remains of it until the morning you shall burn with fire. ¹¹ This is how you shall eat it: with your belt on your waist, your shoes on your feet, and your staff in your hand; and you shall eat it in haste: it is Yahweh's Passover Lamb. ¹² For I will go through the land of Egypt in that night, and will strike all the firstborn in the land of Egypt, both man and animal. Against all the gods of Egypt I will execute judgments: I am Yahweh. ¹³ The blood shall be to you for a token on the houses where you are: and when I see the blood, I will pass over you, and there shall no plague be on you to destroy you, when I strike the land of Egypt.

²¹ Then Moses called for all the elders of Israel, and said to them, "Draw out, and take lambs according to your families, and kill the Passover [lamb]. ²² You shall take a bunch of hyssop, and dip it in the blood that is in the basin, and strike the lintel and the two door posts with the blood that is in the basin; and none of you shall go out of the door of his house until the morning.

A Memorial of Redemption Explained

²³ For Yahweh will pass through to strike the Egyptians; and when he sees the blood on the lintel, and on the two door posts, Yahweh will pass over the door, and will not allow the destroyer to come in to your houses to strike you. ²⁴ You shall observe this thing for an ordinance to you and to your sons forever. ²⁵ It shall happen when you have come to the land which Yahweh will give you, according as he has promised, that you shall keep this service. ²⁶ It will happen, when your children ask you, 'What do you mean by this service?' ²⁷ that you shall say, 'It is the sacrifice of Yahweh's Passover, who passed over the houses of the children of Israel in Egypt, when he struck the Egyptians, and spared our houses.'"

The people bowed their heads and worshiped. ²⁸ The children of Israel went and did so; as Yahweh had commanded Moses and Aaron, so they did.

Judgment of God upon Egypt

²⁹ At midnight, Yahweh struck all the firstborn in the land of Egypt, from the firstborn of Pharaoh who sat on his throne to the firstborn of the captive who was in the dungeon; and all the firstborn of livestock. ³⁰ Pharaoh rose up in the night, he, and all his servants, and all the Egyptians; and there was a great cry in Egypt,

for there was not a house where there was not one dead. ³¹ He called for Moses and Aaron by night, and said, "Rise up, get out from among my people, both you and the children of Israel; and go, serve Yahweh, as you have said! ³² Take both your flocks and your herds, as you have said, and be gone; and bless me also!"

The Exodus of Israel

³³ The Egyptians were urgent with the people, to send them out of the land in haste, for they said, "We are all dead men." ³⁴ The people took their dough before it was leavened, their kneading troughs being bound up in their clothes on their shoulders. ³⁵ The children of Israel did according to the word of Moses; and they asked of the Egyptians jewels of silver, and jewels of gold, and clothing. ³⁶ Yahweh gave the people favor in the sight of the Egyptians, so that they let them have what they asked. They plundered the Egyptians.

³⁷ The children of Israel traveled from Rameses to Succoth, about six hundred thousand on foot who were men, besides children. ³⁸ A mixed multitude went up also with them, with flocks, herds, and even very much livestock. ³⁹ They baked unleavened cakes of the dough which they brought out of Egypt; for it wasn't leavened, because they were thrust out of Egypt, and couldn't wait, and they had not prepared any food for themselves. ⁴⁰ Now the time that the children of Israel lived in Egypt was four hundred thirty years. ⁴¹ At the end of four hundred thirty years, to the day, all of Yahweh's armies [hosts of people] went out from the land of Egypt.

Ordinance of the Passover

⁴² It is a night to be much observed to Yahweh for bringing them out from the land of Egypt. This is that night of Yahweh, to be much observed of all the children of Israel throughout their generations.

1. What sign did God require in order for the destroyer to pass over the homes of the Israelites?
2. How were the Israelites to remember this day in the future?
3. Why do you suppose God wanted them to remember this day?

21. FREE AT LAST
Exodus 14:5-31

After Israel left Egypt, Pharaoh regretted having let the people go and tried to recapture them. We see how the mighty power of God saved His people in the midst of an impossible situation.

Crossing the Red Sea

14 ⁵ The king of Egypt was told that the people had fled; and the heart of Pharaoh and of his servants was changed towards the people, and they said, "What is this we have done, that we have let Israel go from serving us?" ⁶ He prepared his chariot, and took his army with him; ⁷ and he took six hundred chosen chariots, and all the chariots of Egypt, and captains over all them. ⁸

Yahweh hardened the heart of Pharaoh king of Egypt, and he pursued the children of Israel; for the children of Israel went out with a high hand [boldly]. ⁹ The Egyptians pursued them. All the horses and chariots of Pharaoh, his horsemen, and his army overtook them encamping by the sea, beside Pi Hahiroth, before Baal Zephon.

¹⁰ When Pharaoh came near, the children of Israel lifted up their eyes, and behold, the Egyptians were marching after them; and they were very afraid. The children of Israel cried out to Yahweh. ¹¹ They said to Moses, "Because there were no graves in Egypt, have you taken us away to die in the wilderness? Why have you treated us this way, to bring us out of Egypt? ¹² Isn't this the word that we spoke to you in Egypt, saying, 'Leave us alone, that we may serve the Egyptians?' For it were better for us to serve the Egyptians, than that we should die in the wilderness."

¹³ Moses said to the people, "Don't be afraid. Stand still, and see the salvation of Yahweh, which he will work for you today: for the Egyptians whom you have seen today, you shall never see them again. ¹⁴ Yahweh will fight for you, and you shall be still."

God's Triumph over Egypt
¹⁵ Yahweh said to Moses, "Why do you cry to me? Speak to the children of Israel, that they go forward. ¹⁶ Lift up your rod, and stretch out your hand over the sea, and divide it: and the children of Israel shall go into the middle of the sea on dry ground. ¹⁷ Behold, I myself will harden the hearts of the Egyptians, and they shall go in after them: and I will get myself honor over Pharaoh, and over all his armies, over his chariots, and over his horsemen. ¹⁸ The Egyptians shall know that I am Yahweh, when I have gotten myself honor over Pharaoh, over his chariots, and over his horsemen." ¹⁹ The angel of God, who went before the camp of Israel, moved and went behind them; and the pillar of cloud moved from before them, and stood behind them. ²⁰ It came between the camp of Egypt and the camp of Israel; and there was the cloud and the darkness, yet gave it light by night: and one didn't come near the other all night.

The Sea Is Divided
²¹ Moses stretched out his hand over the sea, and Yahweh caused the sea to go back by a strong east wind all night, and made the sea dry land, and the waters were divided.²² The children of Israel went into the middle of the sea on the dry ground, and the waters were a wall to them on their right hand, and on their left. ²³ The Egyptians pursued, and went in after them into the middle of the sea: all of Pharaoh's horses, his chariots, and his horsemen. ²⁴ In the morning watch, Yahweh looked out on the Egyptian army through the pillar of fire and of cloud, and confused the Egyptian army. ²⁵ He took off their chariot wheels [jammed the wheels], and they drove them heavily; so that the Egyptians said, "Let's flee from the face of Israel, for Yahweh fights for them against the Egyptians!"

²⁶ Yahweh said to Moses, "Stretch out your hand over the sea, that the waters

may come again on the Egyptians, on their chariots, and on their horsemen." [27] Moses stretched out his hand over the sea, and the sea returned to its strength when the morning appeared; and the Egyptians fled against it. Yahweh overthrew the Egyptians in the middle of the sea. [28] The waters returned, and covered the chariots and the horsemen, even all Pharaoh's army that went in after them into the sea. There remained not so much as one of them. [29] But the children of Israel walked on dry land in the middle of the sea, and the waters were a wall to them on their right hand, and on their left. [30] Thus Yahweh saved Israel that day out of the hand of the Egyptians; and Israel saw the Egyptians dead on the seashore. [31] Israel saw the great work which Yahweh did to the Egyptians, and the people feared Yahweh; and they believed in Yahweh, and in his servant Moses.

1. *How did God finally deliver the Israelites from the hand of Pharaoh, king of Egypt?*

2. *Think about the characters of God, Pharaoh and Moses.*
   a. Will God always have the last word?
   b. Why was Pharaoh willing to ruin Egypt by his actions?
   c. How did Moses dare to command the Red Sea to divide?

3. *What important lesson did Israel learn from this experience? How did the attitude of the people change?*

D. ISRAEL AND THE WILDERNESS EXPERIENCE

After God took the descendants of Abraham out of Egypt, He began to form them into a new nation called Israel. This was a process that took time and did not come easily. They were instructed to invade, conquer, kill or drive out the inhabitants of Canaan, the Holy Land, and settle there. Israel needed to be prepared for the tremendous struggles ahead. Living and wandering in the desert for 40 years was a unique experience for Israel, but absolutely necessary for their future success. Even though all the needs of the people were divinely provided, and all they had to do was to trust God and obey Him, it still took 40 long years for them to learn how to live with God as their supreme leader and provider. The following selections instructed Israel as to what God expected of the people and how He intended to bless their obedience.

22. GOD PROMISES BREAD AND MEAT
Exodus 15:22-27 and 16:1-35

After the Children of Israel escaped from Egypt, the Israelites had to wander through the deserts of Sinai before they were allowed to settle in Canaan. As Moses led the people, God provided food for them in the desert. God's provision of bread pointed ahead to the time when He would provide the Savior as the "bread of life" for all mankind.

Great Bible Truths

Water, Manna and Quail

15 [22] Moses led Israel onward from the Red Sea, and they went out into the wilderness of Shur; and they went three days in the wilderness, and found no water. [23] When they came to Marah, they couldn't drink from the waters of Marah, for they were bitter. Therefore its name was called Marah. [22] The people murmured against Moses, saying, "What shall we drink?" [25] Then he cried to Yahweh. Yahweh showed him a tree, and he threw it into the waters, and the waters were made sweet. There he made a statute and an ordinance for them, and there he tested them; [26] and he said, "If you will diligently listen to Yahweh your God's voice, and will do that which is right in his eyes, and will pay attention to his commandments, and keep all his statutes, I will put none of the diseases on you, which I have put on the Egyptians; for I am Yahweh who heals you." [27] They came to Elim, where there were twelve springs of water, and seventy palm trees: and they encamped there by the waters.

16 They took their journey from Elim, and all the congregation of the children of Israel came to the wilderness of Sin, which is between Elim and Sinai, on the fifteenth day of the second month after their departing out of the land of Egypt. [2] The whole congregation of the children of Israel murmured against Moses and against Aaron in the wilderness; [3] and the children of Israel said to them, "We wish that we had died by Yahweh's hand in the land of Egypt, when we sat by the meat pots, when we ate our fill of bread, for you have brought us out into this wilderness, to kill this whole assembly with hunger." [4] Then Yahweh said to Moses, "Behold, I will rain bread from the sky for you, and the people shall go out and gather a day's portion every day, that I may test them, whether they will walk in my law, or not. [5] It shall come to pass on the sixth day, that they shall prepare that which they bring in, and it shall be twice as much as they gather daily."

Water, Manna and Quail

[6] Moses and Aaron said to all the children of Israel, "At evening, then you shall know that Yahweh has brought you out from the land of Egypt; [7] and in the morning, then you shall see Yahweh's glory; because he hears your murmurings against Yahweh. Who are we, that you murmur against us?" [8] Moses said, "Now Yahweh shall give you meat to eat in the evening, and in the morning bread to satisfy you; because Yahweh hears your murmurings which you murmur against him. And who are we? Your murmurings are not against us, but against Yahweh." [9] Moses said to Aaron, "Tell all the congregation of the children of Israel, 'Come near before Yahweh, for he has heard your murmurings.'" [10] As Aaron spoke to the whole congregation of the children of Israel, they looked toward the wilderness, and behold, Yahweh's glory appeared in the cloud. [11] Yahweh spoke to Moses, saying, [12] "I have heard the murmurings of the children of Israel. Speak to them, saying, 'At evening you shall eat meat, and in the morning you shall be filled with bread: and you shall know that I am Yahweh your God.'"

¹³ In the evening, quail came up and covered the camp; and in the morning the dew lay around the camp. ¹⁴ When the dew that lay had gone, behold, on the surface of the wilderness was a small round thing, small as the frost on the ground. ¹⁵ When the children of Israel saw it, they said to one another, "What is it?" For they didn't know what it was. Moses said to them, "It is the bread which Yahweh has given you to eat." ¹⁶ This is the thing which Yahweh has commanded: "Gather of it everyone according to his eating; an omer a head, according to the number of your persons, you shall take it, every man for those who are in his tent." ¹⁷ The children of Israel did so, and gathered some more, some less. ¹⁸ When they measured it with an omer [2.3 qt., 2.2 liters], he who gathered much had nothing over, and he who gathered little had no lack. They gathered every man according to his eating. ¹⁹ Moses said to them, "Let no one leave of it until the morning." ²⁰ Notwithstanding they didn't listen to Moses, but some of them left of it until the morning, and it bred worms, and became foul: and Moses was angry with them. ²¹ They gathered it morning by morning, everyone according to his eating. When the sun grew hot, it melted. ²² On the sixth day, they gathered twice as much bread, two omers for each one, and all the rulers of the congregation came and told Moses. ²³ He said to them, "This is that which Yahweh has spoken, 'Tomorrow is a solemn rest, a holy Sabbath to Yahweh. Bake that which you want to bake, and boil that which you want to boil; and all that remains over lay up for yourselves to be kept until the morning.'" ²⁴ They laid it up until the morning, as Moses asked, and it didn't become foul, and there were no worms in it. ²⁵ Moses said, "Eat that today, for today is a Sabbath to Yahweh. Today you shall not find it in the field. ²⁶ Six days you shall gather it, but on the seventh day is the Sabbath. In it there shall be none." ²⁷ On the seventh day, some of the people went out to gather, and they found none. ²⁸ Yahweh said to Moses, "How long do you refuse to keep my commandments and my laws? ²⁹ Behold, because Yahweh has given you the Sabbath, therefore he gives you on the sixth day the bread of two days. Everyone stay in his place. Let no one go out of his place on the seventh day." ³⁰ So the people rested on the seventh day. ³¹ The house of Israel called its name Manna, and it was like coriander seed, white; and its taste was like wafers with honey. ³² Moses said, "This is the thing which Yahweh has commanded, 'Let an omer-full of it be kept throughout your generations, that they may see the bread with which I fed you in the wilderness, when I brought you out of the land of Egypt.'" ³³ Moses said to Aaron, "Take a pot, and put an omer-full of manna in it, and lay it up before Yahweh, to be kept throughout your generations." ³⁴ As Yahweh commanded Moses, so Aaron laid it up before the Testimony, to be kept. ³⁵ The children of Israel ate the manna forty years, until they came to an inhabited land. They ate the manna until they came to the borders of the land of Canaan.

1. How did God provide food for the people in the wilderness?

2. Why did God forbid them to gather manna on the seventh day?

3. What lesson was God trying to teach them as they collected manna every day except the seventh day?

4. Does God still want us to set aside one day each week to rest and worship Him?

23. THE LAWS OF GOD
Deuteronomy 5:1-33

While travelling in the wilderness on the way to the Promised Land, Israel reached Mount Sinai. This is the same mountain where Moses first experienced God within the burning bush. Here the Lord made a covenant with Israel, giving them ten commandments. These became known as The Ten Commandments. These commandments form the basis for mankind's relationship with God and instruct mankind everywhere, for all time, on how God wants all people to live.

The Ten Commandments

5 [1]Moses called to all Israel, and said to them, "Hear, Israel, the statutes and the ordinances which I speak in your ears today, that you may learn them, and observe to do them." [2] Yahweh our God made a covenant with us in Horeb. [3] Yahweh didn't make this covenant with our fathers, but with us, even us, who are all of us here alive today.[4] Yahweh spoke with you face to face on the mountain out of the middle of the fire, [5] (I stood between Yahweh and you at that time, to show you Yahweh's word: for you were afraid because of the fire, and didn't go up onto the mountain;) saying,

[6]"I am Yahweh your God, who brought you out of the land of Egypt, out of the house of bondage.

[7]"You shall have no other gods before me.

[8]"You shall not make an engraved image for yourself, any likeness of what is in heaven above, or what is in the earth beneath, or that is in the water under the earth. [9] You shall not bow yourself down to them, nor serve them; for I, Yahweh, your God, am a jealous God, visiting the iniquity of the fathers on the children, and on the third and on the fourth generation of those who hate me; [10] and showing loving kindness to thousands of those who love me and keep my commandments.

[11]"You shall not take the name of Yahweh your God in vain: for Yahweh will not hold him guiltless who takes his name in vain.

[12]"Observe the Sabbath day, to keep it holy, as Yahweh your God commanded you.[13] You shall labor six days, and do all your work; [14] but the seventh day is a Sabbath to Yahweh your God, in which you shall not do any work, you, nor your son, nor your daughter, nor your male servant, nor your female servant, nor your ox, nor your donkey, nor any of your livestock, nor your stranger who is within your gates; that your male servant and your female servant may rest as well as you. [15] You shall remember that you were a servant in the land of Egypt, and Yahweh your God brought you out of there by a mighty hand and by

Great Bible Truths

an outstretched arm. Therefore Yahweh your God commanded you to keep the Sabbath day.

[16] "Honor your father and your mother, as Yahweh your God commanded you; that your days may be long, and that it may go well with you, in the land which Yahweh your God gives you.

[17] "You shall not murder.

[18] "You shall not commit adultery.

[19] "You shall not steal.

[20] "You shall not give false testimony against your neighbor.

[21] "You shall not covet your neighbor's wife. Neither shall you desire your neighbor's house, his field, or his male servant, or his female servant, his ox, or his donkey, or anything that is your neighbor's."

[22] Yahweh spoke these words to all your assembly on the mountain out of the middle of the fire, of the cloud, and of the thick darkness, with a great voice. He added no more. He wrote them on two stone tablets, and gave them to me. [23] When you heard the voice out of the middle of the darkness, while the mountain was burning with fire, you came near to me, even all the heads of your tribes, and your elders; [24] and you said, "Behold, Yahweh our God has shown us his glory and his greatness, and we have heard his voice out of the middle of the fire. We have seen today that God does speak with man, and he lives. [25] Now therefore why should we die? For this great fire will consume us. If we hear Yahweh our God's voice any more, then we shall die. [26] For who is there of all flesh, that has heard the voice of the living God speaking out of the middle of the fire, as we have, and lived? [27] Go near, and hear all that Yahweh our God shall say, and tell us all that Yahweh our God tells you; and we will hear it, and do it."

[28] Yahweh heard the voice of your words, when you spoke to me; and Yahweh said to me, "I have heard the voice of the words of this people, which they have spoken to you. They have well said all that they have spoken. [29] Oh that there were such a heart in them, that they would fear me, and keep all my commandments always, that it might be well with them, and with their children forever!

[30] "Go tell them, 'Return to your tents.' [31] But as for you, stand here by me, and I will tell you all the commandments, and the statutes, and the ordinances, which you shall teach them, that they may do them in the land which I give them to possess it."

[32] You shall observe to do therefore as Yahweh your God has commanded you. You shall not turn aside to the right hand or to the left. [33] You shall walk in all the way which Yahweh your God has commanded you, that you may live and that it may be well with you, and that you may prolong your days in the land which you shall possess.

1. *The first four commandments deal with man's relationship with God. What do the last six commandments deal with?*

2. *What promise is given to those who honor their parents?*

3. Does God want people to lie, steal and cheat?
4. The tenth commandment shows that even attitudes and thoughts can be sinful. Do you agree?
5. What do these laws tell us about God?

E. THE BLESSINGS OF GOD

Next we see that God's blessings come with conditions. When His conditions of obedience are met, He blesses and prospers His people. Refusal to obey the commandments of God results in poverty and destruction. God leaves the decision to each individual. We must choose whom we will serve and then reap the consequences of God's blessing or curse on our lives.

24. BLESSING AND CURSE
Deuteronomy 6:1-19 and 28:1-6, 15-19

Moses taught the Israelites that obeying the laws of God would result in great blessings for them. On the other hand, refusal to obey God's commands would bring a curse on the land and the people.

Love the Lord Your God

6 ¹Now this is the commandment, the statutes, and the ordinances, which Yahweh your God commanded to teach you, that you might do them in the land where you go over to possess it; ² that you might fear Yahweh your God, to keep all his statutes and his commandments, which I command you; you, and your son, and your son's son, all the days of your life; and that your days may be prolonged. ³ Hear therefore, Israel, and observe to do it; that it may be well with you, and that you may increase mightily, as Yahweh, the God of your fathers, has promised to you, in a land flowing with milk and honey. ⁴ Hear, Israel: Yahweh is our God. Yahweh is one. ⁵ You shall love Yahweh your God with all your heart, with all your soul, and with all your might. ⁶ These words, which I command you today, shall be on your heart; ⁷ and you shall teach them diligently to your children, and shall talk of them when you sit in your house, and when you walk by the way, and when you lie down, and when you rise up. ⁸ You shall bind them for a sign on your hand, and they shall be for frontlets between your eyes. ⁹ You shall write them on the door posts of your house, and on your gates. ¹⁰ It shall be, when Yahweh your God brings you into the land which he swore to your fathers, to Abraham, to Isaac, and to Jacob, to give you, great and goodly cities, which you didn't build, ¹¹ and houses full of all good things, which you didn't fill, and cisterns dug out, which you didn't dig, vineyards and olive trees, which you didn't plant, and you shall eat and be full; ¹² then beware lest you forget Yahweh, who brought you out of the land of Egypt, out of the house of bondage. ¹³ You shall fear Yahweh your God; and you shall serve him, and shall swear by his name. ¹⁴ You shall not go after other gods, of the gods of the peoples who are around you; ¹⁵ for Yahweh your God among you is a jealous God; lest the anger of Yahweh your God be kindled against you, and he destroy you from off the face of the earth. ¹⁶ You shall not tempt Yahweh your God, as you tempted him in Massah. ¹⁷ You shall diligently keep the commandments of Yahweh your God, and his testimonies, and his statutes, which he has commanded you. ¹⁸ You shall do that which is right and good in Yahweh's sight; that it may be well with you, and that you may go in and possess the good land which Yahweh swore to your fathers, ¹⁹ to thrust out all your enemies from before you, as Yahweh has spoken.

Blessings for Obedience

28 It shall happen, if you shall listen diligently to Yahweh your God's voice, to observe to do all his commandments which I command you today, that Yahweh your God will set you high above all the nations of the earth. ² All these blessings will come upon you, and overtake you, if you listen to Yahweh your God's voice. ³ You shall be blessed in the city, and you shall be blessed in the field. ⁴ You shall be blessed in the fruit of your body, the fruit of your ground, the fruit of your animals, the increase of your livestock, and the young of your flock. ⁵ Your basket and your kneading trough shall be blessed. ⁶ You shall be blessed when you come in, and you shall be blessed when you go out.

Curses for Disobedience

¹⁵ But it shall come to pass, if you will not listen to Yahweh your God's voice, to observe to do all his commandments and his statutes which I command you today, that all these curses will come on you, and overtake you. ¹⁶ You will be cursed in the city, and you will be cursed in the field. ¹⁷ Your basket and your kneading trough will be cursed. ¹⁸ The fruit of your body, the fruit of your ground, the increase of your livestock, and the young of your flock will be cursed. ¹⁹ You will be cursed when you come in, and you will be cursed when you go out.

   1. How were the people to remember the law of God?

   2. Did you notice that parents were responsible for teaching the ways of God to their children?

   3. How did God feel about His people worshiping other gods?

25. A PLAN FOR PROSPERITY
Deuteronomy 30:1-20

Moses taught the people that in order to love and obey God, man's heart must be changed from within. Each individual must decide for himself whether or not he will follow God's ways. There are blessings of life and prosperity for those who choose to worship the Lord God.

A Call to Return to God

30 It shall happen, when all these things have come on you, the blessing and the curse, which I have set before you, and you shall call them to mind among all the nations, where Yahweh your God has driven you, ² and return to Yahweh your God, and obey his voice according to all that I command you today, you and your children, with all your heart, and with all your soul; ³ that then Yahweh your God will release you from captivity, have compassion on you, and will return and gather you from all the peoples where Yahweh your God has scattered you. ⁴ If your outcasts are in the uttermost parts of [the earth under] the heavens, from there Yahweh your God will gather you, and from there he will bring you back. ⁵ Yahweh your God will bring you into the land which your fathers possessed, and you will possess it. He will do you good, and increase your numbers more than your fathers. ⁶ Yahweh your God will circumcise [purify] your heart, and the heart of your offspring, to love Yahweh your God with all your heart, and with all your soul, that you may live. ⁷ Yahweh your God will put all these curses on your enemies, and on those who hate you, who persecuted you. ⁸ You shall return and obey Yahweh's voice, and do all his commandments which I command you today. ⁹ Yahweh your God will make you plenteous in all the work of your hand, in the fruit of your body, in the fruit of your livestock, and in the fruit of your ground, for good; for Yahweh will again rejoice over you for good, as he rejoiced over your fathers; ¹⁰ if you will obey Yahweh your God's voice, to keep his commandments and his statutes which are written in this book of the law; if you turn to Yahweh your God with all your heart, and with all your soul.

The Choice of Life or Death
¹¹ For this commandment which I command you today is not too hard for you or too distant. ¹² It is not in heaven, that you should say, "Who will go up for us to heaven, and bring it to us, and proclaim it to us, that we may do it?" ¹³ Neither is it beyond the sea, that you should say, "Who will go over the sea for us, and bring it to us, and proclaim it to us, that we may do it?" ¹⁴ But the word is very near to you, in your mouth and in your heart, that you may do it. ¹⁵ Behold, I have set before you today life and prosperity, and death and evil. ¹⁶ For I command you today to love Yahweh your God, to walk in his ways, and to keep his commandments, his statutes, and his ordinances, that you may live and multiply, and that Yahweh your God may bless you in the land where you go in to possess it. ¹⁷ But if your heart turns away, and you will not hear, but are drawn away, and worship other gods, and serve them; ¹⁸ I denounce to [warn] you today, that you will surely perish. You will not prolong your days in the land where you pass over the Jordan to go in to possess it. ¹⁹ I call heaven and earth to witness against you today, that I have set before you life and death, the blessing and the curse. Therefore choose life, that you may live, you and your descendants; ²⁰ to love Yahweh your God, to obey his voice, and to cling to him; for he is your life, and the length of your days; that you may dwell in the land which Yahweh swore to your fathers, to Abraham, to Isaac, and to Jacob, to give them.

> 1. What did God mean when He said, "When you and your children return to the Lord?" (vv. 2-3)
>
> 2. Describe the blessings of obedience and the curses of disobedience.
>
> 3 Do you think that it is really difficult to obey God?
>
> 4. Who is our life (v.20)? Do you believe this?

26. THE DRY RIVER
Joshua 1:1-11 and 3:1-17

Forty years had passed since Israel left Egypt. The time came for the people to enter the Promised Land. Many hundreds of years before, God promised Abraham that his descendants would possess the land of Canaan. After years of preparation in the wilderness Moses' work was finished, and the people were ready. When Moses died, Joshua took charge, and the promise was fulfilled as Joshua led the people across the Jordan River into Canaan.

The Lord Commands Joshua

1 Now after the death of Moses the servant of Yahweh, Yahweh spoke to Joshua the son of Nun, Moses' servant, saying, ² "Moses my servant is dead. Now therefore arise, go across this Jordan, you, and all these people, to the land which I am giving to them, even to the children of Israel. ³ I have given you every place that the sole of your foot will tread on, as I told Moses. ⁴ From the wilderness, and this Lebanon, even to the great river, the river Euphrates, all the land of the Hittites, and to the great sea toward the going down of the sun, shall be your border. ⁵ No man will be able to stand before you all the days of your life. As I was with Moses, so I will be with you. I will not fail you nor forsake you.

⁶ "Be strong and courageous; for you shall cause this people to inherit the land which I swore to their fathers to give them. ⁷ Only be strong and very courageous. Be careful to observe to do according to all the law, which Moses my servant commanded you. Don't turn from it to the right hand or to the left, that you may have good success wherever you go. ⁸ This book of the law shall not depart from your mouth, but you shall meditate on it day and night, that you may observe to do according to all that is written in it; for then you shall make your way prosperous, and then you shall have good success.⁹ Haven't I commanded you? Be strong and courageous. Don't be afraid. Don't be dismayed, for Yahweh your God is with you wherever you go."

¹⁰ Then Joshua commanded the officers of the people, saying, ¹¹ "Pass through the middle of the camp, and command the people, saying, 'Prepare food; for within three days you are to pass over this Jordan, to go in to possess the land, which Yahweh your God gives you to possess it.'"

Crossing the Jordan

3 Joshua got up early in the morning; and they moved from Shittim, and came to the Jordan, he and all the children of Israel. They camped there before they crossed over.² After three days, the officers went through the middle of the camp; ³ and they commanded the people, saying, "When you see the Ark of Yahweh your God's covenant, and the priests the Levites bearing it, then leave your place, and follow it. ⁴ Yet there shall be a space between you and it, about two thousand cubits by measure. Don't come near it, that you may know the way by which you must go; for you have not passed this way before."

⁵ Joshua said to the people, "Sanctify yourselves; for tomorrow Yahweh will do wonders among you."

⁶ Joshua spoke to the priests, saying, "Take up the Ark of the Covenant, and cross over before the people." They took up the Ark of the Covenant, and went before the people.

⁷ Yahweh said to Joshua, "Today I will begin to magnify you in the sight of all Israel, that they may know that as I was with Moses, so I will be with you. ⁸ You shall command the priests who bear the Ark of the Covenant, saying, 'When you come to the brink of the waters of the Jordan, you shall stand still in the Jordan.'"

⁹ Joshua said to the children of Israel, "Come here, and hear the words of Yahweh your God." ¹⁰ Joshua said, "By this you shall know that the living God is among you, and that he will without fail drive the Canaanite, and the Hittite, and the Hivite, and the Perizzite, and the Girgashite, and the Amorite, and the Jebusite out from before you. ¹¹ Behold, the Ark of the covenant of the Lord of all the earth passes over before you into the Jordan. ¹² Now therefore take twelve men out of the tribes of Israel, for every tribe a man. ¹³ It shall be that when the soles of the feet of the priests who bear the Ark of Yahweh, the Lord of all the earth, rest in the waters of the Jordan, that the waters of the Jordan will be cut off. The waters that come down from above shall stand in one heap."

¹⁴ When the people moved from their tents to pass over the Jordan, the priests who bore the Ark of the covenant being before the people, ¹⁵ and when those who bore the Ark had come to the Jordan, and the feet of the priests who bore the Ark had dipped in the edge of the water (for the Jordan overflows all its banks all the time of harvest), ¹⁶ the waters which came down from above stood, and rose up in one heap, a great way off, at Adam, the city that is beside Zarethan; and those that went down toward the sea of the Arabah, even the Salt Sea, were wholly cut off. Then the people passed over near Jericho. ¹⁷ The priests who bore the Ark of Yahweh's covenant stood firm on dry ground in the middle of the Jordan; and all Israel crossed over on dry ground, until all the nation had passed completely over the Jordan.

1. How did the Lord encourage Joshua?

2. What promises did God make to Joshua?

3. What miracle took place to show the people that God was with Joshua?

27. THE MARCH OF VICTORY
Joshua 6:1-21

God had promised to give Israel the land of Canaan, and the time came for Israel to enter it. However, before the people of Israel could live in the land, they would have to conquer the Canaanites and drive them out. Canaan was controlled by wicked people who worshiped false gods. God decided to completely eliminate the Canaanites because of their sinful ways, and Israel was to be the executioner. God had already spoken to Joshua and told him that He would help Israel win the land. The first city to be conquered was the walled city of Jericho. Although no other army had ever been able to get beyond those high walls, God had a plan.

The Fall of Jericho

6 Now Jericho was tightly shut up because of the children of Israel. No one went out, and no one came in. ² Yahweh said to Joshua, "Behold, I have given Jericho into your hand, with its king and the mighty men of valor. ³ All of your men of war shall march around the city, going around the city once. You shall do this six days. ⁴ Seven priests shall bear seven trumpets of rams' horns before the Ark. On the seventh day, you shall march around the city seven times, and the priests shall blow the trumpets. ⁵ It shall be that when they make a long blast with the ram's horn, and when you hear the sound of the trumpet, all the people shall shout with a great shout; then the city wall will fall down flat, and the people shall go up, every man straight in front of him."

⁶Joshua the son of Nun called the priests, and said to them, "Take up the Ark of the Covenant, and let seven priests bear seven trumpets of rams' horns before Yahweh's ark."

⁷They said to the people, "Advance! March around the city, and let the armed men pass on before Yahweh's ark."

⁸It was so, that when Joshua had spoken to the people, the seven priests bearing the seven trumpets of rams' horns before Yahweh advanced and blew the trumpets, and the Ark of Yahweh's covenant followed them. ⁹ The armed men went before the priests who blew the trumpets, and the ark went after them. The trumpets sounded as they went.

¹⁰ Joshua commanded the people, saying, "You shall not shout, nor let your voice be heard, neither shall any word proceed out of your mouth, until the day I tell you to shout. Then you shall shout." ¹¹ So he caused Yahweh's Ark to go around the city, going about it once. Then they came into the camp, and stayed in the camp. ¹² Joshua rose early in the morning, and the priests took up Yahweh's Ark. ¹³ The seven priests bearing the seven trumpets of rams' horns in front of Yahweh's Ark went on continually, and blew the trumpets. The armed men went in front of them. The rear guard came after Yahweh's Ark. The trumpets sounded as they went. ¹⁴ The second day they marched around the city once, and returned into the camp. They did this six days.

¹⁵ On the seventh day, they rose early at the dawning of the day, and marched around the city in the same way seven times. Only on this day they marched around the city seven times. ¹⁶ At the seventh time, when the priests blew the trumpets, Joshua said to the people, "Shout, for Yahweh has given you the city! ¹⁷ The city shall be devoted, even it and all that is in it, to Yahweh. Only Rahab the prostitute shall live, she and all who are with her in the house, because she hid the messengers that we sent. ¹⁸ But as for you, only keep

yourselves from what is devoted to destruction, lest when you have devoted it, you take of the devoted thing; so you would make the camp of Israel accursed, and trouble it. [19] But all the silver, gold, and vessels of brass and iron, are holy to Yahweh. They shall come into Yahweh's treasury."

[20] So the people shouted and the priests blew the trumpets. When the people heard the sound of the trumpet, the people shouted with a great shout, and the wall fell down flat, so that the people went up into the city, every man straight in front of him, and they took the city. [21] They utterly destroyed all that was in the city, both man and woman, both young and old, and ox, sheep, and donkey, with the edge of the sword.

1. What was God's special plan to capture the city?
2. Jericho was "devoted/cursed (v.17)" to the Lord. This meant that all the inhabitants and everything in the city was to be totally destroyed, no plunder. What did that mean for the ordinary soldier?
3. Can you picture those huge walls suddenly collapsing at the same moment that the Israeli soldiers rushed in from all sides of the city?
4. Did Israel conquer Jericho in its own strength, or did God help them as He had promised?

28. JOSHUA'S CHALLENGE TO ISRAEL
Joshua 23:1-16 and 24:14-28

After defeating Jericho, Israel continued to invade Canaan. With God's special help, they conquered and destroyed some 31 kingdoms, successfully eradicating most of the inhabitants of the land. After this, Joshua divided up the land among the twelve tribes. Israel now had a permanent home. Their leader, Joshua, nearing the end of his life, called all the tribes together to give them his final words of instruction. His words of warning to Israel should be heeded by all peoples of the world, even today. We, too, must choose whom we will serve.

Joshua's Charge
23 After many days, when Yahweh had given rest to Israel from their enemies all around, and Joshua was old and well advanced in years, [2] Joshua called for all Israel, for their elders and for their heads, and for their judges and for their officers, and said to them, "I am old and well advanced in years. [3] You have seen all that Yahweh your God has done to all these nations because of you; for it is Yahweh your God who has fought for you. [4] Behold, I have allotted to you these nations that remain, to be an inheritance for your tribes, from the Jordan, with all the nations that I have cut off, even to the great sea toward the going down of the sun. [5] Yahweh your God will thrust them out from before you, and drive them from out of your sight. You shall possess their land, as Yahweh your God spoke to you.

[6] "Therefore be very courageous to keep and to do all that is written in the

book of the law of Moses, that you not turn aside from it to the right hand or to the left; [7] that you not come among [do not associate with] these nations, these that remain among you; neither make mention of the name of their gods, nor cause to swear by them, neither serve them, nor bow down yourselves to them; [8] but hold fast to Yahweh your God, as you have done to this day.

[9] "For Yahweh has driven great and strong nations out from before you. But as for you, no man has stood before you to this day. [10] One man of you shall chase a thousand; for it is Yahweh your God who fights for you, as he spoke to you. [11] Take good heed therefore to yourselves, that you love Yahweh your God.

[12] "But if you do at all go back, and hold fast to the remnant of these nations, even these who remain among you, and make marriages with them, and go in to them, and they to you; [13] know for a certainty that Yahweh your God will no longer drive these nations from out of your sight; but they shall be a snare and a trap to you, a scourge in your sides, and thorns in your eyes, until you perish from off this good land which Yahweh your God has given you.

[14] "Behold, today I am going the way of all the earth. You know in all your hearts and in all your souls that not one thing has failed of all the good things which Yahweh your God spoke concerning you. All have happened to you. Not one thing has failed of it. [15] It shall happen that as all the good things have come on you of which Yahweh your God spoke to you, so Yahweh will bring on you all the evil things, until he has destroyed you from off this good land which Yahweh your God has given you, [16] when you disobey the covenant of Yahweh your God, which he commanded you, and go and serve other gods, and bow down yourselves to them. Then Yahweh's anger will be kindled against you, and you will perish quickly from off the good land which he has given to you."

The Covenant Renewed

24 [14]"Now therefore fear Yahweh, and serve him in sincerity and in truth. Put away the gods which your fathers served beyond the River, in Egypt; and serve Yahweh. [15] If it seems evil to you to serve Yahweh, choose today whom you will serve; whether the gods which your fathers served that were beyond the River, or the gods of the Amorites, in whose land you dwell; but as for me and my house, we will serve Yahweh."

[16] The people answered, "Far be it from us that we should forsake Yahweh, to serve other gods; [17] for it is Yahweh our God who brought us and our fathers up out of the land of Egypt, from the house of bondage, and who did those great signs in our sight, and preserved us in all the way in which we went, and among all the peoples through the middle of whom we passed. [18] Yahweh drove out from before us all the peoples, even the Amorites who lived in the land. Therefore we also will serve Yahweh; for he is our God."

[19] Joshua said to the people, "You can't serve Yahweh, for he is a holy God. He is a jealous God. He will not forgive your disobedience nor your sins. [20] If you forsake Yahweh, and serve foreign gods, then he will turn and do you evil, and

consume you, after he has done you good."

²¹ The people said to Joshua, "No, but we will serve Yahweh." ²² Joshua said to the people, "You are witnesses against yourselves that you have chosen Yahweh yourselves, to serve him."

They said, "We are witnesses."

²³ "Now therefore put away the foreign gods which are among you, and incline your heart to Yahweh, the God of Israel."

²⁴ The people said to Joshua, "We will serve Yahweh our God, and we will listen to his voice."

²⁵ So Joshua made a covenant with the people that day, and made for them a statute and an ordinance in Shechem. ²⁶ Joshua wrote these words in the book of the law of God; and he took a great stone, and set it up there under the oak that was by the sanctuary of Yahweh. ²⁷ Joshua said to all the people, "Behold, this stone shall be a witness against us, for it has heard all Yahweh's words which he spoke to us. It shall be therefore a witness against you, lest you deny your God."

²⁸ So Joshua sent the people away, each to his own inheritance.

1. *How did Joshua describe the true and living Lord God?*
2. *What did Joshua tell the people about Canaan's idols?*
3. *Why is an idol so dangerous to a person who knows and loves the true God?*
4. *What were Joshua's final words to the people?*
5. *What was the people's answer to Joshua? Whom will they serve?*

F. THE MEN OF GOD

In every period of Israel's history, God chose certain men and women to proclaim His ways to the people. In this section we read how God used judges, prophets, and kings. Only those who remained obedient to Him were allowed to keep their positions. One of these leaders was David. He was Israel's greatest king, and it was from his royal family that God promised to bring the King of Kings, Jesus Christ, to be the Savior of the world. We begin with the leaders who followed Joshua.

29. THE JUDGES
Judges 2:6-23

After Joshua's death, the next generation of Israelites forgot all that the Lord God had done for them. They turned away from the God of their fathers and began to worship idols. God raised up men to be judges, who tried to turn the people back to the Lord. Because the people did not listen, God could no longer protect them from their enemies.

Great Bible Truths

Disobedience and Defeat

2 ⁶Now when Joshua had sent the people away, the children of Israel each went to his inheritance to possess the land. ⁷ The people served Yahweh all the days of Joshua, and all the days of the elders who outlived Joshua, who had seen all the great work of Yahweh that he had worked for Israel. ⁸ Joshua the son of Nun, the servant of Yahweh, died, being one hundred ten years old. ⁹ They buried him in the border of his inheritance in Timnath Heres, in the hill country of Ephraim, on the north of the mountain of Gaash. ¹⁰ After all that generation were gathered to their fathers, another generation arose after them, who didn't know Yahweh, nor the work which he had done for Israel. ¹¹ The children of Israel did that which was evil in Yahweh's sight, and served the Baals. ¹² They abandoned Yahweh, the God of their fathers, who brought them out of the land of Egypt, and followed other gods, of the gods of the peoples who were around them, and bowed themselves down to them; and they provoked Yahweh to anger. ¹³ They abandoned Yahweh, and served Baal and the Ashtaroth. ¹⁴ Yahweh's anger burned against Israel, and he delivered them into the hands of raiders who plundered them. He sold them into the hands of their enemies all around, so that they could no longer stand before their enemies. ¹⁵ Wherever they went out, Yahweh's hand was against them for evil, as Yahweh had spoken, and as Yahweh had sworn to them; and they were very distressed. ¹⁶ Yahweh raised up judges, who saved them out of the hand of those who plundered them. ¹⁷ Yet they didn't listen to their judges; for they prostituted themselves to other gods, and bowed themselves down to them. They turned aside quickly out of the way in which their fathers walked, obeying Yahweh's commandments. They didn't do so. ¹⁸ When Yahweh raised up judges for them, then Yahweh was with the judge, and saved them out of the hand of their enemies all the days of the judge; for it grieved Yahweh because of their groaning by reason of those who oppressed them and troubled them. ¹⁹ But when the judge was dead, they turned back, and dealt more corruptly than their fathers in following other gods to serve them, and to bow down to them. They didn't cease what they were doing, or give up their stubborn ways. ²⁰ Yahweh's anger burned against Israel; and he said, "Because this nation transgressed my covenant which I commanded their fathers, and has not listened to my voice, ²¹ I also will no longer drive out any of the nations that Joshua left when he died from before them; ²² that by them I may test Israel, to see if they will keep the Yahweh's way to walk therein, as their fathers kept it, or not." ²³ So Yahweh left those nations, without driving them out hastily. He didn't deliver them into Joshua's hand.

1. *Why did the next generation turn away from God?*
2. *What happened to Israel when they began to worship idols?*
3. *Why did God allow them to be defeated by their enemies?*
4. *Why did God raise up judges in Israel? What did they do?*

30. THE BOY PROPHET
1 Samuel 1:1-28 and 2:18-26 and 3:1-21

At the end of the time of the judges, Israel was having great difficulties because the people refused to follow the Lord God. However, God is faithful even if man is not. He uses those who love and obey Him. In this passage we see that through the faith and obedience of one childless woman, God raised up Samuel to be His prophet and leader of Israel.

The Birth of Samuel

1 Now there was a certain man of Ramathaim Zophim, of the hill country of Ephraim, and his name was Elkanah, the son of Jeroham, the son of Elihu, the son of Tohu, the son of Zuph, an Ephraimite. ² He had two wives. The name of one was Hannah, and the name of other Peninnah. Peninnah had children, but Hannah had no children. ³ This man went up out of his city from year to year to worship and to sacrifice to Yahweh of Armies [God Almighty] in Shiloh. The two sons of Eli, Hophni and Phinehas, priests to Yahweh, were there. ⁴ When the day came that Elkanah sacrificed, he gave to Peninnah his wife, and to all her sons and her daughters, portions; ⁵ but to Hannah he gave a double portion, for he loved Hannah, but Yahweh had shut up her womb. ⁶ Her rival provoked her severely, to irritate her, because Yahweh had shut up her womb. ⁷ As he did so year by year, when she went up to Yahweh's house. Her rival provoked her; therefore she wept, and didn't eat.⁸ Elkanah her husband said to her, "Hannah, why do you weep? Why don't you eat? Why is your heart grieved? Am I not better to you than ten sons?"

Hannah Cries out to God

So Hannah rose up after they had finished eating and drinking in Shiloh. Now Eli the priest was sitting on his seat by the doorpost of Yahweh's temple. ¹⁰ She was in bitterness of soul, and prayed to Yahweh, weeping bitterly. ¹¹ She vowed a vow, and said, "Yahweh of Armies [God Almighty], if you will indeed look at the affliction of your servant, and remember me, and not forget your servant, but will give to your servant a boy, then I will give him to Yahweh all the days of his life, and no razor shall come on his head."

¹² As she continued praying before Yahweh, Eli saw her mouth. ¹³ Now Hannah spoke in her heart. Only her lips moved, but her voice was not heard. Therefore Eli thought she was drunk. ¹⁴ Eli said to her, "How long will you be drunk? Get rid of your wine!"

¹⁵ Hannah answered, "No, my lord, I am a woman of a sorrowful spirit. I have not been drinking wine or strong drink, but I poured out my soul before Yahweh. ¹⁶ Don't consider your servant a wicked woman; for I have been speaking out of the abundance of my complaint and my provocation."

¹⁷ Then Eli answered, "Go in peace; and may the God of Israel grant your petition that you have asked of him."

Great Bible Truths

¹⁸ She said, "Let your servant find favor in your sight." So the woman went her way, and ate; and her facial expression wasn't sad any more.

¹⁹ They rose up in the morning early, and worshiped before Yahweh, and returned, and came to their house to Ramah. Then Elkanah knew Hannah his wife; and Yahweh remembered her.

²⁰ When the time had come, Hannah conceived, and bore a son; and she named him Samuel, saying, "Because I have asked him of Yahweh."

Hannah Dedicates Samuel

²¹ The man Elkanah, and all his house, went up to offer to Yahweh the yearly sacrifice, and his vow. ²² But Hannah didn't go up; for she said to her husband, "Not until the child is weaned; then I will bring him, that he may appear before Yahweh, and stay there forever."

²³ Elkanah her husband said to her, "Do what seems good to you. Wait until you have weaned him; only may Yahweh establish his word."

So the woman waited and nursed her son, until she weaned him. ²⁴ When she had weaned him, she took him up with her, with three bulls, and one ephah of meal, and a bottle of wine, and brought him to Yahweh's house in Shiloh. The child was young. ²⁵ They killed the bull, and brought the child to Eli. ²⁶ She said, "Oh, my lord, as your soul lives, my lord, I am the woman who stood by you here, praying to Yahweh. ²⁷ I prayed for this child; and Yahweh has given me my petition which I asked of him. ²⁸ Therefore I have also given him to Yahweh. As long as he lives he is given to Yahweh." He worshiped Yahweh there.

2 ¹⁸ But Samuel ministered before Yahweh, being a child, clothed with a linen ephod.¹⁹ Moreover his mother made him a little robe, and brought it to him from year to year, when she came up with her husband to offer the yearly sacrifice. ²⁰ Eli blessed Elkanah and his wife, and said, "May Yahweh give you offspring from this woman for the petition which was asked of Yahweh." Then they went to their own home. ²¹ Yahweh visited Hannah, and she conceived, and bore three sons and two daughters. The child Samuel grew before Yahweh.

A Father's Grief

²² Now Eli was very old; and he heard all that his sons did to all Israel, and how that they slept with the women who served at the door of the Tent of Meeting. ²³ He said to them, "Why do you do such things? for I hear of your evil dealings from all this people. ²⁴ No, my sons; for it is no good report that I hear! You make Yahweh's people disobey. ²⁵ If one man sins against another, God will judge him; but if a man sins against Yahweh, who will intercede for him?" Notwithstanding, they didn't listen to the voice of their father, because Yahweh intended to kill them. ²⁶ The child Samuel grew on, and increased in favor both with Yahweh, and also with men.

The Lord Calls Samuel

3 The child Samuel ministered to Yahweh before Eli. Yahweh's word was rare in those days. There were not many visions then. ² At that time, when Eli was laid down in his place (now his eyes had begun to grow dim, so that he could not see), ³ and God's lamp hadn't yet gone out, and Samuel had laid down in Yahweh's temple, where God's ark was; ⁴ Yahweh called Samuel; and he said, "Here I am." ⁵ He ran to Eli, and said, "Here I am; for you called me."

He said, "I didn't call. Lie down again."

He went and lay down. ⁶ Yahweh called yet again, "Samuel!" Samuel arose and went to Eli, and said, "Here I am; for you called me."

He answered, "I didn't call, my son. Lie down again." ⁷ Now Samuel didn't yet know Yahweh, neither was Yahweh's word yet revealed to him. ⁸ Yahweh called Samuel again the third time. He arose and went to Eli, and said, "Here I am; for you called me."

Eli perceived that Yahweh had called the child. ⁹ Therefore Eli said to Samuel, "Go, lie down. It shall be, if he calls you, that you shall say, 'Speak, Yahweh; for your servant hears.'" So Samuel went and lay down in his place. ¹⁰ Yahweh came, and stood, and called as at other times, "Samuel! Samuel!"

Then Samuel said, "Speak; for your servant hears."

¹¹ Yahweh said to Samuel, "Behold, I will do a thing in Israel, at which both the ears of everyone who hears it will tingle. ¹² In that day I will perform against Eli all that I have spoken concerning his house, from the beginning even to the end. ¹³ For I have told him that I will judge his house forever, for the iniquity which he knew, because his sons brought a curse on themselves, and he didn't restrain them. ¹⁴ Therefore I have sworn to the house of Eli, that the iniquity of Eli's house shall not be removed with sacrifice or offering forever."

¹⁵ Samuel lay until the morning, and opened the doors of Yahweh's house. Samuel feared to show Eli the vision. ¹⁶ Then Eli called Samuel, and said, "Samuel, my son!"

He said, "Here I am."

¹⁷ He said, "What is the thing that he has spoken to you? Please don't hide it from me. God do so to you, and more also, if you hide anything from me of all the things that he spoke to you."

¹⁸ Samuel told him every bit, and hid nothing from him. He said, "It is Yahweh. Let him do what seems good to him."

¹⁹ Samuel grew, and Yahweh was with him, and let none of his words fall to the ground.²⁰ All Israel from Dan even to Beersheba knew that Samuel was established to be a prophet of Yahweh. ²¹ Yahweh appeared again in Shiloh; for Yahweh revealed himself to Samuel in Shiloh by Yahweh's word.

1. How did God hear and answer Hannah's prayer?
2. Discuss Hannah's faithfulness in keeping her vow.
3. What displeased God about Eli's sons?
4. Discuss how Eli himself was part of the problem.
5. How did God show himself to Samuel?

31. THE SHEPHERD KING
1 Samuel 15:17-29 and 16:1-13

The people of Israel wanted to be like the other nations around them. They insisted that God give them a king. God appointed Saul to reign over Israel, but he disobeyed God, and a new king needed to be chosen. God sent the prophet Samuel to anoint a young shepherd lad named David. David was Israel's greatest king. It was from his royal family that God promised to bring the King of Kings, Jesus Christ, to be Savior of the world.

The Lord Rejects Saul as King

15 [17]Samuel said, "Though you were little in your own sight, weren't you made the head of the tribes of Israel? Yahweh anointed you king over Israel; [18] and Yahweh sent you on a journey, and said, 'Go, and utterly destroy the sinners the Amalekites, and fight against them until they are consumed.' [19] Why then didn't you obey Yahweh's voice, but took the plunder, and did that which was evil in Yahweh's sight?"

[20] Saul said to Samuel, "But I have obeyed Yahweh's voice, and have gone the way which Yahweh sent me, and have brought Agag the king of Amalek, and have utterly destroyed the Amalekites. [21] But the people took of the plunder, sheep and cattle, the chief of the devoted things, to sacrifice to Yahweh your God in Gilgal."

[22] Samuel said, "Has Yahweh as great delight in burnt offerings and sacrifices, as in obeying Yahweh's voice? Behold, to obey is better than sacrifice, and to listen than the fat of rams. [23] For rebellion is as the sin of witchcraft, and stubbornness is as idolatry and teraphim [divination]. Because you have rejected Yahweh's word, he has also rejected you from being king."

[24] Saul said to Samuel, "I have sinned; for I have transgressed the commandment of Yahweh, and your words, because I feared the people, and obeyed their voice. [25] Now therefore, please pardon my sin, and turn again with me, that I may worship Yahweh."

[26] Samuel said to Saul, "I will not return with you; for you have rejected Yahweh's word, and Yahweh has rejected you from being king over Israel." [27] As Samuel turned around to go away, Saul grabbed the skirt of his robe, and it tore. [28] Samuel said to him, "Yahweh has torn the kingdom of Israel from you today, and has given it to a neighbor of yours who is better than you. [29] Also the Strength of Israel [God] will not lie nor repent; for he is not a man, that he should repent."

God Chooses a New King for Israel

16 Yahweh said to Samuel, "How long will you mourn for Saul, since I have rejected him from being king over Israel? Fill your horn with oil, and go. I will send you to Jesse the Bethlehemite; for I have provided a king for myself among his sons." [2] Samuel said, "How can I go? If Saul hears it, he will kill me." Yahweh said, "Take a heifer with you, and say, I have come to sacrifice to Yahweh. [3] Call Jesse to the sacrifice, and I will show you what you shall do. You shall anoint to me him whom I name to you."

⁴ Samuel did that which Yahweh spoke, and came to Bethlehem. The elders of the city came to meet him trembling, and said, "Do you come peaceably?"

⁵ He said, "Peaceably; I have come to sacrifice to Yahweh. Sanctify yourselves, and come with me to the sacrifice." He sanctified Jesse and his sons, and called them to the sacrifice. ⁶ When they had come, he looked at Eliab, and said, "Surely Yahweh's anointed is before him."

⁷ But Yahweh said to Samuel, "Don't look on his face, or on the height of his stature, because I have rejected him; for I don't see as man sees. For man looks at the outward appearance, but Yahweh looks at the heart." ⁸ Then Jesse called Abinadab, and made him pass before Samuel. He said, "Yahweh has not chosen this one, either." ⁹ Then Jesse made Shammah to pass by. He said, "Yahweh has not chosen this one, either." ¹⁰ Jesse made seven of his sons to pass before Samuel. Samuel said to Jesse, "Yahweh has not chosen these." ¹¹ Samuel said to Jesse, "Are all your children here?"

He said, "There remains yet the youngest. Behold, he is keeping the sheep." Samuel said to Jesse, "Send and get him, for we will not sit down until he comes here."

¹² He sent, and brought him in. Now he was ruddy, with a handsome face and good appearance. Yahweh said, "Arise! Anoint him, for this is he."

¹³ Then Samuel took the horn of oil, and anointed him in the middle of his brothers. Then Yahweh's Spirit came mightily on David from that day forward. So Samuel rose up and went to Ramah.

1. *Why did God reject Saul and choose David instead to be king?*
2. *Which pleases God more; obedience or sacrifice?*
3. *Is God able to lie? Why not?*
4. *What did the Lord mean when He said, "Man looks at the outward appearance, but the Lord looks at the heart"?*
5. *What change came into David's life after he was anointed by Samuel?*

32. KILLING A GIANT
1 Samuel 17:1-54

Because the presence of the Lord had departed from Saul, he was not able to win any more battles. David, however, trusted in God and was able to confront and kill the giant who threatened to destroy the Israelites.

David and Goliath

17 Now the Philistines gathered together their armies to battle; and they were gathered together at Socoh, which belongs to Judah, and encamped between Socoh and Azekah, in Ephesdammim. ² Saul and the men of Israel were gathered together, and encamped in the valley of Elah, and set the battle in array against the Philistines. ³ The Philistines stood on the mountain on the one side, and Israel stood on the mountain on the other side: and there was a valley between them.

Goliath Defies Israel

⁴ A champion out of the camp of the Philistines named Goliath, of Gath, whose height was six cubits and a span [9 feet 9 inches] went out. ⁵ He had a helmet of brass on his head, and he wore a coat of mail; and the weight of the coat was five thousand shekels [110 pounds] of brass. ⁶ He had brass shin armor on his legs, and a brass javelin between his shoulders. ⁷ The staff of his spear was like a weaver's beam; and his spear's head weighed six hundred shekels [15 pounds] of iron. His shield bearer went before him. ⁸ He stood and cried to the armies of Israel, and said to them, "Why have you come out to set your battle in array? Am I not a Philistine, and you servants to Saul? Choose a man for yourselves, and let him come down to me. ⁹ If he is able to fight with me and kill me, then will we be your servants; but if I prevail against him and kill him, then you will be our servants and serve us." ¹⁰ The Philistine said, "I defy the armies of Israel today! Give me a man, that we may fight together!"

¹¹ When Saul and all Israel heard those words of the Philistine, they were dismayed, and greatly afraid. ¹² Now David was the son of that Ephrathite of Bethlehem Judah, whose name was Jesse; and he had eight sons. The man was an elderly old man in the days of Saul. ¹³ The three oldest sons of Jesse had gone after Saul to the battle: and the names of his three sons who went to the battle were Eliab the firstborn, and next to him Abinadab, and the third Shammah. ¹⁴ David was the youngest; and the three oldest followed Saul.¹⁵ Now David went back and forth from Saul to feed his father's sheep at Bethlehem.¹⁶ The Philistine came near morning and evening, and presented himself forty days.¹⁷ Jesse said to David his son, "Now take for your brothers an ephah [approx. 2/3 bushel] of this parched grain, and these ten loaves, and carry them quickly to the camp to your brothers; ¹⁸ and bring these ten cheeses to the captain of their thousand, and see how your brothers are doing, and bring back news." ¹⁹ Now Saul, and they, and all the men of Israel, were in the valley of Elah, fighting with the Philistines. ²⁰ David rose up early in the morning, and left the sheep with a keeper, and took and went, as Jesse had commanded him. He came to the place of the wagons, as the army which was going out to the fight shouted for the battle. ²¹ Israel and the Philistines put the battle in array, army against army. ²² David left his baggage in the hand of the keeper of the baggage, and ran to the army, and came and greeted his brothers. ²³ As he talked with them, behold, the champion, the Philistine of Gath, Goliath by name, came up out of the ranks of the Philistines, and said the same words; and David heard them. ²⁴ All the men of Israel, when they saw the man, fled from him, and were terrified. ²⁵ The men of Israel said, "Have you seen this man who has come up? He has surely come up

Great Bible Truths

to defy Israel. The king will give great riches to the man who kills him, and will give him his daughter, and make his father's house free in Israel."

David Takes up the Challenge

²⁶ David spoke to the men who stood by him, saying, "What shall be done to the man who kills this Philistine, and takes away the reproach from Israel? For who is this uncircumcised Philistine, that he should defy the armies of the living God?"

²⁷ The people answered him in this way, saying, "So shall it be done to the man who kills him."

²⁸Eliab his oldest brother heard when he spoke to the men; and Eliab's anger burned against David, and he said, "Why have you come down? With whom have you left those few sheep in the wilderness? I know your pride, and the naughtiness of your heart; for you have come down that you might see the battle."

²⁹ David said, "What have I now done? Is there not a cause?" ³⁰ He turned away from him toward another, and spoke like that again; and the people answered him again the same way. ³¹ When the words were heard which David spoke, they rehearsed them before Saul; and he sent for him. ³² David said to Saul, "Let no man's heart fail because of him. Your servant will go and fight with this Philistine."

³³ Saul said to David, "You are not able to go against this Philistine to fight with him; for you are but a youth, and he a man of war from his youth."

³⁴ David said to Saul, "Your servant was keeping his father's sheep; and when a lion or a bear came, and took a lamb out of the flock, ³⁵ I went out after him, and struck him, and rescued it out of his mouth. When he arose against me, I caught him by his beard, and struck him, and killed him. ³⁶ Your servant struck both the lion and the bear. This uncircumcised Philistine shall be as one of them, since he has defied the armies of the living God." ³⁷ David said, "Yahweh who delivered me out of the paw of the lion, and out of the paw of the bear, he will deliver me out of the hand of this Philistine."

Saul said to David, "Go! Yahweh will be with you." ³⁸ Saul dressed David with his clothing. He put a helmet of brass on his head, and he clad him with a coat of mail. ³⁹ David strapped his sword on his clothing, and he tried to move; for he had not tested it. David said to Saul, "I can't go with these; for I have not tested them." Then David took them off.

Five Smooth Stones

⁴⁰ He took his staff in his hand, and chose for himself five smooth stones out of the brook, and put them in the pouch of his shepherd's bag which he had. His sling was in his hand; and he came near to the Philistine. ⁴¹ The Philistine walked and came near to David; and the man who bore the shield went before him. ⁴² When the Philistine looked around, and saw David, he disdained him; for

he was but a youth, and ruddy, and had a good looking face. ⁴³ The Philistine said to David, "Am I a dog, that you come to me with sticks?" The Philistine cursed David by his gods. ⁴⁴ The Philistine said to David, "Come to me, and I will give your flesh to the birds of the sky, and to the animals of the field."

⁴⁵ Then David said to the Philistine, "You come to me with a sword, with a spear, and with a javelin; but I come to you in the name of Yahweh of Armies [God Almighty], the God of the armies of Israel, whom you have defied. ⁴⁶ Today, Yahweh will deliver you into my hand. I will strike you, and take your head from off you. I will give the dead bodies of the army of the Philistines today to the birds of the sky, and to the wild animals of the earth; that all the earth may know that there is a God in Israel, ⁴⁷ and that all this assembly may know that Yahweh doesn't save with sword and spear; for the battle is Yahweh's, and he will give you into our hand."

⁴⁸ When the Philistine arose, and walked and came near to meet David, David hurried, and ran toward the army to meet the Philistine. ⁴⁹ David put his hand in his bag, took a stone, and slung it, and struck the Philistine in his forehead. The stone sank into his forehead, and he fell on his face to the earth. ⁵⁰ So David prevailed over the Philistine with a sling and with a stone, and struck the Philistine, and killed him; but there was no sword in the hand of David. ⁵¹ Then David ran, stood over the Philistine, took his sword, drew it out of its sheath, killed him, and cut off his head with it. When the Philistines saw that their champion was dead, they fled. ⁵² The men of Israel and of Judah arose and shouted, and pursued the Philistines as far as Gath and to the gates of Ekron. The wounded of the Philistines fell down by the way to Shaaraim, even to Gath and to Ekron. ⁵³The children of Israel returned from chasing after the Philistines and they plundered their camp. ⁵⁴ David took the head of the Philistine, and brought it to Jerusalem; but he put his armor in his tent.

1. What did David say to Saul that showed his faith in God alone?
2. What did David mean when he told Goliath, "It is not by sword or spear that the Lord saves."?
3. Describe how David killed Goliath and what happened to the Philistines next.

33. THE COMING KING
2 Samuel 5-1-10 and 7:8-29

David became king over Israel and sought only to serve the Lord God. Although David did fall into sin, he always repented, and he tried to keep his heart pure before God. David was a good king, and the people looked back to his reign as the golden age of Israel. They also looked forward to the time when the Messiah (or Christ, meaning "the anointed King") would appear in the family line of David to rule forever.

Great Bible Truths

David Becomes King over Israel

5 Then all the tribes of Israel came to David at Hebron, and spoke, saying, "Behold, we are your bone and your flesh. ² In times past, when Saul was king over us, it was you who led Israel out and in. Yahweh said to you, 'You will be shepherd of my people Israel, and you will be prince over Israel.'" ³ So all the elders of Israel came to the king to Hebron, and king David made a covenant with them in Hebron before Yahweh; and they anointed David king over Israel. ⁴ David was thirty years old when he began to reign, and he reigned forty years. ⁵ In Hebron he reigned over Judah seven years and six months; and in Jerusalem he reigned thirty-three years over all Israel and Judah.

Jerusalem Becomes the Capital City

⁶ The king and his men went to Jerusalem against the Jebusites, the inhabitants of the land, who spoke to David, saying, "The blind and the lame will keep you out of here"; thinking, "David can't come in here." ⁷ Nevertheless David took the stronghold of Zion. This is David's city. ⁸ David said on that day, "Whoever strikes the Jebusites, let him go up to the watercourse and strike the lame and the blind, who are hated by David's soul." Therefore they say, "The blind and the lame can't come into the house."

⁹ David lived in the stronghold, and called it David's city. David built around from Millo and inward. ¹⁰ David grew greater and greater; for Yahweh, the God of Armies, was with him.

God's Promise to David

7 ⁸ Now therefore tell my servant David this, 'Yahweh of Armies [God Almighty] says, "I took you from the sheep pen, from following the sheep, to be prince over my people, over Israel. ⁹ I have been with you wherever you went, and have cut off all your enemies from before you. I will make you a great name, like the name of the great ones who are in the earth. ¹⁰ I will appoint a place for my people Israel, and will plant them, that they may dwell in their own place, and be moved no more. The children of wickedness will not afflict them anymore, as at the first, ¹¹ and as from the day that I commanded judges to be over my people Israel. I will cause you to rest from all your enemies. Moreover Yahweh tells you that Yahweh will make you a house. ¹² When your days are fulfilled, and you sleep with your fathers, I will set up your offspring after you, who will proceed out of your body, and I will establish his kingdom. ¹³ He will build a house for my name, and I will establish the throne of his kingdom forever. ¹⁴ I will be his father, and he will be my son. If he commits iniquity, I will chasten him with the rod of men, and with the stripes of the children of men; ¹⁵ but my loving kindness will not depart from him, as I took it from Saul, whom I put away before you. ¹⁶ Your house and your kingdom will be made sure forever before you. Your throne will be established forever."' ¹⁷ Nathan spoke to David all these words, and according to all this vision.

Great Bible Truths

David's Prayer of Thanksgiving

[18] Then David the king went in, and sat before Yahweh; and he said, "Who am I, Lord Yahweh, and what is my house, that you have brought me this far? [19] This was yet a small thing in your eyes, Lord Yahweh; but you have spoken also of your servant's house for a great while to come; and this among men, Lord Yahweh! [20] What more can David say to you? For you know your servant, Lord Yahweh. [21] For your word's sake, and according to your own heart, you have worked all this greatness, to make your servant know it. [22] Therefore you are great, Yahweh God. For there is no one like you, neither is there any God besides you, according to all that we have heard with our ears. [23] What one nation in the earth is like your people, even like Israel, whom God went to redeem to himself for a people, and to make himself a name, and to do great things for you, and awesome things for your land, before your people, whom you redeemed to yourself out of Egypt, from the nations and their gods? [24] You established for yourself your people Israel to be your people forever; and you, Yahweh, became their God. [25] Now, Yahweh God, the word that you have spoken concerning your servant, and concerning his house, confirm it forever, and do as you have spoken. [26] Let your name be magnified forever, saying, 'Yahweh of Armies is God over Israel; and the house of your servant David will be established before you.' [27] For you, Yahweh of Armies, the God of Israel, have revealed to your servant, saying, 'I will build you a house.' Therefore your servant has found in his heart to pray this prayer to you.

[28] "Now, O Lord Yahweh, you are God, and your words are truth, and you have promised this good thing to your servant. [29] Now therefore let it please you to bless the house of your servant, that it may continue forever before you; for you, Lord Yahweh, have spoken it. Let the house of your servant be blessed forever with your blessing."

1. *What impressed you most about how God established leaders for the nation of Israel?*

2. *What promises did God make to David after he became king of all Israel?*

3. *What did David praise God for in his prayer of thanks?*

III. GOD REVEALS HIS WAYS

This last section of selections taken from the Old Testament reveals to man the ways of God. We discover what He is like. Through the writings of the kings of Israel we read of the greatness of God and His infinite wisdom. The writings of the prophets of God give us a glimpse of His great mercy and His unwavering judgment against sin. In the last selections, God reveals His plan to send the Savior to pay the price for the sin of all mankind.

A. THE GREATNESS OF GOD

Along with being a great king, David was also a gifted poet. His many songs and poems have been preserved in the book of Psalms. The selected psalms included here reveal the greatness of God through His love, His goodness, and His forgiveness. Only the Lord God of creation is worthy to be praised by man.

34. GOD FORGIVES
Psalm 51:1-17

This psalm was written by David after he committed a terrible sin. David repents of his sin, telling God he is sorry for the wrong he has done. Seeking forgiveness, David asks God to cleanse his heart and make him pure.

David's Prayer for Forgiveness

51 Have mercy on me, God, according to your loving kindness.
   According to the multitude of your tender mercies, blot out my transgressions.
2 Wash me thoroughly from my iniquity.
   Cleanse me from my sin.
3 For I know my transgressions.
   My sin is constantly before me.
4 Against you, and you only, have I sinned,
   and done that which is evil in your sight;
   that you may be proved right when you speak,
   and justified when you judge.
5 Behold, I was born in iniquity.
   In sin my mother conceived me.
6 Behold, you desire truth in the inward parts.
   You teach me wisdom in the inmost place.
7 Purify me with hyssop, and I will be clean.
   Wash me, and I will be whiter than snow.
8 Let me hear joy and gladness,
   That the bones which you have broken may rejoice.
9 Hide your face from my sins,
   and blot out all of my iniquities.
10 Create in me a clean heart, O God.
   Renew a right spirit within me.
11 Don't throw me from your presence,
   and don't take your holy Spirit from me.
12 Restore to me the joy of your salvation.
   Uphold me with a willing spirit.
13 Then I will teach transgressors your ways.
   Sinners shall be converted to you.

¹⁴ Deliver me from the guilt of bloodshed,
    O God, the God of my salvation.
    My tongue shall sing aloud of your righteousness.
¹⁵ Lord, open my lips.
    My mouth shall declare your praise.
¹⁶ For you don't delight in sacrifice, or else I would give it.
    You have no pleasure in burnt offering.
¹⁷ The sacrifices of God are a broken spirit.
    A broken and contrite heart, O God, you will not despise.

> 1. Read aloud the verses in which David confessed and repented of his sin. Make this a prayer of your heart.
>
> 2. Read aloud the verses in which David asked for forgiveness and cleansing. Make this a prayer of your heart too.
>
> 3. What kinds of sacrifices are really pleasing to God?

35. GOD GUIDES
Psalm 32, and 63, and 25

David knew that when he confessed his sin, God would forgive and bless him. A man who is humble and trusts in God will be guided and protected by Him.

It Is Better to Confess Sin

32 ¹ Blessed is he whose disobedience is forgiven,
    whose sin is covered.
² Blessed is the man to whom Yahweh doesn't impute iniquity,
    in whose spirit there is no deceit.
³ When I kept silence, my bones wasted away through
    my groaning all day long.
⁴ For day and night your hand was heavy on me.
    My strength was sapped in the heat of summer. Selah.
⁵ I acknowledged my sin to you.
    I didn't hide my iniquity.
I said, I will confess my transgressions to Yahweh,
    and you forgave the iniquity of my sin. Selah.
⁶ For this, let everyone who is godly pray to you in a time
    when you may be found.
Surely when the great waters overflow,
    they shall not reach to him.
⁷ You are my hiding place.
    You will preserve me from trouble.
You will surround me with songs of deliverance. Selah.
⁸   I will instruct you and teach you in the way which you shall go.
I will counsel you with my eye on you.

⁹ Don't be like the horse, or like the mule, which have no understanding,
   who are controlled by bit and bridle, or else they will not come near to you.
¹⁰ Many sorrows come to the wicked,
   but loving kindness shall surround him who trusts in Yahweh.
¹¹ Be glad in Yahweh, and rejoice, you righteous!
   Shout for joy, all you who are upright in heart!

Wishing to Be near God

63 God, you are my God. I will earnestly seek you.
   My soul thirsts for you. My flesh longs for you,
in a dry and weary land, where there is no water.
² So I have seen you in the sanctuary,
   watching your power and your glory.
³ Because your loving kindness is better than life,
   my lips shall praise you.
⁴ So I will bless you while I live.
   I will lift up my hands in your name.
⁵ My soul shall be satisfied as with the richest food.
   My mouth shall praise you with joyful lips
⁶ when I remember you on my bed,
   and think about you in the night watches.
⁷ For you have been my help.
   I will rejoice in the shadow of your wings.
⁸ My soul stays close to you.
   Your right hand holds me up.
⁹ But those who seek my soul, to destroy it,
   shall go into the lower parts of the earth.
¹⁰ They shall be given over to the power of the sword.
   They shall be jackal food.
¹¹ But the king shall rejoice in God.
   Everyone who swears by him will praise him,
   for the mouth of those who speak lies shall be silenced.

A Prayer for God to Guide

25 To you, Yahweh, do I lift up my soul.
²   My God, I have trusted in you.
 Don't let me be shamed.
   Don't let my enemies triumph over me.
³ Yes, no one who waits for you shall be shamed.
   They shall be shamed who deal treacherously without cause.
⁴ Show me your ways, Yahweh.
   Teach me your paths.
⁵ Guide me in your truth, and teach me,

For you are the God of my salvation,
    I wait for you all day long.
⁶ Yahweh, remember your tender mercies and your loving kindness,
    for they are from old times.
⁷ Don't remember the sins of my youth, nor my transgressions.
    Remember me according to your loving kindness,
    for your goodness' sake, Yahweh.
⁸ Good and upright is Yahweh,
    therefore he will instruct sinners in the way.
⁹ He will guide the humble in justice.
    He will teach the humble his way.
¹⁰ All the paths of Yahweh are loving kindness and truth
    to such as keep his covenant and his testimonies.
¹¹ For your name's sake, Yahweh,
    pardon my iniquity, for it is great.
¹² What man is he who fears Yahweh?
    He shall instruct him in the way that he shall choose.
¹³ His soul shall dwell at ease.
    His offspring shall inherit the land.
¹⁴ The friendship of Yahweh is with those who fear him.
    He will show them his covenant.
¹⁵ My eyes are ever on Yahweh,
    for he will pluck my feet out of the net.
¹⁶ Turn to me, and have mercy on me,
    for I am desolate and afflicted.
¹⁷ The troubles of my heart are enlarged.
    Oh bring me out of my distresses.
¹⁸ Consider my affliction and my travail.
    Forgive all my sins.
¹⁹ Consider my enemies, for they are many.
    They hate me with cruel hatred.
²⁰ Oh keep my soul, and deliver me.
    Let me not be disappointed, for I take refuge in you.
²¹ Let integrity and uprightness preserve me,
    for I wait for you.
²² Redeem Israel, God, out all of his troubles.

1. How did David feel before he confessed his sin?

2. Did God forgive David's sin once he confessed it?

3. What blessings come to the person who fears the Lord and wants to please Him?

36. THE GOD WHO KNOWS
Psalm 1 and 139

The way to right living is to live a life according to God's Word. God watches over those who seek to obey Him. Because God is the creator of each person, He knows everything about us, and it is impossible to hide from Him.

Two Ways to Live

1 Blessed is the man who doesn't walk in the counsel
 of the wicked, nor stand on the path of sinners,
 nor sit in the seat of scoffers;
² but his delight is in Yahweh's law.
 On his law he meditates day and night.
³ He will be like a tree planted by the streams of water,
 that produces its fruit in its season,
 whose leaf also does not wither.
 Whatever he does shall prosper.
⁴ The wicked are not so,
 but are like the chaff which the wind drives away.
⁵ Therefore the wicked shall not stand in the judgment,
 nor sinners in the congregation of the righteous.
⁶ For Yahweh knows the way of the righteous,
 but the way of the wicked shall perish.

God Knows Everything

139 Yahweh, you have searched me,
 and you know me.
² You know my sitting down and my rising up.
 You perceive my thoughts from afar.
³ You search out my path and my lying down,
 and are acquainted with all my ways.
⁴ For there is not a word on my tongue,
 but, behold, Yahweh, you know it altogether.
⁵ You hem me in behind and before.
 You laid your hand on me.
⁶ This knowledge is beyond me.
 It's lofty.
 I can't attain it.
⁷ Where could I go from your Spirit?
 Or where could I flee from your presence?
⁸ If I ascend up into heaven, you are there.
 If I make my bed in Sheol, behold, you are there!
⁹ If I take the wings of the dawn,
 and settle in the uttermost parts of the sea;

¹⁰ Even there your hand will lead me,
    and your right hand will hold me.
¹¹ If I say, "Surely the darkness will overwhelm me;
    the light around me will be night";
¹² even the darkness doesn't hide from you,
    but the night shines as the day.
    The darkness is like light to you.
¹³ For you formed my inmost being.
    You knit me together in my mother's womb.
¹⁴ I will give thanks to you,
    for I am fearfully and wonderfully made.
    Your works are wonderful.
    My soul knows that very well.
¹⁵ My frame wasn't hidden from you,
    when I was made in secret,
    woven together in the depths of the earth.
¹⁶ Your eyes saw my body.
    In your book they were all written,
    the days that were ordained for me,
    when as yet there were none of them.
¹⁷ How precious to me are your thoughts, God!
    How vast is their sum!
¹⁸ If I would count them, they are more in number than the sand.
    When I wake up, I am still with you.
¹⁹ If only you, God, would kill the wicked.
    Get away from me, you bloodthirsty men!
²⁰ For they speak against you wickedly.
    Your enemies take your name in vain.
²¹ Yahweh, don't I hate those who hate you?
    Am I not grieved with those who rise up against you?
²² I hate them with perfect hatred.
    They have become my enemies.
²³ Search me, God, and know my heart.
    Try me, and know my thoughts.
²⁴ See if there is any wicked way in me,
    and lead me in the everlasting way.

    1. What is a righteous person like? Or a wicked person?

    2. Did you contrast the life styles of the righteous and wicked persons?

    3. What one essential element accounts for the differences in the two lives portrayed?

4. Read aloud the verses that show the following:
   a. *We cannot hide from God.*
   b. *We are created by God.*
   c. *God thinks about us.*

5. How can knowing these things about God comfort and challenge us?

6. Please read the last two verses of Psalm 139 as your sincere prayer.

37. GOD'S GLORY
Psalm 8 and 19 and 24

The work of God's hands is evidence of His marvelous glory. The beauty and holiness of God is called His "glory". These psalms speak about the greatness of God as shown in His creation.

The Lord's Greatness

8 Yahweh, our Lord, how majestic is your name in all the earth, who has set your glory above the heavens!

² From the lips of babes and infants you have established strength, because of your adversaries, that you might silence the enemy and the avenger.

³ When I consider your heavens, the work of your fingers, the moon and the stars, which you have ordained;

⁴ what is man, that you think of him? What is the son of man that you care for him?

⁵ For you have made him a little lower than God, and crowned him with glory and honor.

⁶ You make him ruler over the works of your hands. You have put all things under his feet:

⁷ All sheep and cattle, yes, and the animals of the field,

⁸ The birds of the sky, the fish of the sea, and whatever passes through the paths of the seas.

⁹ Yahweh, our Lord, how majestic is your name in all the earth!

God's Works and His Word

19 The heavens declare the glory of God. The expanse shows his handiwork.

² Day after day they pour out speech, and night after night they display knowledge.

³ There is no speech nor language, where their voice is not heard.

⁴ Their voice has gone out through all the earth,

their words to the end of the world.
In them he has set a tent for the sun,
⁵ which is as a bridegroom coming out of his room,
like a strong man rejoicing to run his course.
⁶ His going out is from the end of the heavens,
his circuit to its ends;
There is nothing hidden from its heat.
⁷ Yahweh's law is perfect, restoring the soul,
Yahweh's testimony is sure, making wise the simple.
⁸ Yahweh's precepts are right, rejoicing the heart.
Yahweh's commandment is pure, enlightening the eyes.
⁹ The fear of Yahweh is clean, enduring forever.
Yahweh's ordinances are true, and righteous altogether.
10 More to be desired are they than gold, yes, than much fine gold;
sweeter also than honey and the extract of the honeycomb.
11 Moreover by them is your servant warned.
In keeping them there is great reward.
12 Who can discern his errors?
Forgive me from hidden errors.
¹³ Keep back your servant also from presumptuous sins.
Let them not have dominion over me.
Then I will be upright.
I will be blameless and innocent of great transgression.
¹⁴ Let the words of my mouth and the meditation of my heart
be acceptable in your sight,
Yahweh, my rock, and my redeemer.

The Lord, the Glorious King

24 The earth is Yahweh's, with its fullness;
the world, and those who dwell therein.
² For he has founded it on the seas,
and established it on the floods.
³ Who may ascend to Yahweh's hill?
Who may stand in his holy place?
⁴ He who has clean hands and a pure heart;
who has not lifted up his soul to
falsehood, and has not sworn deceitfully.
⁵ He shall receive a blessing from Yahweh,
righteousness from the God of his salvation.
⁶ This is the generation of those who seek Him,
who seek your face—even Jacob. Selah.
⁷ Lift up your heads, you gates!
Be lifted up, you everlasting doors,
and the King of glory will come in.

⁸ Who is the King of glory?
   Yahweh strong and mighty,
   Yahweh mighty in battle.
⁹ Lift up your heads, you gates;
   yes, lift them up, you everlasting doors,
   and the King of glory will come in.
¹⁰ Who is this King of glory?
   Yahweh of Armies [God Almighty] is the King of glory! Selah.

> 1. Who did God choose to rule over His creation? What does that say about the importance of man?
>
> 2. How do the heavens declare God's glory? Have you seen this glory?
>
> 3. What are "Heaven's Armies" and who is the King of Glory?
>
> 4. Read the last three verses (12-14) of Psalm 19 as a prayer from your own heart.

38. THE GOD WHO LOVES
Psalm 23 and 46

The love of God for man is shown through His promise to always be with us. Through all the problems and difficulties of life, we need not fear when we know the comfort of His loving presence.

The Lord the Shepherd

23 Yahweh is my shepherd:
   I shall lack nothing.
² He makes me lie down in green pastures.
   He leads me beside still waters.
³ He restores my soul.
   He guides me in the paths of righteousness for his name's sake.
⁴ Even though I walk through the valley of the shadow of death,
   I will fear no evil, for you are with me.
   Your rod and your staff,
   they comfort me.
⁵ You prepare a table before me
   in the presence of my enemies.
   You anoint my head with oil.
   My cup runs over.
⁶ Surely goodness and loving kindness shall follow me
   all the days of my life,
   and I will dwell in Yahweh's house forever.

God Protects His People

46 God is our refuge and strength,
   a very present help in trouble.

² Therefore we won't be afraid,
   though the earth changes,
   though the mountains are
   shaken into the heart of the seas;
³ though its waters roar and are troubled,
   though the mountains tremble with their swelling. Selah.
⁴ There is a river, the streams of which make the city of God glad,
   the holy place of the tents of the Most High.
⁵ God is within her. She shall not be moved.
   God will help her at dawn.
⁶ The nations raged. The kingdoms were moved.
   He lifted his voice, and the earth melted.
⁷ Yahweh of Armies [God Almighty] is with us.
   The God of Jacob is our refuge. Selah.
⁸ Come, see Yahweh's works,
   what desolations he has made in the earth.
⁹ He makes wars cease to the end of the earth.
   He breaks the bow, and shatters the spear.
   He burns the chariots in the fire.
¹⁰ "Be still, and know that I am God.
   I will be exalted among the nations.
   I will be exalted in the earth."
¹¹ Yahweh of Armies [God Almighty] is with us.
   The God of Jacob is our refuge.
Selah.

> 1. Name at least ten things God does for us as our shepherd.
>
> 2. Where is God when we face trouble and disasters?
>
> 3. Have these two psalms brought comfort to you in the past? If so, in what ways?

39. GOD IS GOOD
Psalm 100 and 103

In these psalms we see the Lord as a great and holy God who is good. He is also described as a compassionate father who loves His children.

A Call to Praise the Lord
100 Shout for joy to Yahweh [God Almighty], all you lands!
   ² Serve Yahweh [God Almighty] with gladness.
      Come before his presence with singing.
³ Know that Yahweh [God Almighty], he is God.
   It is he who has made us, and we are his.
   We are his people, and the sheep of his pasture.

⁴ Enter into his gates with thanksgiving,
   into his courts with praise.
   Give thanks to him, and bless his name.
⁵ For Yahweh is good.
   His loving kindness endures forever,
   his faithfulness to all generations.

God Cares for His People
103 Praise Yahweh, my soul!
   All that is within me, praise his holy name!
² Praise the Lord, my soul,
   and don't forget all His benefits;
³ who forgives all your sins;
   who heals all your diseases;
⁴ who redeems your life from destruction; who crowns you with
   loving kindness and tender mercies;
⁵ who satisfies your desire with good things,
   so that your youth is renewed like the eagle's.
⁶ Yahweh executes righteous acts,
   and justice for all who are oppressed.
⁷ He made known his ways to Moses,
   his deeds to the children of Israel.
⁸ Yahweh is merciful and gracious,
   slow to anger, and abundant in loving kindness.
⁹ He will not always accuse;
   neither will he stay angry forever.
¹⁰ He has not dealt with us according to our sins,
   nor repaid us for our iniquities.
¹¹ For as the heavens are high above the earth,
¹² As far as the east is from the west,
   so far has he removed our transgressions from us.
¹³ Like a father has compassion on his children,
   so Yahweh has compassion on those who fear him.
¹⁴ For he knows how we are made.
   He remembers that we are dust.
¹⁵ As for man, his days are like grass.
   As a flower of the field, so he flourishes.
¹⁶ For the wind passes over it, and it is gone.
   Its place remembers it no more.
¹⁷ But Yahweh's loving kindness is from everlasting to
   everlasting with those who fear him,
   his righteousness to children's children;
¹⁸ to those who keep his covenant,

to those who remember to obey his precepts.
¹⁹ Yahweh has established his throne in the heavens.
   His kingdom rules over all,
²⁰ Praise Yahweh, you angels of his, who are mighty in
   strength, who fulfill his word, obeying the voice of his word.
²¹ Praise Yahweh, all you armies of his,
   you servants of his, who do his pleasure.
²² Praise Yahweh, all you works of his,
   in all places of his dominion.
   Praise Yahweh, my soul!

> 1. Using Psalm 103, list all the things that God does for those who know and worship Him.
>
> 2. Describe the character of God as found in these two psalms.

40. GOD IS PRAISED
Psalm 148 and 150

To praise God means to think about how great and wonderful He is. It means that our emotions are lifted by thoughts of His glory and His love for us. When we praise God, we let His greatness fill our being.

All Creation Called to Praise the Lord

148 Praise Yahweh from the heavens!
² Praise him in the heights!
   Praise him, all his army!
³ Praise him, sun and moon!
   Praise him, all you shining stars!
⁴ Praise him, you heavens of heavens,
   You waters that are above the heavens.
⁵ Let them praise Yahweh's name,
   For he commanded, and they were created.
⁶ He has also established them forever and ever.
   He has made a decree which will not pass away.
⁷ Praise Yahweh from the earth,
   you great sea creatures, and all depths!
⁸ Lightning and hail, snow and clouds;
   stormy wind, fulfilling his word;
⁹ mountains and all hills;
   fruit trees and all cedars;
¹⁰ wild animals and all livestock;
   small creatures and flying birds;
¹¹ kings of the earth and all peoples;
   princes and all judges of the earth;

¹² both young men and maidens;
   old men and children:
¹³ let them praise Yahweh's name,
   for his name alone is exalted.
   His glory is above the earth and the heavens.
¹⁴ He has lifted up the horn of his people,
   the praise of all his saints;
   even of the children of Israel, a people near to him.
   Praise Yahweh!

Praise the Lord with Music
150 ¹Praise Yahweh!
   Praise God in his sanctuary!
   Praise him in his heavens for his acts of power!
² Praise him for his mighty acts!
   Praise him according to his excellent greatness!
³ Praise him with the sounding of the trumpet!
   Praise him with harp and lyre!
⁴ Praise him with tambourine and dancing!
   Praise him with stringed instruments and flute!
⁵ Praise him with loud cymbals!
   Praise him with resounding cymbals!
⁶ Let everything that has breath praise Yahweh!
   Praise Yahweh!

   1. What are some of the reasons why we are to praise God?
   2. Make a list of all the parts of God's creation which are to praise Him.
   3. Name some of the instruments that we are to use in praising God.

B. THE WISDOM OF GOD

The book of Proverbs was written by David's son Solomon, who followed him as king of Israel. Solomon asked God to give him wisdom so that he could better lead the people. Because God answered this prayer, we have some of the greatest advice on how to live that has ever been written.

41. WISDOM IS GIVEN
1 Kings 3:5-14 and 4:29-34

God answered Solomon's prayer and gave him not only wisdom but riches and honor as well. Solomon was one of the wisest men who ever lived.

Solomon Asks for Wisdom
3 ⁵In Gibeon, Yahweh appeared to Solomon in a dream by night; and God said, "Ask for what I should give you."

⁶ Solomon said, "You have shown to your servant David my father great loving kindness, because he walked before you in truth, in righteousness, and in uprightness of heart with you. You have kept for him this great loving kindness, that you have given him a son to sit on his throne, as it is today. ⁷ Now, Yahweh my God, you have made your servant king instead of David my father. I am just a little child. I don't know how to go out or come in.⁸ Your servant is among your people which you have chosen, a great people, that can't be numbered or counted for multitude. ⁹ Give your servant therefore an understanding heart to judge your people, that I may discern between good and evil; for who is able to judge this great people of yours?"

¹⁰ This request pleased the Lord, that Solomon had asked this thing. ¹¹ God said to him, "Because you have asked this thing, and have not asked for yourself long life, nor have you asked for riches for yourself, nor have you asked for the life of your enemies, but have asked for yourself understanding to discern justice; ¹² behold, I have done according to your word. Behold, I have given you a wise and understanding heart; so that there has been no one like you before you, and after you none will arise like you. ¹³ I have also given you that which you have not asked, both riches and honor, so that there will not be any among the kings like you for all your days. ¹⁴ If you will walk in my ways, to keep my statutes and my commandments, as your father David walked, then I will lengthen your days."

Solomon's Wisdom

4 ²⁹God gave Solomon abundant wisdom and understanding, and very great understanding, even as the sand that is on the seashore. ³⁰ Solomon's wisdom excelled the wisdom of all the children of the east and all the wisdom of Egypt. ³¹ For he was wiser than all men; than Ethan the Ezrahite, Heman, Calcol, and Darda, the sons of Mahol: and his fame was in all the nations all around. ³² He spoke three thousand proverbs; and his songs numbered one thousand five. ³³ He spoke of trees, from the cedar that is in Lebanon even to the hyssop that grows out of the wall; he also spoke of animals, of birds, of creeping things, and of fish. ³⁴ People of all nations came to hear the wisdom of Solomon, sent by all kings of the earth, who had heard of his wisdom.

> 1. What did God promise to give to Solomon in addition to wisdom?
>
> 2. Why do you suppose Solomon asked only for wisdom?
>
> 3. What was Solomon to do in order to have a long life?
>
> 4. How great and wise was Solomon?

42. TRUE WISDOM
Proverbs 2:1-11 and 3:1-35

Here we have the explanation of what true wisdom is and where it comes from. We also learn of the great benefits that come to those who fear God and obey His commandments.

Moral Benefits of Wisdom

2 My son, if you will receive my words,
  and store up my commandments within you;
² So as to turn you ear to wisdom,
  and apply your heart to understanding;
³ Yes, if you call out for discernment,
  and lift up your voice for understanding;
⁴ If you seek her as silver,
  and search for her as for hidden treasures:
⁵ then you will understand the fear of Yahweh,
  and find the knowledge of God.
⁶ For Yahweh gives wisdom.
  Out of his mouth comes knowledge and understanding.
⁷ He lays up sound wisdom for the upright.
  He is a shield to those who walk in integrity;
⁸ that he may guard the paths of justice,
  and preserve the way of his saints.
⁹ Then you will understand righteousness and justice,
  equity and every good path.
¹⁰ For wisdom will enter into your heart.
  Knowledge will be pleasant to your soul.
¹¹ Discretion will watch over you.
  Understanding will keep you,

Further Benefits of Wisdom

3 My son, don't forget my teaching;
  but let your heart keep my commandments:
² For length of days, and years of life,
  and peace, they will add to you.
³ Don't let kindness and truth forsake you.
  Bind them around your neck.
  Write them on the tablet of your heart.
⁴ So you will find favor,
  and good understanding in the sight of God and man.

Always Ask God First

⁵ Trust in Yahweh with all your heart,
  and don't lean on your own understanding.

⁶ In all your ways acknowledge him,
   and he will make your paths straight.
⁷ Don't be wise in your own eyes.
   Fear Yahweh, and depart from evil.
⁸ It will be health to your body,
   and nourishment to your bones.
⁹ Honor Yahweh with your substance,
   with the first fruits of all your increase:
¹⁰ so your barns will be filled with plenty,
   and your vats will overflow with new wine.
¹¹ My son, don't despise Yahweh's discipline,
   neither be weary of his reproof:
¹² for whom Yahweh loves, he reproves;
   even as a father reproves the son in whom he delights.

Wisdom More Precious Than Wealth

¹³ Happy is the man who finds wisdom,
   the man who gets understanding.
¹⁴ For her good profit is better than getting silver,
   and her return is better than fine gold.
¹⁵ She is more precious than rubies.
   None of the things you can desire are to be compared to her.
¹⁶ Length of days is in her right hand.
   In her left hand are riches and honor.
¹⁷ Her ways are ways of pleasantness.
   All her paths are peace.
¹⁸ She is a tree of life to those who lay hold of her.
   Happy is everyone who retains her.
¹⁹ By wisdom Yahweh founded the earth.
   By understanding, he established the heavens.
²⁰ By his knowledge, the depths were broken up,
   and the skies drop down the dew.

Never Walk Away from Wisdom

²¹ My son, let them not depart from your eyes.
   Keep sound wisdom and discretion:
²² so they will be life to your soul,
   and grace for your neck.
²³ Then you shall walk in your way securely.
   Your foot won't stumble.
²⁴ When you lie down, you will not be afraid.
   Yes, you will lie down, and your sleep will be sweet.
²⁵ Don't be afraid of sudden fear,
   neither of the desolation of the wicked, when it comes:

²⁶ for Yahweh will be your confidence,
  and will keep your foot from being taken.
²⁷ Don't withhold good from those to whom it is due,
  when it is in the power of your hand to do it.
²⁸ Don't say to your neighbor, "Go, and come again;
  tomorrow I will give it to you,"
  when you have it by you.
²⁹ Don't devise evil against your neighbor,
  since he dwells securely by you.
³⁰ Don't strive with a man without cause,
  if he has done you no harm.
³¹ Don't envy the man of violence.
  Choose none of his ways.
³² For the perverse is an abomination to Yahweh,
  but his friendship is with the upright.
³³ Yahweh's curse is in the house of the wicked,
  but he blesses the habitation of the righteous.
³⁴ Surely he mocks the mockers,
  but he gives grace to the humble.
³⁵ The wise will inherit glory,
  but shame will be the promotion of fools.

> 1. How can we gain knowledge and wisdom from God?
>
> 2. List the benefits we receive from keeping God's commands and trusting and fearing Him.
>
> 3. According to the wisdom in these passages, how should we behave toward our neighbors?
>
> 4. In your own words, summarize how you would find the Lord's wisdom and apply it to your life.

43. THE GOOD AND THE WICKED
Proverbs 12:1-25

A good man finds favor with the Lord. In these verses we learn about the ways of a good man in contrast to the ways of a wicked man.

Words to Live By
12 Whoever loves correction [or discipline] loves knowledge,
  but he who hates reproof [correction] is stupid.
² A good man shall obtain favor from Yahweh,
  but he will condemn a man of wicked devices.
³ A man shall not be established by wickedness,
  but the root of the righteous shall not be moved.

4 A worthy woman is the crown of her husband,
    but a disgraceful wife is as rottenness in his bones.
5 The thoughts of the righteous are just,
    but the advice of the wicked is deceitful.
6 The words of the wicked are about lying in wait for blood,
    but the speech of the upright rescues them.
7 The wicked are overthrown, and are no more,
    but the house of the righteous shall stand.
8 A man shall be commended according to his wisdom,
    but he who has a warped mind shall be despised.
9 Better is he who is lightly esteemed, and has a servant,
    than he who honors himself, and lacks bread.
10 A righteous man respects the life of his animal,
    but the tender mercies of the wicked are cruel.
11 He who tills his land shall have plenty of bread,
    but he who chases fantasies is void of understanding.
12 The wicked desires the plunder of evil men,
    but the root of the righteous flourishes.
13 An evil man is trapped by sinfulness of lips,
    but the righteous shall come out of trouble.
14 A man shall be satisfied with good by the fruit of his mouth.
    The work of a man's hands shall be rewarded to him.
15 The way of a fool is right in his own eyes,
    but he who is wise listens to counsel
16 A fool shows his annoyance the same day,
    but one who overlooks an insult is prudent.
17 He who is truthful testifies honestly,
    but a false witness lies.
18 There is one who speaks rashly like the piercing of a sword,
    but the tongue of the wise heals.
19 Truth's lips will be established forever,
    but a lying tongue is only momentary.
20 Deceit is in the heart of those who plot evil,
    but joy comes to the promoters of peace.
21 No mischief shall happen to the righteous,
    but the wicked shall be filled with evil.
22 Lying lips are an abomination to Yahweh,
    but those who do the truth are his delight.
23 A prudent man keeps his knowledge,
    but the hearts of fools proclaim foolishness.
24 The hands of the diligent ones shall rule,
    but laziness ends in slave labor.

²⁵ Anxiety in a man's heart weighs it down,
    but a kind word makes it glad.

> 1. Discuss the statement, "Whoever loves discipline, loves knowledge." (v.1)
>
> 2. How does God feel about a person who is truthful?
>
> 3. Describe an evil person and a righteous person.

44. WISDOM TO LIVE BY
Proverbs 21 and 22:1-9

We all need wisdom to know how to live proper lives. Who would know better how to live than the God who created man? That is why God directed Solomon to write Proverbs: to help people live correctly in a world filled with evil. Here are some more practical suggestions that we would be wise to follow.

21 The king's heart is in Yahweh's hand like the watercourses.
    He turns it wherever he desires.
² Every way of a man is right in his own eyes,
    but Yahweh weighs the hearts.
³ To do righteousness and justice
    is more acceptable to Yahweh than sacrifice.
⁴ A high look, and a proud heart,
    the lamp of the wicked, is sin.
⁵ The plans of the diligent surely lead to profit;
    and everyone who is hasty surely rushes to poverty.
⁶ Getting treasures by a lying tongue
    is a fleeting vapor for those who seek death.
⁷ The violence of the wicked will drive them away,
    because they refuse to do what is right.
⁸ The way of the guilty is devious,
    but the conduct of the innocent is upright.
⁹ It is better to dwell in the corner of the housetop,
    than to share a house with a contentious woman.
¹⁰ The soul of the wicked desires evil;
    his neighbor finds no mercy in his eyes.
¹¹ When the mocker is punished, the simple gains wisdom.
    When the wise is instructed, he receives knowledge.
¹² The Righteous One considers the house of the wicked,
    and brings the wicked to ruin.
¹³ Whoever stops his ears at the cry of the poor,
    he will also cry out, but shall not be heard.
¹⁴ A gift in secret pacifies anger;
    and a bribe in the cloak, strong wrath.

¹⁵ It is joy to the righteous to do justice;
   but it is a destruction to the workers of iniquity.
¹⁶ The man who wanders out of the way of understanding
   shall rest in the assembly of the departed spirits.
¹⁷ He who loves pleasure shall be a poor man.
   He who loves wine and oil shall not be rich.
¹⁸ The wicked is a ransom for the righteous;
   the treacherous for the upright.
¹⁹ It is better to dwell in a desert land,
   than with a contentious and fretful woman.
²⁰ There is precious treasure and oil in the dwelling of the wise;
   but a foolish man swallows it up.
²¹ He who follows after righteousness and kindness
   finds life, righteousness, and honor.
²² A wise man scales the city of the mighty,
   and brings down the strength of its confidence.
²³ Whoever guards his mouth and his tongue
   keeps his soul from troubles.
²⁴ The proud and haughty man, "scoffer" is his name;
   he works in the arrogance of pride.
²⁵ The desire of the sluggard kills him,
   for his hands refuse to labor.
²⁶ There are those who covet greedily all day long;
   but the righteous give and don't withhold.
²⁷ The sacrifice of the wicked is an abomination:
   how much more, when he brings it with a wicked mind!
²⁸ A false witness will perish,
   and a man who listens speaks to eternity.
²⁹ A wicked man hardens his face;
   but as for the upright, he establishes his ways.
³⁰ There is no wisdom nor understanding
   nor counsel against Yahweh.
³¹ The horse is prepared for the day of battle;
   but victory is with Yahweh.

22 A good name is more desirable than great riches,
   and loving favor is better than silver and gold.
² The rich and the poor have this in common:
   Yahweh is the maker of them all.
³ A prudent man sees danger, and hides himself;
   but the simple pass on, and suffer for it.
⁴ The result of humility and the fear of Yahweh
   is wealth, honor, and life.

⁵ Thorns and snares are in the path of the wicked:
   whoever guards his soul stays from them.
⁶ Train up a child in the way he should go,
   and when he is old he will not depart from it.
⁷ The rich rule over the poor.
   The borrower is servant to the lender.
⁸ He who sows wickedness reaps trouble,
   and the rod of his fury will be destroyed.
⁹ He who has a generous eye will be blessed;
   for he shares his food with the poor.

> 1. Find the verses that give advice on the following subjects: pride, lying, giving, a quarrelsome wife, and child rearing.
>
> 2. Find the verses that tell how a man obtains wealth and honor.
>
> 3. How can a good name be more valuable than riches?

C. THE JUDGMENT OF GOD

Although King Solomon was very wise, he failed to continue to worship only the Lord God. He married women from the surrounding kingdoms, and they brought many false gods to Israel. After Solomon's death, the nation of Israel split into two kingdoms called Judah and Israel. Many of the kings who followed Solomon also departed from worshiping the one true God. Because of their disobedience, God brought judgment upon the people. Eventually, the two kingdoms were taken over by foreign nations, and most of the people were sent to other lands. During this time, God sent many prophets who tried to turn Israel and Judah back from their wicked ways.

45. A DIVIDED NATION
1 Kings 11:1-13; 12:1-17

Although Solomon was the wisest man who ever lived, he went off the track. His lust for life resulted in his introducing the worship of false gods to Israel. This brought consequences that ended the golden age of Israel. Israel divided into two competing nations. From now on, life was difficult because evil, once introduced in the nations, unfortunately dominated life in both kingdoms. In this next selection we will see how this all came about.

Solomon's Unfaithfulness to God

11 ¹ Now king Solomon loved many foreign women, together with the daughter of Pharaoh, women of the Moabites, Ammonites, Edomites, Sidonians, and Hittites; ² of the nations concerning which Yahweh said to the children of Israel, "You shall not go among them, neither shall they come among you; for surely they will turn away your heart after their gods." Solomon joined to these in love.

³ He had seven hundred wives, princesses, and three hundred concubines; and his wives turned away his heart. ⁴ When Solomon was old, his wives turned away his heart after other gods; and his heart was not perfect with Yahweh his God, as the heart of David his father was. ⁵ For Solomon went after Ashtoreth the goddess of the Sidonians, and after Milcom the abomination of the Ammonites. ⁶ Solomon did that which was evil in Yahweh's sight, and didn't go fully after Yahweh, as David his father did. ⁷ Then Solomon built a high place for Chemosh the abomination of Moab, on the mountain that is before Jerusalem, and for Molech the abomination of the children of Ammon. ⁸ So he did for all his foreign wives, who burnt incense and sacrificed to their gods. ⁹ Yahweh was angry with Solomon, because his heart was turned away from Yahweh, the God of Israel, who had appeared to him twice, ¹⁰ and had commanded him concerning this thing that he should not go after other gods; but he didn't keep that which Yahweh commanded. ¹¹ Therefore Yahweh said to Solomon, "Because this is done by you, and you have not kept my covenant and my statutes, which I have commanded you, I will surely tear the kingdom from you, and will give it to your servant. ¹² Nevertheless, I will not do it in your days, for David your father's sake; but I will tear it out of your son's hand. ¹³ However I will not tear away all the kingdom; but I will give one tribe to your son, for David my servant's sake, and for Jerusalem's sake which I have chosen."

The Northern Tribes Revolt

12 ¹ Rehoboam went to Shechem, for all Israel had come to Shechem to make him king. ² When Jeroboam the son of Nebat heard of it (for he was yet in Egypt, where he had fled from the presence of king Solomon, and Jeroboam lived in Egypt, ³ and they sent and called him), Jeroboam and all the assembly of Israel came, and spoke to Rehoboam, saying, ⁴ "Your father made our yoke difficult. Now therefore make the hard service of your father, and his heavy yoke which he put on us, lighter, and we will serve you."

⁵ He said to them, "Depart for three days, then come back to me."
The people departed.

⁶ King Rehoboam took counsel with the old men, who had stood before Solomon his father while he yet lived, saying, "What counsel do you give me to answer these people?"

⁷ They replied, "If you will be a servant to this people today, and will serve them, and answer them with good words, then they will be your servants forever."

⁸ But he abandoned the counsel of the old men which they had given him, and took counsel with the young men who had grown up with him, who stood before him. ⁹ He said to them, "What counsel do you give, that we may answer these people, who have spoken to me, saying, 'Make the yoke that your father put on us lighter?'"

¹⁰ The young men who had grown up with him said to him, "Tell these

people who spoke to you, saying, 'Your father made our yoke heavy, but make it lighter to us;' tell them, 'My little finger is thicker than my father's waist. ¹¹ Now my father burdened you with a heavy yoke, but I will add to your yoke. My father chastised you with whips, but I will chastise you with scorpions.'"

¹² So Jeroboam and all the people came to Rehoboam the third day, as the king asked, saying, "Come to me again the third day." ¹³ The king answered the people roughly, and abandoned the counsel of the old men which they had given him, ¹⁴ and spoke to them according to the counsel of the young men, saying, "My father made your yoke heavy, but I will add to your yoke. My father chastised you with whips, but I will chastise you with scorpions."

¹⁵ So the king didn't listen to the people; for it was a thing brought about from Yahweh, that he might establish his word, which Yahweh spoke by Ahijah the Shilonite to Jeroboam the son of Nebat. ¹⁶ When all Israel saw that the king didn't listen to them, the people answered the king, saying, "What portion have we in David? We don't have an inheritance in the son of Jesse. To your tents, Israel! Now see to your own house, David." So Israel departed to their tents. ¹⁷ But as for the children of Israel who lived in the cities of Judah, Rehoboam reigned over them.

1. What or who turned Solomon's heart away from the true God?

2. What were the consequences of his actions?

3. How could Solomon, such a brilliant man, be so unwise? What does this say about the fallen nature of mankind?

4. Did Rehoboam show wisdom when he rejected the advice of the older advisors and heeded the advice of the younger men who had no governing experience?

5. Can you see how important it is to have wisdom?

6. What does this story tell us about the importance of faithful obedience to God's commands in order to have wisdom and enjoy God's blessings? What was Joshua's advice on the subject? (See Selection 28, pp. 61-62)

46. GOD'S PROPHETS WARN ISRAEL
1 Kings 12:25-33 and 13:1-6, 33-34 and 16:29-33
and Jeremiah 5:11-19 and 7:1-15

When Israel turned away from the Lord, corruption entered the culture, and soon the people began to do evil to God and to themselves. God hates evil. He sent many prophets to both Israel and Judah to warn the people to come back to him, the true God, and to stop their evil ways. Elijah and Amos were two prophets sent to the northern tribes of Israel. Jeremiah was one of the prophets God sent to Judah. In spite of all the warnings God gave to the people through His messengers, and in spite of the miracles these prophets did by God's power, the obstinate people continued in their evil ways, were finally banished from the Promised Land into foreign captivity. The ten tribes of Israel were captured and taken into exile in Assyria in 722 B.C. The two tribes of Judah were captured and taken into captivity in Babylon in 586 B.C.

Jeroboam Turns from God

12 ²⁵Then Jeroboam built Shechem in the hill country of Ephraim, and lived in it; and he went out from there, and built Penuel. ²⁶ Jeroboam said in his heart, "Now the kingdom will return to David's house. ²⁷ If this people goes up to offer sacrifices in Yahweh's house at Jerusalem, then the heart of this people will turn again to their lord, even to Rehoboam king of Judah; and they will kill me, and return to Rehoboam king of Judah." ²⁸ So the king took counsel, and made two calves of gold; and he said to them, "It is too much for you to go up to Jerusalem. Look and behold your gods, Israel, which brought you up out of the land of Egypt!" ²⁹ He set the one in Bethel, and the other put he in Dan. ³⁰ This thing became a sin; for the people went even as far as Dan to worship before the one there. ³¹ He made houses of high places, and made priests from among all the people, who were not of the sons of Levi. ³²Jeroboam ordained a feast in the eighth month, on the fifteenth day of the month, like the feast that is in Judah, and he went up to the altar. He did so in Bethel, sacrificing to the calves that he had made, and he placed in Bethel the priests of the high places that he had made. ³³ He went up to the altar which he had made in Bethel on the fifteenth day in the eighth month, even in the month which he had devised of his own heart; and he ordained a feast for the children of Israel, and went up to the altar, to burn incense.

A Prophet Warns Jeroboam

13 Behold, a man of God came out of Judah by Yahweh's word to Beth El; and Jeroboam was standing by the altar to burn incense. ² He cried against the altar by Yahweh's word, and said, "Altar! Altar! Yahweh says: 'Behold, a son will be born to David's house, Josiah by name. On you he will sacrifice the priests of the high places who burn incense on you, and they will burn men's bones on you.'" ³ He gave a sign the same day, saying, "This is the sign which Yahweh has spoken: Behold, the altar will be split apart, and the ashes that are on it will be poured out."

⁴When the king heard the saying of the man of God, which he cried against the altar in Bethel, Jeroboam put out his hand from the altar, saying, "Seize him!" His hand, which he put out against him, dried up, so that he could not draw it back again to himself. ⁵The altar was also split apart, and the ashes poured out from the altar, according to the sign which the man of God had given by Yahweh's word. ⁶ The king answered the man of God, "Now intercede for the favor of Yahweh your God, and pray for me, that my hand may be restored me again." The man of God interceded with Yahweh, and the king's hand was restored to

him again, and became as it was before.

³³ After this thing Jeroboam didn't return from his evil way, but again made priests of the high places from among all the people. Whoever wanted to, he consecrated him, that there might be priests of the high places. ³⁴ This thing became sin to the house of Jeroboam, even to cut it off, and to destroy it from off the surface of the earth.

King Ahab Worships Baal

16 ²⁹In the thirty-eighth year of Asa king of Judah, Ahab the son of Omri began to reign over Israel. Ahab the son of Omri reigned over Israel in Samaria twenty-two years. ³⁰ Ahab the son of Omri did that which was evil in Yahweh's sight above all that were before him.³¹ As if it had been a light thing for him to walk in the sins of Jeroboam the son of Nebat, he took as wife Jezebel the daughter of Ethbaal king of the Sidonians, and went and served Baal, and worshiped him. ³² He raised up an altar for Baal in the house of Baal, which he had built in Samaria. ³³ Ahab made the Asherah; and Ahab did more yet to provoke Yahweh, the God of Israel, to anger than all the kings of Israel who were before him.

God Rejects Israel

5 ¹¹For the house of Israel and the house of Judah have dealt very treacherously against me," says Yahweh. ¹² They have denied Yahweh, and said, "It is not he; neither shall evil come on us; neither shall we see sword nor famine. ¹³ The prophets shall become wind, and the word is not in them. Thus shall it be done to them."

¹⁴ Therefore Yahweh, the God of Armies says, "Because you speak this word, behold, I will make my words in your mouth fire, and this people wood, and it shall devour them.¹⁵ Behold, I will bring a nation on you from far, house of Israel," says Yahweh. "It is a mighty nation. It is an ancient nation, a nation whose language you don't know, neither understand what they say. ¹⁶ Their quiver is an open tomb, they are all mighty men.¹⁷ They shall eat up your harvest, and your bread, which your sons and your daughters should eat. They shall eat up your flocks and your herds. They shall eat up your vines and your fig trees. They shall beat down your fortified cities, in which you trust, with the sword. ¹⁸"But even in those days," says Yahweh, "I will not make a full end with you. ¹⁹ It will happen, when you say, 'Why has Yahweh our God done all these things to us?' Then you shall say to them, 'Just like you have forsaken me, and served foreign gods in your land, so you shall serve strangers in a land that is not yours.'

Jeremiah Preaches in the Temple

7 The word that came to Jeremiah from Yahweh, saying, ² "Stand in the gate of Yahweh's house, and proclaim there this word, and say, 'Hear Yahweh's word, all you of Judah, who enter in at these gates to worship Yahweh.'"

³ Yahweh of Armies, the God of Israel says, "Amend your ways and your doings, and I will cause you to dwell in this place. ⁴ Don't trust in lying words, saying,

'Yahweh's temple, Yahweh's temple, Yahweh's temple, are these.' ⁵ For if you thoroughly amend your ways and your doings; if you thoroughly execute justice between a man and his neighbor; ⁶ if you don't oppress the foreigner, the fatherless, and the widow, and don't shed innocent blood in this place, neither walk after other gods to your own hurt: ⁷ then I will cause you to dwell in this place, in the land that I gave to your fathers, from of old even forever more. ⁸ Behold, you trust in lying words, that can't profit. ⁹ Will you steal, murder, and commit adultery, and swear falsely, and burn incense to Baal, and walk after other gods that you have not known, ¹⁰ and come and stand before me in this house, which is called by my name, and say, 'We are delivered;' that you may do all these abominations? ¹¹ Has this house, which is called by my name, become a den of robbers in your eyes? Behold, I, even I, have seen it," says Yahweh.

¹² "But go now to my place which was in Shiloh, where I caused my name to dwell at the first, and see what I did to it for the wickedness of my people Israel.

¹³ Now, because you have done all these works," says Yahweh, "and I spoke to you, rising up early and speaking, but you didn't hear; and I called you, but you didn't answer: ¹⁴ therefore will I do to the house which is called by my name, in which you trust, and to the place which I gave to you and to your fathers, as I did to Shiloh. ¹⁵ I will cast you out of my sight, as I have cast out all your brothers, even the whole offspring of Ephraim.

> 1. Why did Jeroboam set up an alternative worship system? Why was that a bad idea?
>
> 2. Why did Jeremiah tell the people of Judah not to trust their chant: "Yahweh's Temple, Yahweh's Temple"? Why didn't that work for them?
>
> 3. Do you see how the people were substituting being religious for being obedient?

47. THE LIVING GOD
1 Kings 17:1-24 and 18:1-45

Although he was ruler of Israel at this time, King Ahab was controlled by his wife, Queen Jezebel. She worshiped the false god Baal and was persecuting and killing all those who worshiped the true God. In this exciting passage, the prophet Elijah demonstrated the power of the living God.

Elijah, Ahab and Evil Times in Israel

17 Elijah the Tishbite, who was one of the settlers of Gilead, said to Ahab, "As Yahweh, the God of Israel, lives, before whom I stand, there shall not be dew nor rain these years, but according to my word."

² Then Yahweh's word came to him, saying, ³ "Go away from here, turn eastward, and hide yourself by the brook Cherith, that is before the Jordan. ⁴ You

shall drink from the brook. I have commanded the ravens to feed you there." ⁵ So he went and did according to Yahweh's word; for he went and lived by the brook Cherith that is before the Jordan. ⁶The ravens brought him bread and meat in the morning, and bread and meat in the evening; and he drank from the brook. ⁷ After a while, the brook dried up, because there was no rain in the land.

The Widow at Zarephath
⁸ Yahweh's word came to him, saying, ⁹ "Arise, go to Zarephath, which belongs to Sidon, and stay there. Behold, I have commanded a widow there to sustain you." ¹⁰ So he arose and went to Zarephath; and when he came to the gate of the city, behold, a widow was there gathering sticks. He called to her, and said, "Please get me a little water in a jar, that I may drink."

¹¹ As she was going to get it, he called to her, and said, "Please bring me a morsel of bread in your hand."

¹² She said, "As Yahweh your God lives, I don't have a cake, but a handful of meal in a jar, and a little oil in a jar. Behold, I am gathering two sticks, that I may go in and bake it for me and my son, that we may eat it, and die."

¹³ Elijah said to her, "Don't be afraid. Go and do as you have said; but make me a little cake from it first, and bring it out to me, and afterward make some for you and for your son. ¹⁴ For Yahweh, the God of Israel says, 'The jar of meal will not run out, and the jar of oil will not fail, until the day that Yahweh sends rain on the earth.'"

¹⁵ She went and did according to the saying of Elijah; and she, and he, and her house, ate many days. ¹⁶ The jar of meal didn't run out, and the jar of oil did not fail, according to Yahweh's word, which he spoke by Elijah. ¹⁷ After these things, the son of the woman, the mistress of the house, became sick; and his sickness was so severe that there was no breath left in him. ¹⁸ She said to Elijah, "What have I to do with you, you man of God? You have come to me to bring my sin to memory, and to kill my son!"

¹⁹ He said to her, "Give me your son." He took him out of her bosom, and carried him up into the room where he stayed, and laid him on his own bed. ²⁰ He cried to Yahweh, and said, "Yahweh my God, have you also brought evil on the widow with whom I am staying, by killing her son?"

²¹He stretched himself on the child three times, and cried to Yahweh, and said, "Yahweh my God, please let this child's soul come into him again."

²²Yahweh listened to the voice of Elijah; and the soul of the child came into him again, and he revived. ²³ Elijah took the child, and brought him down out of the room into the house, and delivered him to his mother; and Elijah said, "Behold, your son lives."

²⁴ The woman said to Elijah, "Now I know that you are a man of God, and that Yahweh's word in your mouth is truth."

Elijah and Obadiah

18 After many days, Yahweh's word came to Elijah, in the third year, saying, "Go, show yourself to Ahab; and I will send rain on the earth."

² Elijah went to show himself to Ahab. The famine was severe in Samaria. ³ Ahab called Obadiah, who was over the household. (Now Obadiah feared Yahweh greatly; ⁴ for when Jezebel cut off Yahweh's prophets, Obadiah took one hundred prophets, and hid them by fifty in a cave, and fed them with bread and water.) ⁵ Ahab said to Obadiah, "Go through the land, to all the springs of water, and to all the brooks. Perhaps we may find grass and save the horses and mules alive, that we not lose all the animals."

⁶ So they divided the land between them to pass throughout it. Ahab went one way by himself, and Obadiah went another way by himself. ⁷ As Obadiah was on the way, behold, Elijah met him. He recognized him, and fell on his face, and said, "Is it you, my Lord Elijah?"

⁸ He answered him, "It is I. Go, tell your lord, 'Behold, Elijah is here!'"

⁹He said, "How have I sinned, that you would deliver your servant into the hand of Ahab, to kill me? ¹⁰ As Yahweh your God lives, there is no nation or kingdom where my lord has not sent to seek you. When they said, 'He is not here,' he took an oath of the kingdom and nation, that they didn't find you. ¹¹ Now you say, 'Go, tell your lord, "Behold, Elijah is here."' ¹² It will happen, as soon as I leave you, that Yahweh's Spirit will carry you I don't know where; and so when I come and tell Ahab, and he can't find you, he will kill me. But I, your servant, have feared Yahweh from my youth. ¹³ Wasn't it told my lord what I did when Jezebel killed Yahweh's prophets, how I hid one hundred men of Yahweh's prophets with fifty to a cave, and fed them with bread and water? ¹⁴ Now you say, 'Go, tell your lord, "Behold, Elijah is here."' He will kill me."

¹⁵ Elijah said, "As Yahweh of Armies lives, before whom I stand, I will surely show myself to him today." ¹⁶ So Obadiah went to meet Ahab, and told him; and Ahab went to meet Elijah. ¹⁷ When Ahab saw Elijah, Ahab said to him, "Is that you, you troubler of Israel?"

¹⁸He answered, "I have not troubled Israel; but you, and your father's house, in that you have forsaken Yahweh's commandments, and you have followed the Baals. ¹⁹ Now therefore send, and gather to me all Israel to Mount Carmel, and four hundred fifty of the prophets of Baal, and four hundred of the prophets of the Asherah, who eat at Jezebel's table."

Elijah Hosts a Power Encounter on Mt. Carmel

²⁰ So Ahab sent to all the children of Israel, and gathered the prophets together to Mount Carmel. ²¹ Elijah came near to all the people, and said, "How long will you waver between the two sides? If Yahweh is God, follow him; but if Baal, then follow him."

The people didn't say a word.

²² Then Elijah said to the people, "I, even I only, am left as a prophet of

Yahweh; but Baal's prophets are four hundred fifty men. ²³ Let them therefore give us two bulls; and let them choose one bull for themselves, and cut it in pieces, and lay it on the wood, and put no fire under; and I will dress the other bull, and lay it on the wood, and put no fire under it. ²⁴ You call on the name of your god, and I will call on Yahweh's name. The God who answers by fire, let him be God."

All the people answered, "What you say is good."

God vs Baal on Mt. Carmel
²⁵ Elijah said to the prophets of Baal, "Choose one bull for yourselves, and dress it first; for you are many; and call on the name of your god, but put no fire under it."

²⁶They took the bull which was given them, and they dressed it, and called on the name of Baal from morning even until noon, saying, "Baal, hear us!" But there was no voice, and nobody answered. They leaped about the altar which was made. ²⁷ At noon, Elijah mocked them, and said, "Cry aloud; for he is a god. Either he is deep in thought, or he has gone somewhere, or he is on a journey, or perhaps he sleeps and must be awakened." ²⁸ They cried aloud, and cut themselves in their way with knives and lances, until the blood gushed out on them. ²⁹ When midday was past, they prophesied until the time of the evening offering; but there was no voice, no answer, and nobody paid attention.

³⁰ Elijah said to all the people, "Come near to me!"; and all the people came near to him. He repaired the altar of Yahweh that had been thrown down. ³¹ Elijah took twelve stones, according to the number of the tribes of the sons of Jacob, to whom Yahweh's word came, saying, "Israel shall be your name." ³² With the stones he built an altar in Yahweh's name. He made a trench around the altar, large enough to contain two seahs[a] of seed. ³³ He put the wood in order, and cut the bull in pieces, and laid it on the wood. He said, "Fill four jars with water, and pour it on the burnt offering, and on the wood." ³⁴ He said, "Do it a second time"; and they did it the second time. He said, "Do it a third time"; and they did it the third time. ³⁵ The water ran around the altar; and he also filled the trench with water.

³⁶ At the time of the evening offering, Elijah the prophet came near, and said, "Yahweh, the God of Abraham, of Isaac, and of Israel, let it be known today that you are God in Israel, and that I am your servant, and that I have done all these things at your word.³⁷ Hear me, Yahweh, hear me, that this people may know that you, Yahweh, are God, and that you have turned their heart back again."

Fire from Heaven!
³⁸ Then Yahweh's fire fell, and consumed the burnt offering, the wood, the stones, and the dust, and licked up the water that was in the trench. ³⁹ When all the people saw it, they fell on their faces. They said, "Yahweh, he is God! Yahweh, he is God!"

Great Bible Truths

⁴⁰Elijah said to them, "Seize the prophets of Baal! Don't let one of them escape!"

They seized them; and Elijah brought them down to the brook Kishon, and killed them there.

The End of the Drought

⁴¹ Elijah said to Ahab, "Get up, eat and drink; for there is the sound of abundance of rain." ⁴² So Ahab went off to eat and drink, but Elijah climbed to the top of Carmel, bent himself down on the earth, and put his face between his knees.
⁴³ He said to his servant, "Go up now, and look toward the sea."

He went up, and looked, and said, "There is nothing."

He said, "Go again" seven times.

⁴⁴ On the seventh time, he said, "Behold, a small cloud, like a man's hand, is rising out of the sea."

He said, "Go up, tell Ahab, 'Get ready and go down, so that the rain doesn't stop you.'"

⁴⁵In a little while, the sky grew black with clouds and wind, and there was a great rain. Ahab rode, and went to Jezreel.

1. Why did God send a drought to Israel?
2. Can you see how bad leadership affects an entire nation?
3. Describe the miracles that happened in the widow's home.
4. Why do you think it took courage for Elijah to obey the word of the Lord?
5. Why did the people acknowledge that "the Lord, He is God"?

48. GOD'S WARNING
Amos 5:4-15, and 21-27

One of the prophets God used to warn Israel was a man named Amos. Through Amos, God pointed out the lack of justice in the land. Through Amos God told the people to turn away from evil and seek Him, to live righteously so that they might live.

Seek the Lord and Live

5 ⁴For Yahweh says to the house of Israel:
"Seek me, and you will live;
⁵ but don't seek Bethel,
nor enter into Gilgal,
and don't pass to Beersheba:
for Gilgal shall surely go into captivity,
and Bethel shall come to nothing.
⁶ Seek Yahweh, and you will live;
lest he break out like fire in the house of Joseph,
and it devour,

and there be no one to quench it in Bethel.
⁷ You who turn justice to wormwood,
    and cast down righteousness to the earth:
⁸ seek him who made the Pleiades and Orion,
    and turns the shadow of death into the morning,
and makes the day dark with night;
    who calls for the waters of the sea,
and pours them out on the surface of the earth,
    Yahweh is his name,
⁹ who brings sudden destruction on the strong,
    so that destruction comes on the fortress.
¹⁰ They hate him who reproves in the gate,
    and they abhor him who speaks blamelessly.
¹¹ Therefore, because you trample on the poor,
    and take taxes from him of wheat:
You have built houses of cut stone,
    but you will not dwell in them.
You have planted pleasant vineyards,
    but you shall not drink their wine.
¹² For I know how many your offenses,
    and how great are your sins--
you who afflict the just, who take a bribe,
    and who turn aside the needy in the courts.
¹³Therefore a prudent person keeps silent in such a time,
    for it is an evil time.
¹⁴Seek good, and not evil,
    that you may live;
and so Yahweh, the God of Armies, will be with you,
    as you say.
¹⁵Hate evil, love good,
    and establish justice in the courts.
It may be that Yahweh, the God of Armies, will be gracious
    to the remnant of Joseph."
²¹ I hate, I despise your feasts,
    and I can't stand your solemn assemblies.
²² Yes, though you offer me your burnt offerings and meal offerings,
    I will not accept them;
neither will I regard
    the peace offerings of your fat animals.
²³ Take away from me the noise of your songs!
    I will not listen to the music of your harps.
²⁴ But let justice roll on like rivers,

and righteousness like a mighty stream.
²⁵ "Did you bring to me sacrifices and offerings
   in the wilderness forty years, house of Israel?
²⁶ You also carried the tent of your king
   and the shrine of your images, the star of your god,
   which you made for yourselves.
²⁷ Therefore will I cause you to go into captivity beyond Damascus,"
   says Yahweh, whose name is the God of Armies.

   1. Name some of the injustices that took place in Israel.

   2. What were the Lord's instructions to Israel?

49. TAKEN CAPTIVE
2 Kings 17:7-23

In spite of all the warning God gave to the people, they continued to sin against Him. Finally, God brought an end to the Kingdom of Israel (the northern tribes). They were conquered and exiled to Assyria in 722 B.C. God banished those people from the Promised Land forever. They became what history has called, the "ten lost tribes," lost because they were never heard from again.

The End of Israel, a Failed Nation

17 ⁷It was so because the children of Israel had sinned against Yahweh their God, who brought them up out of the land of Egypt from under the hand of Pharaoh king of Egypt, and had feared other gods, ⁸ and walked in the statutes of the nations whom Yahweh cast out from before the children of Israel, and of the kings of Israel, which they made. ⁹ The children of Israel secretly did things that were not right against Yahweh their God; and they built high places for themselves in all their cities, from the tower of the watchmen to the fortified city; ¹⁰ and they set up for themselves pillars and Asherah poles on every high hill, and under every green tree; ¹¹ and there they burnt incense in all the high places, as the nations whom Yahweh carried away before them did; and they did wicked things to provoke Yahweh to anger; ¹² and they served idols, of which Yahweh had said to them, "You shall not do this thing." ¹³ Yet Yahweh testified to Israel, and to Judah, by every prophet, and every seer, saying, "Turn from your evil ways, and keep my commandments and my statutes, according to all the law which I commanded your fathers, and which I sent to you by my servants the prophets." ¹⁴ Notwithstanding, they would not listen, but hardened their neck, like the neck of their fathers, who didn't believe in Yahweh their God. ¹⁵ They rejected his statutes, and his covenant that he made with their fathers, and his testimonies which he testified to them; and they followed vanity, and became vain, and followed the nations that were around them, concerning whom Yahweh had commanded them that they should not do like them. ¹⁶ They abandoned all the commandments of Yahweh their God, and made molten images for themselves, even two calves, and made an Asherah, and worshiped all the army of the sky, and served Baal. ¹⁷ They caused their sons and their daughters to pass through the fire, used divination and enchantments, and sold themselves to do that which was evil in Yahweh's sight, to provoke him to anger. ¹⁸ Therefore Yahweh was very angry with Israel, and removed them out of his sight. There was none left but the tribe of Judah only. ¹⁹ Also Judah didn't keep the commandments of Yahweh their God, but walked in the statutes of Israel which they made. ²⁰ Yahweh rejected all the offspring of Israel, afflicted them, and delivered them into the hands of raiders, until he had cast them out of his sight.²¹ For he tore Israel from David's house; and they made Jeroboam the son of Nebat king; and Jeroboam drove Israel from following Yahweh, and made them sin a great sin. ²² The children of Israel walked in all the sins of Jeroboam which he did; they didn't depart from them ²³ until Yahweh removed Israel out of his sight, as he said by all his servants the prophets. So Israel was carried away out of their own land to Assyria to this day.

1. What were the sins that Israel committed against the Lord?

2. What happened to the people when God "removed them and cast them out of His sight"? Is there a lesson here for today?

3. Do you think that the people deserved their punishment?

50. TURN FROM EVIL
Isaiah 1:1-20

One of the greatest prophets of God was a man named Isaiah. He was sent by God to warn the people of Judah to turn from their sins. Through Isaiah, God spoke as One who hated sin and religious ceremonies. He was willing, however, to cleanse those who were willing to obey Him.

A Rebellious Nation

1 ¹The vision of Isaiah the son of Amoz, which he saw concerning Judah and Jerusalem, in the days of Uzziah, Jotham, Ahaz, and Hezekiah, kings of Judah.
²Hear, heavens, and listen, earth; for Yahweh has spoken:
"I have nourished and brought up children,
and they have rebelled against me.
ʷ³The ox knows his owner, and the donkey his master's crib;
but Israel doesn't know,
my people don't consider."
⁴Ah sinful nation, a people loaded with iniquity,
offspring of evildoers,
children who deal corruptly!
They have forsaken Yahweh.
They have despised the Holy One of Israel.
They are estranged and backward.

⁵ Why should you be beaten more,
> that you revolt more and more?

The whole head is sick,
> and the whole heart faint.

⁶From the sole of the foot even to the head there is no soundness in it:
> wounds, welts, and open sores.

They haven't been closed, neither bandaged, neither soothed with oil.
> ⁷Your country is desolate.

Your cities are burned with fire.
> Strangers devour your land in your presence,

and it is desolate, as overthrown by strangers.
> ⁸The daughter of Zion is left like a shelter in a vineyard,

like a hut in a field of melons,
> like a besieged city.

⁹Unless Yahweh of Armies [God Almighty] had left to us a very small remnant,
> we would have been as Sodom;

we would have been like Gomorrah.
> ¹⁰Hear Yahweh's word, you rulers of Sodom!

Listen to the law of our God, you people of Gomorrah!
> ¹¹"What are the multitude of your sacrifices to me?" says Yahweh.

"I have had enough of the burnt offerings of rams,
> and the fat of fed animals.

I don't delight in the blood of bulls,
> or of lambs,

or of male goats.
> ¹²When you come to appear before me,

who has required this at your hand,
> to trample my courts?

¹³Bring no more vain offerings.
> Incense is an abomination to me;

new moons, Sabbaths, and convocations:
> I can't bear with evil assemblies.

¹⁴ My soul hates your New Moons and your appointed feasts.
> They are a burden to me.

I am weary of bearing them.
> ¹⁵ When you spread out your hands, I will hide my eyes from you.

Yes, when you make many prayers, I will not hear.
> Your hands are full of blood.

¹⁶ Wash yourselves, make yourself clean.
> Put away the evil of your doings from before my eyes.
> Cease to do evil.
> ¹⁷ Learn to do well.

Seek justice.
Relieve the oppressed.
Judge the fatherless. Plead for the widow."
¹⁸ "Come now, and let us reason together," says Yahweh:
"Though your sins be as scarlet, they shall be as white as snow.
Though they be red like crimson, they shall be as wool.
¹⁹ If you are willing and obedient,
you shall eat the good of the land;
²⁰ but if you refuse and rebel,
you shall be devoured with the sword;
for the mouth of Yahweh has spoken it."

> 1. What were the sins of Judah?
>
> 2. How did God feel about religious sacrifices and ceremonies?
>
> 3. What did the people have to do in order to have their sins cleansed?

51. A FALLEN NATION
2 Chronicles 36:11-21

Because the kings and their people refused to listen to the prophets, God was forced to bring judgment on Judah, as He had done to Israel. Judah, (the southern tribes and city of Jerusalem) was conquered by the Babylonians and exiled to Babylon in 586 B.C.

Zedekiah King of Judah

36 ¹¹Zedekiah was twenty-one years old when he began to reign; and he reigned eleven years in Jerusalem: ¹² and he did that which was evil in Yahweh his God's sight; he didn't humble himself before Jeremiah the prophet speaking from the mouth of Yahweh. ¹³ He also rebelled against king Nebuchadnezzar, who had made him swear by God: but he stiffened his neck, and hardened his heart against turning to Yahweh, the God of Israel.¹⁴ Moreover all the chiefs of the priests, and the people, trespassed very greatly after all the abominations of the nations; and they polluted Yahweh's house which he had made holy in Jerusalem.

The Fall of Jerusalem

¹⁵ Yahweh, the God of their fathers, sent to them by his messengers, rising up early and sending[them persistently], because he had compassion on his people, and on his dwelling place: ¹⁶ but they mocked the messengers of God, and despised his words, and scoffed at his prophets, until Yahweh's wrath arose against his people, until there was no remedy. ¹⁷ Therefore he brought on them the king of the Chaldeans, who killed their young men with the sword in the house of their sanctuary [the Temple], and had no compassion on young man or virgin, old man or gray-headed: he gave them all into his hand. ¹⁸ All the vessels

of God's house, great and small, and the treasures of Yahweh's house, and the treasures of the king, and of his princes, all these he brought to Babylon. [19] They burnt God's house, and broke down the wall of Jerusalem, and burnt all its palaces with fire, and destroyed all the goodly vessels of it. [20] He carried those who had escaped from the sword away to Babylon; and they were servants to him and his sons until the reign of the kingdom of Persia: [21] to fulfill Yahweh's word by the mouth of Jeremiah, until the land had enjoyed its Sabbaths. As long as it lay desolate it kept Sabbath, to fulfill seventy years.

1. What did King Nebuchadnezzar do to the people of Judah and to the temple in Jerusalem?

2. This was a terrible disaster that could have been avoided. Consider what good their being Hebrews, their religiosity and their confidence in having the temple building located in Jerusalem did for them. Does God live in a building?

3. God promised to be faithful to the Hebrews, His chosen people, but each generation had to confirm this special relationship by honoring and obeying Him. They did not do this, and God had to punish them severely. He used pagans to do it.

4. What does this story tell us about God's nature and His word?

5. God was depending upon the Hebrews to be the nation out of which His Savior would come. Given this situation, what do you think God will do next?

D. THE MERCY OF GOD

We have seen how God revealed His ways through the nation of Israel. We have seen His greatness, His wisdom and His judgment. Israel's captivity was to be an important learning experience for the Israelites, but God is also merciful. Now we look at His mercy as evidenced through individuals and nations who responded to Him. When people did repent and turn to Him, the Lord always had mercy and blessed them. God is a good God who loves everyone who responds to His love. In this section we see examples of that divine, loving nature.

52. A NATION IN CAPTIVITY
Jeremiah 29:4-14 and Daniel 1

Many of the people of Judah were taken as captives by King Nebuchadnezzar of Babylon. In that foreign land, God told the Jews to make it their home for 70 years, even to pray that Babylon would prosper, but they were also called to remain faithful to the Lord God. It would prove to be challenging for many Jews, like Daniel and his three friends. We see God's mercy in providing a "home" away from home for the Jews.

Jeremiah's Letter to the Exiles

29 ⁴Yahweh of Armies, the God of Israel, says to all the captivity, whom I have caused to be carried away captive from Jerusalem to Babylon: ⁵ Build houses, and dwell in them; and plant gardens, and eat their fruit. ⁶ Take wives, and father sons and daughters; and take wives for your sons, and give your daughters to husbands, that they may bear sons and daughters; and multiply there, and don't be diminished. ⁷ Seek the peace of the city where I have caused you to be carried away captive, and pray to Yahweh for it; for in its peace you shall have peace. ⁸ For Yahweh of Armies, the God of Israel says: Don't let your prophets who are among you, and your diviners, deceive you; neither listen to your dreams which you cause to be dreamed. ⁹ For they prophesy falsely to you in my name: I have not sent them, says Yahweh. ¹⁰ For Yahweh says, After seventy years are accomplished for Babylon, I will visit you, and perform my good word toward you, in causing you to return to this place. ¹¹ For I know the thoughts that I think toward you, says Yahweh, thoughts of peace, and not of evil, to give you hope and a future. ¹² You shall call on me, and you shall go and pray to me, and I will listen to you. ¹³ You shall seek me, and find me, when you shall search for me with all your heart. ¹⁴ I will be found by you, says Yahweh, and I will turn again your captivity, and I will gather you from all the nations, and from all the places where I have driven you, says Yahweh; and I will bring you again to the place from where I caused you to be carried away captive.

Daniel in Nebuchadnezzar's Court

1 In the third year of the reign of Jehoiakim king of Judah came Nebuchadnezzar king of Babylon to Jerusalem, and besieged it. ² The Lord gave Jehoiakim king of Judah into his hand, with part of the vessels of the house of God; and he carried them into the land of Shinar to the house of his god: and he brought the vessels into the treasure house of his god. ³ The king spoke to Ashpenaz the master of his eunuchs, that he should bring in some of the children of Israel, even of the royal offspring and of the nobles; ⁴ youths in whom was no defect, but well-favored, and skillful in all wisdom, and endowed with knowledge, and understanding science, and such as had ability to stand in the king's palace; and that he should teach them the learning and the language of the Chaldeans.⁵ The king appointed for them a daily portion of the king's dainties, and of the wine which he drank, and that they should be nourished three years; that at its end they should stand before the king. ⁶ Now among these were, of the children of Judah, Daniel, Hananiah, Mishael, and Azariah. ⁷ The prince of the eunuchs gave names to them: to Daniel he gave the name Belteshazzar; and to Hananiah, Shadrach; and to Mishael, Meshach; and to Azariah, Abednego. ⁸ But Daniel purposed in his heart that he would not defile himself with the king's dainties, nor with the wine which he drank: therefore he requested of the prince of the eunuchs that he might not defile himself. ⁹ Now God made Daniel to find kindness and compassion in the sight of the prince of the eunuchs. ¹⁰ The prince of the eunuchs said to Daniel, "I fear my lord the king, who has appointed your food and your drink: for why should he see your faces worse looking than the youths who are of your own age? So would you endanger my head with the king." [11] Then Daniel said to the steward whom the prince of the eunuchs had appointed over Daniel, Hananiah, Mishael, and Azariah: [12] "Test your servants, I beg you, ten days; and let them give us vegetables to eat, and water to drink. [13] Then let our faces be looked on before you, and the face of the youths who eat of the king's dainties; and as you see, deal with your servants." [14] So he listened to them in this matter, and proved them ten days. [15] At the end of ten days their faces appeared fairer, and they were fatter in flesh, than all the youths who ate of the king's dainties. [16] So the steward took away their dainties, and the wine that they should drink, and gave them vegetables.

Faithfulness Rewarded
[17] Now as for these four youths, God gave them knowledge and skill in all learning and wisdom: and Daniel had understanding in all visions and dreams. [18] At the end of the days which the king had appointed for bringing them in, the prince of the eunuchs brought them in before Nebuchadnezzar. [19] The king talked with them; and among them all was found no one like Daniel, Hananiah, Mishael, and Azariah: therefore stood they before the king. [20] In every matter of wisdom and understanding, concerning which the king inquired of them, he found them ten times better than all the magicians and enchanters who were in all his realm. [21] Daniel continued even to the first year of king Cyrus.

> 1. How did God in His mercy provide for His people when they were forced to live in a foreign land? Did they have hope for the future of their people and their land?
>
> 2. Daniel and his three friends were placed in prominent positions in the Babylonian empire. How was this part of God's plan for His people?
>
> 3. Why did these four young Jewish boys refuse to eat the kings' food?
>
> 4. What advice did Jeremiah give to the Jewish exiles living in Babylon? How long would their captivity last?
>
> 5. What lessons can we learn from Daniel and his friends on how to live in an environment hostile to our faith?
>
> 6. What lessons can we learn from this story about God's sovereign care for His people when disasters come into our lives?

53. THE FIRE WALKERS
Daniel 3

Many of the people of Judah were taken as captives by King Nebuchadnezzar of Babylon. In that foreign land, some of the Israelites decided that they would not bow down and worship the king's false gods. Three young men risked their lives by remaining faithful to God, and He miraculously saved them from a blazing fire.

Great Bible Truths

The Image and the Fiery Furnace

3 Nebuchadnezzar the king made an image of gold, whose height was sixty cubits, and its width six cubits: he set it up in the plain of Dura, in the province of Babylon. ² Then Nebuchadnezzar the king sent to gather together the satraps, the deputies, and the governors, the judges, the treasurers, the counselors, the sheriffs, and all the rulers of the provinces, to come to the dedication of the image which Nebuchadnezzar the king had set up. ³ Then the satraps, the deputies, and the governors, the judges, the treasurers, the counselors, the sheriffs, and all the rulers of the provinces, were gathered together to the dedication of the image that Nebuchadnezzar the king had set up; and they stood before the image that Nebuchadnezzar had set up.

⁴ Then the herald cried aloud, "To you it is commanded, peoples, nations, and languages, ⁵ that whenever you hear the sound of the horn, flute, zither, lyre, harp, pipe, and all kinds of music, you fall down and worship the golden image that Nebuchadnezzar the king has set up; ⁶ and whoever doesn't fall down and worship shall the same hour be cast into the middle of a burning fiery furnace."

⁷ Therefore at that time, when all the peoples heard the sound of the horn, flute, zither, lyre, harp, pipe, and all kinds of music, all the peoples, the nations, and the languages, fell down and worshiped the golden image that Nebuchadnezzar the king had set up.

⁸ Therefore at that time certain Chaldeans came near, and brought accusation against the Jews. ⁹ They answered Nebuchadnezzar the king, "O king, live forever. ¹⁰ You, O king, have made a decree, that every man that shall hear the sound of the horn, flute, zither, lyre, harp, pipe, and all kinds of music, shall fall down and worship the golden image; ¹¹ and whoever doesn't fall down and worship shall be cast into the middle of a burning fiery furnace. ¹² There are certain Jews whom you have appointed over the affairs of the province of Babylon: Shadrach, Meshach, and Abednego; these men, O king, have not respected you. They don't serve your gods, nor worship the golden image which you have set up."

¹³ Then Nebuchadnezzar in rage and fury commanded to bring Shadrach, Meshach, and Abednego. Then they brought these men before the king. ¹⁴ Nebuchadnezzar answered them, "Is it on purpose, Shadrach, Meshach, and Abednego, that you don't serve my god, nor worship the golden image which I have set up? ¹⁵ Now if you are ready whenever you hear the sound of the horn, flute, zither, lyre, harp, pipe, and all kinds of music to fall down and worship the image which I have made, good: but if you don't worship, you shall be cast the same hour into the middle of a burning fiery furnace; and who is that god that shall deliver you out of my hands?"

¹⁶ Shadrach, Meshach, and Abednego answered the king, "Nebuchadnezzar, we have no need to answer you in this matter. ¹⁷ If it happens, our God whom we serve is able to deliver us from the burning fiery furnace; and he will deliver us

out of your hand, O king. ¹⁸ But if not, let it be known to you, O king, that we will not serve your gods, nor worship the golden image which you have set up."

The Blazing Furnace

¹⁹ Then was Nebuchadnezzar full of fury, and the form of his appearance was changed against Shadrach, Meshach, and Abednego. He spoke, and commanded that they should heat the furnace seven times more than it was usually heated. ²⁰ He commanded certain mighty men who were in his army to bind Shadrach, Meshach, and Abednego, and to cast them into the burning fiery furnace. ²¹ Then these men were bound in their pants, their tunics, and their mantles, and their other clothes, and were cast into the middle of the burning fiery furnace. ²² Therefore because the king's commandment was urgent, and the furnace exceeding hot, the flame of the fire killed those men who took up Shadrach, Meshach, and Abednego. ²³ These three men, Shadrach, Meshach, and Abednego, fell down bound into the middle of the burning fiery furnace.

²⁴ Then Nebuchadnezzar the king was astonished, and rose up in haste: he spoke and said to his counselors, "Didn't we cast three men bound into the middle of the fire?"

They answered the king, "True, O king."

²⁵ He answered, "Look, I see four men loose, walking in the middle of the fire, and they are unharmed; and the aspect of the fourth is like a son of the gods."

²⁶ Then Nebuchadnezzar came near to the mouth of the burning fiery furnace: he spoke and said, "Shadrach, Meshach, and Abednego, you servants of the Most High God, come out, and come here."

Then Shadrach, Meshach, and Abednego came out of the middle of the fire. ²⁷ The satraps, the deputies, and the governors, and the king's counselors, being gathered together, saw these men, that the fire had no power on their bodies, nor was the hair of their head singed, neither were their pants changed, nor had the smell of fire passed on them.

²⁸ Nebuchadnezzar spoke and said, "Blessed be the God of Shadrach, Meshach, and Abednego, who has sent his angel, and delivered his servants who trusted in him, and have changed the king's word, and have yielded their bodies, that they might not serve nor worship any god, except their own God. ²⁹ Therefore I make a decree, that every people, nation, and language, which speak anything evil against the God of Shadrach, Meshach, and Abednego, shall be cut in pieces, and their houses shall be made a dunghill; because there is no other god who is able to deliver after this sort."

³⁰ Then the king promoted Shadrach, Meshach, and Abednego in the province of Babylon.

> *1. Why did the three young men refuse to worship the image?*
>
> *2. Who do you think was the fourth person in the fire?*

3. Discuss the scope of the miracle that occurred that day.

4. What actions did Nebuchadnezzar take afterward that proved that God used this miracle to touch the king's heart?

54. A MAN OF PRINCIPLE
Daniel 6

As the Jewish exile in Babylon continued, God prospered the Jews as He had promised. However, as we saw in a former selection, it was not easy for true believers to live in a pagan culture, where false gods were required to be honored and worshiped. Daniel, one of the original Jewish exiles, held important government positions in each succeeding government. Daniel was always faithful to God, and God blessed him with insights and wisdom, which made him invaluable to the pagan kings. In this selection, we see how Daniel risked his life to stay faithful to God and how God honored his courageous decision in an awesome way.

Conspiracy Against Daniel

6 It pleased Darius to set over the kingdom one hundred twenty satraps, who should be throughout the whole kingdom; ² and over them three presidents, of whom Daniel was one; that these satraps might give account to them, and that the king should have no damage. ³ Then this Daniel was distinguished above the presidents and the satraps, because an excellent spirit was in him; and the king thought to set him over the whole realm.

⁴ Then the presidents and the satraps sought to find occasion against Daniel as touching the kingdom; but they could find no occasion nor fault, because he was faithful, neither was there any error or fault found in him. ⁵ Then these men said, "We shall not find any occasion against this Daniel, except we find it against him concerning the law of his God."

⁶ Then these presidents and satraps assembled together to the king, and said thus to him, "King Darius, live forever. ⁷ All the presidents of the kingdom, the deputies and the satraps, the counselors and the governors, have consulted together to establish a royal statute, and to make a strong decree, that whoever shall ask a petition of any god or man for thirty days, except of you, O king, he shall be cast into the den of lions. ⁸ Now, O king, establish the decree, and sign the writing, that it not be changed, according to the law of the Medes and Persians, which doesn't alter." ⁹ Therefore king Darius signed the writing and the decree. ¹⁰ When Daniel knew that the writing was signed, he went into his house (now his windows were open in his room toward Jerusalem) and he kneeled on his knees three times a day, and prayed, and gave thanks before his God, as he did before.

¹¹ Then these men assembled together, and found Daniel making petition and supplication before his God. ¹² Then they came near, and spoke before the king concerning the king's decree: "Haven't you signed an decree, that every man who shall make petition to any god or man within thirty days, except to you,

O king, shall be cast into the den of lions?" The king answered, "The thing is true, according to the law of the Medes and Persians, which doesn't alter."

¹³ Then answered they and said before the king, "That Daniel, who is of the children of the captivity of Judah, doesn't respect you, O king, nor the decree that you have signed, but makes his petition three times a day." ¹⁴ Then the king, when he heard these words, was very displeased, and set his heart on Daniel to deliver him; and he labored until the going down of the sun to rescue him. ¹⁵ Then these men assembled together to the king, and said to the king, "Know, O king, that it is a law of the Medes and Persians, that neither decree nor statute which the king establishes may be changed."

¹⁶ Then the king commanded, and they brought Daniel, and cast him into the den of lions. The king spoke and said to Daniel, "Your God whom you serve continually, he will deliver you." ¹⁷ A stone was brought, and laid on the mouth of the den; and the king sealed it with his own signet, and with the signet of his lords; that nothing might be changed concerning Daniel. ¹⁸ Then the king went to his palace, and passed the night fasting; neither were instruments of music brought before him: and his sleep fled from him.

Daniel Delivered and His Foes Punished

¹⁹ Then the king arose very early in the morning, and went in haste to the den of lions. ²⁰ When he came near to the den to Daniel, he cried with a lamentable voice; the king spoke and said to Daniel, "Daniel, servant of the living God, is your God, whom you serve continually, able to deliver you from the lions?" ²¹ Then Daniel said to the king, "O king, live forever. ²² My God has sent his angel, and has shut the lions' mouths, and they have not hurt me; because as before him innocence was found in me; and also before you, O king, have I done no hurt."

²³ Then was the king exceeding glad, and commanded that they should take Daniel up out of the den. So Daniel was taken up out of the den, and no kind of harm was found on him, because he had trusted in his God. ²⁴ The king commanded, and they brought those men who had accused Daniel, and they cast them into the den of lions, them, their children, and their wives; and the lions mauled them, and broke all their bones in pieces, before they came to the bottom of the den.

Darius Acknowledges Daniel's God

²⁵ Then king Darius wrote to all the peoples, nations, and languages, who dwell in all the earth: "Peace be multiplied to you. ²⁶ I make a decree, that in all the dominion of my kingdom men tremble and fear before the God of Daniel; for he is the living God, and steadfast forever, His kingdom that which shall not be destroyed; and his dominion shall be even to the end. ²⁷ He delivers and rescues, and he works signs and wonders in heaven and in earth, who has delivered Daniel from the power of the lions." ²⁸ So this Daniel prospered in the reign of Darius, and in the reign of Cyrus the Persian.

1. Why do you think that King Darius agreed to the ingeniously clever request of the other leaders?
2. Why was Daniel willing to risk his life by praying openly before his enemies as he had done before?
3. How did God deliver Daniel from certain death?
4. Why did Darius publicly proclaim God's majesty to the world after Daniel's deliverance?

55. A LEPER IS HEALED
2 Kings 5:1-27

The following four selections took place before Israel went into exile. They are included to tell of God's mercy and miraculous care for His chosen Hebrew people, even for foreigners who were receptive to believe in Him. A man who was not an Israelite was cleansed of his leprosy because he humbled himself and obeyed the prophet Elisha. After his healing, he became a worshiper of the God of Israel.

Naaman Healed of Leprosy

5 Now Naaman, captain of the army of the king of Syria, was a great man with his master, and honorable, because by him Yahweh had given victory to Syria: he was also a mighty man of valor, but he was a leper. ² The Syrians had gone out in bands, and had brought away captive out of the land of Israel a little maiden; and she waited on Naaman's wife. ³ She said to her mistress, "I wish that my lord were with the prophet who is in Samaria! Then he would heal him of his leprosy."

⁴Someone went in, and told his lord, saying, "The maiden who is from the land of Israel said this."

⁵The king of Syria said, "Go now, and I will send a letter to the king of Israel." He departed, and took with him ten talents [756 lbs. or 343 kilograms] of silver, and six thousand pieces of gold, and ten changes of clothing. ⁶ He brought the letter to the king of Israel, saying, "Now when this letter has come to you, behold, I have sent Naaman my servant to you, that you may heal him of his leprosy."

⁷When the king of Israel had read the letter, he tore his clothes, and said, "Am I God, to kill and to make alive, that this man sends to me to heal a man of his leprosy? But please consider and see how he seeks a quarrel against me."

⁸ It was so, when [the prophet] Elisha the man of God heard that the king of Israel had torn his clothes that he sent to the king saying, "Why have you torn your clothes? Let him come now to me, and he shall know that there is a prophet in Israel."

⁹So Naaman came with his horses and with his chariots, and stood at the door of the house of Elisha. ¹⁰ Elisha sent a messenger to him, saying, "Go and wash in the Jordan seven times, and your flesh shall come again to you, and you shall be clean."

¹¹ But Naaman was angry, and went away, and said, "Behold, I thought,

'He will surely come out to me, and stand, and call on the name of Yahweh his God, and wave his hand over the place, and heal the leper.' [12] Aren't Abanah and Pharpar, the rivers of Damascus, better than all the waters of Israel? Couldn't I wash in them, and be clean?" So he turned and went away in a rage. [13] His servants came near, and spoke to him, and said, "My father, if the prophet had asked you do some great thing, wouldn't you have done it? How much rather then, when he says to you, 'Wash, and be clean?'"

[14] Then went he down, and dipped himself seven times in the Jordan, according to the saying of the man of God; and his flesh was restored like the flesh of a little child, and he was clean. [15] He returned to the man of God, he and all his company, and came, and stood before him; and he said, "See now, I know that there is no God in all the earth, but in Israel. Now therefore, please take a gift from your servant."

[16] But he said, "As Yahweh lives, before whom I stand, I will receive none." He urged him to take it; but he refused. [17] Naaman said, "If not, then, please let two mules' burden of earth be given to your servant; for your servant will from now on offer neither burnt offering nor sacrifice to other gods, but to Yahweh. [18] In this thing may Yahweh pardon your servant: when my master goes into the house of Rimmon to worship there, and he leans on my hand, and I bow myself in the house of Rimmon. When I bow myself in the house of Rimmon, may Yahweh pardon your servant in this thing."

[19] He said to him, "Go in peace."

Gehazi's Greed
So he departed from him a little way. [20] But Gehazi the servant of Elisha the man of God, said, "Behold, my master has spared this Naaman the Syrian, in not receiving at his hands that which he brought. As Yahweh lives, I will run after him, and take something from him."

[21] So Gehazi followed after Naaman. When Naaman saw one running after him, he came down from the chariot to meet him, and said, "Is all well?"

[22] He said, "All is well. My master has sent me, saying, 'Behold, even now two young men of the sons of the prophets have come to me from the hill country of Ephraim. Please give them a talent [75 lbs. or 34 kilograms] of silver and two changes of clothing.'"

[23] Naaman said, "Be pleased to take two talents." He urged him, and bound two talents of silver in two bags, with two changes of clothing, and laid them on two of his servants; and they carried them before him. [24] When he came to the hill, he took them from their hand, and stored them in the house. Then he let the men go, and they departed. [25] But he went in, and stood before his master. Elisha said to him, "Where did you come from, Gehazi?"
He said, "Your servant went nowhere."

[26] He said to him, "Didn't my heart go with you, when the man turned from his chariot to meet you? Is it a time to receive money, and to receive garments, and olive groves and vineyards, and sheep and cattle, and male servants and female servants? [27] Therefore the leprosy of Naaman will cling to you and to your offspring forever." He went out from his presence a leper, as white as snow.

1. Who was Naaman? Where did he live, and what did he do?
2. Explain how God used the servant girl from Israel and later Naaman's own servant to help bring about Naaman's healing.
3. What was Naaman's response to his healing, and what promise did he make to Elisha?
4. What was Gehazi's problem, and what happened to him as a result of his greed?
5. Do you see how God can use anyone, even a lowly servant girl, to tell others about their faith in God?

56. A SPY IN THE ENEMY'S CAMP
2 Kings 6:8-23

God often intervenes mercifully in the affairs of men. Here is a story showing God's mercy both to Israel, keeping the people from harm, and to Israel's enemy, who deserved harm but was spared by God for His glory.

Elisha Traps the Syrians

6 [8] Now the king of Syria was at war against Israel; and he took counsel with his servants, saying, "My camp will be in such and such a place."

[9] The man of God sent to the king of Israel, saying, "Beware that you not pass this place; for the Syrians are coming down there." [10] The king of Israel sent to the place which the man of God told him and warned him of; and he saved himself there, not once or twice. [11] The king of Syria's heart was very troubled about this. He called his servants, and said to them, "Won't you show me which of us is for the king of Israel?"

[12] One of his servants said, "No, my lord, O king; but Elisha, the prophet who is in Israel, tells the king of Israel the words that you speak in your bedroom." [13] He said, "Go and see where he is, that I may send and get him."

He was told, "Behold, he is in Dothan."

[14] Therefore he sent horses, chariots, and a great army there. They came by night, and surrounded the city. [15] When the servant of the man of God had risen early, and gone out, behold, an army with horses and chariots was around the city. His servant said to him, "Alas, my master! What shall we do?"

[16] He answered, "Don't be afraid; for those who are with us are more than those who are with them." [17] Elisha prayed, and said, "Yahweh, please open his eyes, that he may see." Yahweh opened the young man's eyes; and he saw: and behold, the mountain was full of horses and chariots of fire around Elisha. [18] When they [the Syrian army] came down to [capture] him, Elisha prayed to Yahweh, and said, "Please strike this people with blindness."

He struck them with blindness according to Elijah's word. [19] Elisha said to

Great Bible Truths

them, "This is not the way, neither is this the city. Follow me, and I will bring you to the man whom you seek." He led them to Samaria. [20] When they had come into Samaria, Elisha said, "Yahweh, open these men's eyes, that they may see."

Yahweh opened their eyes, and they saw; and behold, they were in the middle of Samaria. [21] The king of Israel said to Elisha, when he saw them, "My father, shall I strike them? Shall I strike them?"

[22] He answered, "You shall not strike them. Would you strike those whom you have taken captive with your sword and with your bow? Set bread and water before them, that they may eat and drink, and go to their master."

[23] He prepared great feast for them. When they had eaten and drunk, he sent them away, and they went to their master. So the bands of Syria stopped raiding the land of Israel.

> 1. Does this story demonstrate the majesty of God, who can be anywhere at any time?
>
> 2. Discuss how God can frustrate men's plans, especially plans with evil intent.
>
> 3. How was Elisha's servant able to see the divine host surrounding them when he had been blind to it before that?
>
> 4. God says throughout the Bible that we are to love our enemies. Discuss how this story ends when Israel "loves its enemy," the Syrians, by sparing their lives and hosting them at a banquet.

57. MIRACLES IN ORDINARY LIFE
2 Kings 2:19-22 and 4:1-44 and 6:1-7 and 8:1-6

God truly is merciful. The following selections tell of miracles that happened to ordinary people in Israel before the two kingdoms were captured by their enemies. There were simple everyday problems that needed some divine assistance. These passages show us that God does care for the ordinary people who love and obey Him.

Elisha Makes Water Pure

2 [19]The men of the city said to Elisha, "Behold, please, the situation of this city is pleasant, as my lord sees; but the water is bad, and the land is barren."

[20] He said, "Bring me a new jar, and put salt in it." Then they brought it to him. [21] He went out to the spring of the waters, and threw salt into it, and said, "Yahweh says, 'I have healed these waters. There shall not be from there any more death or barren wasteland.'"[22] So the waters were healed to this day, according to Elijah's word which he spoke.

Elisha Helps a Poor Widow

4 Now a certain woman of the wives of the sons of the prophets cried out to Elisha, saying, "Your servant my husband is dead. You know that your servant feared Yahweh. Now the creditor has come to take for himself my two children to be slaves."

²Elisha said to her, "What should I do for you? Tell me: what do you have in the house?"

She said, "Your servant has nothing in the house, except a pot of oil."

³ Then he said, "Go, borrow empty containers from of all your neighbors. Don't borrow just a few containers. ⁴ Go in and shut the door on you and on your sons, and pour oil into all those containers; and set aside those which are full."

⁵ So she went from him, and shut the door on herself and on her sons. They brought the containers to her, and she poured oil. ⁶ When the containers were full, she said to her son, "Bring me another container."

He said to her, "There isn't another container." Then the oil stopped flowing.

⁷ Then she came and told the man of God. He said, "Go, sell the oil, and pay your debt; and you and your sons live on the rest."

Elisha and the Rich Woman

⁸ One day Elisha went to Shunem, where there was a prominent woman; and she persuaded him to eat bread. So it was, that as often as he passed by, he turned in there to eat bread. ⁹ She said to her husband, "See now, I perceive that this is a holy man of God who passes by us continually. ¹⁰ Please let us make a little room on the roof. Let us set for him there a bed, a table, a chair, and a lamp stand. When he comes to us, he can stay there."

¹¹ One day he came there, and he went to the room and lay there. ¹² He said to Gehazi his servant, "Call this Shunammite." When he had called her, she stood before him. ¹³ He said to him, "Say now to her, 'Behold, you have cared for us with all this care. What is to be done for you? Would you like to be spoken for to the king, or to the captain of the army?'"

She answered, "I [have all that I need here] dwelling among my own people."

¹⁴ He said, "What then is to be done for her?"

Gehazi answered, "Most certainly she has no son, and her husband is old."

¹⁵ He said, "Call her." When he had called her, she stood in the door. ¹⁶ He said, "At this season, when the time comes around, you will embrace a son."

She said, "No, my lord, you man of God, do not lie to your servant."

¹⁷ The woman conceived, and bore a son at that season, when the time came around, as Elisha had said to her. ¹⁸ When the child was grown, one day he went out to his father to the reapers. ¹⁹ He said to his father, "My head! My head!" He said to his servant, "Carry him to his mother."

²⁰ When he had taken him, and brought him to his mother, he sat on her knees until noon, and then died. ²¹ She went up and laid him on the man of God's bed, and shut the door on him, and went out. ²² She called to her husband, and said, "Please send me one of the servants, and one of the donkeys, that I may run to the man of God, and come again."

²³ He said, "Why would you want go to him today? It is not a new moon or a Sabbath."

She said, "It's alright."

²⁴Then she saddled a donkey, and said to her servant, "Drive, and go forward! Don't slow down for me, unless I ask you to."

²⁵ So she went, and came to the man of God to Mount Carmel. When the man of God saw her afar off, he said to Gehazi his servant, "Behold, there is the Shunammite. ²⁶ Please run now to meet her, and ask her, 'Is it well with you? Is it well with your husband? Is it well with your child?'" She answered, "It is well."

²⁷ When she came to the man of God to the hill, she caught hold of his feet. Gehazi came near to thrust her away; but the man of God said, "Leave her alone; for her soul is troubled within her; and Yahweh has hidden it from me, and has not told me."

²⁸ Then she said, "Did I ask you for a son, my lord? Didn't I say, 'Do not deceive me'?"

²⁹ Then he said to Gehazi, "Tuck your cloak into your belt, take my staff in your hand, and go your way. If you meet any man, don't greet him; and if anyone greets you, don't answer him again. Then lay my staff on the child's face."

³⁰The child's mother said, "As Yahweh lives, and as your soul lives, I will not leave you."

So he arose, and followed her.

³¹ Gehazi went ahead of them, and laid the staff on the child's face; but there was no voice and or hearing. Therefore he returned to meet him, and told him, "The child has not awakened."

³² When Elisha had come into the house, behold, the child was dead, and lying on his bed.³³ He went in therefore, and shut the door on them both, and prayed to Yahweh. ³⁴ He went up, and lay on the child, and put his mouth on his mouth, and his eyes on his eyes, and his hands on his hands. He stretched himself on him; and the child's flesh grew warm. ³⁵ Then he returned, and walked in the house once back and forth; and went up, and stretched himself out on him. Then the child sneezed seven times, and the child opened his eyes. ³⁶ He called Gehazi, and said, "Call this Shunammite!" So he called her. When she had come in to him, he said, "Take up your son."

³⁷ Then she went in, fell at his feet, and bowed herself to the ground; then she picked up her son, and went out.

Death in the Pot

³⁸ Elisha came again to Gilgal. There was a famine in the land; and the sons of the prophets were sitting before him; and he said to his servant, "Get the large pot, and boil stew for the sons of the prophets."

³⁹ One went out into the field to gather herbs, and found a wild vine, and gathered a lap full of wild gourds from it, and came and cut them up into the

pot of stew; for they didn't recognize them. ⁴⁰ So they poured out for the men to eat. As they were eating some of the stew, they cried out, and said, "Man of God, there is death in the pot!" And they could not eat it.

⁴¹ But he said, "Then bring meal." He threw it into the pot; and he said, "Serve it to the people, that they may eat." And there was nothing harmful in the pot.

Feeding of a Hundred

⁴² A man from Baal Shalishah came, and brought the man of God bread some of the first fruits: twenty loaves of barley, and fresh ears of grain in his sack. He said, "Give to the people, that they may eat."

⁴³ His servant said, "What, should I set this before a hundred men?" But he said, "Give the people that they may eat; for Yahweh says, 'They will eat, and will have some left over.'"

⁴⁴ So he set it before them, and they ate, and had some left over, according to Yahweh's word.

An Axhead Floats

6 The sons of the prophets said to Elisha, "See now, the place where we live and meet with you is too small for us. ² Please let us go to the Jordan, and each man take a beam from there, and let us make us a place there, where we may live." He answered, "Go!"

³ One said, "Please be pleased to go with your servants."
He answered, "I will go." ⁴ So he went with them. When they came to the Jordan, they cut down wood. ⁵ But as one was cutting down a tree, the ax head fell into the water. Then he cried, and said, "Alas, my master! For it was borrowed."

⁶ The man of God asked, "Where did it fall?" He showed him the place. He cut down a stick, threw it in there, and made the iron float. ⁷ He said, "Take it." So he put out his hand and took it.

The Shunammite's Land Restored

8 Now Elisha had spoken to the woman whose son he had restored to life, saying, "Arise, and go, you and your household, and stay for a while wherever you can; for Yahweh has called for a famine. It will also come on the land for seven years."

² The woman arose, and did according to the man of God's word. She went with her household, and lived in the land of the Philistines for seven years. ³ At the end of seven years, the woman returned from the land of the Philistines. Then she went out to beg the king for her house and for her land. ⁴ Now the king was talking with Gehazi the servant of the man of God, saying, "Please tell me all the great things that Elisha has done." ⁵ As he was telling the king how he had restored to life him who was dead, behold, the woman, whose son he had restored to life, begged the king for her house and for her land. Gehazi said, "My lord, O king, this is the woman, and this is her son, whom Elisha restored to life."

⁶ When the king asked the woman, she told him. So the king appointed to her

Great Bible Truths

a certain officer, saying, "Restore all that was hers, and all the fruits of the field since the day that she left the land, even until now."

1. Which miracle story did you enjoy the most?
2. Can miracles happen to ordinary people today?
3. Have you ever had a miraculous event happen to you? What was your reaction to it?

58. A NATION REPENTS
Jonah 1 and 2:1-2, 9-10 and 3:1-10

God chose a reluctant man named Jonah to take his message to the wicked people of the land of Nineveh. When those people decided to turn from their evil ways, God had mercy on them and saved them from destruction.

Jonah Flees from the Lord

1 Now Yahweh's word came to Jonah the son of Amittai, saying, ² "Arise, go to Nineveh, that great city, and preach against it, for their wickedness has come up before me." ³ But Jonah rose up to flee to Tarshish from the presence of Yahweh. He went down to Joppa, and found a ship going to Tarshish; so he paid its fare, and went down into it, to go with them to Tarshish from the presence of Yahweh. ⁴ But Yahweh sent out a great wind on the sea, and there was a mighty storm on the sea, so that the ship was likely to break up. ⁵ Then the mariners were afraid, and every man cried to his god. They threw the cargo that was in the ship into the sea to lighten the ship. But Jonah had gone down into the innermost parts of the ship, and he was laying down, and was fast asleep. ⁶ So the ship master came to him, and said to him, "What do you mean, sleeper? Arise, call on your God! Maybe your God will notice us, so that we won't perish."

⁷ They all said to each other, "Come, let us cast lots, that we may know who is responsible for this evil that is on us." So they cast lots, and the lot fell on Jonah. ⁸ Then they asked him, "Tell us, please, for whose cause this evil is on us. What is your occupation? Where do you come from? What is your country? Of what people are you?"

⁹ He said to them, "I am a Hebrew, and I fear Yahweh, the God of heaven, who has made the sea and the dry land."

¹⁰ Then were the men exceedingly afraid, and said to him, "What is this that you have done?" For the men knew that he was fleeing from the presence of Yahweh, because he had told them. ¹¹ Then they said to him, "What shall we do to you, that the sea may be calm to us?" For the sea grew more and more stormy. ¹² He said to them, "Take me up, and throw me into the sea. Then the sea will be calm for you; for I know that because of me this great storm is on you."

¹³ Nevertheless the men rowed hard to get them back to the land; but they could not, for the sea grew more and more stormy against them. ¹⁴ Therefore they cried to Yahweh, and said, "We beg you, Yahweh, we beg you, don't let us

die for this man's life, and don't lay on us innocent blood; for you, Yahweh, have done as it pleased you." ¹⁵ So they took up Jonah, and threw him into the sea; and the sea ceased its raging. ¹⁶ Then the men feared Yahweh exceedingly; and they offered a sacrifice to Yahweh, and made vows.

¹⁷ Yahweh prepared a great fish to swallow up Jonah, and Jonah was in the belly of the fish three days and three nights.

Jonah's Prayer

2 Then Jonah prayed to Yahweh, his God, out of the fish's belly. ² He said,
"I called because of my affliction to Yahweh.
He answered me.
Out of the belly of Sheol I cried.
You heard my voice.
⁹But I will sacrifice to you with the voice of thanksgiving.
I will pay that which I have vowed.
Salvation belongs to Yahweh."

¹⁰ Yahweh spoke to the fish, and it vomited out Jonah on the dry land.

Nineveh Repents

3 Yahweh's word came to Jonah the second time, saying, ² "Arise, go to Nineveh, that great city, and preach to it the message that I give you."

³ So Jonah arose, and went to Nineveh, according to Yahweh's word. Now Nineveh was an exceedingly great city, three days' journey across. ⁴ Jonah began to enter into the city a day's journey, and he cried out, and said, "In forty days, Nineveh will be overthrown!"

⁵ The people of Nineveh believed God; and they proclaimed a fast, and put on sackcloth, from their greatest even to their least. ⁶ The news reached the king of Nineveh, and he arose from his throne, and took off his royal robe, covered himself with sackcloth, and sat in ashes. ⁷ He made a proclamation and published through Nineveh by the decree of the king and his nobles, saying, "Let neither man nor animal, herd nor flock, taste anything; let them not feed, nor drink water; ⁸ but let them be covered with sackcloth, both man and animal, and let them cry mightily to God. Yes, let them turn everyone from his evil way, and from the violence that is in his hands. ⁹ Who knows whether God will not turn and relent, and turn away from his fierce anger, so that we might not perish?"

¹⁰ God saw their works, that they turned from their evil way. God relented of the disaster which he said he would do to them, and he didn't do it.

1. *Why didn't Jonah's plan of escape work for him?*

2. *How do we know that God heard Jonah's prayer?*

3. *How did the king and his people respond to Jonah's message?*

4. *Explain how God's promise to Abraham, "that in you all nations will be blessed," applies to Nineveh.*

59. THE HAPPY HOMECOMING
Ezra 1:1-11 and 3:1-3, 10-13 and Nehemiah 1:1-4 and 2:4-18 and 6:15-16

Seventy years after the people of Judah were taken into captivity; they were permitted by King Cyrus of Persia, in 516 B.C., to return to their homeland. God allowed a small remnant to be brought back to Jerusalem to reestablish the nation of Israel. It was through this group of people that God fulfilled His promise to bring the Savior into the world. Once again, this showed God's mercy to Israel, giving the Israelites another opportunity to be the people He had called them to be.

Cyrus Helps the Exiles to Return

1 It was in the first year of Cyrus king of Persia, that Yahweh's word by the mouth of Jeremiah might be accomplished, Yahweh stirred up the spirit of Cyrus king of Persia, so that he made a proclamation throughout all his kingdom, and put it also in writing, saying, ² "Thus says Cyrus king of Persia, 'Yahweh, the God of heaven, has given me all the kingdoms of the earth; and he has commanded me to build him a house in Jerusalem, which is in Judah. ³ Whoever there is among you of all his people, may his God be with him, and let him go up to Jerusalem, which is in Judah, and build the house of Yahweh, the God of Israel (he is God), which is in Jerusalem. ⁴ Whoever is left, in any place where he lives, let the men of his place help him with silver, with gold, with goods, and with animals, besides the freewill offering for God's house which is in Jerusalem.'" ⁵ Then the heads of fathers' households of Judah and Benjamin, and the priests, and the Levites, even all whose spirit God had stirred to go up rose up to build Yahweh's house which is in Jerusalem. ⁶ All those who were around them strengthened their hands with vessels of silver, with gold, with goods, and with animals, and with precious things, besides all that was willingly offered. ⁷ Also Cyrus the king brought out the vessels of Yahweh's house, which Nebuchadnezzar had brought out of Jerusalem, and had put in the house of his gods; ⁸ even those, Cyrus king of Persia brought out by the hand of Mithredath the treasurer, and numbered them to Sheshbazzar, the prince of Judah. ⁹ This is the number of them: thirty platters of gold, one thousand platters of silver, twenty-nine knives, ¹⁰ thirty bowls of gold, silver bowls of a second sort four hundred and ten, and other vessels one thousand. ¹¹ All the vessels of gold and of silver were five thousand and four hundred. Sheshbazzar brought all these up, when the captives were brought up from Babylon to Jerusalem.

Rebuilding the Altar

3 ¹When the seventh month had come, and the children of Israel were in the cities, the people gathered themselves together as one man to Jerusalem. ² Then Jeshua the son of Jozadak stood up with his brothers the priests, and Zerubbabel the son of Shealtiel and his brothers, and built the altar of the God of Israel, to offer burnt offerings on it, as it is written in the law of Moses the man of God. ³ In spite of their fear because of the peoples of the surrounding lands, they set the altar on its base; and they offered burnt offerings on it to Yahweh, even burnt offerings morning and evening.

Rebuilding the Temple

¹⁰ When the builders laid the foundation of Yahweh's temple, they set the priests in their clothing with trumpets, with the Levites the sons of Asaph with cymbals, to praise Yahweh, according to the directions of David king of Israel. ¹¹ They sang to one another in praising and giving thanks to Yahweh, "For he is good, for his loving kindness endures forever toward Israel." All the people shouted with a great shout, when they praised Yahweh, because the foundation of Yahweh's house had been laid. ¹¹But many of the priests and Levites and heads of fathers' households, the old men who had seen the first house, when the foundation of this house was laid before their eyes, wept with a loud voice. Many also shouted aloud for joy, ¹³ so that the people could not discern the noise of the shout of joy from the noise of the weeping of the people; for the people shouted with a loud shout, and the noise was heard far away.

God Calls Nehemiah to Return to Jerusalem

1 The words of Nehemiah the son of Hacaliah. Now in the month Chislev, in the twentieth year, as I was in Shushan the palace, ² Hanani, one of my brothers, came, he and certain men out of Judah; and I asked them concerning the Jews who had escaped, who were left of the captivity, and concerning Jerusalem. ³ They said to me, "The remnant who are left of the captivity there in the province are in great affliction and reproach. The wall of Jerusalem also is broken down, and its gates are burned with fire." ⁴ When I heard these words, I sat down and wept, and mourned certain days; and I fasted and prayed before the God of heaven.

Nehemiah Rebuilds Jerusalem

2 ⁴Then the king said to me, "For what do you make request?"
So I prayed to the God of heaven. ⁵ I said to the king, "If it pleases the king, and if your servant has found favor in your sight, that you would send me to Judah, to the city of my fathers' tombs, that I may build it."
⁶ The king said to me (the queen was also sitting by him), "For how long shall your journey be? And when will you return?"
So it pleased the king to send me; and I set him a time. ⁷ Moreover I said to the king, "If it pleases the king, let letters be given me to the governors beyond the River, that they may let me pass through until I come to Judah; ⁸ and a letter to Asaph the keeper of the king's forest, that he may give me timber to make beams for the gates of the citadel by the temple, for the wall of the city, and for the house that I shall enter into."

The king granted my requests, because of the good hand of my God on me. ⁹ Then I came to the governors beyond the River, and gave them the king's letters. Now the king had sent with me captains of the army and horsemen. ¹⁰ When

Sanballat the Horonite, and Tobiah the servant, the Ammonite, heard of it, it grieved them exceedingly, because a man had come to seek the welfare of the children of Israel. [11] So I came to Jerusalem, and was there three days. [12] I arose in the night, I and some few men with me; neither told I any man what my God put into my heart to do for Jerusalem; neither was there any animal with me, except the animal that I rode on. [13] I went out by night by the valley gate, even toward the jackal's well, and to the dung gate, and viewed the walls of Jerusalem, which were broken down, and its gates were consumed with fire. [14] Then I went on to the spring gate and to the king's pool: but there was no place for the animal that was under me to pass. [15] Then went I up in the night by the brook, and viewed the wall; and I turned back, and entered by the valley gate, and so returned. [16] The rulers didn't know where I went, or what I did; neither had I as yet told it to the Jews, nor to the priests, nor to the nobles, nor to the rulers, nor to the rest who did the work. [17] Then I said to them, "You see the evil case that we are in, how Jerusalem lies waste, and its gates are burned with fire. Come, let us build up the wall of Jerusalem, that we won't be disgraced." [18] I told them of the hand of my God which was good on me, as also of the king's words that he had spoken to me.

They said, "Let's rise up and build." So they strengthened their hands for the good work.

6 [15]So the wall was finished in the twenty-fifth day of Elul, in fifty-two days.

[16] When all our enemies heard of it, all the nations that were around us were afraid, and were much cast down in their own eyes; for they perceived that this work was worked of our God.

> 1. Why did Cyrus decide to let the people of Judah return to Jerusalem?
>
> 2. Why did the people both weep and rejoice when the temple foundation was laid?
>
> 3. Why was Nehemiah concerned about the city walls?
>
> 4. Why do you suppose the three men mentioned in Nehemiah 2:10 were against Nehemiah helping the Jews?

E. THE PLAN OF GOD

Throughout the Old Testament we have seen God's promise to Abraham being brought to the point of final fulfillment. In these next six selections, we will see how God set forth His plan to send the Savior long before the actual promise was fulfilled. God spoke through His prophets, giving the signs and events to come that would reveal the Savior to those who were looking for His coming.

60. SIGNS OF HIS COMING
Isaiah 7:14; 9:2-7; 11:1-5; 61: 1-3; Malachi 3:1-5

The prophet Isaiah wrote that the Savior of the world would be born to a virgin and be a member of the royal family of David. God's great promise that all the families of the earth would be blessed through Abraham's descendants would be fulfilled. The name Immanuel means that God has come down to be with man. The Savior's coming would be as if a great light had appeared in the midst of darkness, bringing forgiveness and healing to the lives of men.

The Sign of Immanuel
7 ¹⁴Therefore the Lord himself will give you a sign.
> Behold, the virgin will conceive, and bear a son,
> and shall call his name Immanuel.

A New Day Coming
9 ²The people who walked in darkness have seen a great light. Those who lived in the land of the shadow of death, on them the light has shined.

³ You have multiplied the nation.
You have increased their joy.
> They rejoice before you according to the joy in harvest,
> as men rejoice when they divide the plunder.

⁴ For the yoke of his burden, and the staff of his shoulder,
the rod of his oppressor, you have broken as in the day of Midian.

⁵ For all the armor of the armed man in the noisy battle, and the garments rolled in blood, will be for burning, fuel for the fire.

⁶ For to us a child is born. To us a son is given;
and the government will be on his shoulders.
> His name will be called Wonderful, Counselor, Mighty God,
> Everlasting Father, Prince of Peace.

⁷ Of the increase of his government and of peace
there shall be no end, on David's throne, and on his kingdom,
> to establish it, and to uphold it with justice
and with righteousness from that time on, even forever.
> The zeal of Yahweh [God Almighty] of Armies will perform this.

The Branch of Jesse
11 A shoot will come out of the stock of Jesse,
> and a branch out of his roots will bear fruit.

² Yahweh's Spirit will rest on him:
> the spirit of wisdom and understanding,
the spirit of counsel and might,
> the spirit of knowledge and of the fear of Yahweh.

³ His delight will be in the fear of Yahweh.

He will not judge by the sight of his eyes
neither decide by the hearing of his ears;
⁴ but with righteousness he will judge the poor,
and decide with equity for the humble of the earth.
He will strike the earth with the rod of his mouth;
and with the breath of his lips he will kill the wicked.
⁵ Righteousness will be the belt of his waist,
and faithfulness the belt of his waist.

The Year of the Lord's Favor

61 The Lord Yahweh's Spirit is on me;
   because Yahweh has anointed me
   to preach good news to the humble.
He has sent me to bind up the broken hearted,
   to proclaim liberty to the captives,
   and release to those who are bound;
² to proclaim the year of Yahweh's favor,
   and the day of vengeance of our God;
to comfort all who mourn;
³   to provide for those who mourn in Zion,
to give to them a garland for ashes,
   the oil of joy for mourning,
   the garment of praise
   for the spirit of heaviness;
that they may be called trees of righteousness,
   the planting of Yahweh,
   that he may be glorified.

The Messiah's Coming Predicted

3 "Behold, I send my messenger, and he will prepare the way before me; and the Lord, whom you seek, will suddenly come to his temple; and the messenger of the covenant, whom you desire, behold, he comes!" says Yahweh of Armies [God Almighty]. ² "But who can endure the day of his coming? And who will stand when he appears? For he is like a refiner's fire, and like launderer's soap; ³ and he will sit as a refiner and purifier of silver, and he will purify the sons of Levi, and refine them as gold and silver; and they shall offer to Yahweh [God Almighty] offerings in righteousness. ⁴ Then the offering of Judah and Jerusalem will be pleasant to Yahweh, as in the days of old, and as in ancient years.
⁵ I will come near to you to judgment; and I will be a swift witness against the sorcerers, and against the adulterers, and against the perjurers, and against those who oppress the hireling in his wages, the widow, and the fatherless, and who deprive the foreigner of justice, and don't fear me," says Yahweh of Armies [God Almighty].

1. What titles were given to the Savior?
2. Describe the qualities that the Savior would possess.
3. What would the Savior do for man?

61. THE SUFFERING SERVANT
Isaiah 53

In this chapter from Isaiah we learn of the great work that the Savior would accomplish when He came. Taking upon Himself the punishment of sin for all mankind, the Savior would experience the horror of spiritual death. He would become the innocent lamb sacrificed for man's sin of rebellion and disobedience.

The Innocent Lamb

53 ¹ Who has believed our message?
   To whom has the arm of Yahweh been revealed?
² For he grew up before him as a tender plant,
   and as a root out of dry ground.
He has no good looks or majesty.
   When we see him, there is no beauty that we should desire him.
³ He was despised, and rejected by men;
   a man of suffering, and acquainted with disease.
He was despised as one from whom men hide their face;
   and we didn't respect him.
⁴ Surely he has borne our sickness,
   and carried our suffering;
yet we considered him plagued,
   struck by God, and afflicted.
⁵ But he was pierced for our transgressions.
   He was crushed for our iniquities.
The punishment that brought our peace was on him;
   and by his wounds we are healed.
⁶ All we like sheep have gone astray.
   Everyone has turned to his own way;
and Yahweh has laid on him
   the iniquity of us all.
⁷ He was oppressed, yet when he was afflicted
   he didn't open his mouth.
As a lamb that is led to the slaughter,
   and as a sheep that before its shearers is silent,
   so he didn't open his mouth.
⁸ He was taken away by oppression and judgment;
   and as for his generation, who considered
that he was cut off out of the land of the living
   and stricken for the disobedience of my people?
⁹ They made his grave with the wicked,
   and with a rich man in his death;

although he had done no violence,
>   nor was any deceit in his mouth.
[10] Yet it pleased Yahweh to bruise him. He has caused him to suffer.
>   When you make his soul an offering for sin,
> he will see his offspring. He will prolong his days,
>   and Yahweh's pleasure will prosper in his hand.
[11] After the suffering of his soul,
>   he will see the light and be satisfied.
> My righteous servant will justify many by the knowledge of himself;
>   and he will bear their iniquities.
[12] Therefore will I give him a portion with the great,
>   and he will divide the plunder with the strong;
> because he poured out his soul to death
>   and was numbered with the transgressors;
> yet he bore the sin of many,
>   and made intercession for the transgressors.

> 1. Describe the emotional suffering that the Savior endured for us.
> 2. What would be the results of the Savior's suffering for all mankind?

62. THE SUFFERING SAVIOR
Psalm 22

God also gave King David a vision of the Savior's suffering on the cross. This passage, like the previous one from Isaiah, is very accurate in predicting the details of the physical sufferings of Jesus Christ. It is amazing to realize that these accounts were written hundreds of years before the birth of Jesus. Only God could have revealed to men the cry of the Savior's heart.

Prayer of a Suffering Man

22 [1] My God, my God, why have you forsaken me?
>   Why are you so far from helping me,
> and from the words of my groaning?
[2] My God, I cry in the daytime, but you don't answer;
>   in the night season, and am not silent.
[3] But you are holy,
>   you who inhabit the praises of Israel.
[4] Our fathers trusted in you.
>   They trusted, and you delivered them.
[5] They cried to you, and were delivered.
>   They trusted in you, and were not disappointed.
[6] But I am a worm, and no man;
>   a reproach of men, and despised by the people.
[7] All those who see me mock me.
>   They insult me with their lips. They shake their heads, saying,
[8] "He trusts in Yahweh;
>   let him deliver him.

Let him rescue him,
   since he delights in him."
⁹ But you brought me out of the womb.
   You made me trust at my mother's breasts.
¹⁰ I was thrown on you from my mother's womb.
   You are my God since my mother bore me.
¹¹ Don't be far from me,
   for trouble is near.
   For there is no one to help.
¹² Many bulls have surrounded me.
   Strong bulls of Bashan have encircled me.
¹³ They open their mouths wide against me,
   lions tearing prey and roaring.
¹⁴ I am poured out like water.
   All my bones are out of joint.
My heart is like wax;
   it is melted within me.
¹⁵ My strength is dried up like a potsherd.
   My tongue sticks to the roof of my mouth.
   You have brought me into the dust of death.
¹⁶ For dogs have surrounded me.
   A company of evildoers have enclosed me.
   They have pierced my hands and feet.
¹⁷ I can count all of my bones.
   They look and stare at me.
¹⁸ They divide my garments among them.
   They cast lots for my clothing.
¹⁹ But don't be far off, Yahweh.
   You are my help: hurry to help me.
²⁰ Deliver my soul from the sword,
   my precious life from the power of the dog.
²¹ Save me from the lion's mouth!
   Yes, from the horns of the wild oxen, you have answered me.
²² I will declare your name to my brothers.
   Among the assembly, I will praise you.
²³ You who fear Yahweh, praise him!
   All you descendants of Jacob, glorify him!
   Stand in awe of him, all you descendants of Israel!
²⁴ For he has not despised nor abhorred the affliction of the afflicted,
Neither has he hidden his face from him;
   but when he cried to him, he heard.
²⁵ Of you comes my praise in the great assembly.
   I will pay my vows before those who fear him.
²⁶ The humble shall eat and be satisfied.
   They shall praise Yahweh who seek after him.

Let your hearts live forever.
²⁷ All the ends of the earth
    shall remember and turn to Yahweh.
All the relatives of the nations
    shall worship before you.
²⁸ For the kingdom is Yahweh's.
    He is the ruler over the nations.
²⁹ All the rich ones of the earth shall eat and worship.
    All those who go down to the dust shall bow before him,
    even he who can't keep his soul alive.
³⁰ Posterity shall serve him.
    Future generations shall be told about the Lord.
³¹ They shall come and shall declare his righteousness
to a people that shall be born, for he has done it.

> 1. Describe the physical suffering of the Savior.
> 2. What would be the worldwide results and rewards of the Savior's suffering?

63. GOD'S INVITATION TO MAN
Isaiah 55

Because of the suffering and death of the Savior, the price was paid for the sin of all mankind. The way of salvation was made possible, and forgiveness of sin became a free gift to man. Anyone who calls upon God and truly turns from his sin will find that God abundantly pardons him.

God's Offer of Mercy
55 "Come, everyone who thirsts, to the waters!
    Come, he who has no money, buy, and eat!
Yes, come, buy wine and milk
    without money and without price.
² Why do you spend money for that which is not bread,
    and your labor for that which doesn't satisfy?
Listen diligently to me, and eat that which is good,
    and let your soul delight itself in richness.
³ Turn your ear, and come to me.
    Hear, and your soul will live:
and I will make an everlasting covenant with you,
    even the sure mercies of David.
⁴ Behold, I have given him for a witness to the peoples,
    a leader and commander to the peoples.
⁵ Behold, you shall call a nation that you don't know;
    and a nation that didn't know you shall run to you,
because of Yahweh your God,
    and for the Holy One of Israel;
for he has glorified you."

⁶ Seek Yahweh while he may be found.
   Call on him while he is near.
⁷ Let the wicked forsake his way,
   the unrighteous man his thoughts.
Let him return to Yahweh, and he will have mercy on him;
   and to our God, for he will freely pardon.
⁸ "For my thoughts are not your thoughts, and your ways are not my ways,"
   says Yahweh.
⁹ "For as the heavens are higher than the earth,
   so are my ways higher than your ways,
   and my thoughts than your thoughts.
¹⁰ For as the rain comes down
   and the snow from the sky,
and doesn't return there,
   but waters the earth,
and makes it grow and bud,
   and gives seed to the sower and bread to the eater;
¹¹ so is my word that goes out of my mouth:
   it will not return to me void,
but it will accomplish that which I please,
   and it will prosper in the thing I sent it to do.
¹² For you shall go out with joy,
   and be led out with peace.
The mountains and the hills will break out before you into singing;
and all the trees of the fields
   will clap their hands.
¹³ Instead of the thorn the cypress tree will come up;
   and instead of the brier the myrtle tree will come up:
and it will make a name for Yahweh,
   for an everlasting sign that will not be cut off."

1. *What are the conditions that man must fulfill in order to receive God's pardon?*

2. *Describe the power of the Word of God that goes out from His mouth.*

3. *Describe the blessings that come to those who have received God's pardon.*

4. *Can you see that God's invitation is to every living person, and that every person is able to accept God's invitation?*

64. A NEW HEART AND SPIRIT
Jeremiah 17:5-10 and 24:7 and 31:31-34 and 32:39-41
also Ezekiel 11:19-20 and 36:25-28

We see God's plan unfolding, another wonderful Bible truth. When Jeremiah and Ezekiel witnessed the terrible consequences caused by Israel's continual inability to follow the Lord's commands, God used these two prophets to explain what He was going to do in the future. It involved changing man's fundamental motivational source, his heart. The heart is a person's center for physical, emotional, intellectual and moral action. God describes the heart as being full of evil and wickedness. This is the reason why man fails in his efforts to keep right with God. The Law, given earlier to Moses, contained commands to obey. It was a list of do's and don'ts but it did not work. No one can keep the Law, even if he wants to, because his sinful nature, inherited from Adam, has corrupted his every good intent. However, God had a plan. Man needed a new motivational source, a new heart. As God restored Israel to the Promised Land after 70 years of exile, we see that God also planned a spiritual restoration. God would give man a new heart and a new spirit, said Jeremiah and Ezekiel. It was God's will to provide forgiveness through the promised Savior and also provide a new heart and spirit so that man would be able to obey God and keep His commandments. Please read these passages carefully, and ask God for understanding. This important Bible truth will be referred to again in the New Testament selections.

Wisdom from God

17 [5] Yahweh says: Cursed is the man who trusts in man,
  and makes flesh his arm,
  and whose heart departs from Yahweh.
[6] For he shall be like a bush in the desert,
  and shall not see when good comes,
but shall inhabit the parched places in the wilderness,
  an uninhabited salt land.
[7] Blessed is the man who trusts in Yahweh,
  and whose trust Yahweh is.
[8] For he shall be as a tree planted by the waters,
  who spreads out its roots by the river,
and shall not fear when heat comes,
  but its leaf shall be green;
and shall not be careful in the year of drought,
  neither shall cease from yielding fruit.
[9] The heart is deceitful above all things, and it is exceedingly corrupt:
  who can know it?
[10] I, Yahweh, search the mind, I try the heart,
  even to give every man according to his ways,
  according to the fruit of his doings.

A Promised New Heart

24 [7] I will give them a heart to know me, that I am Yahweh: and they shall be my people, and I will be their God; for they shall return to me with their whole heart.

Great Bible Truths

A New Covenant

31 [31] Behold, the days come, says Yahweh, that I will make a new covenant with the house of Israel, and with the house of Judah: [32] not according to the covenant that I made with their fathers in the day that I took them by the hand to bring them out of the land of Egypt; which my covenant they broke, although I was a husband to them, says Yahweh. [33] But this is the covenant that I will make with the house of Israel after those days, says Yahweh: I will put my law in their inward parts, and in their heart will I write it; and I will be their God, and they shall be my people: [34] and they shall teach no more every man his neighbor, and every man his brother, saying, Know Yahweh; for they shall all know me, from their least to their greatest, says Yahweh: for I will forgive their iniquity, and their sin will I remember no more.

32 [39] and I will give them one heart and one way, that they may fear me forever, for their good, and of their children after them: [40] and I will make an everlasting covenant with them, that I will not turn away from following them, to do them good; and I will put my fear in their hearts, that they may not depart from me. [41] Yes, I will rejoice over them to do them good, and I will plant them in this land assuredly with my whole heart and with my whole soul.

A Promised New Spirit

11 [19] I will give them one heart, and I will put a new spirit within you; and I will take the stony heart out of their flesh, and will give them a heart of flesh; [20] that they may walk in my statutes, and keep my ordinances, and do them: and they shall be my people, and I will be their God.

36 [25] I will sprinkle clean water on you, and you shall be clean: from all your filthiness, and from all your idols, will I cleanse you. [26] I will also give you a new heart, and I will put a new spirit within you; and I will take away the stony heart out of your flesh, and I will give you a heart of flesh. [27] I will put my Spirit within you, and cause you to walk in my statutes, and you shall keep my ordinances, and do them. [28] You shall dwell in the land that I gave to your fathers; and you shall be my people, and I will be your God.

> 1. Describe the condition of the man whose heart turns away from God.
>
> 2. Describe the condition of the man whose heart is changed by God.
>
> 3. Do you understand the fundamental change that a follower of God experiences in his daily life?
>
> 4. Can you picture the heart of stone being softened by the steady "rain" of God's indwelling Spirit?
>
> 5. Can you imagine how the world could be changed by believers who would obey God?

65. GOD IS GREAT
Isaiah 40

We end the Old Testament selections with a passage that tells how God is great and wonderful beyond human comparisons. Not only is He the Creator and Ruler of the universe, but He is also the Savior of the world. He has provided Himself as the sacrifice for the sin of all mankind.

Comfort for God's People

40 "Comfort, comfort my people," says your God.
   ² "Speak comfortably to Jerusalem;
      and call out to her
that her warfare is accomplished,
      that her iniquity is pardoned,
that she has received of Yahweh's hand
      double for all her sins."
³ The voice of one who calls out,
      "Prepare the way of Yahweh in the wilderness!
Make a level highway
      in the desert for our God.
⁴ Every valley shall be exalted,
      and every mountain and hill shall be made low.
The uneven shall be made level,
      And the rough places a plain.
⁵ Yahweh's glory shall be revealed,
      and all flesh shall see it together;
      for the mouth of Yahweh has spoken it."
⁶ The voice of one saying, "Cry!"
      One said, "What shall I cry?"
"All flesh is like grass,
      and all its glory is like the flower of the field.
⁷ The grass withers, the flower fades,
      because Yahweh's breath blows on it.
      Surely the people are like grass.
⁸ The grass withers, the flower fades;
      but the word of our God stands forever."
⁹ You who tell good news to Zion,
      go up on a high mountain.
You who tell good news to Jerusalem,
      lift up your voice with strength.
Lift it up. Don't be afraid.
      Say to the cities of Judah, "Behold, your God!"
¹⁰ Behold, the Lord Yahweh will come as a mighty one,

and his arm will rule for him.
Behold, his reward is with him,
> and his recompense before him.

¹¹ He will feed his flock like a shepherd.
> He will gather the lambs in his arm,
and carry them in his bosom.
> He will gently lead those who have their young.

¹² Who has measured the waters in the hollow of his hand,
> and marked off the sky with his span,
and calculated the dust of the earth in a measuring basket,
> and weighed the mountains in scales, and the hills in a balance?

¹³ Who has directed Yahweh's Spirit,
> or has taught him as his counselor?

¹⁴ Who did he take counsel with, and who instructed him,
> and taught him in the path of justice,
and taught him knowledge,
> and showed him the way of understanding?

¹⁵ Behold, the nations are like a drop in a bucket,
> and are regarded as a speck of dust on a balance.
> Behold, he lifts up the islands like a very little thing.

¹⁶ Lebanon is not sufficient to burn,
> nor its animals sufficient for a burnt offering.

¹⁷ All the nations are like nothing before him.
> They are regarded by him as less than nothing, and vanity.

¹⁸ To whom then will you liken God?
> Or what likeness will you compare to him?

¹⁹ A workman has cast an image, and the goldsmith overlays it with gold,
> and casts silver chains for it.

²⁰ He who is too impoverished for such an offering
> chooses a tree that will not rot.
He seeks a skillful workman to set up an engraved image
> for him that will not be moved.

²¹ Haven't you known?
> Haven't you heard, yet?
Haven't you been told from the beginning?
> Haven't you understood from the foundations of the earth?

²² It is he who sits above the circle of the earth,
> and its inhabitants are like grasshoppers;
who stretches out the heavens like a curtain,
> and spreads them out like a tent to dwell in;

²³ Who brings princes to nothing;
> who makes the judges of the earth meaningless.

²⁴ They are planted scarcely.
    They are sown scarcely.
    Their stock has scarcely taken root in the ground.
He merely blows on them, and they wither,
    and the whirlwind takes them away as stubble.
²⁵ "To whom then will you liken me?
    Who is my equal?" says the Holy One.
²⁶ Lift up your eyes on high,
    and see who has created these,
who brings out their army by number.
    He calls them all by name.
By the greatness of his might, and because he is strong in power,
    Not one is lacking.
²⁷ Why do you say, Jacob,
    and speak, Israel,
"My way is hidden from Yahweh,
    and the justice due me is disregarded by my God?"
²⁸ Haven't you known?
    Haven't you heard?
The everlasting God, Yahweh,
    The Creator of the ends of the earth, doesn't faint.
He isn't weary.
    His understanding is unsearchable.
²⁹ He gives power to the weak.
    He increases the strength of him who has no might.
³⁰ Even the youths faint and get weary,
    and the young men utterly fall;
³¹ But those who wait for Yahweh will renew their strength.
    They will mount up with wings like eagles.
They will run, and not be weary.
    They will walk and not faint.

> 1. *Since the Lord is like a shepherd, what will He do for you?*
>
> 2. *Find the verses that tell us that God is the Creator of the universe.*
>
> 3. *Find the verses that tell us that God is in control of nations and rulers.*
>
> 4. *What does God give to those who are weak and who trust in Him?*

END OF PART ONE:
SELECTIONS FROM THE OLD TESTAMENT

Bible Time Line
The New Testament Period

6-4 B.C.	The birth of Christ
30 A.D.	Jesus begins his public ministry.
33 A.D.	Jesus' death, resurrection and ascension into heaven.
33-44 A.D.	The Apostles begin to preach the gospel in Jerusalem, Judea, Samaria and the surrounding areas of Palestine.
44-67 A.D.	The Apostle Paul's ministry and missionary travels:
	44-50 A.D. 1st missionary journey
	51-53 A.D. 2nd missionary journey
	54-57 A.D. 3rd missionary journey
	58-60 A.D. Paul is arrested in Jerusalem.
	60-63 A.D. Paul sails to Rome and is under house arrest in Rome.
	63-67 A.D. Paul's second imprisonment and martyrdom under Nero.
70-A.D.	The fall of Jerusalem as Jesus had predicted.
67-96 A.D.	The close of the Apostolic Age with the letters of John to the churches and the book of Revelation, which he received while exiled on the island of Patmos.

The Bible and the Growth of the Christian Movement

100 A.D. The gospels and the letters of Paul were gathered into unified handwritten scrolls.

200 A.D. The unity of the entire New Testament was recognized and recorded on various scrolls of parchment.

300-400 A.D. Jerome translated all the different scrolls into Latin, into one book called The Vulgate. It replaced multiple scrolls and became the official Bible of the Church.

1380-1382 A.D. Wycliffe translated the entire Bible into English.

1455 Gutenberg produces the first printed Bible on his new invention, the printing press

1516 Erasmus made the first Greek-Latin New Testament, which became the basis for modern Bible versions. He expressed the wish that the "holy text be in every language."

1517 The Reformation rode on the crest of a growing desire that the Holy Scriptures be available in the common languages. Personal knowledge of Scripture is what ordinary people most need for their own spiritual good.

1534 Luther translated the Bible into German.

1535 The Cloverdale was first Authorized Great English Bible.

1609 The Douay Version was made for the Catholic Church.

1611 The King James Version, called Authorized Version, used by English-speaking churches for 250 years.

1804 The United Bible Society was founded in England. Today there are 150 Bible Societies working in 240 countries.

19th century The Bible was translated in whole or part into about 400 new languages.

20th century The Bible was translated into whole or part into about 800 new languages.

21st century In 2022 there are 7.36 billion people who speak 7388 languages. There is at least some Scripture in 3589 languages. A complete Bible is available in 724 languages and is partially translated into 2865 languages. Approximately 2644 languages still do not have Scriptures which includes about 203 million people.

PART TWO

Selections from the New Testament

We read in the Old Testament the story of God's promise to send a Savior and the way in which God worked to fulfill that promise. Throughout the entire Old Testament age, God sought to preserve a special people, the twelve tribes of the nation of Israel. Even though this nation sinned again and again, God pardoned and forgave them. Finally, having exhausted God's patience, ten of Israel's tribes were scattered over all the earth. The remaining two tribes were also driven out of the Promised Land. Later a small group of these people returned to Jerusalem to rebuild the temple and the city and resettle there. It was from this remnant of people that God brought the Savior into the world.

The New Testament begins with the Good News about the birth of the Savior. The life, teachings, death and resurrection of Jesus Christ are recorded by His followers. Following these accounts, the important events in the formation of the early Christian church are described. The leaders of the New Testament church were moved by God to write letters of instruction to the people of the different churches, giving them guidelines for their lives. In the final book of the New Testament the events of the last days of the history of the world are vividly described in God's revelation to the disciple John.

IV. GOD FULFILLS HIS PROMISE

God finally fulfilled His promise to Israel to bring the long-awaited Savior. God sent His Son to save not only Israel but the whole world from the judgment of sin. Jesus Christ came to do two things for us. First, He came to live a perfect, sinless life. Second, He came to die on the cross to pay the price for the sins of all humanity. Jesus came to make it possible for us to live a life free from sin and to set us free from the penalty of sin which is eternal death. These first selections from the New Testament are taken from the Gospels, which were written by four of Jesus' followers: Matthew, Mark, Luke, and John. They tell us about the birth of Jesus and His life and ministry, describing His many miracles and practical teachings. We read of Jesus' death on the cross and His glorious resurrection from the dead that proves He is truly the Son of God.

A. THE SON OF GOD

God sent His Son from His home in heaven to come to earth and be born as a humble baby. Jesus Christ is truly the Son of God because of the miraculous nature of His birth and the special events that surrounded this greatest moment in history, including the unusual birth of John the Baptist, the last Old Testament prophet, who was called to prepare the people of Israel for Christ's coming.

66. THE GREATEST PROPHET
Luke 1:5-45 and 57-80

Shortly before the birth of Jesus, a prophet greater than all the prophets of the Old Testament was born. His unusual birth was an indication that God had chosen John to fulfill a special purpose. He was to prepare the people of Israel for the coming of the Savior. John was to identify Jesus as the one about whom the prophets of the Old Testament had written.

The Birth of John the Baptist Foretold

1 ⁵There was in the days of Herod, the king of Judea, a certain priest named Zacharias, of the priestly division of Abijah. He had a wife of the daughters of Aaron, and her name was Elizabeth. ⁶ They were both righteous before God, walking blamelessly in all the commandments and ordinances of the Lord.
⁷ But they had no child, because Elizabeth was barren, and they both were well advanced in years.
⁸ Now while he executed the priest's office before God in the order of his division, ⁹ according to the custom of the priest's office, his lot was to enter into the temple of the Lord and burn incense. ¹⁰ The whole multitude of the people were praying outside at the hour of incense.
¹¹ An angel of the Lord appeared to him, standing on the right side of the altar of incense.¹² Zacharias was troubled when he saw him, and fear fell upon him. ¹³ But the angel said to him, "Don't be afraid, Zacharias, because your request has been heard, and your wife, Elizabeth, will bear you a son, and you shall call his name John. ¹⁴ You will have joy and gladness; and many will rejoice at his birth. ¹⁵ For he will be great in the sight of the Lord, and he will drink no wine nor strong drink. He will be filled with the Holy Spirit, even from his mother's womb. ¹⁶ He will turn many of the children of Israel to the Lord, their God.¹⁷ He will go before him in the spirit and power of Elijah, 'to turn the hearts of the fathers to the children,' and the disobedient to the wisdom of the just; to prepare a people prepared for the Lord."
¹⁸ Zacharias said to the angel, "How can I be sure of this? For I am an old man, and my wife is well advanced in years."
¹⁹ The angel answered him, "I am Gabriel, who stands in the presence of God. I was sent to speak to you, and to bring you this good news. ²⁰ Behold, you will be silent and not able to speak, until the day that these things will happen, because you didn't believe my words, which will be fulfilled in their proper time."

²¹ The people were waiting for Zacharias, and they marveled that he delayed in the temple. ²² When he came out, he could not speak to them, and they perceived that he had seen a vision in the temple. He continued making signs to them, and remained mute.

²³ When the days of his service were fulfilled, he departed to his house.
²⁴ After these days Elizabeth, his wife, conceived, and she hid herself five months, saying, ²⁵ "Thus has the Lord done to me in the days in which he looked at me, to take away my reproach among men."

The Birth of Jesus Foretold

²⁶ Now in the sixth month, the angel Gabriel was sent from God to a city of Galilee, named Nazareth, ²⁷ to a virgin pledged to be married to a man whose name was Joseph, of David's house. The virgin's name was Mary. ²⁸ Having come in, the angel said to her, "Rejoice, you highly favored one! The Lord is with you. Blessed are you among women!"

²⁹ But when she saw him, she was greatly troubled at the saying, and considered what kind of salutation this might be. ³⁰ The angel said to her, "Don't be afraid, Mary, for you have found favor with God. ³¹ Behold, you will conceive in your womb, and give birth to a son, and will call his name 'Jesus.' ³² He will be great, and will be called the Son of the Most High. The Lord God will give him the throne of his father, David, ³³ and he will reign over the house of Jacob forever. There will be no end to his Kingdom."

³⁴ Mary said to the angel, "How can this be, seeing I am a virgin?"

³⁵ The angel answered her, "The Holy Spirit will come on you, and the power of the Most High will overshadow you. Therefore also the holy one who is born from you will be called the Son of God. ³⁶ Behold, Elizabeth, your relative, also has conceived a son in her old age; and this is the sixth month with her who was called barren. ³⁷ For nothing spoken by God is impossible."

³⁸ Mary said, "Behold, the servant of the Lord; let it be done to me according to your word." The angel departed from her.

Mary Visits Elizabeth

³⁹ Mary arose in those days and went into the hill country with haste, into a city of Judah, ⁴⁰ and entered into the house of Zacharias and greeted Elizabeth.
⁴¹ When Elizabeth heard Mary's greeting, the baby leaped in her womb, and Elizabeth was filled with the Holy Spirit. ⁴² She called out with a loud voice, and said, "Blessed are you among women, and blessed is the fruit of your womb!
⁴³ Why am I so favored, that the mother of my Lord should come to me? ⁴⁴ For behold, when the voice of your greeting came into my ears, the baby leaped in my womb for joy! ⁴⁵ Blessed is she who believed, for there will be a fulfillment of the things which have been spoken to her from the Lord!"

The Birth of John the Baptist

⁵⁷ Now the time that Elizabeth should give birth was fulfilled, and she gave birth to a son. ⁵⁸ Her neighbors and her relatives heard that the Lord had

magnified his mercy towards her, and they rejoiced with her. ⁵⁹ On the eighth day, they came to circumcise the child; and they would have called him Zacharias, after the name of the father. ⁶⁰ His mother answered, "Not so; but he will be called John."

⁶¹ They said to her, "There is no one among your relatives who is called by this name."⁶² They made signs to his father, what he would have him called.
⁶³ He asked for a writing tablet, and wrote, "His name is John." They all marveled. ⁶⁴ His mouth was opened immediately, and his tongue freed, and he spoke, blessing God. ⁶⁵ Fear came on all who lived around them, and all these sayings were talked about throughout all the hill country of Judea. ⁶⁶ All who heard them laid them up in their heart, saying, "What then will this child be?" The hand of the Lord was with him.

Zechariah Praises God

⁶⁷His father, Zacharias, was filled with the Holy Spirit, and prophesied, saying,
⁶⁸"Blessed be the Lord, the God of Israel,
    for he has visited and redeemed his people;
⁶⁹and has raised up a horn of salvation for us
    in the house of his servant David
⁷⁰(as he spoke by the mouth of his holy prophets who have been from of old),
⁷¹salvation from our enemies,
    and from the hand of all who hate us;
⁷²to show mercy towards our fathers,
    to remember his holy covenant,
⁷³the oath which he spoke to Abraham, our father,
⁷⁴to grant to us that we, being delivered out of the hand of our enemies,
    should serve him without fear,
⁷⁵In holiness and righteousness before him all the days of our life.
⁷⁶And you, child, will be called a prophet of the Most High,
    for you will go before the face of the Lord to prepare his ways,
⁷⁷to give knowledge of salvation to his people
    by the remission of their sins,
⁷⁸because of the tender mercy of our God,
    whereby the dawn from on high will visit us,
⁷⁹to shine on those who sit in darkness
    and the shadow of death;
    to guide our feet into the way of peace."
⁸⁰The child was growing, and becoming strong in spirit, and was in the desert until the day of his public appearance to Israel.

    1. What did the angel tell Zechariah the work of John would be?

    2. What did the angel tell Mary about Jesus?

    3. What did Zechariah prophesy concerning his newborn child?

67. THE SAVIOR IS BORN
Matthew 1:18-25 and Luke 2:1-20

In the previous passage we read of the angel's visit to Mary and the conception of Jesus by the Holy Spirit. We now read how the virgin birth of Jesus provided conclusive proof that He is truly the Son of God. Because there was no place for Joseph and Mary to lodge, Jesus was born in a simple animal shelter. This indicated to the world that He had come as a humble servant to meet the needs of God's lost and dying world.

The Birth of Jesus Christ

1 [18]Now the birth of Jesus Christ was like this; for after his mother, Mary, was engaged to Joseph, before they came together, she was found pregnant by the Holy Spirit. [19] Joseph, her husband, being a righteous man, and not willing to make her a public example, intended to put her away secretly.

[20] But when he thought about these things, behold, an angel of the Lord appeared to him in a dream, saying, "Joseph, son of David, don't be afraid to take to yourself Mary, your wife, for that which is conceived in her is of the Holy Spirit. [21] She shall give birth to a son. You shall call his name Jesus, for it is he who shall save his people from their sins."

[22] Now all this has happened, that it might be fulfilled which was spoken by the Lord through the prophet, saying,
[23]"Behold, the virgin shall be with child, and shall give birth to a son.
They shall call his name Immanuel"; which is, being interpreted, "God with us."

[24] Joseph arose from his sleep, and did as the angel of the Lord commanded him, and took his wife to himself; [25] and didn't know her sexually until she had given birth to her firstborn son. He named him Jesus.

The Birth of Jesus

2 [1]Now in those days, a decree went out from Caesar Augustus that all the world should be enrolled. [2] This was the first enrollment made when Quirinius was governor of Syria.[3] All went to enroll themselves, everyone to his own city.

[4] Joseph also went up from Galilee, out of the city of Nazareth, into Judea, to David's city, which is called Bethlehem, because he was of the house and family of David; [5] to enroll himself with Mary, who was pledged to be married to him as wife, being pregnant.
[6] While they were there, the day had come for her to give birth. [7] She gave birth to her firstborn son. She wrapped him in bands of cloth, and laid him in a feeding trough, because there was no room for them in the inn.

The Shepherds and the Angels

[8] There were shepherds in the same country staying in the field, and keeping watch by night over their flock. [9] Behold, an angel of the Lord stood by them, and the glory of the Lord shone around them, and they were terrified. [10] The angel said to them, "Don't be afraid, for behold, I bring you good news of great joy

which will be to all the people. ¹¹ For there is born to you today, in David's city, a Savior, who is Christ the Lord. ¹² This is the sign to you: you will find a baby wrapped in strips of cloth, lying in a feeding trough [manger]."

¹³ Suddenly, there was with the angel a multitude of the heavenly army praising God, and saying,

> ¹⁴"Glory to God in the highest,
> on earth peace, good will toward men."

¹⁵ When the angels went away from them into the sky, the shepherds said to one another, "Let's go to Bethlehem, now, and see this thing that has happened, which the Lord has made known to us."

¹⁶ They came with haste, and found both Mary and Joseph, and the baby was lying in the feeding trough [manger]. ¹⁷ When they saw it, they publicized widely the saying which was spoken to them about this child. ¹⁸ All who heard it wondered at the things which were spoken to them by the shepherds. ¹⁹ But Mary kept all these sayings, pondering them in her heart. ²⁰ The shepherds returned, glorifying and praising God for all the things that they had heard and seen, just as it was told them.

1. Scholars have found some 324 prophecies in the Old Testament about the coming of the Savior. Do you remember reading any of these earlier in this book? Find one that you remember.

2. What do the names Jesus and Immanuel mean?

3. What did the angel say about this newborn baby? How did Mary respond to this news?

4. What was Mary's response to all the things that had happened?

68. VISIT OF THE WISE MEN
Matthew 2:1-23

The promises God made to King David were fulfilled as Jesus Christ was born in Bethlehem, the city of David. Writings of the Old Testament prophets came to pass when wise men from Persia visited the newborn King. The Roman ruler, King Herod, plotted to have the baby Jesus killed. Prophecy was again fulfilled as Joseph fled with his family to Egypt and then returned to Galilee several years later.

The Visit of the Magi
2 Now when Jesus was born in Bethlehem of Judea in the days of King Herod, behold, wise men from the east came to Jerusalem, saying, ² "Where is he who is born King of the Jews? For we saw his star in the east, and have come to worship him." ³ When King Herod heard it, he was troubled, and all Jerusalem with him. ⁴ Gathering together all the chief priests and scribes of the people, he asked them where the Christ would be born.

⁵ They said to him, "In Bethlehem of Judea, for this is written through the prophet,

> ⁶'You Bethlehem, land of Judah,
> are in no way least among the princes of Judah:
> for out of you shall come a governor,
> who shall shepherd my people, Israel.'"

⁷ Then Herod secretly called the wise men, and learned from them exactly what time the star appeared. ⁸ He sent them to Bethlehem, and said, "Go and search diligently for the young child. When you have found him, bring me word, so that I also may come and worship him."

⁹ They, having heard the king, went their way; and behold, the star, which they saw in the east, went before them, until it came and stood over where the young child was. ¹⁰ When they saw the star, they rejoiced with exceedingly great joy. ¹¹They came into the house and saw the young child with Mary, his mother, and they fell down and worshiped him. Opening their treasures, they offered to him gifts: gold, frankincense, and myrrh.¹² Being warned in a dream that they shouldn't return to Herod, they went back to their own country another way.

The Escape to Egypt

¹³ Now when they had departed, behold, an angel of the Lord appeared to Joseph in a dream, saying, "Arise and take the young child and his mother, and flee into Egypt, and stay there until I tell you, for Herod will seek the young child to destroy him." ¹⁴ He arose and took the young child and his mother by night, and departed into Egypt, ¹⁵ and was there until the death of Herod; that it might be fulfilled which was spoken by the Lord through the prophet, saying, "Out of Egypt I called my son."

Herod Kills the Baby Boys

¹⁶ Then Herod, when he saw that he was mocked [tricked] by the wise men, was exceedingly angry, and sent out, and killed all the male children who were in Bethlehem and in all the surrounding countryside, from two years old and under, according to the exact time which he had learned from the wise men. ¹⁷ Then that which was spoken by Jeremiah the prophet was fulfilled, saying,

> ¹⁸ A voice was heard in Ramah,
> lamentation, weeping and great mourning,
> Rachel weeping for her children;
> she wouldn't be comforted,
> because they are no more."(Jeremiah 31:15)

The Return to Nazareth

¹⁹ But when Herod was dead, behold, an angel of the Lord appeared in a dream to Joseph in Egypt, saying, ²⁰ "Arise and take the young child and his mother, and go into the land of Israel, for those who sought the young child's life are dead."

²¹ He arose and took the young child and his mother, and came into the land

of Israel.²² But when he heard that Archelaus was reigning over Judea in the place of his father, Herod, he was afraid to go there. Being warned in a dream, he withdrew into the region of Galilee, ²³ and came and lived in a city called Nazareth; that it might be fulfilled which was spoken through the prophets: "He will be called a Nazarene."

1. How did the chief priests know where the Messiah Christ was to be born?
2. What prophecy was fulfilled when Joseph took his family to Egypt?
3. What had the prophet Jeremiah said concerning the brutal murder of the innocent infant boys?
4. What prophecy was fulfilled when Joseph settled in Nazareth?

69. THE SON OF MAN
John 1:1-18 and Matthew 1:1-17 and Luke 2:40-52

This Jesus who was born was actually God, the Son. He was one with the Father and had always existed before He came into this world. The term "word" refers to a person's "mind," "reason" or "wisdom." John used this Greek concept to communicate the fact that Jesus, the Second Person of the Divine Trinity, was the self-expression of God to the world. If you want to know what God is all about, look at Jesus. God did a new thing when He sent Jesus to reveal Himself to men. God chose the lowly means of a virgin's womb to bring His Son into the world to become a man. Jesus was born into a family directly descended from Abraham and David. Thus, Jesus, the very Son of God is also the Son of Man. He is called the Christ, meaning the anointed King, the promised Savior of all men and women. These Bible passages show both His divine and human natures. In them we see how God revealed Himself to mankind by being born as a baby and growing up to adulthood in a normal family situation. Jesus is fully God and fully human. It is a divine mystery of two distinct natures united in one Person forever.

God Comes to Man

1 In the beginning was the Word, and the Word was with God, and the Word was God.² The same was in the beginning with God.

³ All things were made through him. Without him was not anything made that has been made. ⁴ In him was life, and the life was the light of men. ⁵ The light shines in the darkness, and the darkness hasn't overcome it.

⁶ There came a man, sent from God, whose name was John. ⁷ The same came as a witness, that he might testify about the light, that all might believe through him. ⁸ He was not the light, but was sent that he might testify about the light. ⁹ The true light that enlightens everyone was coming into the world.

¹⁰ He was in the world, and the world was made through him, and the world

didn't recognize him. ¹¹ He came to his own, and those who were his own didn't receive him.¹² But as many as received him, to them he gave the right to become God's children, to those who believe in his name: ¹³ who were born not of blood, nor of the will of the flesh, nor of the will of man, but of God.

¹⁴ The Word became flesh, and lived among us. We saw his glory, such glory as of the one and only Son of the Father, full of grace and truth.

¹⁵ John testified about him. He cried out, saying, "This was he of whom I said, 'He who comes after me has surpassed me, for he was before me.'" ¹⁶ From his fullness we all received grace upon grace. ¹⁷ For the law was given through Moses. Grace and truth were realized through Jesus Christ. ¹⁸ No one has seen God at any time. The one and only Son, who is in the bosom of the Father, he has declared him.

The Human Genealogy of Jesus

1 The book of the genealogy of Jesus Christ, the son of David, the son of Abraham.

² Abraham became the father of Isaac.
Isaac became the father of Jacob.
Jacob became the father of Judah and his brothers.
³ Judah became the father of Perez and Zerah by Tamar.
Perez became the father of Hezron.
Hezron became the father of Ram.
⁴ Ram became the father of Amminadab.
Amminadab became the father of Nahshon.
Nahshon became the father of Salmon.
⁵ Salmon became the father of Boaz by Rahab.
Boaz became the father of Obed by Ruth.
Obed became the father of Jesse.
⁶ Jesse became the father of King David.
David became the father of
Solomon by her who had been Uriah's wife.
⁷ Solomon became the father of Rehoboam.
Rehoboam became the father of Abijah.
Abijah became the father of Asa.
⁸ Asa became the father of Jehoshaphat.
Jehoshaphat became the father of Joram.
Joram became the father of Uzziah.
⁹ Uzziah became the father of Jotham.
Jotham became the father of Ahaz.

Ahaz became the father of Hezekiah.
¹⁰ Hezekiah became the father of Manasseh.
Manasseh became the father of Amon.
Amon became the father of Josiah.
¹¹ Josiah became the father of Jechoniah and his brothers,
at the time of the exile to Babylon.
¹² After the exile to Babylon, Jechoniah became the father of Shealtiel.
Shealtiel became the father of Zerubbabel.
¹³ Zerubbabel became the father of Abiud.
Abiud became the father of Eliakim.
Eliakim became the father of Azor.
¹⁴ Azor became the father of Zadok.
Zadok became the father of Achim.
Achim became the father of Eliud.
¹⁵ Eliud became the father of Eleazar.
Eleazar became the father of Matthan.
Matthan became the father of Jacob.
¹⁶ Jacob became the father of Joseph, the husband of Mary,
from whom was born Jesus, who is called Christ.

¹⁷ So all the generations from Abraham to David are fourteen generations; from David to the exile to Babylon fourteen generations; and from the carrying away to Babylon to the Christ, fourteen generations.

Jesus as a Boy

2 ⁴⁰The child was growing, and was becoming strong in spirit, being filled with wisdom, and the grace of God was upon him. ⁴¹ His parents went every year to Jerusalem at the feast of the Passover.

⁴² When he was twelve years old, they went up to Jerusalem according to the custom of the feast, ⁴³ and when they had fulfilled the days, as they were returning, the boy Jesus stayed behind in Jerusalem. Joseph and his mother didn't know it, ⁴⁴ but supposing him to be in the company, they went a day's journey, and they looked for him among their relatives and acquaintances. ⁴⁵ When they didn't find him, they returned to Jerusalem, looking for him. ⁴⁶ After three days they found him in the temple, sitting in the middle of the teachers, both listening to them, and asking them questions. ⁴⁷ All who heard him were amazed at his understanding and his answers.

⁴⁸ When they saw him, they were astonished, and his mother said to him,
"Son, why have you treated us this way? Behold, your father and I were anxiously looking for you."

⁴⁹ He said to them, "Why were you looking for me? Didn't you know that I must be in my Father's house?" ⁵⁰ They didn't understand the saying which he spoke to them. ⁵¹ And he went down with them, and came to Nazareth. He was subject to them, and his mother kept all these sayings in her heart. ⁵² And Jesus increased in wisdom and stature, and in favor with God and men.

1. Did Jesus exist when God created the world?
2. Who revealed God to us?
3. Can you recognize some of the family line we studied earlier in this book who were Jesus' ancestors?
4. What right does God give to those who believe in Jesus?

B. THE POWER OF GOD

During the years He was growing into manhood, Jesus lived with His family. He probably worked with His father, Joseph, who was a carpenter. When He was about thirty years old, Jesus was given the power of God to do the work that He had been sent to do. He was given authority over all the works of Satan: sin, disease, demons and even death. In these next five selections we will read of Jesus' miracle-working power, which meets all the needs of those who believe in Him.

70. THE SPIRIT OF POWER
Luke 3:1-18 and Matthew 3:13-17
Luke 4:1-15 and Matthew 4:12-17

John, the great prophet, prepared the way for Jesus to begin His public ministry. John called upon the people to give up their evil ways and corrupt practices so that they might be ready to welcome the Christ. At the baptism of Jesus, the Spirit of God came upon Him, giving Jesus the power He needed to do the works of God and to overcome Satan.

John the Baptist Prepares the Way

3 Now in the fifteenth year of the reign of Tiberius Caesar, Pontius Pilate being governor of Judea, and Herod being tetrarch of Galilee, and his brother Philip tetrarch of the region of Ituraea and Trachonitis, and Lysanias tetrarch of Abilene, ² in the high priesthood of Annas and Caiaphas, the word of God came to John, the son of Zacharias, in the wilderness. ³ He came into the entire region around the Jordan, preaching the baptism of repentance for remission of sins. ⁴ As it is written in the book of the words of Isaiah the prophet,

> "The voice of one crying in the wilderness,
> 'Make ready the way of the Lord.
> Make his paths straight.
> Every valley will be filled.
> ⁵Every mountain and hill will be brought low.

The crooked will become straight,
and the rough ways smooth.
⁶ All flesh will see God's salvation.'"

⁷ He said therefore to the multitudes who went out to be baptized by him, "You offspring of vipers, who warned you to flee from the wrath to come? ⁸ Therefore produce fruits worthy of repentance, and don't begin to say among yourselves, 'We have Abraham for our father;' for I tell you that God is able to raise up children to Abraham from these stones! ⁹ Even now the ax also lies at the root of the trees. Every tree therefore that doesn't produce good fruit is cut down, and thrown into the fire."

¹⁰ The multitudes asked him, "What then must we do?"
¹¹ He answered them, "He who has two coats, let him give to him who has none. He who has food, let him do likewise."
¹² Tax collectors also came to be baptized, and they said to him, "Teacher, what must we do?"
¹³ He said to them, "Collect no more than that which is appointed to you."
¹⁴ Soldiers also asked him, saying, "What about us? What must we do?" He said to them, "Extort from no one by violence, neither accuse anyone wrongfully. Be content with your wages."
¹⁵ As the people were in expectation, and all men reasoned in their hearts concerning John, whether perhaps he was the Christ, ¹⁶ John answered them all, "I indeed baptize you with water, but he comes who is mightier than I, the strap of whose sandals I am not worthy to loosen. He will baptize you in the Holy Spirit and fire, ¹⁷ whose fan is in his hand, and he will thoroughly cleanse his threshing floor, and will gather the wheat into his barn; but he will burn up the chaff with unquenchable fire." ¹⁸ Then with many other exhortations he preached good news to the people.

The Baptism of Jesus

3 ¹³Then Jesus came from Galilee to the Jordan to John, to be baptized by him.
¹⁴ But John would have hindered him, saying, "I need to be baptized by you, and you come to me?"

¹⁵ But Jesus, answering, said to him, "Allow it now, for this is the fitting way for us to fulfill all righteousness." Then he allowed him.
¹⁶ Jesus, when he was baptized, went up directly from the water: and behold, the heavens were opened to him. He saw the Spirit of God descending as a dove, and coming on him. ¹⁷ Behold, a voice out of the heavens said, "This is my beloved Son, with whom I am well pleased."

The Temptation of Jesus

4 ¹Jesus, full of the Holy Spirit, returned from the Jordan, and was led by the Spirit into the wilderness ² for forty days, being tempted by the devil. He ate nothing in those days. Afterward, when they were completed, he was hungry.

Great Bible Truths

³ The devil said to him, "If you are the Son of God, command this stone to become bread."

⁴Jesus answered him saying, "It is written, 'Man shall not live by bread alone, but by every word of God.'"

⁵ The devil, leading him up on a high mountain, showed him all the kingdoms of the world in a moment of time. ⁶ The devil said to him, "I will give you all this authority, and their glory, for it has been delivered to me; and I give it to whomever I want. ⁷ If you therefore will worship before me, it will all be yours."

⁸ Jesus answered him, "Get behind me Satan! For it is written, 'You shall worship the Lord your God, and you shall serve him only.'"

⁹ He led him to Jerusalem, and set him on the pinnacle of the temple, and said to him, "If you are the Son of God, cast yourself down from here, ¹⁰ for it is written,

He will put his angels in charge of you, to guard you;"

¹¹And, on their hands they will bear you up,

Lest perhaps you dash your foot against a stone."

¹² Jesus answering, said to him, "It has been said, 'You shall not tempt the Lord your God.'"

¹³ When the devil had completed every temptation, he departed from him until another time.¹⁴ Jesus returned in the power of the Spirit into Galilee, and news about him spread through all the surrounding area. ¹⁵ He taught in their synagogues, being glorified by all.

Jesus Begins to Preach

4 ¹²Now when Jesus heard that John was delivered up, he withdrew into Galilee. ¹³ Leaving Nazareth, he came and lived in Capernaum, which is by the sea, in the region of Zebulun and Naphtali, ¹⁴that it might be fulfilled which was spoken through Isaiah the prophet, saying,

¹⁵"The land of Zebulun and the land of Naphtali, toward the sea, beyond the Jordan, Galilee of the Gentiles,

¹⁶ the people who sat in darkness saw a great light,

to those who sat in the region and shadow of death,

to them light has dawned."

¹⁷ From that time, Jesus began to preach, and to say, "Repent! For the Kingdom of Heaven is at hand."

   1. In what practical ways did John the Baptist advise people to change?

   2. What kind of baptism did John offer to the people?

   3. How did John describe Jesus the Christ?

   4. When Jesus was baptized, what did God the Father say about His Son? What were the Father's words?

   5. How did Jesus overcome each of the devil's temptations?

71. POWER OVER SIN AND EVIL
Luke 4:14-37 and 5:12-26

Jesus was anointed by the Spirit of God to bring good news of freedom and healing to those bound by Satan. He was given power over evil spirits as well as authority from God to forgive sins, bringing healing for both the body and soul of man.

Jesus Rejected at Nazareth

4 ¹⁴Jesus returned in the power of the Spirit into Galilee, and news about him spread through all the surrounding area. ¹⁵ He taught in their synagogues, being glorified by all.

¹⁶ He came to Nazareth, where he had been brought up. He entered, as was his custom, into the synagogue on the Sabbath day, and stood up to read. ¹⁷ The book of the prophet Isaiah was handed to him. He opened the book, and found the place where it was written,

> ¹⁸ "The Spirit of the Lord is on me,
> because he has anointed me
> to preach good news to the poor.
> He has sent me to heal the broken hearted,
> to proclaim release to the captives,
> recovering of sight to the blind,
> to deliver those who are crushed,
> ¹⁹ and to proclaim the acceptable year of the Lord."

²⁰ He closed the book, gave it back to the attendant, and sat down. The eyes of all in the synagogue were fastened on him. ²¹ He began to tell them, "Today, this Scripture has been fulfilled in your hearing."

²² All testified about him, and wondered at the gracious words which proceeded out of his mouth, and they said, "Isn't this Joseph's son?"

²³ He said to them, "Doubtless you will tell me this parable, 'Physician, heal yourself! Whatever we have heard done at Capernaum, do also here in your home town.'" ²⁴ He said, "Most certainly I tell you, no prophet is acceptable in his hometown. ²⁵ But truly I tell you, there were many widows in Israel in the days of Elijah, when the sky was shut up three years and six months, when a great famine came over all the land. ²⁶ Elijah was sent to none of them, except to Zarephath, in the land of Sidon, to a woman who was a widow. ²⁷ There were many lepers in Israel in the time of Elisha the prophet, yet not one of them was cleansed, except Naaman, the Syrian."

²⁸ They were all filled with wrath in the synagogue, as they heard these things. ²⁹ They rose up, threw him out of the city, and led him to the brow of the hill that their city was built on, that they might throw him off the cliff. ³⁰ But he, passing through the middle of them, went his way.

Jesus Drives out an Evil Spirit

³¹ He came down to Capernaum, a city of Galilee. He was teaching them on the Sabbath day, ³² and they were astonished at his teaching, for his word was with

authority. ³³ In the synagogue there was a man who had a spirit of an unclean demon, and he cried out with a loud voice, ³⁴ saying, "Ah! what have we to do with you, Jesus of Nazareth? Have you come to destroy us? I know you who you are: the Holy One of God!"

³⁵ Jesus rebuked him, saying, "Be silent, and come out of him!" When the demon had thrown him down in the middle of them, he came out of him, having done him no harm.

³⁶ Amazement came on all, and they spoke together, one with another, saying, "What is this word? For with authority and power he commands the unclean spirits, and they come out!" ³⁷ News about him went out into every place of the surrounding region.

The Man with Leprosy

5 ¹²While he was in one of the cities, behold, there was a man full of leprosy. When he saw Jesus, he fell on his face, and begged him, saying, "Lord, if you want to, you can make me clean." ¹³ He stretched out his hand, and touched him, saying, "I want to. Be made clean." Immediately the leprosy left him. ¹⁴ He commanded him to tell no one, "But go your way, and show yourself to the priest, and offer for your cleansing according to what Moses commanded, for a testimony to them." ¹⁵ But the report concerning him spread much more, and great multitudes came together to hear, and to be healed by him of their infirmities. ¹⁶ But he withdrew himself into the desert, and prayed.

Jesus Heals a Paralytic

¹⁷ On one of those days, he was teaching; and there were Pharisees and teachers of the law sitting by, who had come out of every village of Galilee, Judea, and Jerusalem. The power of the Lord was with him to heal them. ¹⁸ Behold, men brought a paralyzed man on a cot, and they sought to bring him in to lay before Jesus. ¹⁹ Not finding a way to bring him in because of the multitude, they went up to the housetop, and let him down through the tiles with his cot into the middle before Jesus.

²⁰ Seeing their faith, he said to him, "Man, your sins are forgiven you."

²¹ The scribes and the Pharisees began to reason, saying, "Who is this that speaks blasphemies? Who can forgive sins, but God alone?"

²² But Jesus, perceiving their thoughts, answered them, "Why are you reasoning so in your hearts? ²³ Which is easier to say, 'Your sins are forgiven you;' or to say, 'Arise and walk?' ²⁴ But that you may know that the Son of Man has authority on earth to forgive sins" (he said to the paralyzed man), "I tell you, arise, and take up your cot, and go to your house."

²⁵ Immediately he rose up before them, and took up that which he was laying on, and departed to his house, glorifying God. ²⁶ Amazement took hold on all, and they glorified God. They were filled with fear, saying, "We have seen strange things today."

1. Do you see how Jesus fulfilled Isaiah's prophecy as He began His ministry?
2. Why did the people in Capernaum receive Jesus while the people in Nazareth, His own home town, rejected Him?
3. Why was Jesus willing to touch the leper and heal him?
4. What did Jesus see in the men who brought the paralytic?
5. Why were the Pharisees concerned when Jesus told the man his sins were forgiven?

72. POWER OVER NATURE
John 2:1-11 and 6:1-21 and Luke 8:22-25

Because He was sent from God, who created the world and everything in it, Jesus had authority over the laws of nature. Here we read of His miraculous power over water, food, gravity and the weather.

Jesus Changes Water into Wine

2 The third day, there was a marriage in Cana of Galilee. Jesus' mother was there. ² Jesus also was invited, with his disciples, to the marriage. ³ When the wine ran out, Jesus' mother said to him, "They have no wine."

⁴ Jesus said to her, "Woman, what does that have to do with you and me? My hour has not yet come."

⁵ His mother said to the servants, "Whatever he says to you, do it." ⁶ Now there were six water pots of stone set there after the Jews' way of purifying, containing two or three metretes apiece.

⁷ Jesus said to them, "Fill the water pots with water." They filled them up to the brim.

⁸ He said to them, "Now draw some out, and take it to the ruler of the feast." So they took it. ⁹ When the ruler of the feast tasted the water now become wine, and didn't know where it came from (but the servants who had drawn the water knew), the ruler of the feast called the bridegroom, ¹⁰ and said to him, "Everyone serves the good wine first, and when the guests have drunk freely, then that which is worse. You have kept the good wine until now!"

¹¹ This beginning of his signs Jesus did in Cana of Galilee, and revealed his glory; and his disciples believed in him.

Jesus Feeds the Five Thousand

6 After these things, Jesus went away to the other side of the sea of Galilee, which is also called the Sea of Tiberias. ² A great multitude followed him, because they saw his signs which he did on those who were sick. ³ Jesus went up into the mountain, and he sat there with his disciples. ⁴ Now the Passover, the feast of the Jews, was at hand.

⁵ Jesus therefore lifting up his eyes, and seeing that a great multitude was

coming to him, said to Philip, "Where are we to buy bread that these may eat?" ⁶ This he said to test him, for he himself knew what he would do.

⁷Philip answered him, "Two hundred denarii worth of bread is not sufficient for them, that everyone of them may receive a little."

⁸One of his disciples, Andrew, Simon Peter's brother, said to him, ⁹ "There is a boy here who has five barley loaves and two fish, but what are these among so many?"

¹⁰ Jesus said, "Have the people sit down." Now there was much grass in that place. So the men sat down, in number about five thousand. ¹¹ Jesus took the loaves; and having given thanks, he distributed to the disciples, and the disciples to those who were sitting down; likewise also of the fish as much as they desired.

¹² When they were filled, he said to his disciples, "Gather up the broken pieces which are left over, that nothing be lost." ¹³ So they gathered them up, and filled twelve baskets with broken pieces from the five barley loaves, which were left over by those who had eaten.

¹⁴ When therefore the people saw the sign which Jesus did, they said, "This is truly the prophet who comes into the world."¹⁵ Jesus therefore, perceiving that they were about to come and take him by force, to make him king, withdrew again to the mountain by himself.

Jesus Walks on Water

¹⁶ When evening came, his disciples went down to the sea, ¹⁷ and they entered into the boat, and were going over the sea to Capernaum. It was now dark, and Jesus had not come to them. ¹⁸ The sea was tossed by a great wind blowing. ¹⁹ When therefore they had rowed about twenty-five or thirty stadia [3-4 miles or 5-6 km], they saw Jesus walking on the sea, and drawing near to the boat; and they were afraid. ²⁰ But he said to them, "It is I. Don't be afraid." ²¹ They were willing therefore to receive him into the boat. Immediately the boat was at the land where they were going.

Jesus Calms the Storm

8 ²²Now on one of those days, he entered into a boat, himself and his disciples, and he said to them, "Let's go over to the other side of the lake." So they launched out. ²³ But as they sailed, he fell asleep. A wind storm came down on the lake, and they were taking on dangerous amounts of water.

²⁴ They came to him, and awoke him, saying, "Master, master, we are dying!"

He awoke, and rebuked the wind and the raging of the water, and they ceased, and it was calm.²⁵ He said to them, "Where is your faith?"

Being afraid they marveled, saying to one another, "Who is this, then, that he commands even the winds and the water, and they obey him?"

1. What did Jesus reveal about himself when He changed water into wine?
2. What was the reaction of the people to the miracle of the multiplied bread and fish?
3. Why were the disciples terrified when they saw Jesus walking on the water?
4. After the storm was calmed, what question did Jesus ask His disciples? Why?
5. How did the disciples react to Jesus' control over the weather?

73. POWER OVER DEMONS AND DISEASE
Luke 8:26-39 and Matthew 8:5-17

Since the beginning of time, Satan has attempted to destroy men and women by using demons and disease. Because Jesus is one with the Father, He is able to overcome the works of the devil through the power of God's Spirit. Jesus made it very clear that it is faith that causes God's power to bring healing.

Healing of the Demon-possessed Man

8 [26]They arrived at the country of the Gadarenes, which is opposite Galilee. [27] When Jesus stepped ashore, a certain man out of the city who had demons for a long time met him. He wore no clothes, and didn't live in a house, but in the tombs. [28] When he saw Jesus, he cried out, and fell down before him, and with a loud voice said, "What do I have to do with you, Jesus, you Son of the Most High God? I beg you, don't torment me!" [29] For Jesus was commanding the unclean spirit to come out of the man. For the unclean spirit had often seized the man. He was kept under guard, and bound with chains and fetters. Breaking the bands apart, he was driven by the demon into the desert.

[30] Jesus asked him, "What is your name?"

He said, "Legion," for many demons had entered into him. [31] They begged him that he would not command them to go into the abyss. [32] Now there was there a herd of many pigs feeding on the mountain, and they begged him that he would allow them to enter into those. He allowed them. [33] The demons came out of the man, and entered into the pigs, and the herd rushed down the steep bank into the lake, and were drowned.

[34] When those who fed them saw what had happened, they fled, and told it in the city and in the country. [35] People went out to see what had happened. They came to Jesus, and found the man from whom the demons had gone out, sitting at Jesus' feet, clothed and in his right mind; and they were afraid. [36] Those who saw it told them how he who had been possessed by demons was healed. [37] All the people of the surrounding country of the Gadarenes asked him to depart from them, for they were very much afraid. He entered into the boat, and returned.

[38] But the man from whom the demons had gone out begged him that he

might go with him, but Jesus sent him away, saying, ³⁹ "Return to your house, and declare what great things God has done for you." He went his way, proclaiming throughout the whole city what great things Jesus had done for him.

The Faith of the Centurion

8 ⁵When he came into Capernaum, a centurion came to him, asking him, ⁶ and saying, "Lord, my servant lies in the house paralyzed, grievously tormented."

⁷ Jesus said to him, "I will come and heal him."

⁸ The centurion answered, "Lord, I'm not worthy for you to come under my roof. Just say the word, and my servant will be healed. ⁹For I am also a man under authority, having under myself soldiers. I tell this one, 'Go,' and he goes; and tell another, 'Come,' and he comes; and tell my servant, 'Do this,' and he does it."

¹⁰ When Jesus heard it, he marveled, and said to those who followed, "Most certainly I tell you, I haven't found so great a faith, not even in Israel. ¹¹ I tell you that many will come from the east and the west, and will sit down with Abraham, Isaac, and Jacob in the Kingdom of Heaven, ¹² but the children of the Kingdom will be thrown out into the outer darkness. There will be weeping and gnashing of teeth."

¹³ Jesus said to the centurion, "Go your way. Let it be done for you as you have believed." His servant was healed in that hour.

Jesus Heals Many

¹⁴ When Jesus came into Peter's house, he saw his wife's mother lying sick with a fever.¹⁵ He touched her hand, and the fever left her. She got up and served him.

¹⁶ When evening came, they brought to him many possessed with demons. He cast out the spirits with a word, and healed all who were sick; ¹⁷ that it might be fulfilled which was spoken through Isaiah the prophet, saying,

"He took our infirmities, and bore our diseases."

> 1. Did you notice how the demons feared Jesus?
>
> 2. How did that community react to the man's healing? Why did they react this way?
>
> 3. What did the man do after Jesus healed him?
>
> 4. Why was Jesus so impressed with the centurion's faith?
>
> 5. Is Isaiah's prophecy still being fulfilled today?

74. POWER OVER DEATH
John 11:17-45 and Luke 8:40-56

We have seen that Jesus had divine power over sin and evil, over demons and disease and even over nature. In the following selection we see that Jesus had power over physical death as well when he raised his friend Lazarus from the dead and restored life to a lifeless young girl. Jesus promises life that never ends to those who believe in Him. Because of Jesus, we will never, ever, have to fear death again.

Great Bible Truths

Jesus Comforts the Sisters

11 ¹⁷So when Jesus came, he found that he, [Lazarus], had been in the tomb four days already. ¹⁸ Now Bethany was near Jerusalem, about fifteen stadia [1.7 miles or 2.8 km] away. ¹⁹ Many of the Jews had joined the women around Martha and Mary, to console them concerning their brother. ²⁰ Then when Martha heard that Jesus was coming, she went and met him, but Mary stayed in the house.

²¹ Therefore Martha said to Jesus, "Lord, if you would have been here, my brother wouldn't have died. ²² Even now I know that, whatever you ask of God, God will give you."

²³ Jesus said to her, "Your brother will rise again."

²⁴ Martha said to him, "I know that he will rise again in the resurrection at the last day."

²⁵ Jesus said to her, "I am the resurrection and the life. He who believes in me will still live, even if he dies. ²⁶ Whoever lives and believes in me will never die. Do you believe this?"

²⁷ She said to him, "Yes, Lord. I have come to believe that you are the Christ, God's Son, he who comes into the world."

²⁸ When she had said this, she went away, and called Mary, her sister, secretly, saying, "The Teacher is here, and is calling you." ²⁹ When she heard this, she arose quickly, and went to him. ³⁰ Now Jesus had not yet come into the village, but was in the place where Martha met him. ³¹ Then the Jews who were with her in the house, and were consoling her, when they saw Mary, that she rose up quickly and went out, followed her, saying, "She is going to the tomb to weep there."

³² Therefore when Mary came to where Jesus was, and saw him, she fell down at his feet, saying to him, "Lord, if you would have been here, my brother wouldn't have died."

³³ When Jesus therefore saw her weeping, and the Jews weeping who came with her, he groaned in the spirit, and was troubled, ³⁴ and said, "Where have you laid him?"

They told him, "Lord, come and see." ³⁵ Jesus wept.

³⁶ The Jews therefore said, "See how much affection he had for him!"

³⁷ Some of them said, "Couldn't this man, who opened the eyes of him who was blind, have also kept this man from dying?"

Jesus Raises Lazarus from the Dead

³⁸ Jesus therefore, again groaning in himself, came to the tomb. Now it was a cave, and a stone lay against it. ³⁹ Jesus said, "Take away the stone."

Martha, the sister of him who was dead, said to him, "Lord, by this time there is a stench, for he has been dead four days."

⁴⁰Jesus said to her, "Didn't I tell you that if you believed, you would see God's glory?"

⁴¹ So they took away the stone from the place where the dead man was lying.

Great Bible Truths

Jesus lifted up his eyes, and said, "Father, I thank you that you listened to me. ⁴² I know that you always listen to me, but because of the multitude that stands around I said this, that they may believe that you sent me." ⁴³ When he had said this, he cried with a loud voice, "Lazarus, come out!"

⁴⁴ He who was dead came out, bound hand and foot with wrappings, and his face was wrapped around with a cloth.

Jesus said to them, "Free him, and let him go." ⁴⁵ Therefore many of the Jews, who came to Mary and saw what Jesus did, believed in him.

A Dead Girl and a Sick Woman

8 ⁴⁰When Jesus returned, the multitude welcomed him, for they were all waiting for him.⁴¹ Behold, there came a man named Jairus, and he was a ruler of the synagogue. He fell down at Jesus' feet, and begged him to come into his house, ⁴² for he had an only daughter, about twelve years of age, and she was dying.

But as he went, the multitudes pressed against him. ⁴³ A woman who had a flow of blood for twelve years, who had spent all her living on physicians, and could not be healed by any, ⁴⁴ came behind him, and touched the fringe of his cloak, and immediately the flow of her blood stopped.

⁴⁵ Jesus said, "Who touched me?"

When all denied it, Peter and those with him said, "Master, the multitudes press and jostle you, and you say, 'Who touched me?'"

⁴⁶ But Jesus said, "Someone did touch me, for I perceived that power has gone out of me." ⁴⁷ When the woman saw that she was not hidden, she came trembling, and falling down before him declared to him in the presence of all the people the reason why she had touched him, and how she was healed immediately. ⁴⁸ He said to her, "Daughter, cheer up. Your faith has made you well. Go in peace."

Jesus Raises a Dead Girl

⁴⁹While he still spoke, one from the ruler of the synagogue's house came, saying to him, "Your daughter is dead. Don't trouble the Teacher."

⁵⁰ But Jesus hearing it, answered him, "Don't be afraid. Only believe, and she will be healed."

⁵¹When he came to the house, he didn't allow anyone to enter in, except Peter, John, James, the father of the child, and her mother. ⁵² All were weeping and mourning her, but he said, "Don't weep. She isn't dead, but sleeping."

⁵³ They were ridiculing him, knowing that she was dead. ⁵⁴ But he put them all outside, and taking her by the hand, he called, saying, "Child, arise!" ⁵⁵ Her spirit returned, and she rose up immediately. He commanded that something be given to her to eat. ⁵⁶ Her parents were amazed, but he commanded them to tell no one what had been done.

1. *What important comforting words did Jesus give to Martha?*

2. *Who did Jesus tell Martha He was, and what awesome implications did this statement have?*

3. Why did Jesus weep at Lazarus' grave?

4. Why do you think the woman was healed that day?

5. How do we know that Jesus has power over death?

C. THE NAMES OF CHRIST

Jesus identifies Himself in many ways, sometimes using names that are allegorical. These names symbolize, or represent, truths of human life. Jesus used these word pictures in order that we might more easily understand how He came to meet the needs of all mankind in all situations. These different names tell people about Himself in order to make it possible for ordinary people to grasp the awesome, wonderful truth of God's love and care for every person who comes to believe in Him. In these next four selections, we read about Jesus' relationship to His Heavenly Father and how we can know God by believing in Jesus as God's son.

75. THE SON OF GOD
John 5:16-47

As He was doing the work of His Father, there were times when Jesus would heal people on the Jewish holy day, called the Sabbath. This made the Jewish leaders very angry because they did not believe that Jesus was the Son of God. They thought that He was just an ordinary man who was flouting the inflexible Sabbath rules. Jesus told them that the proof that God had sent Him could be seen in the very work the Father had given Him to do.

Life Through the Son

5 [16]For this cause the Jews persecuted Jesus, and sought to kill him, because he did these things on the Sabbath. [17] But Jesus answered them, "My Father is still working, so I am working, too." [18] For this cause therefore the Jews sought all the more to kill him, because he not only broke the Sabbath, but also called God his own Father, making himself equal with God.

[19] Jesus therefore answered them, "Most certainly, I tell you, the Son can do nothing of himself, but what he sees the Father doing. For whatever things he does, these the Son also does likewise. [20] For the Father has affection for the Son, and shows him all things that he himself does. He will show him greater works than these that you may marvel. [21] For as the Father raises the dead and gives them life, even so the Son also gives life to whom he desires. [22] For the Father judges no one, but he has given all judgment to the Son, [23] that all may honor the Son, even as they honor the Father. He who doesn't honor the Son doesn't honor the Father who sent him.

[24] "Most certainly I tell you, he who hears my word, and believes him who sent me, has eternal life, and doesn't come into judgment, but has passed out of death into life. [25] Most certainly, I tell you, the hour comes, and now is, when the dead will hear the Son of God's voice; and those who hear will live. [26] For as the

Great Bible Truths

Father has life in himself, even so he gave to the Son also to have life in himself. ²⁷ He also gave him authority to execute judgment, because he is a son of man.

²⁸ Don't marvel at this, for the hour comes, in which all that are in the tombs will hear his voice, ²⁹ and will come out; those who have done good, to the resurrection of life; and those who have done evil, to the resurrection of judgment. ³⁰ I can of myself do nothing. As I hear, I judge, and my judgment is righteous; because I don't seek my own will, but the will of my Father who sent me.

Testimonies About Jesus

³¹ "If I testify about myself, my witness is not valid. ³² It is another who testifies about me. I know that the testimony which he testifies about me is true.

³³ You have sent to John, and he has testified to the truth. ³⁴ But the testimony which I receive is not from man. However, I say these things that you may be saved. ³⁵ He was the burning and shining lamp, and you were willing to rejoice for a while in his light.

³⁶ But the testimony which I have is greater than that of John, for the works which the Father gave me to accomplish, the very works that I do, testify about me, that the Father has sent me. ³⁷ The Father himself, who sent me, has testified about me. You have neither heard his voice at any time, nor seen his form. ³⁸ You don't have his word living in you; because you don't believe him whom he sent. ³⁹ "You search the Scriptures, because you think that in them you have eternal life; and these are they which testify about me. ⁴⁰ Yet you will not come to me, that you may have life.

⁴¹ I don't receive glory from men. ⁴² But I know you, that you don't have God's love in yourselves. ⁴³ I have come in my Father's name, and you don't receive me. If another comes in his own name, you will receive him. ⁴⁴ How can you believe, who receive glory from one another, and you don't seek the glory that comes from the only God?

⁴⁵ "Don't think that I will accuse you to the Father. There is one who accuses you, even Moses, on whom you have set your hope. ⁴⁶ For if you believed Moses, you would believe me; for he wrote about me. ⁴⁷ But if you don't believe his writings, how will you believe my words?"

1. *What were the two reasons the Jews were angry with Jesus?*

2. *Who did Jesus say gave Him the power to do miracles?*

3. *Is it possible to honor God without honoring Jesus? Why not?*

4. *What two things did Jesus say that testified that He was sent from God?*

5. *What promise did Jesus give to those who heard His word and believed?*

76. THE BREAD OF LIFE
John 6:25-59

After Jesus miraculously fed the five thousand, many people followed Him because they wanted to continue to receive food. Jesus told them not to seek physical food but to look to Him as the bread of life, which is everlasting.

Jesus the Bread of Life

6 [25] When they found him on the other side of the sea, they asked him, "Rabbi, when did you come here?"

[26] Jesus answered them, "Most certainly I tell you, you seek me, not because you saw signs, but because you ate of the loaves, and were filled. [27] Don't work for the food which perishes, but for the food which remains to eternal life, which the Son of Man will give to you. For God the Father has sealed him."

The Work of God

[28] They said therefore to him, "What must we do, that we may work the works of God?"

[29] Jesus answered them, "This is the work of God, that you believe in him whom he has sent."

[30] They said therefore to him, "What then do you do for a sign, that we may see, and believe you? What work do you do? [31] Our fathers ate the manna in the wilderness. As it is written, 'He gave them bread out of heaven to eat.'"

[32] Jesus therefore said to them, "Most certainly, I tell you, it wasn't Moses who gave you the bread out of heaven, but my Father gives you the true bread out of heaven. [33] For the bread of God is that which comes down out of heaven, and gives life to the world."

[34] They said therefore to him, "Lord, always give us this bread."

[35] Jesus said to them, "I am the bread of life. He who comes to me will not be hungry, and he who believes in me will never be thirsty. [36] But I told you that you have seen me, and yet you don't believe. [37] All those whom the Father gives me will come to me. He who comes to me I will in no way throw out. [38] For I have come down from heaven, not to do my own will, but the will of him who sent me. [39] This is the will of my Father who sent me, that of all he has given to me I should lose nothing, but should raise him up at the last day. [40] This is the will of the one who sent me, that everyone who sees the Son, and believes in him, should have eternal life; and I will raise him up at the last day."

[41] The Jews therefore murmured concerning him, because he said, "I am the bread which came down out of heaven." [42] They said, "Isn't this Jesus, the son of Joseph, whose father and mother we know? How then does he say, 'I have come down out of heaven?'"

[43] Therefore Jesus answered them, "Don't murmur among yourselves. [44] No one can come to me unless the Father who sent me draws him, and I will raise him up in the last day. [45] It is written in the prophets, 'They will all be taught by

Great Bible Truths

God.' Therefore everyone who hears from the Father, and has learned, comes to me. ⁴⁶ Not that anyone has seen the Father, except he who is from God. He has seen the Father. ⁴⁷ Most certainly, I tell you, he who believes in me has eternal life. ⁴⁸ I am the bread of life. ⁴⁹ Your fathers ate the manna in the wilderness, and they died. ⁵⁰ This is the bread which comes down out of heaven, that anyone may eat of it and not die. ⁵¹ I am the living bread which came down out of heaven. If anyone eats of this bread, he will live forever. Yes, the bread which I will give for the life of the world is my flesh."

⁵² The Jews therefore contended with one another, saying, "How can this man give us his flesh to eat?"

⁵³ Jesus therefore said to them, "Most certainly I tell you, unless you eat the flesh of the Son of Man and drink his blood, you don't have life in yourselves. ⁵⁴ He who eats my flesh and drinks my blood has eternal life, and I will raise him up at the last day. ⁵⁵ For my flesh is food indeed, and my blood is drink indeed. ⁵⁶ He who eats my flesh and drinks my blood lives in me, and I in him. ⁵⁷ As the living Father sent me, and I live because of the Father; so he who feeds on me, he will also live because of me. ⁵⁸ This is the bread which came down out of heaven—not as our fathers ate the manna, and died. He who eats this bread will live forever." ⁵⁹ He said these things in the synagogue, as he taught in Capernaum.

1. *The people asked what work they had to do to please God. Jesus' answer was, "The work of God is....(your answer here)*

2. *Intrigued by unusual miraculous signs, the people asked for more supernatural signs, real evidence of blessing for themselves, such as food. The divine sign from God was actually standing before their eyes. Who was He? Can you see how they were oblivious of the truth?*

3. *The Father's will is simple. What is it? (v. 40)*

4. *What promise did Jesus make to those who came to Him as the bread of life?*

77. THE LIGHT OF THE WORLD
John 8:12-59

Because Jesus was sent from God, He is the Light of the World who brings people out of darkness and sets them free from the bondage of sin. The Jewish leadership did not believe Jesus' words because they refused to admit that they were sinners. They also refused to believe that Jesus was divinely sent from God to bring divine light into a dark world lost in sin. In this passage Jesus referred several times to His divinity. Unfortunately, few had the spiritual insight to believe in Him.

The Validity of Jesus' Testimony

8 ¹²Again, therefore, Jesus spoke to them, saying, "I am the light of the world. He who follows me will not walk in the darkness, but will have the light of life."

[13]The Pharisees therefore said to him, "You testify about yourself. Your testimony is not valid."

[14] Jesus answered them, "Even if I testify about myself, my testimony is true, for I know where I came from, and where I am going; but you don't know where I came from, or where I am going. [15] You judge according to the flesh. I judge no one. [16] Even if I do judge, my judgment is true, for I am not alone, but I am with the Father who sent me.[17] It's also written in your law that the testimony of two people is valid. [18] I am one who testifies about myself, and the Father who sent me testifies about me."

[19] They said therefore to him, "Where is your Father?"

Jesus answered, "You know neither me, nor my Father. If you knew me, you would know my Father also." [20] Jesus spoke these words in the treasury, as he taught in the temple. Yet no one arrested him, because his hour had not yet come.

The People Misunderstand Jesus

[21] Jesus said therefore again to them, "I am going away, and you will seek me, and you will die in your sins. Where I go, you can't come."

[22] The Jews therefore said, "Will he kill himself, that he says, 'Where I am going, you can't come'?"

[23] He said to them, "You are from beneath. I am from above. You are of this world. I am not of this world. [24] I said therefore to you that you will die in your sins; for unless you believe that I am he, you will die in your sins."

[25] They said therefore to him, "Who are you?"

Jesus said to them, "Just what I have been saying to you from the beginning. [26] I have many things to speak and to judge concerning you. However he who sent me is true; and the things which I heard from him, these I say to the world."

[27] They didn't understand that he spoke to them about the Father. [28] Jesus therefore said to them, "When you have lifted up the Son of Man, then you will know that I am he, and I do nothing of myself, but as my Father taught me, I say these things. [29] He who sent me is with me. The Father hasn't left me alone, for I always do the things that are pleasing to him." [30] As he spoke these things, many believed in him.

Obeying Jesus' Teachings Brings True Liberty of Right Living

[31] Jesus therefore said to those Jews who had believed him, "If you remain in my word, then you are truly my disciples. [32] You will know the truth, and the truth will make you free."

The True Children of Abraham

[33]They answered him, "We are Abraham's offspring, and have never been in bondage to anyone. How do you say, 'You will be made free'?"

[34] Jesus answered them, "Most certainly I tell you, everyone who commits sin is the bondservant of sin. [35] A bondservant doesn't live in the house forever. A son remains forever. [36] If therefore the Son makes you free, you will be free

indeed. ³⁷ I know that you are Abraham's offspring, yet you seek to kill me, because my word finds no place in you. ³⁸ I say the things which I have seen with my Father; and you also do the things which you have seen with your father."

³⁹ They answered him, "Our father is Abraham."

Jesus said to them, "If you were Abraham's children, you would do the works of Abraham. ⁴⁰ But now you seek to kill me, a man who has told you the truth, which I heard from God. Abraham didn't do this. ⁴¹ You do the works of your father."

They said to him, "We were not born of sexual immorality. We have one Father, God."

The Children of the Devil

⁴² Therefore Jesus said to them, "If God were your father, you would love me, for I came out and have come from God. For I haven't come of myself, but he sent me. ⁴³ Why don't you understand my speech? Because you can't hear my word. ⁴⁴ You are of your father, the devil, and you want to do the desires of your father. He was a murderer from the beginning, and doesn't stand in the truth, because there is no truth in him. When he speaks a lie, he speaks on his own; for he is a liar, and its father. ⁴⁵ But because I tell the truth, you don't believe me. ⁴⁶ Which of you convicts me of sin? If I tell the truth, why do you not believe me? ⁴⁷ He who is of God hears the words of God.

For this cause you don't hear, because you are not of God."

The Claims of Jesus About Himself

⁴⁸ Then the Jews answered him, "Don't we say well that you are a Samaritan, and have a demon?"

⁴⁹ Jesus answered, "I don't have a demon, but I honor my Father, and you dishonor me. ⁵⁰ But I don't seek my own glory. There is one who seeks and judges. ⁵¹ Most certainly, I tell you, if a person keeps my word, he will never see death."

⁵² Then the Jews said to him, "Now we know that you have a demon. Abraham died, and the prophets; and you say, 'If a man keeps my word, he will never taste of death.' ⁵³ Are you greater than our father, Abraham, who died? The prophets died. Who do you make yourself out to be?"

⁵⁴ Jesus answered, "If I glorify myself, my glory is nothing. It is my Father who glorifies me, of whom you say that he is our God. ⁵⁵ You have not known him, but I know him. If I said, 'I don't know him,' I would be like you, a liar. But I know him, and keep his word. ⁵⁶ Your father Abraham rejoiced to see my day. He saw it, and was glad."

⁵⁷ The Jews therefore said to him, "You are not yet fifty years old, and have you seen Abraham?"

⁵⁸ Jesus said to them, "Most certainly, I tell you, before Abraham came into existence, I AM."

⁵⁹ Therefore they took up stones to throw at him, but Jesus was hidden, and went out of the temple, having gone through the middle of them, and so passed by.

1. Why did Jesus call Himself the Light of the World?

2. What is it that sets us free?

3. Can we know God the Father without knowing Jesus?

4. How did Jesus describe Satan?

5. Who in the Old Testament said that his name was I AM? Jesus used the same statement about Himself. Is He God?

6. Find the examples where Jesus claimed to be God in this passage.

7. What did Jesus say was the ultimate test to show who belongs to God? (See verses 42-47)

8. What did Jesus say was at stake in this discussion? (v.24)

9. What do you think was the real reason that the Jews did not believe in Jesus?

78. THE GOOD SHEPHERD
John 10:1-42

Jesus is the Good Shepherd. He committed Himself to protecting and caring for His sheep. The sheep of Jesus' flock were those who listened to His voice and followed Him, receiving eternal life because they believed.

The Shepherd and His Flock

10 "Most certainly, I tell you, one who doesn't enter by the door into the sheep fold, but climbs up some other way, the same is a thief and a robber. ² But one who enters in by the door is the shepherd of the sheep. ³ The gatekeeper opens the gate for him, and the sheep listen to his voice. He calls his own sheep by name, and leads them out.⁴ Whenever he brings out his own sheep, he goes before them, and the sheep follow him, for they know his voice. ⁵ They will by no means follow a stranger, but will flee from him; for they don't know the voice of strangers." ⁶ Jesus spoke this parable to them, but they didn't understand what he was telling them.

⁷ Jesus therefore said to them again, "Most certainly, I tell you, I am the sheep's door.⁸ All who came before me are thieves and robbers, but the sheep didn't listen to them. ⁹ I am the door. If anyone enters in by me, he will be saved, and will go in and go out, and will find pasture. ¹⁰ The thief only comes to steal, kill, and destroy. I came that they may have life, and may have it abundantly.

¹¹ I am the good shepherd. The good shepherd lays down his life for the sheep. ¹² He who is a hired hand, and not a shepherd, who doesn't own the sheep, sees the wolf coming, leaves the sheep, and flees. The wolf snatches the

sheep, and scatters them. ¹³ The hired hand flees because he is a hired hand, and doesn't care for the sheep. ¹⁴ I am the good shepherd. I know my own, and I'm known by my own; ¹⁵ even as the Father knows me, and I know the Father. I lay down my life for the sheep. ¹⁶ I have other sheep, which are not of this fold. I must bring them also, and they will hear my voice. They will become one flock with one shepherd. ¹⁷ Therefore the Father loves me, because I lay down my life, that I may take it again. ¹⁸ No one takes it away from me, but I lay it down by myself. I have power to lay it down, and I have power to take it again. I received this commandment from my Father."

¹⁹ Therefore a division arose again among the Jews because of these words. ²⁰ Many of them said, "He has a demon, and is insane! Why do you listen to him?" ²¹ Others said, "These are not the sayings of one possessed by a demon. It isn't possible for a demon to open the eyes of the blind, is it?"

The Unbelief of the Jews

²² It was the Feast of the Dedication at Jerusalem. ²³ It was winter, and Jesus was walking in the temple, in Solomon's porch. ²⁴ The Jews therefore came around him and said to him, "How long will you hold us in suspense? If you are the Christ, tell us plainly."

²⁵ Jesus answered them, "I told you, and you don't believe. The works that I do in my Father's name, these testify about me. ²⁶ But you don't believe, because you are not of my sheep, as I told you. ²⁷ My sheep hear my voice, and I know them, and they follow me. ²⁸ I give eternal life to them. They will never perish, and no one will snatch them out of my hand. ²⁹ My Father, who has given them to me, is greater than all. No one is able to snatch them out of my Father's hand. ³⁰ I and the Father are one."

³¹ Therefore Jews took up stones again to stone him. ³² Jesus answered them, "I have shown you many good works from my Father. For which of those works do you stone me?"

³³ The Jews answered him, "We don't stone you for a good work, but for blasphemy: because you, being a man, make yourself God."

³⁴ Jesus answered them, "Isn't it written in your law, 'I said, you are gods?' ³⁵ If he called them gods, to whom the word of God came (and the Scripture can't be broken),³⁶ do you say of him whom the Father sanctified and sent into the world, 'You blaspheme,' because I said, 'I am the Son of God?' ³⁷ If I don't do the works of my Father, don't believe me. ³⁸ But if I do them, though you don't believe me, believe the works; that you may know and believe that the Father is in me, and I in the Father."

³⁹ They sought again to seize him, and he went out of their hand. ⁴⁰ He went away again beyond the Jordan into the place where John was baptizing at first, and there he stayed.⁴¹ Many came to him. They said, "John indeed did no sign, but everything that John said about this man is true." ⁴² Many believed in him there.

1. *How committed was Jesus to His followers? How was He different from a hired man?*
2. *For whom was Jesus willing to lay down His life. Why?*
3. *If a sheep should become Jesus' disciple – could anyone steal him away from Jesus? Why not? (v.28)*
4. *What did Jesus give the sheep that followed Him?*
5. *Who are the "other sheep" Jesus must bring in also?*

Pause for reflection: *Why do you think that the Jews could not bring themselves to believe in Jesus, even though they saw the divine wonders He did among them? What accounted for their stubborn unbelief?*

D. THE FOLLOWERS OF JESUS

Those who followed Jesus held different positions in society and came from different cultures. It was not only the love and compassion that Jesus showed through His many miracles that drew them. They chose to follow Jesus because they believed Him to be the Son of God, who came to set them free from the sin in their lives.

79. THE CHOSEN TWELVE
Luke 5:1-11; 27-32 and 6:12-16 and 9:1-6

Although there were many people who followed Jesus, He chose twelve special disciples who would continue the work that He had begun. Jesus gave them power and authority to do the same works that He Himself was doing.

Peter, James and John Become Jesus' Disciples

5 Now while the multitude pressed on him and heard the word of God, he was standing by the lake of Gennesaret. ² He saw two boats standing by the lake, but the fishermen had gone out of them, and were washing their nets. ³ He entered into one of the boats, which was Simon's, and asked him to put out a little from the land. He sat down and taught the multitudes from the boat.

⁴ When he had finished speaking, he said to Simon, "Put out into the deep, and let down your nets for a catch."

⁵ Simon answered him, "Master, we worked all night, and took nothing; but at your word I will let down the net."

⁶ When they had done this, they caught a great multitude of fish, and their net was breaking. ⁷ They beckoned to their partners in the other boat, that they should come and help them. They came, and filled both boats, so that they began to sink. ⁸ But Simon Peter, when he saw it, fell down at Jesus' knees, saying, "Depart from me, for I am a sinful man, Lord." ⁹ For he was amazed, and all who were with him, at the catch of fish which they had caught; ¹⁰ and so also were James and John, sons of Zebedee, who were partners with Simon.

Jesus said to Simon, "Don't be afraid. From now on you will be catching people alive."

¹¹ When they had brought their boats to land, they left everything, and followed him.

The Calling of Levi

²⁷ After these things he went out, and saw a tax collector named Levi sitting at the tax office, and said to him, "Follow me!" ²⁸ He left everything, and rose up and followed him.

²⁹ Levi made a great feast for him in his house. There was a great crowd of tax collectors and others who were reclining with them. ³⁰ Their scribes and the Pharisees murmured against his disciples, saying, "Why do you eat and drink with the tax collectors and sinners?"

³¹ Jesus answered them, "Those who are healthy have no need for a physician, but those who are sick do. ³² I have not come to call the righteous, but sinners to repentance."

The Twelve Apostles

6 ¹²In these days, he went out to the mountain to pray, and he continued all night in prayer to God. ¹³ When it was day, he called his disciples, and from them he chose twelve, whom he also named apostles: ¹⁴ Simon, whom he also named Peter; Andrew, his brother; James; John; Philip; Bartholomew; ¹⁵ Matthew; Thomas; James, the son of Alphaeus; Simon, who was called the Zealot; ¹⁶ Judas the son of James; and Judas Iscariot, who also became a traitor.

Jesus Commissions the Twelve to Preach and Heal

9 ¹He called the twelve together, and gave them power and authority over all demons, and to cure diseases. ² He sent them out to preach God's Kingdom and to heal the sick.³ He said to them, "Take nothing for your journey—neither staffs, nor wallet, nor bread, nor money; neither have two coats apiece. ⁴ Into whatever house you enter, stay there, and depart from there. ⁵ As many as don't receive you, when you depart from that city, shake off even the dust from your feet for a testimony against them." ⁶They departed, and went throughout the villages, preaching the Good News, and healing everywhere.

1. *What was the occupation of the first three men who chose to follow Jesus?*

2. *To whom did Jesus come to call to repent of their sins?*

3. *What things were the twelve apostles given power to do?*

80. A RELIGIOUS MAN SEEKS THE TRUTH
John 3:1-21

It was not only uneducated fishermen and government officials who chose to follow Jesus. Some of the highly educated religious leaders, like the man Nicodemus, also came to believe in Jesus as their Savior. Nicodemus honestly sought answers to his curiosity about who Jesus was. Jesus' answer to Nicodemus is the most cited Bible verse ever (v.16). And, although spoken privately to one man, the message was meant for all the world's people.

Jesus Teaches Nicodemus

3 Now there was a man of the Pharisees named Nicodemus, a ruler of the Jews. ² The same came to him by night, and said to him, "Rabbi, we know that you are a teacher come from God, for no one can do these signs that you do, unless God is with him."

³ Jesus answered him, "Most certainly, I tell you, unless one is born anew, he can't see God's Kingdom."

⁴ Nicodemus said to him, "How can a man be born when he is old? Can he enter a second time into his mother's womb, and be born?"

⁵ Jesus answered, "Most certainly I tell you, unless one is born of water and spirit, he can't enter into God's Kingdom! ⁶ That which is born of the flesh is flesh. That which is born of the Spirit is spirit. ⁷ Don't marvel that I said to you, 'You must be born anew.' ⁸ The wind blows where it wants to, and you hear its sound, but don't know where it comes from and where it is going. So is everyone who is born of the Spirit."

⁹ Nicodemus answered him, "How can these things be?"

¹⁰ Jesus answered him, "Are you the teacher of Israel, and don't understand these things? ¹¹ Most certainly I tell you, we speak that which we know, and testify of that which we have seen, and you don't receive our witness. ¹² If I told you earthly things and you don't believe, how will you believe if I tell you heavenly things? ¹³ No one has ascended into heaven, but he who descended out of heaven, the Son of Man, who is in heaven. ¹⁴ As Moses lifted up the serpent in the wilderness, even so must the Son of Man be lifted up, ¹⁵ that whoever believes in him should not perish, but have eternal life.

¹⁶For God so loved the world, that he gave his one and only Son, that whoever believes in him should not perish, but have eternal life. ¹⁷ For God didn't send his Son into the world to judge the world, but that the world should be saved through him. ¹⁸ He who believes in him is not judged. He who doesn't believe has been judged already, because he has not believed in the name of the one and only Son of God. ¹⁹ This is the judgment, that the light has come into the world, and men loved the darkness rather than the light; for their works were evil. ²⁰ For everyone who does evil hates the light, and doesn't come to the light, lest his works would be exposed. ²¹ But he who does the truth comes to the light, that his works may be revealed, that they have been done in God."

1. What things about Jesus made Nicodemus seek Him out? Why do you think Nicodemus was interested in knowing about Jesus?

2. What did Jesus say must happen to a man for him to enter the Kingdom of God?

3. Please repeat verses 16 and 17 out loud to yourself. Why did God give His only Son?

4. What must a person do so that he might not perish? What is the reward for believing in Jesus?

5. Why do some people refuse to come to the light of the truth?

81. THE WOMAN AT THE WELL
John 4:1-42

Jesus came to meet the needs of all people, regardless of their position or level in society. As Jesus spoke to an immoral village woman, He revealed the real source of life and true worship.

Jesus Talks with a Samaritan Woman

4 ¹Therefore when the Lord knew that the Pharisees had heard that Jesus was making and baptizing more disciples than John ² (although Jesus himself didn't baptize, but his disciples), ³ he left Judea, and departed into Galilee. ⁴ He needed to pass through Samaria. ⁵ So he came to a city of Samaria, called Sychar, near the parcel of ground that Jacob gave to his son, Joseph. ⁶ Jacob's well was there. Jesus therefore, being tired from his journey, sat down by the well. It was about the sixth hour. ⁷ A woman of Samaria came to draw water. Jesus said to her, "Give me a drink." ⁸ For his disciples had gone away into the city to buy food.

⁹ The Samaritan woman therefore said to him, "How is it that you, being a Jew, ask for a drink from me, a Samaritan woman?" (For Jews have no dealings with Samaritans.)

¹⁰ Jesus answered her, "If you knew the gift of God, and who it is who says to you, 'Give me a drink,' you would have asked him, and he would have given you living water."

¹¹ The woman said to him, "Sir, you have nothing to draw with, and the well is deep. So where do you get that living water? ¹² Are you greater than our father, Jacob, who gave us the well, and drank of it himself, as did his children, and his livestock?"

¹³ Jesus answered her, "Everyone who drinks of this water will thirst again, ¹⁴ but whoever drinks of the water that I will give him will never thirst again; but the water that I will give him will become in him a well of water springing up to eternal life."

¹⁵ The woman said to him, "Sir, give me this water, so that I don't get thirsty, neither come all the way here to draw."

¹⁶ Jesus said to her, "Go, call your husband, and come here."

¹⁷ The woman answered, "I have no husband."

Jesus said to her, "You said well, 'I have no husband,' ¹⁸ for you have had five husbands; and he whom you now have is not your husband. This you have said truly."

¹⁹ The woman said to him, "Sir, I perceive that you are a prophet. ²⁰ Our fathers worshiped in this mountain, and you Jews say that in Jerusalem is the place where people ought to worship."

Great Bible Truths

²¹ Jesus said to her, "Woman, believe me, the hour comes, when neither in this mountain, nor in Jerusalem, will you worship the Father. ²² You worship that which you don't know. We worship that which we know; for salvation is from the Jews. ²³ But the hour comes, and now is, when the true worshipers will worship the Father in spirit and truth, for the Father seeks such to be his worshipers. ²⁴ God is spirit, and those who worship him must worship in spirit and truth."

²⁵ The woman said to him, "I know that Messiah comes, he who is called Christ. When he has come, he will declare to us all things."

²⁶ Jesus said to her, "I am he, the one who speaks to you."

The Disciples Rejoin Jesus

²⁷ At this, his disciples came. They marveled that he was speaking with a woman; yet no one said, "What are you looking for?" or, "Why do you speak with her?"

²⁸ So the woman left her water pot, and went away into the city, and said to the people, ²⁹ "Come, see a man who told me everything that I did. Can this be the Christ?"

³⁰ They went out of the city, and were coming to him. ³¹ In the meanwhile, the disciples urged him, saying, "Rabbi, eat."

³² But he said to them, "I have food to eat that you don't know about."

³³ The disciples therefore said to one another, "Has anyone brought him something to eat?"

³⁴ Jesus said to them, "My food is to do the will of him who sent me, and to accomplish his work. ³⁵ Don't you say, 'There are yet four months until the harvest?' Behold, I tell you, lift up your eyes, and look at the fields, that they are white for harvest already. ³⁶ He who reaps receives wages, and gathers fruit to eternal life; that both he who sows and he who reaps may rejoice together. ³⁷ For in this the saying is true, 'One sows, and another reaps.' ³⁸ I sent you to reap that for which you haven't labored. Others have labored, and you have entered into their labor."

Many Samaritans Believe

³⁹ From that city many of the Samaritans believed in him because of the word of the woman, who testified, "He told me everything that I did." ⁴⁰ So when the Samaritans came to him, they begged him to stay with them. He stayed there two days. ⁴¹ Many more believed because of his word. ⁴² They said to the woman, "Now we believe, not because of your speaking; for we have heard for ourselves, and know that this is indeed the Christ, the Savior of the world."

> 1. In this encounter can you see how Jesus' concern for people went beyond racial and religious prejudices?
>
> 2. Describe the "living water" that Jesus offers all peoples? How is that different from the water we drink?

3. What is a true worshiper? What kind of worshipers is God the Father seeking?

4. Did you notice that Jesus was drawing people to Himself and not to a religion?

5. Why did the people of the town come to believe in Jesus?

82. BLIND EYES SEE
John 9:1-41

As it was with this blind man, those whom Jesus healed became His faithful followers. Others, who claimed to be religious, such as the Jewish Pharisees, chose to remain spiritually blind because they refused to believe that Jesus was sent from God.

Jesus Heals a Man Born Blind

9 [1] As he passed by, he saw a man blind from birth. [2] His disciples asked him, "Rabbi, who sinned, this man or his parents, that he was born blind?"

[3] Jesus answered, "Neither did this man sin, nor his parents; but, that the works of God might be revealed in him. [4] I must work the works of him who sent me, while it is day. The night is coming, when no one can work. [5] While I am in the world, I am the light of the world."

[6] When he had said this, he spat on the ground, made mud with the saliva, anointed the blind man's eyes with the mud, [7] and said to him, "Go, wash in the pool of Siloam" (which means "Sent"). So he went away, washed, and came back seeing.

[8] The neighbors therefore, and those who saw that he was blind before, said, "Isn't this he who sat and begged?"

[9] Others were saying, "It is he." Still others were saying, "He looks like him."

He said, "I am he." [10] They therefore were asking him, "How were your eyes opened?"

[11] He answered, "A man called Jesus made mud, anointed my eyes, and said to me, 'Go to the pool of Siloam, and wash.' So I went away and washed, and I received sight."

[12] Then they asked him, "Where is he?"

He said, "I don't know."

The Pharisees Investigate the Healing

[13] They brought him who had been blind to the Pharisees. [14] It was a Sabbath when Jesus made the mud and opened his eyes. [15] Again therefore the Pharisees also asked him how he received his sight. He said to them, "He put mud on my eyes, I washed, and I see."

[16] Some therefore of the Pharisees said, "This man is not from God, because he doesn't keep the Sabbath."

Others said, "How can a man who is a sinner do such signs?" There was division among them. ¹⁷ Therefore they asked the blind man again, "What do you say about him, because he opened your eyes?"

He said, "He is a prophet."

¹⁸ The Jews therefore did not believe concerning him, that he had been blind, and had received his sight, until they called the parents of him who had received his sight, ¹⁹ and asked them, "Is this your son, whom you say was born blind? How then does he now see?"

²⁰ His parents answered them, "We know that this is our son, and that he was born blind; ²¹ but how he now sees, we don't know; or who opened his eyes, we don't know. He is of age. Ask him. He will speak for himself." ²² His parents said these things because they feared the Jews; for the Jews had already agreed that if any man would confess him as Christ, he would be put out of the synagogue. ²³ Therefore his parents said, "He is of age. Ask him."

²⁴ So they called the man who was blind a second time, and said to him, "Give glory to God. We know that this man is a sinner."

²⁵ He therefore answered, "I don't know if he is a sinner. One thing I do know: that though I was blind, now I see."

²⁶ They said to him again, "What did he do to you? How did he open your eyes?"

²⁷ He answered them, "I told you already, and you didn't listen. Why do you want to hear it again? You don't also want to become his disciples, do you?"

²⁸ They insulted him and said, "You are his disciple, but we are disciples of Moses. ²⁹ We know that God has spoken to Moses. But as for this man, we don't know where he comes from."

³⁰ The man answered them, "How amazing! You don't know where he comes from, yet he opened my eyes. ³¹ We know that God doesn't listen to sinners, but if anyone is a worshiper of God, and does his will, he listens to him. ³² Since the world began it has never been heard of that anyone opened the eyes of someone born blind. ³³ If this man were not from God, he could do nothing."

³⁴ They answered him, "You were altogether born in sins, and do you teach us?" They threw him out.

Spiritual Blindness

³⁵ Jesus heard that they had thrown him out, and finding him, he said, "Do you believe in the Son of God?"

³⁶ He answered, "Who is he, Lord, that I may believe in him?"

³⁷ Jesus said to him, "You have both seen him, and it is he who speaks with you."

⁸ He said, "Lord, I believe!" and he worshiped him.

³⁹ Jesus said, "I came into this world for judgment, that those who don't see may see; and that those who see may become blind."

⁴⁰ Those of the Pharisees who were with him heard these things, and said to him, "Are we also blind?"

⁴¹ Jesus said to them, "If you were blind, you would have no sin; but now you say, 'We see.' Therefore your sin remains.

> 1. Why was this man born blind?
>
> 2. Describe how his eyes were opened.
>
> 3. In spite of this miracle, why did the Pharisees think that Jesus was not from God?
>
> 4. Why did Jesus tell the Pharisees that they were guilty of sin? What was their sin?

83. CHANGED LIVES
John 8:1-11 and Luke 7:36-50; 18:35-43 and 19:1-10

Jesus was always ready to forgive those who admitted that they were sinners and needed His forgiveness. Here are several people from different levels of society whose lives were dramatically changed when they met Jesus. Nevertheless, it was those who were too proud to confess their own sin who were always eager to condemn others.

The Woman Caught in Adultery

8 ¹ But Jesus went to the Mount of Olives. ² Now very early in the morning, he came again into the temple, and all the people came to him. He sat down, and taught them. ³ The scribes and the Pharisees brought a woman taken in adultery. Having set her in the middle, ⁴ they told him, "Teacher, we found this woman in adultery, in the very act. ⁵ Now in our law, Moses commanded us to stone such women. What then do you say about her?" ⁶ They said this testing him, that they might have something to accuse him of.

But Jesus stooped down, and wrote on the ground with his finger. ⁷ But when they continued asking him, he looked up and said to them, "He who is without sin among you, let him throw the first stone at her." ⁸ Again he stooped down, and with his finger wrote on the ground.

⁹They, when they heard it, being convicted by their conscience, went out one by one, beginning from the oldest, even to the last. Jesus was left alone with the woman where she was, in the middle. ¹⁰ Jesus, standing up, saw her and said, "Woman, where are your accusers? Did no one condemn you?"

¹¹ She said, "No one, Lord."

Jesus said, "Neither do I condemn you. Go your way. From now on, sin no more."

Jesus Anointed by a Sinful Woman

7 ³⁶One of the Pharisees invited him to eat with him. He entered into the Pharisee's house, and sat at the table. ³⁷ Behold, a woman in the city who was a sinner, when she knew that he was reclining in the Pharisee's house, she brought an alabaster jar of ointment.³⁸ Standing behind at his feet weeping, she began to wet his feet with her tears, and she wiped them with the hair of her head, kissed his feet, and anointed them with the ointment.

[39] Now when the Pharisee who had invited him saw it, he said to himself, "This man, if he were a prophet, would have perceived who and what kind of woman this is who touches him, that she is a sinner."

[40] Jesus answered him, "Simon, I have something to tell you."

He said, "Teacher, say on."

[41] A certain lender had two debtors. The one owed five hundred denarii, and the other fifty. [42] When they couldn't pay, he forgave them both. Which of them therefore will love him most?"

[43] Simon answered, "He, I suppose, to whom he forgave the most."

He said to him, "You have judged correctly."

[44] Turning to the woman, he said to Simon, "Do you see this woman? I entered into your house, and you gave me no water for my feet, but she has wet my feet with her tears, and wiped them with the hair of her head. [45] You gave me no kiss, but she, since the time I came in, has not ceased to kiss my feet. [46] You didn't anoint my head with oil, but she has anointed my feet with ointment. [47] Therefore I tell you, her sins, which are many, are forgiven, for she loved much. But to whom little is forgiven, the same loves little."

[48] He said to her, "Your sins are forgiven."

[49] Those who sat at the table with him began to say to themselves, "Who is this who even forgives sins?"

[50] He said to the woman, "Your faith has saved you. Go in peace."

A Blind Beggar Receives His Sight

18 [35] As he came near Jericho, a certain blind man sat by the road, begging. [36] Hearing a multitude going by, he asked what this meant. [37] They told him that Jesus of Nazareth was passing by.

[38] He cried out, "Jesus, you son of David, have mercy on me!"

[39] Those who led the way rebuked him, that he should be quiet; but he cried out all the more, "You son of David, have mercy on me!"

[40] Standing still, Jesus commanded him to be brought to him. When he had come near, he asked him, [41] "What do you want me to do?"

He said, "Lord, that I may see again."

Jesus said to him, "Receive your sight. Your faith has healed you." Immediately he received his sight, and followed him, glorifying God. All the people, when they saw it, praised God.

Zacchaeus the Tax Collector

19 [1] He entered and was passing through Jericho. [2] There was a man named Zacchaeus. He was a chief tax collector, and he was rich. [3] He was trying to see who Jesus was, and couldn't because of the crowd, because he was short. [4] He ran on ahead, and climbed up into a sycamore tree to see him, for he was going to pass that way.

[5] When Jesus came to the place, he looked up and saw him, and said to him, "Zacchaeus, hurry and come down, for today I must stay at your house." [6] He hurried, came down, and received him joyfully.

⁷ When they saw it, they all murmured, saying, "He has gone in to lodge with a man who is a sinner."

⁸ Zacchaeus stood and said to the Lord, "Behold, Lord, half of my goods I give to the poor. If I have wrongfully exacted anything of anyone, I restore four times as much."

⁹ Jesus said to him, "Today, salvation has come to this house, because he also is a son of Abraham. ¹⁰ For the Son of Man came to seek and to save that which was lost."

> 1. Why did none of the Pharisees throw a stone at the woman? How did Jesus' response exemplify the "grace and truth" that we saw in John 1:17? (see selection #69 John.1:14)
>
> 2. Why did the woman anoint the feet of Jesus?
>
> 3. What did Jesus see in this woman that Simon did not?
>
> 4. Tell what Jesus said to each of these women.
>
> 5. Why did Jesus heal the blind beggar? If Jesus asked, "What do you want me to do for you?" What would you say?
>
> 6. How do we know that Zacchaeus' life was changed?

E. THE MESSAGE OF CHRIST

Jesus said that He must preach the good news of the Kingdom of God because that was why He was sent. This was His message to all who would listen, that God was making it possible for all who would repent of their sins to come into His kingdom. Jesus made it very clear that He did not come to set up an earthly kingdom, but He did want to rule in the hearts of all who would receive Him as their Savior.

84. LOST AND FOUND
Luke 15:1-32

Jesus wanted people to know that God searches like a shepherd and waits like a father to receive those who want to come to Him. Like the son in this story, we must be willing to turn from our sin as we seek the Father's forgiveness.

The Story of the Lost Sheep

15 ¹Now all the tax collectors and sinners were coming close to him to hear him. ² The Pharisees and the scribes murmured, saying, "This man welcomes sinners, and eats with them."

³ He told them this parable. ⁴ "Which of you men, if you had one hundred sheep, and lost one of them, wouldn't leave the ninety-nine in the wilderness, and go after the one that was lost, until he found it? ⁵ When he has found it, he carries it on his shoulders, rejoicing. ⁶ When he comes home, he calls together his friends and his neighbors, saying to them, 'Rejoice with me, for I have found my sheep which was lost!' ⁷ I tell you that even so there will be more joy in

heaven over one sinner who repents, than over ninety-nine righteous people who need no repentance.

The Story of the Lost Coin
[8] Or what woman, if she had ten drachma coins, if she lost one drachma coin, wouldn't light a lamp, sweep the house, and seek diligently until she found it? [9] When she has found it, she calls together her friends and neighbors, saying, 'Rejoice with me, for I have found the drachma which I had lost.' [10] Even so, I tell you, there is joy in the presence of the angels of God over one sinner repenting."

The Story of the Lost Son
[11] He said, "A certain man had two sons. [12] The younger of them said to his father, 'Father, give me my share of your property.' He divided his livelihood between them.

[13] Not many days after, the younger son gathered all of this together and traveled into a far country. There he wasted his property with riotous living. [14] When he had spent all of it, there arose a severe famine in that country, and he began to be in need. [15] He went and joined himself to one of the citizens of that country, and he sent him into his fields to feed pigs. [16] He wanted to fill his belly with the husks that the pigs ate, but no one gave him any.

[17] But when he came to himself he said, 'How many hired servants of my father's have bread enough to spare, and I'm dying with hunger! [18] I will get up and go to my father, and will tell him, "Father, I have sinned against heaven, and in your sight. [19] I am no more worthy to be called your son. Make me as one of your hired servants."'

[20] "He arose, and came to his father. But while he was still far off, his father saw him, and was moved with compassion, and ran, and fell on his neck, and kissed him.

[21] The son said to him, 'Father, I have sinned against heaven, and in your sight. I am no longer worthy to be called your son.'

[22] "But the father said to his servants, 'Bring out the best robe, and put it on him. Put a ring on his hand, and shoes on his feet. [23] Bring the fattened calf, kill it, and let us eat, and celebrate; [24] for this, my son, was dead, and is alive again. He was lost, and is found.' They began to celebrate.

[25] "Now his elder son was in the field. As he came near to the house, he heard music and dancing. [26] He called one of the servants to him, and asked what was going on. [27] He said to him, 'Your brother has come, and your father has killed the fattened calf, because he has received him back safe and healthy.'

[28] But he was angry, and would not go in. Therefore his father came out, and begged him. [29] But he answered his father, 'Behold, these many years I have served you, and I never disobeyed a commandment of yours, but you never gave me a goat, that I might celebrate with my friends. [30] But when this, your son, came, who has devoured your living with prostitutes, you killed the fattened calf for him.'

Great Bible Truths

³¹ "He said to him, 'Son, you are always with me, and all that is mine is yours. ³² But it was appropriate to celebrate and be glad, for this, your brother, was dead, and is alive again. He was lost, and is found.'"

1. Is every person in the world valuable in God's eyes?
2. Why is there rejoicing in heaven?
3. Why did the son decide to return home to the father?
4. How did the father react when he saw his son returning?
5. What did the son say to the father that showed he was sorry for his sin?
6. Why did the father want to celebrate?

85. SECRETS OF THE KINGDOM
Matthew 13:1-23 and 44-52; Luke 17:20-21

Jesus taught the secrets of the Kingdom in stories called parables. In the parable of the sower Jesus showed how different people received His message and allowed it to either die or grow in their hearts.

The Parable of the Sower

13 ¹On that day Jesus went out of the house, and sat by the seaside. ² Great multitudes gathered to him, so that he entered into a boat, and sat, and all the multitude stood on the beach. ³ He spoke to them many things in parables, saying, "Behold, a farmer went out to sow. ⁴ As he sowed, some seeds fell by the roadside, and the birds came and devoured them. ⁵ Others fell on rocky ground, where they didn't have much soil, and immediately they sprang up, because they had no depth of earth. ⁶ When the sun had risen, they were scorched. Because they had no root, they withered away. ⁷ Others fell among thorns. The thorns grew up and choked them. ⁸ Others fell on good soil, and yielded fruit: some one hundred times as much, some sixty, and some thirty. ⁹ He who has ears to hear, let him hear."

Why Jesus Used Stories (Parables) to Teach

¹⁰ The disciples came, and said to him, "Why do you speak to them in parables?"

¹¹ He answered them, "To you it is given to know the mysteries of the Kingdom of Heaven, but it is not given to them. ¹² For whoever has, to him will be given, and he will have abundance, but whoever doesn't have, from him will be taken away even that which he has. ¹³ Therefore I speak to them in parables, because seeing they don't see, and hearing, they don't hear, neither do they understand. ¹⁴ In them the prophecy of Isaiah is fulfilled, which says,

> 'By hearing you will hear, and will in no way understand;
> Seeing you will see, and will in no way perceive:
> ¹⁵for this people's heart has grown callous,

> their ears are dull of hearing,
> they have closed their eyes;
>> or else perhaps they might perceive with their eyes,
> hear with their ears, understand with their heart,
>> and would turn again;
> and I would heal them.

[16] "But blessed are your eyes, for they see; and your ears, for they hear. [17] For most certainly I tell you that many prophets and righteous men desired to see the things which you see, and didn't see them; and to hear the things which you hear, and didn't hear them.

The Parable of the Sower Explained

[18] "Hear, then, the parable of the farmer. [19] When anyone hears the word of the Kingdom, and doesn't understand it, the evil one comes, and snatches away that which has been sown in his heart. This is what was sown by the roadside. [20] What was sown on the rocky places, this is he who hears the word, and immediately with joy receives it; [21] yet he has no root in himself, but endures for a while. When oppression or persecution arises because of the word, immediately he stumbles. [22] What was sown among the thorns, this is he who hears the word, but the cares of this age and the deceitfulness of riches choke the word, and he becomes unfruitful. [23] What was sown on the good ground, this is he who hears the word, and understands it, who most certainly bears fruit, and produces, some one hundred times as much, some sixty, and some thirty."

Parables of the Hidden Treasure, the Pearl and the Dragnet

[44] "Again, the Kingdom of Heaven is like a treasure hidden in the field, which a man found, and hid. In his joy, he goes and sells all that he has, and buys that field.

[45] "Again, the Kingdom of Heaven is like a man who is a merchant seeking fine pearls, [46] who having found one pearl of great price, he went and sold all that he had, and bought it. [47] "Again, the Kingdom of Heaven is like a dragnet, that was cast into the sea, and gathered some fish of every kind, [48] which, when it was filled, they drew up on the beach. They sat down, and gathered the good into containers, but the bad they threw away. [49] So will it be in the end of the world. The angels will come and separate the wicked from among the righteous, [50] and will cast them into the furnace of fire. There will be the weeping and the gnashing of teeth."

[51] Jesus said to them, "Have you understood all these things?" They answered him, "Yes, Lord."

[52] He said to them, "Therefore every scribe who has been made a disciple in the Kingdom of Heaven is like a man who is a householder, who brings out of his treasure new and old things."

Great Bible Truths

Coming of the Kingdom of God
17 [20]Being asked by the Pharisees when God's Kingdom would come, he answered them, "God's Kingdom doesn't come with observation; [21] neither will they say, 'Look, here!' or, 'Look, there!' for behold, God's Kingdom is within you."

   1. Why did Jesus speak to the people in parables?
   2. What was the seed and who was the farmer/sower?
   3. Looking at the four types of soils Jesus mentioned, what were the characteristics of each, and what happened to the seed in each soil?
   4. Which soil best describes the condition of your heart right now?
   5. What is the Kingdom of God like, and where is the Kingdom of God?

86. THE RICH AND THE POOR
Mark 12:41-44 and Luke 12:13-21, 32-34 and 18:18-30

The values of God's Kingdom are much different from those of the world. Jesus taught that we should not seek material riches but desire the treasures of heaven, which have eternal value.

The Widow's Offering, True Giving
12 [41]Jesus sat down opposite the treasury, and saw how the multitude cast money into the treasury. Many who were rich cast in much. [42] A poor widow came, and she cast in two small brass coins, which equal a quadrans coin.

[43] He called his disciples to himself, and said to them, "Most certainly I tell you, this poor widow gave more than all those who are giving into the treasury, [44] for they all gave out of their abundance, but she, out of her poverty, gave all that she had to live on."

Parable of the Pathetic Foolish Man
12 [13]One of the multitude said to him, "Teacher, tell my brother to divide the inheritance with me."

[14] But he said to him, "Man, who made me a judge or an arbitrator over you?" [15] He said to them, "Beware! Keep yourselves from covetousness, for a man's life doesn't consist of the abundance of the things which he possesses."

[16] He spoke a parable to them, saying, "The ground of a certain rich man produced abundantly. [17] He reasoned within himself, saying, 'What will I do, because I don't have room to store my crops?'

[18] He said, 'This is what I will do. I will pull down my barns, and build bigger ones, and there I will store all my grain and my goods. [19] I will tell my soul, "Soul, you have many goods laid up for many years. Take your ease, eat, drink, be merry."'

[20] "But God said to him, 'You foolish one, tonight your soul is required of you. The things which you have prepared—whose will they be?'

²¹ So is he who lays up treasure for himself, and is not rich toward God."

³² Don't be afraid, little flock, for it is your Father's good pleasure to give you the Kingdom. ³³ Sell that which you have, and give gifts to the needy. Make for yourselves purses which don't grow old, a treasure in the heavens that doesn't fail, where no thief approaches, neither moth destroys. ³⁴For where your treasure is, there will your heart be also.

A Rich Man's Question

18 ¹⁸A certain ruler asked him, saying, "Good Teacher, what shall I do to inherit eternal life?"

¹⁹ Jesus asked him, "Why do you call me good? No one is good, except one—God. ²⁰ You know the commandments: 'Don't commit adultery,' 'Don't murder,' 'Don't steal,' 'Don't give false testimony,' 'Honor your father and your mother.'"

²¹ He said, "I have observed all these things from my youth up."

²² When Jesus heard these things, he said to him, "You still lack one thing. Sell all that you have, and distribute it to the poor. You will have treasure in heaven. Come, follow me."

²³ But when he heard these things, he became very sad, for he was very rich. ²⁴ Jesus, seeing that he became very sad, said, "How hard it is for those who have riches to enter into God's Kingdom! ²⁵ For it is easier for a camel to enter in through a needle's eye, than for a rich man to enter into God's Kingdom."

Who Can Be Saved

²⁶ Those who heard it said, "Then who can be saved?"

²⁷ But he said, "The things which are impossible with men are possible with God."

²⁸ Peter said, "Look, we have left everything, and followed you."

²⁹ He said to them, "Most certainly I tell you, there is no one who has left house, or wife, or brothers, or parents, or children, for God's Kingdom's sake, ³⁰ who will not receive many times more in this time, and in the world to come, eternal life."

> 1. Why did Jesus say that the widow put more money into the treasury than all the others?
>
> 2. Why was the rich fool not rich toward God?
>
> 3. Where did Jesus say that our heart is? Why?
>
> 4. Why did the rich ruler who came to see Jesus become sad and disappointed? What was his dilemma?
>
> 5. What are the rewards for those who have left all to follow Jesus?

87. HEAVEN OR HELL
Matthew 13:24-30; 36-43 and Luke 14:15-24
and Luke 16:19-31

Jesus explained that after death there are rich rewards in heaven for the righteous sons of His Kingdom. There is also a place of terrible torment, called hell, for those who refuse to believe in Jesus and choose the way of the evil one. All of us are invited to the Kingdom of God, but only those who are humble in heart will taste of God's banquet.

The Parable of the Weeds

13 ²⁴He set another parable before them, saying, "The Kingdom of Heaven is like a man who sowed good seed in his field, ²⁵ but while people slept, his enemy came and sowed darnel weeds also among the wheat, and went away. ²⁶ But when the blade sprang up and produced fruit, then the darnel weeds appeared also.

²⁷ The servants of the householder came and said to him, 'Sir, didn't you sow good seed in your field? Where did these darnel weeds come from?'

²⁸ "He said to them, 'An enemy has done this.'
"The servants asked him, 'Do you want us to go and gather them up?'

²⁹ "But he said, 'No, lest perhaps while you gather up the darnel weeds, you root up the wheat with them. ³⁰ Let both grow together until the harvest, and in the harvest time I will tell the reapers, "First, gather up the darnel weeds, and bind them in bundles to burn them; but gather the wheat into my barn."'"

The Parable of the Weeds Explained

³⁶Then Jesus sent the multitudes away, and went into the house. His disciples came to him, saying, "Explain to us the parable of the darnel weeds of the field."

³⁷He answered them, "He who sows the good seed is the Son of Man, ³⁸ the field is the world; and the good seed, these are the children of the Kingdom; and the darnel weeds are the children of the evil one. ³⁹ The enemy who sowed them is the devil. The harvest is the end of the age, and the reapers are angels.

⁴⁰ As therefore the darnel weeds are gathered up and burned with fire; so will it be at the end of this age. ⁴¹ The Son of Man will send out his angels, and they will gather out of his Kingdom all things that cause stumbling, and those who do iniquity, ⁴² and will cast them into the furnace of fire. There will be weeping and the gnashing of teeth. ⁴³ Then the righteous will shine like the sun in the Kingdom of their Father. He who has ears to hear, let him hear.

The Parable of the Great Banquet

14 ¹⁵When one of those who sat at the table with him heard these things, he said to him, "Blessed is he who will feast in God's Kingdom!"

¹⁶ But he said to him, "A certain man made a great supper, and he invited many people.¹⁷ He sent out his servant at supper time to tell those who were invited, 'Come, for everything is ready now.'

¹⁸ They all as one began to make excuses. "The first said to him, 'I have bought a field, and I must go and see it. Please have me excused.'

¹⁹"Another said, 'I have bought five yoke of oxen, and I must go try them out. Please have me excused.'

²⁰"Another said, 'I have married a wife, and therefore I can't come.'

²¹"That servant came, and told his lord these things. Then the master of the house, being angry, said to his servant, 'Go out quickly into the streets and lanes of the city, and bring in the poor, maimed, blind, and lame.'

²²"The servant said, 'Lord, it is done as you commanded, and there is still room.'

²³"The lord said to the servant, 'Go out into the highways and hedges, and compel them to come in, that my house may be filled. ²⁴ For I tell you that none of those men who were invited will taste of my supper.'"

The Rich Man and Lazarus

16 ¹⁹"Now there was a certain rich man, and he was clothed in purple and fine linen, living in luxury every day. ²⁰ A certain beggar, named Lazarus, was laid at his gate, full of sores,²¹ and desiring to be fed with the crumbs that fell from the rich man's table. Yes, even the dogs came and licked his sores.

²² The beggar died, and he was carried away by the angels to Abraham's bosom. The rich man also died, and was buried. ²³ In Hades, he lifted up his eyes, being in torment, and saw Abraham far off, and Lazarus at his bosom.²⁴ He cried and said, 'Father Abraham, have mercy on me, and send Lazarus, that he may dip the tip of his finger in water, and cool my tongue! For I am in anguish in this flame.'

²⁵ "But Abraham said, 'Son, remember that you, in your lifetime, received your good things, and Lazarus, in the same way, bad things. But now here he is comforted and you are in anguish. ²⁶ Besides all this, between us and you there is a great gulf fixed, that those who want to pass from here to you are not able, and that no one may cross over from there to us.'

²⁷ "He said, 'I ask you therefore, father, that you would send him to my father's house;²⁸ for I have five brothers, that he may testify to them, so they won't also come into this place of torment.'

²⁹"But Abraham said to him, 'They have Moses and the prophets. Let them listen to them.'

³⁰"He said, 'No, father Abraham, but if one goes to them from the dead, they will repent.'

³¹"He said to him, 'If they don't listen to Moses and the prophets, neither will they be persuaded if one rises from the dead.'"

> 1. Tell what each of these represent: the sower, the field, the good seed, the enemy, the weeds and the harvest
>
> 2. What was the enemy trying to accomplish by sowing weeds among the good seed? Why was the farmer patient in letting the weeds stay until harvest time?

3. At the end of the age, what will happen to those who do evil? What will happen to the righteous? Do you see the conflict between good and evil in today's world?

4. What do you think the "great banquet" (v.16) represented?

5. Who did the master choose to invite after the proud and satisfied people rejected his invitation?

6. Jesus makes it clear that life continues after death. What happened to Lazarus after he died? What happened to the rich man? Why?

7. Why did Abraham refuse to send someone to warn the rich man's brothers?

8. Can a person go from hell to heaven, even if he sees his errors and wants to change his lifestyle?

F. THE TEACHINGS OF JESUS

During the three years of Jesus' ministry, He did more than heal the sick and perform miracles. He also spent much time teaching His disciples by giving them instructions on how to live lives that would be pleasing to God. The next Bible selections are taken from what is called Jesus' Sermon on the Mount, as well as from other teachings.

88. WORDS TO LIVE BY
Matthew 5:1-26

Jesus said that those who are blessed in God's sight are not the rich and the proud but those whose hearts are pure before Him. Jesus gave his followers special instructions by which to live and promised great rewards for those who practiced His words.

The Beatitudes

5 ¹Seeing the multitudes, he went up onto the mountain. When he had sat down, his disciples came to him. ² He opened his mouth and taught them, saying,
"Blessed are the poor in spirit,
for theirs is the Kingdom of Heaven.
⁴ Blessed are those who mourn,
for they shall be comforted.
⁵ Blessed are the gentle,
for they shall inherit the earth.
⁶ Blessed are those who hunger and thirst after righteousness,
for they shall be filled.
⁷ Blessed are the merciful,
for they shall obtain mercy.

> ⁸ Blessed are the pure in heart,
>> for they shall see God.
> ⁹ Blessed are the peacemakers,
>> for they shall be called children of God.
> ¹⁰Blessed are those who have been persecuted
>> for righteousness' sake,
>>> for theirs is the Kingdom of Heaven.
> ¹¹ "Blessed are you when people reproach you, persecute you,
>> and say all kinds of evil against you falsely, for my sake.
> ¹² Rejoice, and be exceedingly glad,
>> for great is your reward in heaven.
> For that is how they persecuted the prophets
>> who were before you.

Salt and Light

¹³ "You are the salt of the earth, but if the salt has lost its flavor, with what will it be salted? It is then good for nothing, but to be cast out and trodden under the feet of men.¹⁴ You are the light of the world. A city located on a hill can't be hidden. ¹⁵ Neither do you light a lamp, and put it under a measuring basket, but on a stand; and it shines to all who are in the house. ¹⁶ Even so, let your light shine before men; that they may see your good works, and glorify your Father who is in heaven.

Fulfillment of the Law

¹⁷ "Don't think that I came to destroy the law or the prophets. I didn't come to destroy, but to fulfill. ¹⁸ For most certainly, I tell you, until heaven and earth pass away, not even one smallest letter or one tiny pen stroke shall in any way pass away from the law, until all things are accomplished. ¹⁹ Whoever, therefore, shall break one of these least commandments, and teach others to do so, shall be called least in the Kingdom of Heaven; but whoever shall do and teach them shall be called great in the Kingdom of Heaven. ²⁰ For I tell you that unless your righteousness exceeds that of the scribes and Pharisees, there is no way you will enter into the Kingdom of Heaven.

Murder

²¹ "You have heard that it was said to the ancient ones, 'You shall not murder;' and 'Whoever murders will be in danger of the judgment.' ²² But I tell you, that everyone who is angry with his brother without a cause will be in danger of the judgment; and whoever says to his brother, 'Raca!' will be in danger of the council; and whoever says, 'You fool!' will be in danger of the fire of Gehenna [Hell].

Reconciliation Makes the Heart Pure

²³ "If therefore you are offering your gift at the altar, and there remember that your brother has anything against you, ²⁴ leave your gift there before the altar, and go your way. First be reconciled to your brother, and then come and offer

Great Bible Truths

your gift. ²⁵ Agree with your adversary quickly, while you are with him on the way; lest perhaps the prosecutor deliver you to the judge, and the judge deliver you to the officer, and you be cast into prison. ²⁶ Most certainly I tell you, you shall by no means get out of there, until you have paid the last penny.

> 1. Jesus described a godly character in the first eight beatitudes. Can you see that they describe who we are, not what we must do?
>
> 2. How are Jesus' followers to be salt and light to the world?
>
> 3. Do you see the connection between anger and murder?
>
> 4. Why is it so important to be reconciled to our brothers and also to our adversaries?

89. THE ISSUES OF LIFE
Matthew 5:27-48

Jesus dealt with many issues of life that are faced by all people all the time. His teachings required His followers to live lives that were holy, which was much different from the way they had lived before.

Adultery

5 ²⁷"You have heard that it was said, 'You shall not commit adultery;' ²⁸ but I tell you that everyone who gazes at a woman to lust after her has committed adultery with her already in his heart. ²⁹ If your right eye causes you to stumble, pluck it out and throw it away from you. For it is more profitable for you that one of your members should perish, than for your whole body to be cast into Gehenna [Hell]. ³⁰ If your right hand causes you to stumble, cut it off, and throw it away from you. For it is more profitable for you that one of your members should perish, than for your whole body to be cast into Gehenna [Hell].

Divorce

³¹ "It was also said, 'Whoever shall put away his wife, let him give her a writing of divorce,' ³² but I tell you that whoever puts away his wife, except for the cause of sexual immorality, makes her an adulteress; and whoever marries her when she is put away commits adultery.

Oaths

³³ "Again you have heard that it was said to them of old time, 'You shall not make false vows, but shall perform to the Lord your vows,' ³⁴ but I tell you, don't swear at all: neither by heaven, for it is the throne of God; ³⁵ nor by the earth, for it is the footstool of his feet; nor by Jerusalem, for it is the city of the great King. ³⁶ Neither shall you swear by your head, for you can't make one hair white or black. ³⁷ But let your 'Yes' be 'Yes' and your 'No' be 'No.' Whatever is more than these is of the evil one.

Revenge

38 "You have heard that it was said, 'An eye for an eye, and a tooth for a tooth.' 39 But I tell you, don't resist him who is evil; but whoever strikes you on your right cheek, turn to him the other also. 40 If anyone sues you to take away your coat, let him have your cloak also. 41 Whoever compels you to go one mile, go with him two. 42 Give to him who asks you, and don't turn away him who desires to borrow from you.

Love for Enemies

43 "You have heard that it was said, 'You shall love your neighbor and hate your enemy.' 44 But I tell you, love your enemies, bless those who curse you, do good to those who hate you, and pray for those who mistreat you and persecute you, 45 that you may be children of your Father who is in heaven. For he makes his sun to rise on the evil and the good, and sends rain on the just and the unjust. 46 For if you love those who love you, what reward do you have? Don't even the tax collectors do the same? 47 If you only greet your friends, what more do you do than others? Don't even the tax collectors do the same? 48 Therefore you shall be perfect, just as your Father in heaven is perfect.

> 1. How do people commit adultery or any other sin in their hearts?
>
> 2. How should we act toward those who have done wrong to us?
>
> 3. In behavior toward others, what unique characteristic distinguishes Jesus' followers from pagans?

90. TREASURE AND REWARDS
Matthew 6:1-34

Jesus taught His disciples that they should live to please God and not men. If we follow His instructions, we will be given all that we need for this life, as well as rich rewards in heaven.

Giving to the Needy

6 "Be careful that you don't do your charitable giving before men, to be seen by them, or else you have no reward from your Father who is in heaven. 2 Therefore when you do merciful deeds, don't sound a trumpet before yourself, as the hypocrites do in the synagogues and in the streets, that they may get glory from men. Most certainly I tell you, they have received their reward. 3 But when you do merciful deeds, don't let your left hand know what your right hand does, 4 so that your merciful deeds may be in secret, then your Father who sees in secret will reward you openly.

Prayer

⁵ "When you pray, you shall not be as the hypocrites, for they love to stand and pray in the synagogues and in the corners of the streets, that they may be seen by men. Most certainly, I tell you, they have received their reward. ⁶ But you, when you pray, enter into your inner room, and having shut your door, pray to your Father who is in secret, and your Father who sees in secret will reward you openly. ⁷ In praying, don't use vain repetitions, as the Gentiles do; for they think that they will be heard for their much speaking. ⁸ Therefore don't be like them, for your Father knows what things you need, before you ask him.

The Lord's Prayer

⁹ Pray like this:

> 'Our Father in heaven,
> may your name be kept holy.
> ¹⁰ Let your Kingdom come.
> Let your will be done, as in heaven, so on earth.
> ¹¹ Give us today our daily bread.
> ¹² Forgive us our debts,
> as we also forgive our debtors.
> ¹³ Bring us not into temptation,
> but deliver us from the evil one.
> For yours is the Kingdom,
> the power, and the glory forever. Amen.

¹⁴ "For if you forgive men their trespasses, your heavenly Father will also forgive you. ¹⁵ But if you don't forgive men their trespasses, neither will your Father forgive your trespasses.

Fasting

¹⁶ "Moreover when you fast, don't be like the hypocrites, with sad faces. For they disfigure their faces, that they may be seen by men to be fasting. Most certainly I tell you, they have received their reward. ¹⁷ But you, when you fast, anoint your head, and wash your face; ¹⁸ so that you are not seen by men to be fasting, but by your Father who is in secret, and your Father, who sees in secret, will reward you.

Treasures in Heaven

¹⁹ "Don't lay-up treasures for yourselves on the earth, where moth and rust consume, and where thieves break through and steal; ²⁰ but lay up for yourselves treasures in heaven, where neither moth nor rust consume, and where thieves don't break through and steal; ²¹ for where your treasure is, there your heart will be also.

Watch Your Eyes

²² "The lamp of the body is the eye. If therefore your eye is sound, your whole body will be full of light. ²³ But if your eye is evil, your whole body will be full

of darkness. If therefore the light that is in you is darkness, how great is the darkness!

²⁴"No one can serve two masters, for either he will hate the one and love the other; or else he will be devoted to one and despise the other. You can't serve both God and Mammon.

Do Not Worry

²⁵Therefore I tell you, don't be anxious for your life: what you will eat, or what you will drink; nor yet for your body, what you will wear. Isn't life more than food, and the body more than clothing? ²⁶ See the birds of the sky, that they don't sow, neither do they reap, nor gather into barns. Your heavenly Father feeds them. Aren't you of much more value than they?

²⁷ "Which of you, by being anxious, can add one moment to his lifespan? ²⁸ Why are you anxious about clothing? Consider the lilies of the field, how they grow. They don't toil, neither do they spin, ²⁹yet I tell you that even Solomon in all his glory was not dressed like one of these. ³⁰ But if God so clothes the grass of the field, which today exists, and tomorrow is thrown into the oven, won't he much more clothe you, you of little faith?

³¹ "Therefore don't be anxious, saying, 'What will we eat?', 'What will we drink?' or, 'With what will we be clothed?' ³² For the Gentiles seek after all these things; for your heavenly Father knows that you need all these things.

Seek First the Kingdom of God

³³ But seek first God's Kingdom, and his righteousness; and all these things will be given to you as well. ³⁴ Therefore don't be anxious for tomorrow, for tomorrow will be anxious for itself. Each day's own evil is sufficient.

1. How are we supposed to give?

2. How does God want us to pray?

3. Why do we need to forgive others?

4. What is the connection between the eye and the body?

5. Why can't we serve both God and money?

6. Why does Jesus tell us not to worry?

7. What simple advice does Jesus give that insures that we can live as He wants us to? (v.33)

91. THE NARROW ROAD
Matthew 7:1-29

Living as Jesus tells us to is not always easy and requires walking on the narrow road. Jesus' followers are known by the good fruit in their lives and they are blessed for their wisdom.

Judging Others

7 "Don't judge, so that you won't be judged. [2] For with whatever judgment you judge, you will be judged; and with whatever measure you measure, it will be measured to you. [3] Why do you see the speck that is in your brother's eye, but don't consider the beam that is in your own eye? [4] Or how will you tell your brother, 'Let me remove the speck from your eye;' and behold, the beam is in your own eye? [5] You hypocrite! First remove the beam out of your own eye, and then you can see clearly to remove the speck out of your brother's eye.

Be Discerning and Discreet with the Truth

[6] "Don't give that which is holy to the dogs, neither throw your pearls before the pigs, lest perhaps they trample them under their feet, and turn and tear you to pieces.

Ask, Seek, Knock

[7] "Ask, and it will be given you. Seek, and you will find. Knock, and it will be opened for you. [8] For everyone who asks receives. He who seeks finds. To him who knocks it will be opened. [9] Or who is there among you, who, if his son asks him for bread, will give him a stone? [10] Or if he asks for a fish, who will give him a serpent? [11] If you then, being evil, know how to give good gifts to your children, how much more will your Father who is in heaven give good things to those who ask him!

Jesus Explains the Golden Rule

[12] Therefore whatever you desire for men to do to you, you shall also do to them; for this is the law and the prophets.

The Narrow and Wide Gates

[13] "Enter in by the narrow gate; for wide is the gate and broad is the way that leads to destruction, and many are those who enter in by it. [14] How narrow is the gate, and restricted is the way that leads to life! Few are those who find it.

A Tree and Its Fruits

[15] "Beware of false prophets, who come to you in sheep's clothing, but inwardly are ravening wolves. [16] By their fruits you will know them. Do you gather grapes from thorns, or figs from thistles? [17] Even so, every good tree produces good fruit; but the corrupt tree produces evil fruit. [18] A good tree can't produce evil fruit, neither can a corrupt tree produce good fruit. [19] Every tree that doesn't grow good fruit is cut down, and thrown into the fire. [20] Therefore by their fruits you will know them. [21] Not everyone who says to me, 'Lord, Lord,' will enter into the Kingdom of Heaven; but he who does the will of my Father who is in heaven. [22] Many will tell me in that day, 'Lord, Lord, didn't we prophesy in your name, in your name cast out demons, and in your name do many mighty works?' [23] Then I will tell them, 'I never knew you. Depart from me, you who work iniquity.'

The Wise and Foolish Builders

[24] "Everyone therefore who hears these words of mine, and does them, I will liken him to a wise man, who built his house on a rock. [25] The rain came down,

the floods came, and the winds blew, and beat on that house; and it didn't fall, for it was founded on the rock.²⁶ Everyone who hears these words of mine, and doesn't do them will be like a foolish man, who built his house on the sand. ²⁷ The rain came down, the floods came, and the winds blew, and beat on that house; and it fell—and great was its fall."
²⁸ When Jesus had finished saying these things, the multitudes were astonished at his teaching, ²⁹ for he taught them with authority, and not like the scribes.

1. Why should we be careful not to judge others?

2. How do we know that our heavenly Father hears and answers our prayers?

3. Do you practice the "Golden Rule" in your life?

4. For you personally, what makes the "broad road" most tempting or the "narrow road" difficult? Who will enter heaven?

5. Describe the man who practices the words of Jesus and the man who does not obey Him. How is your spiritual foundation?

6. What teaching from the Sermon on the Mount, (the last four selections) is the most meaningful to you?

92. THE CLEAN AND THE UNCLEAN
Mark 7:1-23

Jesus taught the important truth that it is not outward rituals or ceremonies or eating of special foods, which were all part of Jewish religious rules that make a person clean before God. It is the purity of a person's heart and mind that make one clean in God's sight.

Jesus Teaches About Inner Purity

7 Then the Pharisees and some of the scribes gathered together to him, having come from Jerusalem. ² Now when they saw some of his disciples eating bread with defiled, that is unwashed, hands, they found fault. ³ (For the Pharisees and all the Jews, don't eat unless they wash their hands and forearms, holding to the tradition of the elders. ⁴ They don't eat when they come from the marketplace unless they bathe themselves, and there are many other things, which they have received to hold to: washings of cups, pitchers, bronze vessels, and couches.)
⁵ The Pharisees and the scribes asked him, "Why don't your disciples walk according to the tradition of the elders, but eat their bread with unwashed hands?"

⁶ He answered them, "Well did Isaiah prophesy of you hypocrites, as it is written,

> 'This people honors me with their lips,
> but their heart is far from me.
> ⁷ But they worship me in vain,
> teaching as doctrines the commandments of men.'"

⁸ "For you set aside the commandment of God, and hold tightly to the tradition of men—the washing of pitchers and cups, and you do many other such things." ⁹ He said to them, "Full well do you reject the commandment of God, that you may keep your tradition.¹⁰ For Moses said, 'Honor your father and your mother;' and, 'He who speaks evil of father or mother, let him be put to death.' ¹¹ But you say, 'If a man tells his father or his mother, "Whatever profit you might have received from me is Corban, that is to say, given to God";' ¹² then you no longer allow him to do anything for his father or his mother, ¹³ making void the word of God by your tradition, which you have handed down. You do many things like this."

¹⁴ He called all the multitude to himself, and said to them, "Hear me, all of you, and understand. ¹⁵ There is nothing from outside of the man, that going into him can defile him; but the things which proceed out of the man are those that defile the man. ¹⁶ If anyone has ears to hear, let him hear!"

¹⁷ When he had entered into a house away from the multitude, his disciples asked him about the parable. ¹⁸ He said to them, "Are you also without understanding? Don't you perceive that whatever goes into the man from outside can't defile him, ¹⁹ because it doesn't go into his heart, but into his stomach, then into the latrine, thus purifying all foods?" ²⁰ He said, "That which proceeds out of the man, that defiles the man. ²¹ For from within, out of the hearts of men, proceed evil thoughts, adulteries, sexual sins, murders, thefts, ²² covetings, wickedness, deceit, lustful desires, an evil eye, blasphemy, pride, and foolishness. ²³ All these evil things come from within, and defile the man."

1. *What really makes a person unclean?*
2. *Can you see how fulfilling human traditions can interfere with obeying God's commands?*
3. *What is a hypocrite?*
4. *What sins come out of men's hearts?*

93. THE PLACE OF HONOR
Luke 14:7-14; Matthew 20:20-28 and Mark 9:33-37

We continue to learn how to live our lives. In this selection Jesus teaches His disciples that those who want to become great among them must humble themselves to be as a servant and a child.

A Lesson in Humility

14 ⁷He spoke a parable to those who were invited, when he noticed how they chose the best seats, and said to them, ⁸ "When you are invited by anyone to a marriage feast, don't sit in the best seat, since perhaps someone more honorable than you might be invited by him, ⁹ and he who invited both of you would come and tell you, 'Make room for this person.' Then you would begin, with shame, to take the lowest place. [10] But when you are invited, go and sit in the lowest place, so that when he who invited you comes, he may tell you, 'Friend, move up higher.' Then you will be honored in the presence of all who sit at the table with you. [11] For everyone who exalts himself will be humbled, and whoever humbles himself will be exalted."

[12] He also said to the one who had invited him, "When you make a dinner or a supper, don't call your friends, nor your brothers, nor your kinsmen, nor rich neighbors, or perhaps they might also return the favor, and pay you back. [13] But when you make a feast, ask the poor, the maimed, the lame, or the blind; [14] and you will be blessed, because they don't have the resources to repay you. For you will be repaid in the resurrection of the righteous."

A Mother's Request

20 [20]Then the mother of the sons of Zebedee came to him with her sons, kneeling and asking a certain thing of him. [21] He said to her, "What do you want?" She said to him, "Command that these, my two sons, may sit, one on your right hand, and one on your left hand, in your Kingdom."

[22] But Jesus answered, "You don't know what you are asking. Are you able to drink the cup that I am about to drink, and be baptized with the baptism that I am baptized with?"

They said to him, "We are able."

[23] He said to them, "You will indeed drink my cup, and be baptized with the baptism that I am baptized with, but to sit on my right hand and on my left hand is not mine to give; but it is for whom it has been prepared by my Father."

[24] When the ten heard it, they were indignant with the two brothers.

[25] But Jesus summoned them, and said, "You know that the rulers of the nations lord it over them, and their great ones exercise authority over them. [26] It shall not be so among you, but whoever desires to become great among you shall be your servant. [27] Whoever desires to be first among you shall be your bondservant, [28]even as the Son of Man came not to be served, but to serve, and to give his life as a ransom for many."

Jesus Defines "Greatness"

9 [33]He came to Capernaum, and when he was in the house he asked them, "What were you arguing among yourselves on the way?"

[34] But they were silent, for they had disputed one with another on the way about who was the greatest.

[35] He sat down, and called the twelve; and he said to them, "If any man wants to be first, he shall be last of all, and servant of all." [36] He took a little child, and set him in the middle of them. Taking him in his arms, he said to them, [37] "Whoever receives one such little child in my name, receives me, and whoever receives me, doesn't receive me, but him who sent me."

1. *What happens to a person who humbles himself?*
2. *What contrast did Jesus make between God's Kingdom and the world we live in?*
3. *Why did Jesus use a child as an object lesson on true greatness?*
4. *Why did Jesus come to earth? (v.28)*
5. *How did Jesus define greatness? How must we act if we want to be great in God's sight?*

94. THE IMPORTANCE OF FORGIVENESS
Matthew 18:15-35

Jesus emphasized the importance of forgiveness. He taught that there are no limits to our forgiveness of others. Like the merciful king in this parable, God forgives us according to the way we have forgiven those who have wronged us.

When a Person Sins Against You

18 [15]"If your brother sins against you, go, show him his fault between you and him alone. If he listens to you, you have gained back your brother. [16] But if he doesn't listen, take one or two more with you, that at the mouth of two or three witnesses every word may be established. [17] If he refuses to listen to them, tell it to the assembly. If he refuses to hear the assembly also, let him be to you as a Gentile or a tax collector. [18] Most certainly I tell you, whatever things you bind on earth will have been bound in heaven, and whatever things you release on earth will have been released in heaven.

[19] Again, assuredly I tell you, that if two of you will agree on earth concerning anything that they will ask, it will be done for them by my Father who is in heaven. [20] For where two or three are gathered together in my name, there I am in the middle of them."

The Necessity for Forgiveness

[21]Then Peter came and said to him, "Lord, how often shall my brother sin against me, and I forgive him? Until seven times?"

[22]Jesus said to him, "I don't tell you until seven times, but, until seventy times seven.

Parable of the Unforgiving Servant

[23] Therefore the Kingdom of Heaven is like a certain king, who wanted to reconcile accounts with his servants. [24] When he had begun to reconcile, one was brought to him who owed him ten thousand talents. [25] But because he couldn't pay, his lord commanded him to be sold, with his wife, his children, and all that he had, and payment to be made. [26] The servant therefore fell down and knelt before him, saying, 'Lord, have patience with me, and I will repay you all!'

[27] The lord of that servant, being moved with compassion, released him, and forgave him the debt.

²⁸ "But that servant went out, and found one of his fellow servants, who owed him one hundred denarii, and he grabbed him, and took him by the throat, saying, 'Pay me what you owe!'

²⁹ "So his fellow servant fell down at his feet and begged him, saying, 'Have patience with me, and I will repay you!' ³⁰ He would not, but went and cast him into prison, until he should pay back that which was due. ³¹ So when his fellow servants saw what was done, they were exceedingly sorry, and came and told to their lord all that was done. ³² Then his lord called him in, and said to him, 'You wicked servant! I forgave you all that debt, because you begged me. ³³ Shouldn't you also have had mercy on your fellow servant, even as I had mercy on you?'

³⁴ His lord was angry, and delivered him to the tormentors, until he should pay all that was due to him. ³⁵ So my heavenly Father will also do to you, if you don't each forgive your brother from your hearts for his misdeeds."

1. How many stages of reconciliation are there? How many witnesses are necessary before a matter can be confirmed?
2. What does this passage say about the importance of having counsel, of accountability?
3. What promises does God make to those who agree together to ask God for something?
4. Describe the king in the parable that Jesus told.
5. Why did the king call the servant "wicked"?
6. Can we expect God's forgiveness if we have not forgiven others?

G. THE PROMISES OF JESUS

At the end of his earthly ministry, Jesus made many precious promises to His disciples and followers. Jesus also told them of His coming death and His being raised back to life before he would be taken to heaven to be with His Father. As He prophesied the events to come at the end of the age, Jesus told of His eventual return to earth, when all people would be judged.

95. WORDS FROM THE FATHER
Matthew 16:13-28 and 17:1-13

As Jesus prepared to go to Jerusalem, He knew that soon He would be killed and then raised from the dead. Knowing the suffering that Jesus must endure, God the Father spoke words of love and encouragement. Jesus' divinity was revealed to His disciples.

Peter's Bold Affirmation

16 ¹³Now when Jesus came into the parts of Caesarea Philippi, he asked his disciples, saying, "Who do men say that I, the Son of Man, am?"

¹⁴ They said, "Some say John the Baptizer, some, Elijah, and others, Jeremiah, or one of the prophets."

¹⁵ He said to them, "But who do you say that I am?"

¹⁶ Simon Peter answered, "You are the Christ, the Son of the living God."

¹⁷Jesus answered him, "Blessed are you, Simon Bar Jonah, for flesh and blood has not revealed this to you, but my Father who is in heaven. ¹⁸ I also tell you that you are Peter, and on this rock I will build my assembly, and the gates of Hades will not prevail against it. ¹⁹ I will give to you the keys of the Kingdom of Heaven, and whatever you bind on earth will have been bound in heaven; and whatever you release on earth will have been released in heaven." ²⁰ Then he commanded the disciples that they should tell no one that he was Jesus the Christ.

Jesus Predicts His Death

²¹ From that time, Jesus began to show his disciples that he must go to Jerusalem and suffer many things from the elders, chief priests, and scribes, and be killed, and the third day be raised up.

²² Peter took him aside, and began to rebuke him, saying, "Far be it from you, Lord! This will never be done to you."

²³ But he turned, and said to Peter, "Get behind me, Satan! You are a stumbling block to me, for you are not setting your mind on the things of God, but on the things of men."

The Cost of Following Jesus

²⁴Then Jesus said to his disciples, "If anyone desires to come after me, let him deny himself, and take up his cross, and follow me. ²⁵For whoever desires to save his life will lose it, and whoever will lose his life for my sake will find it. ²⁶ For what will it profit a man, if he gains the whole world, and forfeits his life? Or what will a man give in exchange for his life? ²⁷ For the Son of Man will come in the glory of his Father with his angels, and then he will render to everyone according to his deeds. ²⁸ Most certainly I tell you, there are some standing here who will in no way taste of death, until they see the Son of Man coming in his Kingdom."

The Transfiguration, a Glimpse of Christ's Glory

17 ¹After six days, Jesus took with him Peter, James, and John his brother, and brought them up into a high mountain by themselves. ² He was transfigured before them. His face shone like the sun, and his garments became as white as the light. ³ Behold, Moses and Elijah appeared to them talking with him. ⁴Peter answered, and said to Jesus, "Lord, it is good for us to be here. If you want, let's make three tents here: one for you, one for Moses, and one for Elijah." ⁵ While he was still speaking, behold, a bright cloud overshadowed them. Behold, a voice came out of the cloud saying, "This is my beloved Son in whom I am well pleased. Listen to him."

⁶ When the disciples heard it, they fell on their faces, and were very afraid. ⁷Jesus came and touched them and said, "Get up, and don't be afraid." ⁸ Lifting up their eyes, they saw no one, except Jesus alone. ⁹ As they were coming down from the mountain, Jesus commanded them, saying, "Don't tell anyone what you saw,

until the Son of Man has risen from the dead."

¹⁰ His disciples asked him, saying, "Then why do the scribes say that Elijah must come first?"

¹¹Jesus answered them, "Elijah indeed comes first, and will restore all things, ¹² but I tell you that Elijah has come already, and they didn't recognize him, but did to him whatever they wanted to. Even so the Son of Man will also suffer by them." ¹³ Then the disciples understood that he spoke to them of John the Baptizer.

1. Who did Peter say Jesus was?

2. What did Jesus say would happen when he went to Jerusalem?

3. What did God the Father say concerning His Son?

4. What instructions did Jesus give to anyone who wanted to follow Him?

96. THE WAY TO GOD
John 14:1-14 and 15:1-17

After Peter's confession that Jesus was the Christ, the Son God, and the transfiguration experience, Jesus changed the direction of His teaching. While spending His last days on earth, He concentrated on preparing His disciples for both the immediate future and the life to follow. In this selection, Jesus told His disciples that He would return to heaven to prepare a place for them. There is only one way to reach heaven, and that is by believing that Jesus is the Son of God and obeying His commandments.

Jesus Comforts His Disciples with Spiritual Truths

14 "Don't let your heart be troubled. Believe in God. Believe also in me. ² In my Father's house are many homes. If it weren't so, I would have told you. I am going to prepare a place for you. ³ If I go and prepare a place for you, I will come again, and will receive you to myself; that where I am, you may be there also. ⁴ Where I go, you know, and you know the way."

Jesus the Way to the Father

⁵Thomas said to him, "Lord, we don't know where you are going. How can we know the way?"

⁶Jesus said to him, "I am the way, the truth, and the life. No one comes to the Father, except through me. ⁷ If you had known me, you would have known my Father also. From now on, you know him, and have seen him."

⁸ Philip said to him, "Lord, show us the Father, and that will be enough for us."

⁹Jesus said to him, "Have I been with you such a long time, and do you not know me, Philip? He who has seen me has seen the Father. How do you say, 'Show us the Father?'¹⁰ Don't you believe that I am in the Father, and the Father in me? The words that I tell you, I speak not from myself; but the Father who lives in me does his works. ¹¹ Believe me that I am in the Father, and the Father in me; or else

believe me for the very works' sake. ¹² Most certainly I tell you, he who believes in me, the works that I do, he will do also; and he will do greater works than these, because I am going to my Father. ¹³ Whatever you will ask in my name, that will I do, that the Father may be glorified in the Son. ¹⁴ If you will ask anything in my name, I will do it.

Jesus Teaches Importance of Union with Himself

15 ¹"I am the true vine, and my Father is the farmer. ² Every branch in me that doesn't bear fruit, he takes away. Every branch that bears fruit, he prunes, that it may bear more fruit. ³ You are already pruned clean because of the word which I have spoken to you.⁴ Remain in me, and I in you. As the branch can't bear fruit by itself, unless it remains in the vine, so neither can you, unless you remain in me. ⁵ I am the vine. You are the branches. He who remains in me, and I in him, the same bears much fruit, for apart from me you can do nothing. ⁶ If a man doesn't remain in me, he is thrown out as a branch, and is withered; and they gather them, throw them into the fire, and they are burned. ⁷ If you remain in me, and my words remain in you, you will ask whatever you desire, and it will be done for you.
⁸ "In this is my Father glorified, that you bear much fruit; and so you will be my disciples.⁹ Even as the Father has loved me, I also have loved you. Remain in my love. ¹⁰ If you keep my commandments, you will remain in my love; even as I have kept my Father's commandments, and remain in his love. ¹¹ I have spoken these things to you, that my joy may remain in you, and that your joy may be made full.
¹² "This is my commandment, that you love one another, even as I have loved you.¹³ Greater love has no one than this, that someone lay down his life for his friends. ¹⁴ You are my friends, if you do whatever I command you. ¹⁵ No longer do I call you servants, for the servant doesn't know what his lord does. But I have called you friends, for everything that I heard from my Father, I have made known to you. ¹⁶ You didn't choose me, but I chose you, and appointed you, that you should go and bear fruit, and that your fruit should remain; that whatever you will ask of the Father in my name, he may give it to you.
¹⁷ "I command these things to you, that you may love one another.

1. *Who did Jesus say that he was?*

2. *How can we know the way to heaven?*

3. *How do we know what God, the heavenly Father is like?*

4. *How does a follower of Jesus "bear fruit," i.e., live the way God wants him to and have an effective, productive life?*

5. *What did Jesus say that indicates that He will hear and answer our prayers?*

6. *How is God the Father glorified?*

7. *What is Jesus' command that we must obey in order to remain in His love?*

97. THE SPIRIT OF TRUTH
John 14:15-31 and 16:5-16

Although Jesus continued to speak of His return to His heavenly Father, He promised not to leave His disciples alone. The Father sends the Holy Spirit to be a divine personal presence in each follower's life. The Holy Spirit is our counselor and teacher, and He leads us into all truth.

Jesus Promises the Holy Spirit

14 [15]If you love me, keep my commandments. [16] I will pray to the Father, and he will give you another Counselor, that he may be with you forever, [17] the Spirit of truth, whom the world can't receive; for it doesn't see him, neither knows him. You know him, for he lives with you, and will be in you. [18] I will not leave you orphans. I will come to you. [19] Yet a little while, and the world will see me no more; but you will see me. Because I live, you will live also. [20] In that day you will know that I am in my Father, and you in me, and I in you. [21] One who has my commandments, and keeps them, that person is one who loves me. One who loves me will be loved by my Father, and I will love him, and will reveal myself to him."

[22] Judas (not Iscariot) said to him, "Lord, what has happened that you are about to reveal yourself to us, and not to the world?"

[23] Jesus answered him, "If a man loves me, he will keep my word. My Father will love him, and we will come to him, and make our home with him. [24] He who doesn't love me doesn't keep my words. The word which you hear isn't mine, but the Father's who sent me. [25] I have said these things to you, while still living with you. [26] But the Counselor, the Holy Spirit, whom the Father will send in my name, he will teach you all things, and will remind you of all that I said to you. [27] Peace I leave with you. My peace I give to you; not as the world gives, give I to you. Don't let your heart be troubled, neither let it be fearful. [28] You heard how I told you, 'I go away, and I come to you.' If you loved me, you would have rejoiced, because I said 'I am going to my Father;' for the Father is greater than I. [29] Now I have told you before it happens so that, when it happens, you may believe. [30] I will no more speak much with you, for the prince of the world comes, and he has nothing in me. [31] But that the world may know that I love the Father, and as the Father commanded me, even so I do. Arise, let us go from here.

The Work of the Holy Spirit

16 [5]But now I am going to him who sent me, and none of you asks me, 'Where are you going?' [6] But because I have told you these things, sorrow has filled your heart. [7] Nevertheless I tell you the truth: It is to your advantage that I go away, for if I don't go away, the Counselor won't come to you. But if I go, I will send him to you. [8]When he has come, he will convict the world about sin, about righteousness, and about judgment; [9] about sin, because they don't believe in me; [10] about righteousness, because I am going to my Father, and you won't see me anymore; ¹¹ about judgment, because the prince of this world has been judged.

¹² "I have yet many things to tell you, but you can't bear them now. ¹³ However when he, the Spirit of truth, has come, he will guide you into all truth, for he will not speak from himself; but whatever he hears, he will speak. He will declare to you things that are coming. ¹⁴ He will glorify me, for he will take from what is mine, and will declare it to you. ¹⁵ All things whatever the Father has are mine; therefore I said that he takes of mine, and will declare it to you. ¹⁶ A little while, and you will not see me. Again a little while, and you will see me."

> 1. Jesus described the Holy Spirit as a divine person, not an impersonal supernatural force. Regarding the Holy Spirit:
>   a. Where did Jesus say that He came from?
>   b. How did Jesus say that we would know Him?
>
> 2. How do we show Jesus that we love Him? Can you see that the Holy Spirit will help you to obey Jesus' commands?
>
> 3. Name six things Jesus said the Holy Spirit would do.
>
> 4. Where does real truth originate? Who brings it to your mind?
>
> 5. Jesus promised His followers peace. Is there any reason to have stress in your life if Jesus will give you His peace?
>
> 6. Who is the prince of this world who stands condemned?

98. THE PRAYER OF JESUS
John 17:1-26

Near the end of Jesus' life on earth, He prayed this intimate prayer to His heavenly Father. Jesus not only prayed for Himself and His disciples, but also for all those everywhere who would come to believe in Him.

Jesus Prays for Himself

17 Jesus said these things, and lifting up his eyes to heaven, he said, "Father, the time has come. Glorify your Son, that your Son may also glorify you; ² even as you gave him authority over all flesh, he will give eternal life to all whom you have given him. ³ This is eternal life, that they should know you, the only true God, and him whom you sent, Jesus Christ. ⁴ I glorified you on the earth. I have accomplished the work which you have given me to do. ⁵ Now, Father, glorify me with your own self with the glory which I had with you before the world existed.

Jesus Prays for His Disciples

⁶ I revealed your name to the people whom you have given me out of the world. They were yours, and you have given them to me. They have kept your word. ⁷ Now they have known that all things whatever you have given me are from you, ⁸

for the words which you have given me I have given to them, and they received them, and knew for sure that I came from you, and they have believed that you sent me. ⁹ I pray for them. I don't pray for the world, but for those whom you have given me, for they are yours. ¹⁰ All things that are mine are yours, and yours are mine, and I am glorified in them. ¹¹ I am no more in the world, but these are in the world, and I am coming to you. Holy Father, keep them through your name which you have given me, that they may be one, even as we are. ¹² While I was with them in the world, I kept them in your name. Those whom you have given me I have kept. None of them is lost, except the son of destruction, that the Scripture might be fulfilled. ¹³ But now I come to you, and I say these things in the world, that they may have my joy made full in themselves. ¹⁴ I have given them your word. The world hated them, because they are not of the world, even as I am not of the world. ¹⁵ I pray not that you would take them from the world, but that you would keep them from the evil one. ¹⁶ They are not of the world even as I am not of the world. ¹⁷ Sanctify them in your truth. Your word is truth. ¹⁸ As you sent me into the world, even so I have sent them into the world. ¹⁹ For their sakes I sanctify myself, that they themselves also may be sanctified in truth.

Jesus Prays for All Believers

²⁰ Not for these only do I pray, but for those also who believe in me through their word, ²¹ that they may all be one; even as you, Father, are in me, and I in you, that they also may be one in us; that the world may believe that you sent me. ²² The glory which you have given me, I have given to them; that they may be one, even as we are one; ²³ I in them, and you in me, that they may be perfected into one; that the world may know that you sent me, and loved them, even as you loved me. ²⁴ Father, I desire that they also whom you have given me be with me where I am, that they may see my glory, which you have given me, for you loved me before the foundation of the world. ²⁵ Righteous Father, the world hasn't known you, but I knew you; and these knew that you sent me. ²⁶ I made known to them your name, and will make it known; that the love with which you loved me may be in them, and I in them."

> 1. *What did Jesus say eternal life is?*
>
> 2. *Why did the world hate those who believed in Jesus?*
>
> 3. *What did Jesus say truth is? Where does it originate?*
>
> 4. *What did Jesus mean when He asked the Father "that they may be one"? What was the result of this unity? (v.21)*
>
> 5. *If you were to become a follower of Jesus, could you see that Jesus' prayer was for you too?*

99. THE SECOND COMING
Matthew 24:1-51

Jesus told His disciples about the events that would take place near the end of the world when He would come again. His second coming would not be as a humble baby but as a king with power and great glory. The exact time of His coming is hidden from everyone except God, the heavenly Father.

Signs of the End of the Age

24 Jesus went out from the temple, and was going on his way. His disciples came to him to show him the buildings of the temple. ² But he answered them, "You see all of these things, don't you? Most certainly I tell you, there will not be left here one stone on another, that will not be thrown down."

Troubles and Persecutions

³ As he sat on the Mount of Olives, the disciples came to him privately, saying, "Tell us, when these things will be? What is the sign of your coming, and of the end of the age?"

⁴ Jesus answered them, "Be careful that no one leads you astray. ⁵ For many will come in my name, saying, 'I am the Christ,' and will lead many astray. ⁶ You will hear of wars and rumors of wars. See that you aren't troubled, for all this must happen, but the end is not yet. ⁷ For nation will rise against nation, and kingdom against kingdom; and there will be famines, plagues, and earthquakes in various places. ⁸ But all these things are the beginning of birth pains. ⁹ Then they will deliver you up to oppression, and will kill you. You will be hated by all of the nations for my name's sake. ¹⁰ Then many will stumble, and will deliver up one another, and will hate one another. ¹¹ Many false prophets will arise, and will lead many astray. ¹² Because iniquity will be multiplied, the love of many will grow cold. ¹³ But he who endures to the end, the same will be saved. ¹⁴ This Good News of the Kingdom will be preached in the whole world for a testimony to all the nations, and then the end will come.

Terrible Times at the End

¹⁵ "When, therefore, you see the abomination of desolation, which was spoken of through Daniel the prophet, standing in the holy place (let the reader understand), ¹⁶ then let those who are in Judea flee to the mountains. ¹⁷ Let him who is on the housetop not go down to take out things that are in his house. ¹⁸ Let him who is in the field not return back to get his clothes. ¹⁹ But woe to those who are with child and to nursing mothers in those days! ²⁰ Pray that your flight will not be in the winter, nor on a Sabbath, ²¹ for then there will be great oppression, such as has not been from the beginning of the world until now, no, nor ever will be. ²² Unless those days had been shortened, no flesh would have been saved. But for the sake of the chosen ones, those days will be shortened.

²³ "Then if any man tells you, 'Behold, here is the Christ,' or, 'There,' don't

believe it. ²⁴ For there will arise false christs, and false prophets, and they will show great signs and wonders, so as to lead astray, if possible, even the chosen ones.

²⁵ "Behold, I have told you beforehand. ²⁶ If therefore they tell you, 'Behold, he is in the wilderness,' don't go out; 'Behold, he is in the inner rooms,' don't believe it. ²⁷ For as the lightning flashes from the east, and is seen even to the west, so will be the coming of the Son of Man. ²⁸ For wherever the carcass is, there is where the vultures gather together.

The Coming of the Son of Man
²⁹ But immediately after the oppression of those days, the sun will be darkened, the moon will not give its light, the stars will fall from the sky, and the powers of the heavens will be shaken; ³⁰ and then the sign of the Son of Man will appear in the sky. Then all the tribes of the earth will mourn, and they will see the Son of Man coming on the clouds of the sky with power and great glory. ³¹ He will send out his angels with a great sound of a trumpet, and they will gather together his chosen ones from the four winds, from one end of the sky to the other.

The Lesson of the Fig Tree
³² "Now from the fig tree learn this parable. When its branch has now become tender, and produces its leaves, you know that the summer is near. ³³ Even so you also, when you see all these things, know that it is near, even at the doors. ³⁴ Most certainly I tell you, this generation will not pass away, until all these things are accomplished. ³⁵ Heaven and earth will pass away, but my words will not pass away.

The Day and Hour Unknown
³⁶But no one knows of that day and hour, not even the angels of heaven, but my Father only.

³⁷"As the days of Noah were, so will be the coming of the Son of Man. ³⁸ For as in those days which were before the flood they were eating and drinking, marrying and giving in marriage, until the day that Noah entered into the ship, ³⁹ and they didn't know until the flood came, and took them all away, so will be the coming of the Son of Man. ⁴⁰ Then two men will be in the field: one will be taken and one will be left; ⁴¹ two women grinding at the mill, one will be taken and one will be left. ⁴² Watch therefore, for you don't know in what hour your Lord comes.

⁴³ But know this, that if the master of the house had known in what watch of the night the thief was coming, he would have watched, and would not have allowed his house to be broken into. ⁴⁴ Therefore also be ready, for in an hour that you don't expect, the Son of Man will come.

The Faithful Versus the Unfaithful Servant
⁴⁵ "Who then is the faithful and wise servant, whom his lord has set over his household, to give them their food in due season? ⁴⁶ Blessed is that servant whom his lord finds doing so when he comes. ⁴⁷ Most certainly I tell you that he will

set him over all that he has.[48] But if that evil servant should say in his heart, 'My lord is delaying his coming,' [49] and begins to beat his fellow servants, and eat and drink with the drunkards, [50] the lord of that servant will come in a day when he doesn't expect it, and in an hour when he doesn't know it, [51] and will cut him in pieces, and appoint his portion with the hypocrites. There is where the weeping and grinding of teeth will be.

> 1. Name at least ten signs that will show it is the end of the age.
> 2. Why should we not believe people who claim to be the Christ, sent from God?
> 3. Where will the Good News of the Kingdom be preached?
> 4. Describe how Jesus, the Son of Man, will return to earth.
> 5. Describe what people will be doing when Jesus returns.
> 6. What should His followers be doing?

100. THE COMING JUDGEMENT
Matthew 25:1-46

Jesus taught His followers through several parables that they must be ready at all times for His return to earth. When He comes, all people will be judged by Jesus and given rewards or punishment according to their faithfulness.

The Parable of the Ten Virgins

25 [1]"Then the Kingdom of Heaven will be like ten virgins, who took their lamps, and went out to meet the bridegroom. [2] Five of them were foolish, and five were wise. [3] Those who were foolish, when they took their lamps, took no oil with them, [4] but the wise took oil in their vessels with their lamps.

[5] Now while the bridegroom delayed, they all slumbered and slept. [6] But at midnight there was a cry, 'Behold! The bridegroom is coming! Come out to meet him!' [7] Then all those virgins arose, and trimmed their lamps. [8] The foolish said to the wise, 'Give us some of your oil, for our lamps are going out.'

[9] But the wise answered, saying, 'What if there isn't enough for us and you? You go rather to those who sell, and buy for yourselves.' [10] While they went away to buy, the bridegroom came, and those who were ready went in with him to the marriage feast, and the door was shut.

[11] Afterward the other virgins also came, saying, 'Lord, Lord, open to us.' [12] But he answered, 'Most certainly I tell you, I don't know you.' [13] Watch therefore, for you don't know the day nor the hour in which the Son of Man is coming.

The Parable of the Three Servants

[14] "For it is like a man, going into another country, who called his own servants, and entrusted his goods to them. [15] To one he gave five talents, to another two, to another one; to each according to his own ability. Then he went on his journey.

¹⁶ Immediately he who received the five talents went and traded with them, and made another five talents. ¹⁷ In the same way, he also who got the two gained another two. ¹⁸ But he who received the one talent went away and dug in the earth, and hid his lord's money.

¹⁹ "Now after a long time the lord of those servants came, and reconciled accounts with them. ²⁰ He who received the five talents came and brought another five talents, saying, 'Lord, you delivered to me five talents. Behold, I have gained another five talents besides them.'

²¹ "His lord said to him, 'Well done, good and faithful servant. You have been faithful over a few things, I will set you over many things. Enter into the joy of your lord.'

²² "He also who got the two talents came and said, 'Lord, you delivered to me two talents. Behold, I have gained another two talents besides them.'

²³ "His lord said to him, 'Well done, good and faithful servant. You have been faithful over a few things, I will set you over many things. Enter into the joy of your lord.'

²⁴ "He also who had received the one talent came and said, 'Lord, I knew you that you are a hard man, reaping where you did not sow, and gathering where you did not scatter. ²⁵ I was afraid, and went away and hid your talent in the earth. Behold, you have what is yours.'

²⁶ "But his lord answered him, 'You wicked and slothful servant. You knew that I reap where I didn't sow, and gather where I didn't scatter. ²⁷ You ought therefore to have deposited my money with the bankers, and at my coming I should have received back my own with interest. ²⁸ Take away therefore the talent from him, and give it to him who has the ten talents. ²⁹ For to everyone who has will be given, and he will have abundance, but from him who doesn't have, even that which he has will be taken away. ³⁰ Throw out the unprofitable servant into the outer darkness, where there will be weeping and gnashing of teeth.'

The King Will Judge All People

³¹ "But when the Son of Man comes in his glory, and all the holy angels with him, then he will sit on the throne of his glory. ³² Before him all the nations will be gathered, and he will separate them one from another, as a shepherd separates the sheep from the goats. ³³ He will set the sheep on his right hand, but the goats on the left. ³⁴ Then the King will tell those on his right hand, 'Come, blessed of my Father, inherit the Kingdom prepared for you from the foundation of the world; ³⁵ for I was hungry, and you gave me food to eat. I was thirsty, and you gave me drink. I was a stranger, and you took me in. ³⁶ I was naked, and you clothed me. I was sick, and you visited me. I was in prison, and you came to me.'

³⁷ "Then the righteous will answer him, saying, 'Lord, when did we see you hungry, and feed you; or thirsty, and give you a drink? ³⁸ When did we see you as a stranger, and take you in; or naked, and clothe you? ³⁹ When did we see you sick, or in prison, and come to you?'

⁴⁰ "The King will answer them, 'Most certainly I tell you, because you did it to

one of the least of these my brothers, you did it to me.' ⁴¹ Then he will say also to those on the left hand, 'Depart from me, you cursed, into the eternal fire which is prepared for the devil and his angels; ⁴² for I was hungry, and you didn't give me food to eat; I was thirsty, and you gave me no drink; ⁴³ I was a stranger, and you didn't take me in; naked, and you didn't clothe me; sick, and in prison, and you didn't visit me.'

⁴⁴ "Then they will also answer, saying, 'Lord, when did we see you hungry, or thirsty, or a stranger, or naked, or sick, or in prison, and didn't help you?'

⁴⁵ "Then he will answer them, saying, 'Most certainly I tell you, because you didn't do it to one of the least of these, you didn't do it to me.' ⁴⁶ These will go away into eternal punishment, but the righteous into eternal life."

1. What was the difference between the wise and the foolish virgins?
2. What two key points was Jesus teaching about His eventual return to earth?
3. What were the master's expectations of his servants while he was away?
4. What did the master say to the two faithful servants?
5. How did the third servant fail to carry-out his responsibility?
6. What differentiates the lives of the two groups of people (the sheep and the goats) on Judgment Day?
   a. What is the reward for the people on the right of Jesus? Why?
   b. What happens to the people on the left of Jesus? Why?
7. What does this tell us about Jesus' concern for people who suffer hardships and His expectation of our help for those less fortunate than we are?

H. DEATH AND RESURRECTION OF JESUS CHRIST

Jesus knew that the time had come for Him to fulfill God's purpose in sending Him to earth. He must suffer and die on the cross to save God's creation from eternal death. Jesus willingly became the sacrifice for the sins of mankind, knowing that He would be raised to a new life and would return to be with His Father in heaven. The death of Jesus made new life possible for all who believe that His blood paid the price for their sin. Now all who have their sins forgiven can enjoy peace and freedom from sin in this life as well as the glories of heaven in the life to come.

101. FRIENDS AND ENEMIES
Matthew 26:1-16 and John 13:1-30

It was the time of year when the Jewish people celebrated the Passover feast, the celebration that commemorated the day of their deliverance from Egypt. Since Jesus' time, Christians have called this event The Last Supper. It was the last time before Jesus was arrested that He and His disciples were together. At that time Jesus prepared Himself to become the Passover Lamb, who would deliver mankind from the slavery and penalty of sin and save all who believed in Him.

The Plot Against Jesus

26 ¹When Jesus had finished all these words, he said to his disciples, ² "You know that after two days the Passover is coming, and the Son of Man will be delivered up to be crucified."

³ Then the chief priests, the scribes, and the elders of the people were gathered together in the court of the high priest, who was called Caiaphas. ⁴ They took counsel together that they might take Jesus by deceit, and kill him. ⁵ But they said, "Not during the feast, lest a riot occur among the people."

Perfume for Jesus' Burial

⁶ Now when Jesus was in Bethany, in the house of Simon the leper, ⁷ a woman came to him having an alabaster jar of very expensive ointment, and she poured it on his head as he sat at the table.

⁸ But when his disciples saw this, they were indignant, saying, "Why this waste? ⁹ For this ointment might have been sold for much, and given to the poor."

¹⁰ However, knowing this, Jesus said to them, "Why do you trouble the woman? Because she has done a good work for me. ¹¹ For you always have the poor with you; but you don't always have me. ¹² For in pouring this ointment on my body, she did it to prepare me for burial. ¹³ Most certainly I tell you, wherever this Good News is preached in the whole world, what this woman has done will also be spoken of as a memorial of her."

Judas Becomes an Enemy of Jesus

¹⁴ Then one of the twelve, who was called Judas Iscariot, went to the chief priests, ¹⁵ and said, "What are you willing to give me, that I should deliver him to you?" They weighed out for him thirty pieces of silver. ¹⁶ From that time he sought opportunity to betray him.

Jesus Washes His Disciples' Feet

13 Now before the feast of the Passover, Jesus, knowing that his time had come that he would depart from this world to the Father, having loved his own who were in the world, he loved them to the end. ² During supper, the devil having already put into the heart of Judas Iscariot, Simon's son, to betray him, ³ Jesus, knowing that the Father had given all things into his hands, and that he came from God, and was going to God, ⁴ arose from supper, and laid aside his outer garments. He took a towel, and wrapped a towel around his waist. ⁵ Then he poured water into the basin, and began to wash the disciples' feet, and to wipe them with the towel that was wrapped around him. ⁶ Then he came to Simon Peter. He said to him, "Lord, do you wash my feet?" ⁷Jesus answered him, "You don't know what I'm doing now, but you will understand later."

⁸ Peter said to him, "You will never wash my feet!"

Jesus answered him, "If I don't wash you, you have no part with me."

⁹ Simon Peter said to him, "Lord, not my feet only, but also my hands and my head!"

[10] Jesus said to him, "Someone who has bathed only needs to have his feet washed, but is completely clean. You are clean, but not all of you." [11] For he knew him who would betray him, therefore he said, "You are not all clean." [12] So when he had washed their feet, put his outer garment back on, and sat down again, he said to them, "Do you know what I have done to you? [13] You call me, 'Teacher' and 'Lord.' You say so correctly, for so I am. [14] If I then, the Lord and the Teacher, have washed your feet, you also ought to wash one another's feet. [15] For I have given you an example, that you also should do as I have done to you. [16] Most certainly I tell you, a servant is not greater than his lord, neither one who is sent greater than he who sent him. [17] If you know these things, blessed are you if you do them.

Jesus Predicts His Betrayal

[18] I don't speak concerning all of you. I know whom I have chosen. But that the Scripture may be fulfilled, 'He who eats bread with me has lifted up his heel against me.'

[19] From now on, I tell you before it happens, that when it happens, you may believe that I am he. [20] Most certainly I tell you, he who receives whomever I send, receives me; and he who receives me, receives him who sent me."

[21] When Jesus had said this, he was troubled in spirit, and testified, "Most certainly I tell you that one of you will betray me."

[22] The disciples looked at one another, perplexed about whom he spoke. [23] One of his disciples, whom Jesus loved, was at the table, leaning against Jesus' breast. [24] Simon Peter therefore beckoned to him, and said to him, "Tell us who it is of whom he speaks."

[25] He, leaning back, as he was, on Jesus' breast, asked him, "Lord, who is it?"

[26] Jesus therefore answered, "It is he to whom I will give this piece of bread when I have dipped it." So when he had dipped the piece of bread, he gave it to Judas, the son of Simon Iscariot. [27] After the piece of bread, then Satan entered into him.

Then Jesus said to him, "What you do, do quickly."

[28] Now no man at the table knew why he said this to him. [29] For some thought, because Judas had the money box, that Jesus said to him, "Buy what things we need for the feast," or that he should give something to the poor. [30] Therefore having received that morsel, he went out immediately. It was night.

1. *Why did Jesus say the woman had done a beautiful thing for Him? How did Jesus use this event to teach His disciples about life's priorities?*

2. *Why did Jesus wash the disciples' feet? What lesson was taught by this action?*

3. *Why do you think Judas betrayed Jesus?*

102. THE ARREST OF JESUS
Matthew 26:26-56

As Jesus and the remaining eleven disciples continued to eat the Passover meal together, He told them of the new covenant that He was making with them. The old covenant began with Israel's liberation from slavery in Egypt. Blood from the sacrificial lamb was sprinkled upon each Israeli doorway so that the angel of death would "pass over" each Jewish home. Passover was celebrated every year as a remembrance of that momentous event. Now Jesus was to be the sacrificial lamb for the new covenant between God and man. This covenant would require the shedding of His blood as the sacrifice for the sins of mankind. All those who believe in Jesus as their Savior receive forgiveness of their sins and are welcomed into God's Kingdom. Just as Israel celebrated the Passover as a remembrance of God's gift of deliverance from Egypt, Christians everywhere celebrate Holy Communion, derived from The Last Supper, as a remembrance of God's gift of Jesus. He sacrificed Himself for our freedom from Satan's bondage so we could have access to God and eternal life with Him.

The Last Supper in the Upper Room

26 ^{26}As they were eating, Jesus took bread, gave thanks for it, and broke it. He gave to the disciples, and said, "Take, eat; this is my body."

^{27} He took the cup, gave thanks, and gave to them, saying, "All of you drink it, ^{28} for this is my blood of the new covenant, which is poured out for many for the remission of sins. ^{29} But I tell you that I will not drink of this fruit of the vine from now on, until that day when I drink it anew with you in my Father's Kingdom."

^{30} When they had sung a hymn, they went out to the Mount of Olives.

Jesus Predicts Peter's Denial

^{31} Then Jesus said to them, "All of you will be made to stumble because of me tonight, for it is written, 'I will strike the shepherd, and the sheep of the flock will be scattered.' ^{32} But after I am raised up, I will go before you into Galilee."

^{33} But Peter answered him, "Even if all will be made to stumble because of you, I will never be made to stumble."

^{34}Jesus said to him, "Most certainly I tell you that tonight, before the rooster crows, you will deny me three times."

^{35} Peter said to him, "Even if I must die with you, I will not deny you." All of the disciples also said likewise.

Jesus at Gethsemane

^{36} Then Jesus came with them to a place called Gethsemane, and said to his disciples, "Sit here, while I go there and pray." ^{37} He took with him Peter and the two sons of Zebedee, and began to be sorrowful and severely troubled. ^{38} Then he said to them, "My soul is exceedingly sorrowful, even to death. Stay here, and watch with me."

⁳⁹ He went forward a little, fell on his face, and prayed, saying, "My Father, if it is possible, let this cup pass away from me; nevertheless, not what I desire, but what you desire."

⁴⁰ He came to the disciples, and found them sleeping, and said to Peter, "What, couldn't you watch with me for one hour? ⁴¹ Watch and pray, that you don't enter into temptation. The spirit indeed is willing, but the flesh is weak."

⁴² Again, a second time he went away, and prayed, saying, "My Father, if this cup can't pass away from me unless I drink it, your desire be done." ⁴³ He came again and found them sleeping, for their eyes were heavy. ⁴⁴ He left them again, went away, and prayed a third time, saying the same words.

⁴⁵ Then he came to his disciples, and said to them, "Sleep on now, and take your rest. Behold, the hour is at hand, and the Son of Man is betrayed into the hands of sinners. ⁴⁶ Arise, let's be going. Behold, he who betrays me is at hand."

Jesus Is Arrested

⁴⁷ While he was still speaking, behold, Judas, one of the twelve, came, and with him a great multitude with swords and clubs, from the chief priest and elders of the people.⁴⁸ Now he who betrayed him gave them a sign, saying, "Whoever I kiss, he is the one. Seize him." ⁴⁹ Immediately he came to Jesus, and said, "Hail, Rabbi!" and kissed him.

⁵⁰ Jesus said to him, "Friend, why are you here?"

Then they came and laid hands on Jesus, and took him. ⁵¹ Behold, one of those who were with Jesus stretched out his hand, and drew his sword, and struck the servant of the high priest, and struck off his ear.⁵² Then Jesus said to him, "Put your sword back into its place, for all those who take the sword will die by the sword. ⁵³ Or do you think that I couldn't ask my Father, and he would even now send me more than twelve legions of angels? ⁵⁴ How then would the Scriptures be fulfilled that it must be so?"

⁵⁵ In that hour Jesus said to the multitudes, "Have you come out as against a robber with swords and clubs to seize me? I sat daily in the temple teaching, and you didn't arrest me. ⁵⁶ But all this has happened, that the Scriptures of the prophets might be fulfilled."

Then all the disciples left him, and fled.

> 1. Do you see the significant symbolism between the Passover and the moment when Jesus said that the broken bread was His body and the poured out wine was His blood?
>
> 2. How did Jesus feel when He was in Gethsemane?
>
> 3. What did Jesus pray for three times?
>
> 4. Why did the disciples abandon Him? How do you think He felt then?

103. SENTENCED TO DIE
Luke 22:54-71 and 23:1-25

Jesus surrendered His will to the Father's at Gethsemane. Jesus yielded Himself to His captors without a struggle. Although He was innocent, having lived a perfect life without sin, Jesus was falsely accused, subjected to horrible indignities and treated as a common criminal.

Peter Denies Jesus

22 ⁵⁴They seized him, and led him away, and brought him into the high priest's house. But Peter followed from a distance. ⁵⁵ When they had kindled a fire in the middle of the courtyard, and had sat down together, Peter sat among them. ⁵⁶ A certain servant girl saw him as he sat in the light, and looking intently at him, said, "This man also was with him."

⁵⁷ He denied Jesus, saying, "Woman, I don't know him."

⁵⁸ After a little while someone else saw him, and said, "You also are one of them!"

But Peter answered, "Man, I am not!"

⁵⁹ After about one hour passed, another confidently affirmed, saying, "Truly this man also was with him, for he is a Galilean!" ⁶⁰ But Peter said, "Man, I don't know what you are talking about!" Immediately, while he was still speaking, a rooster crowed. ⁶¹ The Lord turned, and looked at Peter. Then Peter remembered the Lord's word, how he said to him, "Before the rooster crows you will deny me three times." ⁶² He went out, and wept bitterly.

People Make Fun of Jesus

⁶³The men who held Jesus mocked him and beat him. ⁶⁴ Having blindfolded him, they struck him on the face and asked him, "Prophesy! Who is the one who struck you?"⁶⁵ They spoke many other things against him, insulting him.

Jesus on Trial Before the Jewish Religious Leaders

⁶⁶ As soon as it was day, the assembly of the elders of the people was gathered together, both chief priests and scribes, and they led him away into their council, saying, ⁶⁷ "If you are the Christ, tell us."

But he said to them, "If I tell you, you won't believe, ⁶⁸ and if I ask, you will in no way answer me or let me go. ⁶⁹ From now on, the Son of Man will be seated at the right hand of the power of God."

⁷⁰ They all said, "Are you then the Son of God?" He said to them, "You say it, because I am. ⁷¹ and they said, `What need yet have we of testimony? for we ourselves did hear [it] from his mouth.'

Jesus Before Pilate and Herod

23 The whole company of them rose up and brought him before Pilate. ² They began to accuse him, saying, "We found this man perverting the nation, forbidding paying taxes to Caesar, and saying that he himself is Christ, a king."

³ Pilate asked him, "Are you the King of the Jews?"

He answered him, "So you say."

⁴ Pilate said to the chief priests and the multitudes, "I find no basis for a charge against this man."

⁵ But they insisted, saying, "He stirs up the people, teaching throughout all Judea, beginning from Galilee even to this place." ⁶ But when Pilate heard Galilee mentioned, he asked if the man was a Galilean. ⁷ When he found out that he was in Herod's jurisdiction, he sent him to Herod, who was also in Jerusalem during those days.

⁸ Now when Herod saw Jesus, he was exceedingly glad, for he had wanted to see him for a long time, because he had heard many things about him. He hoped to see some miracle done by him.

⁹ He questioned him with many words, but he gave no answers. ¹⁰ The chief priests and the scribes stood, vehemently accusing him. ¹¹ Herod with his soldiers humiliated him and mocked him. Dressing him in luxurious clothing, they sent him back to Pilate. ¹² Herod and Pilate became friends with each other that very day, for before that they were enemies with each other.

Jesus Must Die

¹³ Pilate called together the chief priests and the rulers and the people, ¹⁴ and said to them, "You brought this man to me as one that perverts the people, and see, I have examined him before you, and found no basis for a charge against this man concerning those things of which you accuse him. ¹⁵ Neither has Herod, for I sent you to him, and see, nothing worthy of death has been done by him. ¹⁶ I will therefore chastise him and release him."

¹⁷ Now he had to release one prisoner to them at the feast. ¹⁸ But they all cried out together, saying, "Away with this man! Release to us Barabbas!" ¹⁹ one who was thrown into prison for a certain revolt in the city, and for murder.

²⁰ Then Pilate spoke to them again, wanting to release Jesus, ²¹ but they shouted, saying, "Crucify! Crucify him!"

²² He said to them the third time, "Why? What evil has this man done? I have found no capital crime in him. I will therefore chastise him and release him." ²³ But they were urgent with loud voices, asking that he might be crucified. Their voices and the voices of the chief priests prevailed. ²⁴ Pilate decreed that what they asked for should be done.²⁵ He released him who had been thrown into prison for insurrection and murder, for whom they asked, but he delivered Jesus up to their will.

1. *Why did Peter weep so bitterly?*

2. *What law had Jesus broken? Were the accusations true?*

3. *Why did Pilate want to release Jesus?*

4. *Why do you think the religious leaders hated Jesus so much that they wanted him crucified?*

5. *Why did Pilate change his decision?*

104. DEATH OF THE KING
Luke 23:26-43 and John 19:23-27 and
Luke 23:44-45 and Mark 15:33-36 and
John 19:30a and Luke 23:46-56

Having been tried and sentenced to death, Jesus was beaten and then forced to walk outside the city to the place of execution. The words spoken by Jesus as He hung dying on the cross give us a perfect picture of who He was and what He came to do. As Jesus took the sin of all mankind upon Himself, God the Father was forced to turn away from His suffering Son. Jesus not only experienced a tortuous physical death, but He also felt the tormenting spiritual agony of separation from His holy, heavenly Father, who could not look upon sin.

Jesus Is Crucified

23 [26]When they led him away, they grabbed one Simon of Cyrene, coming from the country, and laid on him the cross, to carry it after Jesus. [27] A great multitude of the people followed him, including women who also mourned and lamented him. [28] But Jesus, turning to them, said, "Daughters of Jerusalem, don't weep for me, but weep for yourselves and for your children. [29] For behold, the days are coming in which they will say, 'Blessed are the barren, the wombs that never bore, and the breasts that never nursed.'

[30] Then they will begin to tell the mountains, 'Fall on us!'
and tell the hills, 'Cover us.'

[31] For if they do these things in the green tree, what will be done in the dry?"

[32] There were also others, two criminals, led with him to be put to death. [33] When they came to the place that is called The Skull, they crucified him there with the criminals, one on the right and the other on the left.

[34] Jesus said, "Father, forgive them, for they don't know what they are doing." Dividing his garments among them, they cast lots. [35] The people stood watching. The rulers with them also scoffed at him, saying, "He saved others. Let him save himself, if this is the Christ of God, his chosen one!"

[36] The soldiers also mocked him, coming to him and offering him vinegar, [37] and saying, "If you are the King of the Jews, save yourself!"

[38] An inscription was also written over him in letters of Greek, Latin, and Hebrew:

"THIS IS THE KING OF THE JEWS."

[39] One of the criminals who was hanged insulted him, saying, "If you are the Christ, save yourself and us!"

[40] But the other answered, and rebuking him said, "Don't you even fear God, seeing you are under the same condemnation? [41] And we indeed justly, for we receive the due reward for our deeds, but this man has done nothing wrong." [42] He said to Jesus, "Lord, remember me when you come into your Kingdom."

⁴³ Jesus said to him, "Assuredly I tell you, today you will be with me in Paradise."
19 ²³Then the soldiers, when they had crucified Jesus, took his garments and made four parts, to every soldier a part; and also the coat. Now the coat was without seam, woven from the top throughout. ²⁴ Then they said to one another, "Let's not tear it, but cast lots for it to decide whose it will be," that the Scripture might be fulfilled, which says,
> "They parted my garments among them.
>> For my cloak they cast lots."

Therefore the soldiers did these things.
²⁵ But there were standing by the cross of Jesus his mother, and his mother's sister, Mary the wife of Clopas, and Mary Magdalene.²⁶ Therefore when Jesus saw his mother, and the disciple whom he loved standing there, he said to his mother, "Woman, behold your son!" ²⁷ Then he said to the disciple, "Behold, your mother!" From that hour, the disciple took her to his own home.

Jesus Dies
23 ⁴⁴It was now about the sixth hour, [noon 12 pm] and darkness came over the whole land until the ninth hour. ⁴⁵ The sun was darkened, and the veil of the temple was torn in two.
15 ³³When the sixth hour had come, there was darkness over the whole land until the ninth hour. ³⁴ At the ninth hour [about 3 pm] Jesus cried with a loud voice, saying, "Eloi, Eloi, lama sabachthani?" which is, being interpreted, "My God, my God, why have you forsaken me?"

³⁵ Some of those who stood by, when they heard it, said, "Behold, he is calling Elijah."

³⁶ One ran, and filling a sponge full of vinegar, put it on a reed, and gave it to him to drink, saying, "Let him be. Let's see whether Elijah comes to take him down."
19 ³⁰When Jesus therefore had received the vinegar, he said,
> "It is finished."

23 ⁴⁶Jesus, crying with a loud voice, said, "Father, into your hands I commit my spirit!" Having said this, he breathed his last. ⁴⁷ When the centurion saw what was done, he glorified God, saying, "Certainly this was a righteous man."

⁴⁸ All the multitudes that came together to see this, when they saw the things that were done, returned home beating their breasts. ⁴⁹ All his acquaintances, and the women who followed with him from Galilee, stood at a distance, watching these things.

Jesus Is Buried
⁵⁰ Behold, a man named Joseph, who was a member of the council, a good and righteous man ⁵¹ (he had not consented to their counsel and deed), from Arimathaea, a city of the Jews, who was also waiting for God's Kingdom: ⁵² this man went to Pilate, and asked for Jesus' body. ⁵³ He took it down, and wrapped it in a linen cloth, and laid him in a tomb that was cut in stone, where no one had ever been laid. ⁵⁴ It was the Day of the Preparation, and the Sabbath was drawing near. ⁵⁵ The women, who had come with him out of Galilee, followed after, and

saw the tomb, and how his body was laid. ⁵⁶ They returned, and prepared spices and ointments. On the Sabbath they rested according to the commandment.

1. What did Jesus say to the women who were mourning over Him?
2. After He was crucified, what was the first thing Jesus said from the cross?
3. What promise did Jesus make to the criminal who believed in Him?
4. What words spoken by Jesus tell us that He experienced spiritual as well as physical death? Why did God the Father forsake Him?
5. Why did Jesus say, "It is finished"?
6. What did the centurion say about Jesus when Jesus committed His spirit to the Father?
7. If you had been there, what would you have said?

105. ALIVE AGAIN!
Matthew 27:62-66 and 28:1-15 and John 20:3-18

Although sealed and guarded, the tomb could not hold back the risen Christ. God raised Jesus from the dead, showing that He had power even over death and the grave. The resurrection of Jesus Christ proved that God had accepted His death as complete payment for the sins of mankind. Therefore, anyone who believes in Jesus Christ will have his destiny changed from death to life.

The Guard at the Tomb

27 ⁶²Now on the next day, which was the day after the Preparation Day, the chief priests and the Pharisees were gathered together to Pilate, ⁶³ saying, "Sir, we remember what that deceiver said while he was still alive: 'After three days I will rise again.' ⁶⁴ Command therefore that the tomb be made secure until the third day, lest perhaps his disciples come at night and steal him away, and tell the people, 'He is risen from the dead;' and the last deception will be worse than the first."

⁶⁵ Pilate said to them, "You have a guard. Go, make it as secure as you can."
⁶⁶ So they went with the guard and made the tomb secure, sealing the stone.

Jesus Rises from the Dead

28 Now after the Sabbath, as it began to dawn on the first day of the week, Mary Magdalene and the other Mary came to see the tomb. ² Behold, there was a great earthquake, for an angel of the Lord descended from the sky, and came and rolled away the stone from the door, and sat on it. ³ His appearance was like lightning, and his clothing white as snow. ⁴ For fear of him, the guards shook, and became like dead men.⁵ The angel answered the women, "Don't be afraid, for I know that you seek Jesus, who has been crucified. ⁶ He is not here, for he has risen, just like he said. Come, see the place where the Lord was lying. ⁷ Go quickly and tell his disciples, 'He has risen from the dead, and behold, he goes before you into Galilee; there you will see him.'

Behold, I have told you."

⁸ They departed quickly from the tomb with fear and great joy, and ran to bring his disciples word. ⁹ As they went to tell his disciples, behold, Jesus met them, saying, "Rejoice!" They came and took hold of his feet, and worshiped him. ¹⁰ Then Jesus said to them, "Don't be afraid. Go tell my brothers that they should go into Galilee, and there they will see me."

The Guard's Report

¹¹ Now while they were going, behold, some of the guards came into the city, and told the chief priests all the things that had happened. ¹² When they were assembled with the elders, and had taken counsel, they gave a large amount of silver to the soldiers,¹³ saying, "Say that his disciples came by night, and stole him away while we slept. ¹⁴ If this comes to the governor's ears, we will persuade him and make you free of worry. ¹⁵So they took the money and did as they were told. This saying was spread abroad among the Jews, and continues until today.

The Disciples View the Empty Tomb

20 ³Therefore Peter and the other disciple went out, and they went toward the tomb. ⁴ They both ran together. The other disciple outran Peter, and came to the tomb first. ⁵ Stooping and looking in, he saw the linen cloths lying, yet he didn't enter in. ⁶ Then Simon Peter came, following him, and entered into the tomb. He saw the linen cloths lying, ⁷ and the cloth that had been on his head, not lying with the linen cloths, but rolled up in a place by itself. ⁸ So then the other disciple who came first to the tomb also entered in, and he saw and believed. ⁹ For as yet they didn't know the Scripture, that he must rise from the dead.¹⁰ So the disciples went away again to their own homes.

Jesus Appears to Mary Magdalene

¹¹ But Mary was standing outside at the tomb weeping. So, as she wept, she stooped and looked into the tomb, ¹² and she saw two angels in white sitting, one at the head, and one at the feet, where the body of Jesus had lain. ¹³ They told her, "Woman, why are you weeping?"

She said to them, "Because they have taken away my Lord, and I don't know where they have laid him." ¹⁴ When she had said this, she turned around and saw Jesus standing, and didn't know that it was Jesus. ¹⁵ Jesus said to her, "Woman, why are you weeping? Who are you looking for?" She, supposing him to be the gardener, said to him, "Sir, if you have carried him away, tell me where you have laid him, and I will take him away."

¹⁶Jesus said to her, "Mary."

She turned and said to him, "Rabboni!" which is to say, "Teacher!"[

¹⁷Jesus said to her, "Don't hold me, for I haven't yet ascended to my Father; but go to my brothers, and tell them, 'I am ascending to my Father and your Father, to my God and your God.'"

¹⁸Mary Magdalene came and told the disciples that she had seen the Lord, and that he had said these things to her.

    1. Why was the tomb sealed and a guard posted?

    2. What did the angel say to the women?

    3. Why did the other disciple (John) believe?

    4. What did Jesus say to Mary after she recognized Him?

    5. What new things did you learn about Jesus' death and resurrection?

106. WALKING WITH JESUS
Luke 24:13-49 and John 20:24-31

When God raised Jesus from the dead, He gave Him a new body, yet left the scars from His wounds to remind us of His suffering for our sins. Jesus appeared and spoke to His disciples explaining to them all that the Old Testament writers and prophets had written about Him. Although we have not seen Jesus, as Thomas did, we can believe by faith that He is the Christ, the Son of God.

On the Road to Emmaus

24 ¹³Behold, two of them were going that very day to a village named Emmaus, which was sixty stadia [7 miles, 11.6 km] from Jerusalem. ¹⁴ They talked with each other about all of these things which had happened. ¹⁵ While they talked and questioned together, Jesus himself came near, and went with them. ¹⁶ But their eyes were kept from recognizing him. ¹⁷ He said to them, "What are you talking about as you walk, and are sad?"

¹⁸ One of them, named Cleopas, answered him, "Are you the only stranger in Jerusalem who doesn't know the things which have happened there in these days?"

¹⁹ He said to them, "What things?"

They said to him, "The things concerning Jesus, the Nazarene, who was a prophet mighty in deed and word before God and all the people; ²⁰ and how the chief priests and our rulers delivered him up to be condemned to death, and crucified him. ²¹ But we were hoping that it was he who would redeem Israel. Yes, and besides all this, it is now the third day since these things happened. ²² Also, certain women of our company amazed us, having arrived early at the tomb; ²³ and when they didn't find his body, they came saying that they had also seen a vision of angels, who said that he was alive. ²⁴ Some of us went to the tomb, and found it just like the women had said, but they didn't see him."

²⁵He said to them, "Foolish men, and slow of heart to believe in all that the prophets have spoken! ²⁶ Didn't the Christ have to suffer these things and to enter into his glory?" ²⁷ Beginning from Moses and from all the prophets, he explained to them in all the Scriptures the things concerning himself.

²⁸ They came near to the village, where they were going, and he acted like he would go further. ²⁹ They urged him, saying, "Stay with us, for it is almost

evening, and the day is almost over."

He went in to stay with them. ³⁰ When he had sat down at the table with them, he took the bread and gave thanks. Breaking it, he gave to them. ³¹ Their eyes were opened, and they recognized him, and he vanished out of their sight. ³² They said to one another, "Weren't our hearts burning within us, while he spoke to us along the way, and while he opened the Scriptures to us?" ³³ They rose up that very hour, returned to Jerusalem, and found the eleven gathered together, and those who were with them, ³⁴ saying, "The Lord is risen indeed, and has appeared to Simon!" ³⁵ They related the things that happened along the way, and how he was recognized by them in the breaking of the bread.

Jesus Appears to His Disciples

³⁶ As they said these things, Jesus himself stood among them, and said to them, "Peace be to you."

³⁷ But they were terrified and filled with fear, and supposed that they had seen a spirit.

³⁸ He said to them, "Why are you troubled? Why do doubts arise in your hearts? ³⁹ See my hands and my feet, that it is truly me. Touch me and see, for a spirit doesn't have flesh and bones, as you see that I have." ⁴⁰ When he had said this, he showed them his hands and his feet. ⁴¹ While they still didn't believe for joy, and wondered, he said to them, "Do you have anything here to eat?"

⁴² They gave him a piece of a broiled fish and some honeycomb. ⁴³ He took them, and ate in front of them. ⁴⁴ He said to them, "This is what I told you, while I was still with you, that all things which are written in the Law of Moses, the prophets, and the psalms, concerning me must be fulfilled."

⁴⁵ Then he opened their minds, that they might understand the Scriptures. ⁴⁶ He said to them, "Thus it is written, and thus it was necessary for the Christ to suffer and to rise from the dead the third day, ⁴⁷ and that repentance and remission of sins should be preached in his name to all the nations, beginning at Jerusalem. ⁴⁸ You are witnesses of these things. ⁴⁹ Behold, I send out the promise of my Father on you. But wait in the city of Jerusalem until you are clothed with power from on high."

Jesus Confronts the Doubting Thomas

20 ²⁴But Thomas, one of the twelve, called Didymus, wasn't with them when Jesus came.²⁵ The other disciples therefore said to him, "We have seen the Lord!" But he said to them, "Unless I see in his hands the print of the nails, and put my hand into his side, I will not believe."

²⁶ After eight days again his disciples were inside, and Thomas was with them. Jesus came, the doors being locked, and stood in the middle, and said, "Peace be to you."²⁷ Then he said to Thomas, "Reach here your finger, and see my hands. Reach here your hand, and put it into my side. Don't be unbelieving, but believing."

²⁸ Thomas answered him, "My Lord and my God!"

²⁹ Jesus said to him, "Because you have seen me, you have believed. Blessed are those who have not seen, and have believed."

Why John Wrote This Book
³⁰ Therefore Jesus did many other signs in the presence of his disciples, which are not written in this book; ³¹ but these are written, that you may believe that Jesus is the Christ, the Son of God, and that believing you may have life in his name.

1. What caused the two disciples to recognize Jesus? Why?

2. How did Jesus prove to His disciples that he really was alive and not a ghost?

3. What parts of Scripture did Jesus use to show the fulfillment of all that was written about Him? Can you find some of these portions in the Old Testament section of Great Bible Truths?

4. What did Thomas say that showed he believed?

5. The disciples were witnesses of all that had occurred in Jesus' life and ministry. Read what Jesus told His disciples would happen in the future. Jesus had a special work for them. What would that be (see v. 47)?

6. What was the reason John gave for writing about the life and ministry of Jesus?

107. THE RETURN TO HEAVEN
John 21:1-19 and Matthew 28:16-20 and Luke 24:50-53

After His resurrection, Jesus remained on earth forty days. During that time He appeared many times to His disciples and other followers. As the time came for Him to return to His Father in heaven, Jesus gave the mandate and authority to His disciples to carry on His work. It is the responsibility of all who believe and follow Him to tell other people about the Good News of salvation and teach them the commandments of Jesus.

Jesus and the Miraculous Catch of Fish
21 After these things, Jesus revealed himself again to the disciples at the sea of Tiberias. He revealed himself this way. ² Simon Peter, Thomas called Didymus, Nathanael of Cana in Galilee, and the sons of Zebedee, and two others of his disciples were together. ³ Simon Peter said to them, "I'm going fishing."

They told him, "We are also coming with you." They immediately went out, and entered into the boat. That night, they caught nothing. ⁴ But when day had already come, Jesus stood on the beach, yet the disciples didn't know that it was Jesus. ⁵ Jesus therefore said to them, "Children, have you anything to eat?"

They answered him, "No."

⁶ He said to them, "Cast the net on the right side of the boat, and you will find some."

They cast it therefore, and now they weren't able to draw it in for the multitude of fish.⁷ That disciple therefore whom Jesus loved said to Peter, "It's the Lord!"

So when Simon Peter heard that it was the Lord, he wrapped his coat around him (for he was naked), and threw himself into the sea. ⁸ But the other disciples came in the little boat (for they were not far from the land, but about two hundred cubits [100 yards] away), dragging the net full of fish. ⁹ So when they got out on the land, they saw a fire of coals there, and fish laid on it, and bread. ¹⁰ Jesus said to them, "Bring some of the fish which you have just caught."

¹¹ Simon Peter went up, and drew the net to land, full of great fish, one hundred fifty-three; and even though there were so many, the net wasn't torn.

¹² Jesus said to them, "Come and eat breakfast." None of the disciples dared inquire of him, "Who are you?" knowing that it was the Lord.

¹³ Then Jesus came and took the bread, gave it to them, and the fish likewise. ¹⁴ This is now the third time that Jesus was revealed to his disciples, after he had risen from the dead.

Jesus Reinstates Peter
¹⁵ So when they had eaten their breakfast, Jesus said to Simon Peter, "Simon, son of Jonah, do you love me more than these?"

He said to him, "Yes, Lord; you know that I have affection for you."

He said to him, "Feed my lambs." ¹⁶ He said to him again a second time, "Simon, son of Jonah, do you love me?"

He said to him, "Yes, Lord; you know that I have affection for you."

He said to him, "Tend my sheep." ¹⁷ He said to him the third time, "Simon, son of Jonah, do you have affection for me?"

Peter was grieved because he asked him the third time, "Do you have affection for me? "He said to him, "Lord, you know everything. You know that I have affection for you."

Jesus said to him, "Feed my sheep. ¹⁸ Most certainly I tell you, when you were young, you dressed yourself, and walked where you wanted to. But when you are old, you will stretch out your hands, and another will dress you, and carry you where you don't want to go."

¹⁹ Now he said this, signifying by what kind of death he would glorify God. When he had said this, he said to him, "Follow me."

Jesus Commissions His Disciples
28 ¹⁶But the eleven disciples went into Galilee, to the mountain where Jesus had sent them.¹⁷ When they saw him, they bowed down to him, but some doubted.

¹⁸ Jesus came to them and spoke to them, saying, "All authority has been given to me in heaven and on earth. ¹⁹ Go, and make disciples of all nations, baptizing them in the name of the Father and of the Son and of the Holy Spirit, ²⁰ teaching them to observe all things that I commanded you. Behold, I am with you always, even to the end of the age." Amen.

Jesus Goes Back to Heaven

24 ⁵⁰He led them out as far as Bethany, and he lifted up his hands, and blessed them.⁵¹ While he blessed them, he withdrew from them, and was carried up into heaven.⁵² They worshiped him, and returned to Jerusalem with great joy, ⁵³ and were continually in the temple, praising and blessing God. Amen.

1. Why do you think Jesus asked Peter three times, "Do you truly love me?"
2. What three commands did Jesus give to Peter?
3. In commissioning the eleven disciples for the work ahead, what three things did Jesus tell them to do?
4. What promise did Jesus give His disciples before He ascended into heaven?
5. What did the disciples do after Jesus was taken up into heaven?

V. CHRIST BUILDS HIS CHURCH

We have previously read how God chose the descendants of Abraham and the nation of Israel to work out His plan of salvation for the whole world. Although God used Israel, this salvation was not just for one nation or one race of people. Jesus Christ came to earth to die and be raised again to pay the penalty for the sins of every man, woman and child who received Him as their Savior. After Jesus returned to heaven, the Holy Spirit was sent by God the Father so that the Spirit of Jesus might come and live in the hearts of everyone who believed in Him. It is the presence of the Holy Spirit within a believer that makes him or her a new person with a new spirit that can respond to God. Those who become these new persons are called Christians, and they belong to the body of believers called the Church. The Church is not a building or a place; the Church is people from every nation, race and culture who are united by their love and obedience to Jesus Christ. In the following selections we will read how God took Jesus' disciples and used them to build the foundation of His Church, beginning at Jerusalem and spreading to all the nations of the then-known world.

A. THE GROWTH OF THE CHURCH

The beginning and growth of the Church of Jesus Christ are recorded in a book called the Acts of the Apostles. As God poured His Holy Spirit upon the followers of Jesus, they received the power they needed to act as the Body of Christ in the world. We read how ordinary men and women who were filled with the Holy Spirit were able to do the same works and miracles that Jesus did while He was on earth. As the message of the Good News of salvation was preached, people of Israel and other nations came to believe in Jesus as their Savior. It was these believers who became the Church in the different places where they lived.

108. THE COMING OF THE HOLY SPIRIT
Acts 1:1-14 and 2:1-41

Luke, who was not a Jew, wrote one of the Gospel accounts of the life of Jesus Christ. He also wrote the book of the Acts of the Apostles. His plan was to record of the history of the life of Jesus Christ and the events following Jesus' return to heaven along with the beginning, the growth and expansion of the Christian movement. Acts begins with an account of Jesus' last days on earth, his return to heaven and His instructions to the disciples. We will see that Jesus told the disciples to wait for the coming of the Holy Spirit which would give them divine power which they would need to be His ambassadors, fulfilling the commission that He gave to them to go throughout the world to preach the Gospel and make disciples of all peoples.

Very soon on the day of Pentecost, 120 disciples were praying together when the Holy Spirit was poured out upon them, giving them the power they needed to be his witnesses. They were a filled with joy and began to praise God and speak in languages they had never learned. At that time Jerusalem happened to be filled with visitors from faraway places who heard those disciples praising God in their own languages. A crowd formed which was very curious to learn what was going on. Peter's explanation of what was happening and his powerful message resulted in thousands of people receiving Jesus Christ as their Savior. It was an unforgettable day that began a movement that changed the world.

Luke Writes Another Book

1 The first book I wrote, Theophilus, concerned all that Jesus began both to do and to teach, ² until the day in which he was received up, after he had given commandment through the Holy Spirit to the apostles whom he had chosen. ³ To these he also showed himself alive after he suffered, by many proofs, appearing to them over a period of forty days, and speaking about God's Kingdom. ⁴ Being assembled together with them, he commanded them, "Don't depart from Jerusalem, but wait for the promise of the Father, which you heard from me. ⁵ For John indeed baptized in water, but you will be baptized in the Holy Spirit not many days from now."

Jesus Taken up into Heaven

⁶ Therefore when they had come together, they asked him, "Lord, are you now restoring the kingdom to Israel?"

⁷ He said to them, "It isn't for you to know times or seasons which the Father has set within his own authority. ⁸ But you will receive power when the Holy Spirit has come upon you. You will be witnesses to me in Jerusalem, in all Judea and Samaria, and to the uttermost parts of the earth."

⁹ When he had said these things, as they were looking, he was taken up, and a cloud received him out of their sight. ¹⁰ While they were looking steadfastly into the sky as he went, behold, two men stood by them in white clothing, ¹¹ who also said, "You men of Galilee, why do you stand looking into the sky? This Jesus, who was received up from you into the sky will come back in the same way as you saw him going into the sky."

¹² Then they returned to Jerusalem from the mountain called Olivet, which

is near Jerusalem, a Sabbath day's journey away. ¹³ When they had come in, they went up into the upper room, where they were staying; that is Peter, John, James, Andrew, Philip, Thomas, Bartholomew, Matthew, James the son of Alphaeus, Simon the Zealot, and Judas the son of James. ¹⁴ All these with one accord continued steadfastly in prayer and supplication, along with the women, and Mary the mother of Jesus, and with his brothers.

The Holy Spirit Comes at Pentecost

2 Now when the day of Pentecost had come, they were all with one accord in one place. ² Suddenly there came from the sky a sound like the rushing of a mighty wind, and it filled all the house where they were sitting. ³ Tongues like fire appeared and were distributed to them, and one sat on each of them. ⁴ They were all filled with the Holy Spirit, and began to speak with other languages, as the Spirit gave them the ability to speak.

⁵ Now there were dwelling in Jerusalem Jews, devout men, from every nation under the sky. ⁶ When this sound was heard, the multitude came together, and were bewildered, because everyone heard them speaking in his own language.

⁷ They were all amazed and marveled, saying to one another, "Behold, aren't all these who speak Galileans? ⁸ How do we hear, everyone in our own native language? ⁹ Parthians, Medes, Elamites, and people from Mesopotamia, Judea, Cappadocia, Pontus, Asia, ¹⁰ Phrygia, Pamphylia, Egypt, the parts of Libya around Cyrene, visitors from Rome, both Jews and proselytes, ¹¹ Cretans and Arabians: we hear them speaking in our languages the mighty works of God!" ¹² They were all amazed, and were perplexed, saying to one another, "What does this mean?" ¹³ Others, mocking, said, "They are filled with new wine."

Peter Addresses the Crowd

¹⁴ But Peter, standing up with the eleven, lifted up his voice, and spoke out to them, "You men of Judea, and all you who dwell at Jerusalem, let this be known to you, and listen to my words. ¹⁵ For these aren't drunken, as you suppose, seeing it is only the third hour of the day. ¹⁶ But this is what has been spoken through the prophet Joel:

¹⁷'it will be in the last days, says God
that I will pour out my Spirit on all flesh.
Your sons and your daughters will prophesy.
Your young men will see visions.
Your old men will dream dreams.
¹⁸Yes, and on my servants and on my handmaidens in those days,
I will pour out my Spirit, and they will prophesy.
¹⁹ I will show wonders in the sky above,
and signs on the earth beneath;
blood, and fire, and billows of smoke.
²⁰ The sun will be turned into darkness,
and the moon into blood,
before the great and glorious day of the Lord comes.
²¹It will be that whoever will call on the name of the Lord will be saved.'

²² "Men of Israel, hear these words! Jesus of Nazareth, a man approved by God

to you by mighty works and wonders and signs which God did by him among you, even as you yourselves know, ²³ him, being delivered up by the determined counsel and foreknowledge of God, you have taken by the hand of lawless men, crucified and killed; ²⁴ whom God raised up, having freed him from the agony of death, because it was not possible that he should be held by it. ²⁵ For David says concerning him,

> 'I saw the Lord always before my face,
> For he is on my right hand, that I should not be moved.
> ²⁶Therefore my heart was glad, and my tongue rejoiced.
> Moreover my flesh also will dwell in hope;
> ²⁷because you will not leave my soul in Hades,
> neither will you allow your Holy One to see decay.
> ²⁸You made known to me the ways of life.
> You will make me full of gladness with your presence.'

²⁹ "Brothers, I may tell you freely of the patriarch David, that he both died and was buried, and his tomb is with us to this day. ³⁰ Therefore, being a prophet, and knowing that God had sworn with an oath to him that of the fruit of his body, according to the flesh, he would raise up the Christ to sit on his throne, ³¹ he foreseeing this spoke about the resurrection of the Christ, that neither was his soul left in Hades, nor did his flesh see decay. ³² This Jesus God raised up, to which we all are witnesses. ³³ Being therefore exalted by the right hand of God, and having received from the Father the promise of the Holy Spirit, he has poured out this, which you now see and hear. ³⁴ For David didn't ascend into the heavens, but he says himself,

> 'The Lord said to my Lord, "Sit by my right hand,
> ³⁵until I make your enemies a footstool for your feet."'

³⁶ "Let all the house of Israel therefore know certainly that God has made him both Lord and Christ, this Jesus whom you crucified."

³⁷ Now when they heard this, they were cut to the heart, and said to Peter and the rest of the apostles, "Brothers, what shall we do?"

³⁸ Peter said to them, "Repent, and be baptized, every one of you, in the name of Jesus Christ for the forgiveness of sins, and you will receive the gift of the Holy Spirit. ³⁹ For the promise is to you, and to your children, and to all who are far off, even as many as the Lord our God will call to himself." ⁴⁰ With many other words he testified, and exhorted them, saying, "Save yourselves from this crooked generation!"

⁴¹ Then those who gladly received his word were baptized. There were added that day about three thousand souls.

> 1. What did Jesus tell the disciples to do just before He was taken up into heaven? Why?
>
> 2. What happened when the Holy Spirit descended upon the praying disciples? Why were the Jews so amazed at what was happening?
>
> 3. How were the disciples different after the Holy Spirit arrived? What were they supposed to do with this new divine resource? (v.8)

4. Note how Peter's demeanor has changed after receiving the Holy Spirit! Carefully read his sermon. Did you learn something new?
5. What did Peter tell the people to do? Why?
6. To whom was the promise given? What was the promise?
7. How many people responded to Peter's message to form the early Church?

109. THE NAME OF JESUS
Acts 2:42-47 and 3:1-26

As the group of believers grew, we read of their devotion to God and their love for one another. This was the beginning of the Christian Church. The healing of a crippled beggar by the power of the Holy Spirit, through the name of Jesus Christ, gave Peter an opportunity to tell the people about Jesus. Peter said Jesus was the long-promised Messiah, sent by God to Israel and calling the people to repentance, to return to God so that He could bless them once again.

Description of the New Church in Jerusalem

2 ⁴²They continued steadfastly in the apostles' teaching and fellowship, in the breaking of bread, and prayer. ⁴³ Fear came on every soul, and many wonders and signs were done through the apostles. ⁴⁴ All who believed were together, and had all things in common.⁴⁵ They sold their possessions and goods, and distributed them to all, according as anyone had need. ⁴⁶ Day by day, continuing steadfastly with one accord in the temple, and breaking bread at home, they took their food with gladness and singleness of heart,⁴⁷ praising God, and having favor with all the people. The Lord added to the assembly day by day those who were being saved.

Peter Heals the Crippled Beggar

3 ¹Peter and John were going up into the temple at the hour of prayer, the ninth hour. ² A certain man who was lame from his mother's womb was being carried, whom they laid daily at the door of the temple which is called Beautiful, to ask gifts for the needy of those who entered into the temple. ³ Seeing Peter and John about to go into the temple, he asked to receive gifts for the needy. ⁴ Peter, fastening his eyes on him, with John, said, "Look at us." ⁵ He listened to them, expecting to receive something from them. ⁶ But Peter said, "Silver and gold have I none, but what I have, that I give you. In the name of Jesus Christ of Nazareth, get up and walk!" ⁷ He took him by the right hand, and raised him up. Immediately his feet and his ankle bones received strength. ⁸ Leaping up, he stood, and began to walk. He entered with them into the temple, walking, leaping, and praising God.⁹ All the people saw him walking and praising God. ¹⁰ They recognized him, that it was he who used to sit begging for gifts for the needy at the Beautiful Gate of the temple. They were filled with wonder and amazement at what had happened to him.

Peter Speaks to the Onlookers

¹¹As the lame man who was healed held on to Peter and John, all the people ran together to them in the porch that is called Solomon's, greatly wondering.

¹²When Peter saw it, he responded to the people, "You men of Israel, why do you marvel at this man? Why do you fasten your eyes on us, as though by our own power or godliness we had made him walk? ¹³ The God of Abraham, Isaac, and Jacob, the God of our fathers, has glorified his Servant Jesus, whom you delivered up, and denied in the presence of Pilate, when he had determined to release him. ¹⁴ But you denied the Holy and Righteous One, and asked for a murderer to be granted to you, ¹⁵ and killed the Prince of life, whom God raised from the dead, to which we are witnesses. ¹⁶ By faith in his name, his name has made this man strong, whom you see and know. Yes, the faith which is through him has given him this perfect soundness in the presence of you all.

¹⁷ "Now, brothers, I know that you did this in ignorance, as did also your rulers. ¹⁸ But the things which God announced by the mouth of all his prophets, that Christ should suffer, he thus fulfilled.

¹⁹ "Repent therefore, and turn again, that your sins may be blotted out, so that there may come times of refreshing from the presence of the Lord, ²⁰ and that he may send Christ Jesus, who was ordained for you before, ²¹ whom heaven must receive until the times of restoration of all things, which God spoke long ago by the mouth of his holy prophets.

²² For Moses indeed said to the fathers, 'The Lord God will raise up a prophet for you from among your brothers, like me. You shall listen to him in all things whatever he says to you. ²³ It will be that every soul that will not listen to that prophet will be utterly destroyed from among the people.' ²⁴ Yes, and all the prophets from Samuel and those who followed after, as many as have spoken, they also told of these days. ²⁵ You are the children of the prophets, and of the covenant which God made with our fathers, saying to Abraham, 'In your offspring will all the families of the earth be blessed. ²⁶ God, having raised up his servant Jesus, sent him to you first to bless you, in turning away every one of you from your wickedness."

   1. Describe the life style of new believers in Jerusalem.

   2. What did Peter say was the reason the man was healed? (v.16)

   3. What did Peter tell the people they must do to respond to his message?

110. BOLDNESS TO SPEAK
Acts 4:1-31

The healing of the lame man was an astounding event that caused a curious crowd to form. When Peter and John explained the miracle to the people and urged them to believe in Jesus, many responded in faith to the message of salvation. The Jewish leaders arrested the two disciples and with menacing threats commanded them to stop speaking about Jesus Christ. Yet, just as Jesus had promised, the Holy Spirit gave the disciples the power and boldness they needed to continue to be witnesses for Him without fear.

Peter and John at the Council

4 ¹As they spoke to the people, the priests and the captain of the temple and the Sadducees came to them, ² being upset because they taught the people and proclaimed in Jesus the resurrection from the dead. ³ They laid hands on them, and put them in custody until the next day, for it was now evening. ⁴ But many of those who heard the word believed, and the number of the men came to be about five thousand.

⁵In the morning, their rulers, elders, and scribes were gathered together in Jerusalem.⁶ Annas the high priest was there, with Caiaphas, John, Alexander, and as many as were relatives of the high priest. ⁷ When they had stood them in the middle of them, they inquired, "By what power, or in what name, have you done this?"

⁸ Then Peter, filled with the Holy Spirit, said to them, "You rulers of the people, and elders of Israel, ⁹ if we are examined today concerning a good deed done to a crippled man, by what means this man has been healed, ¹⁰ be it known to you all, and to all the people of Israel, that in the name of Jesus Christ of Nazareth, whom you crucified, whom God raised from the dead, in him does this man stand here before you whole. ¹¹ He is 'the stone which was regarded as worthless by you, the builders, which has become the head of the corner.' ¹² There is salvation in none other, for neither is there any other name under heaven, that is given among men, by which we must be saved!"

¹³ Now when they saw the boldness of Peter and John, and had perceived that they were unlearned and ignorant men, they marveled. They recognized that they had been with Jesus. ¹⁴ Seeing the man who was healed standing with them, they could say nothing against it. ¹⁵ But when they had commanded them to go aside out of the council, they conferred among themselves, ¹⁶ saying, "What shall we do to these men? Because indeed a notable miracle has been done through them, as can be plainly seen by all who dwell in Jerusalem, and we can't deny it. ¹⁷ But so that this spreads no further among the people, let's threaten them, that from now on they don't speak to anyone in this name." ¹⁸ They called them, and commanded them not to speak at all nor teach in the name of Jesus.

¹⁹ But Peter and John answered them, "Whether it is right in the sight of God to listen to you rather than to God, judge for yourselves, ²⁰ for we can't help telling the things which we saw and heard."

²¹ When they had further threatened them, they let them go, finding no way to punish them, because of the people; for everyone glorified God for that which was done. ²² For the man on whom this miracle of healing was performed was more than forty years old.

The Believers Pray for Courage

²³ Being let go, they came to their own company, and reported all that the chief priests and the elders had said to them. ²⁴ When they heard it, they lifted up their voice to God with one accord, and said, "O Lord, you are God, who made the heaven, the earth, the sea, and all that is in them; ²⁵ who by the mouth of your servant, David, said,

> 'Why do the nations rage,
> and the peoples plot a vain thing?
> ²⁶ The kings of the earth take a stand,
> and the rulers take council together, against the Lord,
> and against his Christ.'

²⁷ "For truly, in this city against your holy servant, Jesus, whom you anointed, both Herod and Pontius Pilate, with the Gentiles and the people of Israel, were gathered together ²⁸ to do whatever your hand and your council foreordained to happen. ²⁹ Now, Lord, look at their threats, and grant to your servants to speak your word with all boldness, ³⁰ while you stretch out your hand to heal; and that signs and wonders may be done through the name of your holy Servant Jesus."

³¹ When they had prayed, the place was shaken where they were gathered together. They were all filled with the Holy Spirit, and they spoke the word of God with boldness.

1. Why were the priests and Sadducees so disturbed?
2. By what power and in whose Name did Peter say the crippled man was healed?
3. Read v.12. Are there many ways to salvation? Why not?
4. What specifically did the believers ask for when they prayed to God?
5. Did God answer their prayers? How?

111. SPREADING THE GOOD NEWS
Acts 5:12-42 and 6:7

The Christian movement was growing fast. The Holy Spirit inspired preaching the Good News of Salvation in Jesus name was aided by the many signs and wonders performed by the apostles. The divine message was confirmed by divine miracles. The result was a continual growth of the early Christian Church. The Jewish leaders became jealous and put the apostles in jail. However, man cannot thwart the purposes of God, and His power proved to be greater than prison doors or religious thinking. Rejoicing because they were counted worthy to suffer for His name, the disciples continued to spread the Good News that Jesus was the Christ – the promised Savior sent from God.

Great Bible Truths

The Apostles Heal Many

5 [12] By the hands of the apostles many signs and wonders were done among the people. They were all with one accord in Solomon's porch. [13] None of the rest dared to join them, however the people honored them. [14] More believers were added to the Lord, multitudes of both men and women. [15] They even carried out the sick into the streets, and laid them on cots and mattresses, so that as Peter came by, at the least his shadow might overshadow some of them. [16] Multitudes also came together from the cities around Jerusalem, bringing sick people, and those who were tormented by unclean spirits: and they were all healed.

Apostles Persecuted

[17] But the high priest rose up, and all those who were with him (which is the sect of the Sadducees), and they were filled with jealousy, [18] and laid hands on the apostles, and put them in public custody.

God Opens Prison Doors

[19] But an angel of the Lord opened the prison doors by night, and brought them out, and said, [20] "Go stand and speak in the temple to the people all the words of this life."

[21] When they heard this, they entered into the temple about daybreak, and taught. But the high priest came, and those who were with him, and called the council together, and all the senate of the children of Israel, and sent to the prison to have them brought. [22] But the officers who came didn't find them in the prison. They returned and reported, [23] "We found the prison shut and locked, and the guards standing before the doors, but when we opened them, we found no one inside!"

[24] Now when the high priest, the captain of the temple, and the chief priests heard these words, they were very perplexed about them and what might become of this. [25] One came and told them, "Behold, the men whom you put in prison are in the temple, standing and teaching the people."

[26] Then the captain went with the officers, and brought them without violence, for they were afraid that the people might stone them.

[27] When they had brought them, they set them before the council. The high priest questioned them, [28] saying, "Didn't we strictly command you not to teach in this name? Behold, you have filled Jerusalem with your teaching, and intend to bring this man's blood on us."

[29] But Peter and the apostles answered, "We must obey God rather than men. [30] The God of our fathers raised up Jesus, whom you killed, hanging him on a tree. [31] God exalted him with his right hand to be a Prince and a Savior, to give repentance to Israel, and remission of sins. [32] We are His witnesses of these things; and so also is the Holy Spirit, whom God has given to those who obey him."

Gamaliel's Advice

[33] But they, when they heard this, were cut to the heart, and determined to kill them. [34] But one stood up in the council, a Pharisee named Gamaliel, a teacher

of the law, honored by all the people, and commanded to put the apostles out for a little while. ³⁵ He said to them, "You men of Israel, be careful concerning these men, what you are about to do. ³⁶ For before these days Theudas rose up, making himself out to be somebody; to whom a number of men, about four hundred, joined themselves: who was slain; and all, as many as obeyed him, were dispersed, and came to nothing. ³⁷ After this man, Judas of Galilee rose up in the days of the enrollment, and drew away some people after him. He also perished, and all, as many as obeyed him, were scattered abroad. ³⁸ Now I tell you, withdraw from these men, and leave them alone. For if this counsel or this work is of men, it will be overthrown. ³⁹ But if it is of God, you will not be able to overthrow it, and you would be found even to be fighting against God!"

⁴⁰ They agreed with him. Summoning the apostles, they beat them and commanded them not to speak in the name of Jesus, and let them go. ⁴¹ They therefore departed from the presence of the council, rejoicing that they were counted worthy to suffer dishonor for Jesus' name.

⁴² Every day, in the temple and at home, they never stopped teaching and preaching Jesus, the Christ.

6 ⁷The word of God increased and the number of the disciples multiplied in Jerusalem exceedingly. A great company of the priests were obedient to the faith.

> 1. What miracles were being performed by the Apostles?
>
> 2. Why did Peter insist that they must continue to teach about Jesus? Who was their ultimate authority?
>
> 3. Did Gamaliel give wise advice to the Sanhedrin? Why?
>
> 4. Where did the apostles proclaim the Good News, and what was the result?

112. THE FIRST CHRISTIAN MARTYR
Acts 6:8-15; 7:1-60; and 8:1-3

Opposition from the Jewish religious leaders continued and became even stronger as they focused their hatred against a prominent believer named Stephen. He was accused of opposing Judaism. Stephen's defense was a comprehensive review of God's miraculous dealings with Israel beginning with Abraham. He condemned the leadership for exchanging true faith in God for religiosity, for not really loving God or listening to him, and always opposing the Holy Spirit as they made their religion satisfactory and convenient for themselves. Stephen infuriated them, and they took their anger out on Stephen by killing him. Although the Sanhedrin succeeded in destroying Stephen's body, it was unable to crush his spirit or his love for Jesus. Stephen became the first of many in the Church to die as a martyr, giving his life because of his faith in Jesus Christ.

Stephen Is Seized and Accused

6 [8]Stephen, full of faith and power, performed great wonders and signs among the people. [9] But some of those who were of the synagogue called "The Libertines", and of the Cyrenians, of the Alexandrians, and of those of Cilicia and Asia arose, disputing with Stephen. [10] They weren't able to withstand the wisdom and the Spirit by which he spoke. [11] Then they secretly induced men to say, "We have heard him speak blasphemous words against Moses and God." [12] They stirred up the people, the elders, and the scribes, and came against him and seized him, and brought him in to the council, [13] and set up false witnesses who said, "This man never stops speaking blasphemous words against this holy place and the law. [14] For we have heard him say that this Jesus of Nazareth will destroy this place, and will change the customs which Moses delivered to us." [15] All who sat in the council, fastening their eyes on him, saw his face like it was the face of an angel.

Stephen's Speech to the Sanhedrin

7 [1] The high priest said, "Are these things so?" [2] He [Stephen] said, "Brothers and fathers, listen. The God of glory appeared to our father Abraham, when he was in Mesopotamia, before he lived in Haran, [3] and said to him, 'Get out of your land, and from your relatives, and come into a land which I will show you.' [4] Then he came out of the land of the Chaldaeans, and lived in Haran. From there, when his father was dead, God moved him into this land, where you are now living. [5] He gave him no inheritance in it, no, not so much as to set his foot on. He promised that he would give it to him for a possession, and to his offspring after him, when he still had no child. [6] God spoke in this way: that his offspring would live as aliens in a strange land, and that they would be enslaved and mistreated for four hundred years. [7] 'I will judge the nation to which they will be in bondage,' said God, 'and after that will they come out, and serve me in this place.' [8] He gave him the covenant of circumcision. So Abraham became the father of Isaac, and circumcised him the eighth day. Isaac became the father of Jacob, and Jacob became the father of the twelve patriarchs.

[9] "The patriarchs, moved with jealousy against Joseph, sold him into Egypt. God was with him, [10] and delivered him out of all his afflictions, and gave him favor and wisdom before Pharaoh, king of Egypt. He made him governor over Egypt and all his house. [11] Now a famine came over all the land of Egypt and Canaan, and great affliction. Our fathers found no food. [12] But when Jacob heard that there was grain in Egypt, he sent out our fathers the first time. [13] On the second time Joseph was made known to his brothers, and Joseph's race was revealed to Pharaoh. [14] Joseph sent, and summoned Jacob, his father, and all his relatives, seventy-five souls. [15] Jacob went down into Egypt, and he died, himself and our fathers, [16] and they were brought back to Shechem, and laid in the tomb that Abraham bought for a price in silver from the children of Hamor of Shechem.

[17] "But as the time of the promise came close which God had sworn to Abraham, the people grew and multiplied in Egypt, [18] until there arose a

different king, who didn't know Joseph. ¹⁹ The same took advantage of our race, and mistreated our fathers, and forced them to throw out their babies, so that they wouldn't stay alive. ²⁰ At that time Moses was born, and was exceedingly handsome. He was nourished three months in his father's house. ²¹ When he was thrown out, Pharaoh's daughter took him up, and reared him as her own son. ²² Moses was instructed in all the wisdom of the Egyptians. He was mighty in his words and works. ²³ But when he was forty years old, it came into his heart to visit his brothers, the children of Israel. ²⁴ Seeing one of them suffer wrong, he defended him, and avenged him who was oppressed, striking the Egyptian. ²⁵ He supposed that his brothers understood that God, by his hand, was giving them deliverance; but they didn't understand.

²⁶ "The day following, he appeared to them as they fought, and urged them to be at peace again, saying, 'Sirs, you are brothers. Why do you wrong one another?' ²⁷ But he who did his neighbor wrong pushed him away, saying, 'Who made you a ruler and a judge over us? ²⁸ Do you want to kill me, as you killed the Egyptian yesterday?' ²⁹ Moses fled at this saying, and became a stranger in the land of Midian, where he became the father of two sons.

³⁰ "When forty years were fulfilled, an angel of the Lord appeared to him in the wilderness of Mount Sinai, in a flame of fire in a bush. ³¹ When Moses saw it, he wondered at the sight. As he came close to see, a voice of the Lord came to him, ³² 'I am the God of your fathers, the God of Abraham, the God of Isaac, and the God of Jacob. Moses trembled, and dared not look. ³³ The Lord said to him, 'Take your sandals off of your feet, for the place where you stand is holy ground. ³⁴ I have surely seen the affliction of my people that is in Egypt, and have heard their groaning. I have come down to deliver them. Now come, I will send you into Egypt.'

³⁵ "This Moses, whom they refused, saying, 'Who made you a ruler and a judge?'—God has sent him as both a ruler and a deliverer by the hand of the angel who appeared to him in the bush. ³⁶ This man led them out, having worked wonders and signs in Egypt, in the Red Sea, and in the wilderness for forty years. ³⁷ This is that Moses, who said to the children of Israel, 'The Lord our God will raise up a prophet for you from among your brothers, like me.' ³⁸ This is he who was in the assembly in the wilderness with the angel that spoke to him on Mount Sinai, and with our fathers, who received living revelations to give to us, ³⁹ to whom our fathers wouldn't be obedient, but rejected him, and turned back in their hearts to Egypt, ⁴⁰ saying to Aaron, 'Make us gods that will go before us, for as for this Moses, who led us out of the land of Egypt, we don't know what has become of him. ⁴¹ They made a calf in those days, and brought a sacrifice to the idol, and rejoiced in the works of their hands. ⁴² But God turned, and gave them up to serve the army of the sky, [to worship the sun, moon and stars] as it is written in the book of the prophets,

'Did you offer to me slain animals and sacrifices
    forty years in the wilderness, O house of Israel?
⁴³ You took up the tabernacle of Moloch,
    the star of your god Rephan,

the figures [idols] which you made to worship.
I will carry you away beyond Babylon.'

⁴⁴ "Our fathers had the tabernacle of the testimony in the wilderness, even as he who spoke to Moses commanded him to make it according to the pattern that he had seen; ⁴⁵ which also our fathers, in their turn, brought in with Joshua when they entered into the possession of the nations, whom God drove out before the face of our fathers, to the days of David, ⁴⁶ who found favor in the sight of God, and asked to find a habitation for the God of Jacob. ⁴⁷ But Solomon built him a house. ⁴⁸ However, the Most High doesn't dwell in temples made with hands, as the prophet says,

⁴⁹'heaven is my throne,
and the earth a footstool for my feet.
'What kind of house will you build me? says the Lord;
or what is the place of my rest?
⁵⁰Didn't my hand make all these things?'

⁵¹ "You stiff-necked and uncircumcised in heart and ears, you always resist the Holy Spirit! As your fathers did, so you do. ⁵² Which of the prophets didn't your fathers persecute? They killed those who foretold the coming of the Righteous One, of whom you have now become betrayers and murderers. ⁵³ You received the law as it was ordained by angels, and didn't keep it!"

Stephen Put to Death

⁵⁴ Now when they heard these things, they were cut to the heart, and they gnashed at him with their teeth. ⁵⁵ But he, being full of the Holy Spirit, looked up steadfastly into heaven, and saw the glory of God, and Jesus standing on the right hand of God, ⁵⁶ and said, "Behold, I see the heavens opened, and the Son of Man standing at the right hand of God!" ⁵⁷ But they cried out with a loud voice, and stopped their ears, and rushed at him with one accord. ⁵⁸ They threw him out of the city, and stoned him. The witnesses placed their garments at the feet of a young man named Saul. ⁵⁹ They stoned Stephen as he called out, saying, "Lord Jesus, receive my spirit!" ⁶⁰ He kneeled down, and cried with a loud voice, "Lord, don't hold this sin against them!" When he had said this, he fell asleep.

The Church Persecuted and Scattered

8 ¹Saul was consenting to his death. A great persecution arose against the assembly which was in Jerusalem in that day. They were all scattered abroad throughout the regions of Judea and Samaria, except for the apostles. ² Devout men buried Stephen, and lamented greatly over him. ³ But Saul ravaged the assembly, entering into every house, and dragged both men and women off to prison.

> 1. Describe the kind of man that Stephen was.
>
> 2. Did Stephen's recap of Israel's history help you to better understand why God had to send Jesus to Israel? Can you see how religion can deviate from true faith?

3. Why did the Sanhedrin become so angry with Stephen?
4. What did Stephen see when he looked up into heaven?
5. What did Stephen pray as he was being stoned?
6. What happened to the Church after Stephen's martyrdom?
7. How were the people of the Church persecuted? By whom?

113. CHRISTIANITY EXPANDS
Acts 8:4-40

We see the beginning of the expansion of the Christian movement in the next three selections. Remember that Jesus had told His disciples that they would be His witnesses, bringing the Good News of Salvation to all nations, beginning at Jerusalem. However, until now, the Church was well established in Jerusalem, but nowhere else. When the Jerusalem Christians began to be persecuted, many were forced to leave Jerusalem and were scattered throughout the region of Palestine and surrounding provinces of Judea. They took the Gospel of Jesus Christ with them and shared it with non-Jewish people whom God had already prepared to hear and to believe in Jesus. Jesus said that miraculous signs would accompany those who believed. These divine manifestations of power validated their preaching, showing the world that the Kingdom of God had indeed arrived in their midst. It is through the preaching of a disciple named Philip that the people of Samaria heard the Good News. They came to believe on the name of Jesus and received the power of the Holy Spirit. Later Philip was sent to an Ethiopian, who also believed that Jesus Christ was the Son of God and immediately wanted to be baptized in water.

Philip Preaches in Samaria

8 [4]Therefore those who were scattered abroad went around preaching the word. [5] Philip went down to the city of Samaria, and proclaimed to them the Christ. [6] The multitudes listened with one accord to the things that were spoken by Philip, when they heard and saw the signs which he did. [7] For unclean spirits came out of many of those who had them. They came out, crying with a loud voice. Many who had been paralyzed and lame were healed. [8] There was great joy in that city.

Simon the Sorcerer

[9] But there was a certain man, Simon by name, who used to practice sorcery in the city, and amazed the people of Samaria, making himself out to be some great one, [10] to whom they all listened, from the least to the greatest, saying, "This man is that great power of God." [11] They listened to him, because for a long time he had amazed them with his sorceries. [12] But when they believed Philip preaching good news concerning God's Kingdom and the name of Jesus Christ, they were baptized, both men and women.[13] Simon himself also believed. Being baptized, he continued with Philip. Seeing signs and great miracles occurring, he was amazed.

[14] Now when the apostles who were at Jerusalem heard that Samaria had received the word of God, they sent Peter and John to them, [15] who, when they

had come down, prayed for them, that they might receive the Holy Spirit; ¹⁶ for as yet He had fallen on none of them. They had only been baptized in the name of Christ Jesus. ¹⁷ Then they laid their hands on them, and they received the Holy Spirit. ¹⁸ Now when Simon saw that the Holy Spirit was given through the laying on of the apostles' hands, he offered them money, ¹⁹ saying, "Give me also this power, that whomever I lay my hands on may receive the Holy Spirit." ²⁰ But Peter said to him, "May your silver perish with you, because you thought you could obtain the gift of God with money! ²¹ You have neither part nor lot in this matter, for your heart isn't right before God. ²² Repent therefore of this, your wickedness, and ask God if perhaps the thought of your heart may be forgiven you. ²³ For I see that you are in the gall of bitterness and in the bondage of iniquity."

²⁴ Simon answered, "Pray for me to the Lord, that none of the things which you have spoken happen to me."

²⁵ They therefore, when they had testified and spoken the word of the Lord, returned to Jerusalem, and preached the Good News to many villages of the Samaritans.

Philip and the Ethiopian

²⁶ But an angel of the Lord spoke to Philip, saying, "Arise, and go toward the south to the way that goes down from Jerusalem to Gaza. This is a desert."

²⁷ He arose and went; and behold, there was a man of Ethiopia, a eunuch of great authority under Candace, queen of the Ethiopians, who was over all her treasure, who had come to Jerusalem to worship. ²⁸ He was returning and sitting in his chariot, and was reading the prophet Isaiah.

²⁹ The Spirit said to Philip, "Go near, and join yourself to this chariot."

³⁰ Philip ran to him, and heard him reading Isaiah the prophet, and said, "Do you understand what you are reading?"

³¹ He said, "How can I, unless someone explains it to me?" He begged Philip to come up and sit with him. ³² Now the passage of the Scripture which he was reading was this,

> "He was led as a sheep to the slaughter.
> As a lamb before his shearer is silent,
> so he doesn't open his mouth.
> ³³In his humiliation, his judgment was taken away.
> Who will declare His generation?
> For his life is taken from the earth."

³⁴ The eunuch answered Philip, "Who is the prophet talking about? About himself, or about someone else?"

³⁵ Philip opened his mouth, and beginning from this Scripture, preached to him Jesus. ³⁶ As they went on the way, they came to some water, and the eunuch said, "Behold, here is water. What is keeping me from being baptized?" ³⁷ And Philip said, "If you believe with all your heart, you may." The eunuch answered, "I believe that Jesus Christ is the Son of God."

³⁸ He commanded the chariot to stand still, and they both went down into the water, both Philip and the eunuch, and he baptized him.

³⁹ When they came up out of the water, the Spirit of the Lord caught Philip away, and the eunuch didn't see him anymore, for he went on his way rejoicing. ⁴⁰ But Philip was found at Azotus. Passing through, he preached the Good News to all the cities, until he came to Caesarea.

> 1. What miraculous signs did Philip do? How did the people react? Why was there great joy in the city?
>
> 2. Why did Peter tell Simon that his heart was not right before God?
>
> 3. How do we know that Philip knew how to obey God?
>
> 4. Why did Philip agree to baptize the Ethiopian?

114. CHANGED BY JESUS
Acts 9:1-43

Saul of Tarsus, a fanatic religious Jew, was convinced that Jesus was not the promised Messiah and that Jesus' followers had to be stopped. Saul became one of the worst persecutors of the Church. When this treacherous man met Jesus on the road to Damascus, his life was immediately transformed. Saul, whose name was later changed to Paul, became one of the Church's first and greatest missionaries, taking the Good News about Jesus Christ to people in many parts of the world. However, he paid a price for his new life as a believer in Jesus because he was sought after by the Jews, who wanted to kill him. However, because he was God's chosen instrument, God protected him and saved him from death many times.

Saul's Conversion

9 But Saul, still breathing threats and slaughter against the disciples of the Lord, went to the high priest, ² and asked for letters from him to the synagogues of Damascus, that if he found any who were of the Way, whether men or women, he might bring them bound to Jerusalem. ³ As he traveled, he got close to Damascus, and suddenly a light from the sky shone around him. ⁴ He fell on the earth, and heard a voice saying to him, "Saul, Saul, why do you persecute me?"

⁵ He said, "Who are you, Lord?"

The Lord said, "I am Jesus, whom you are persecuting. ⁶ But rise up, and enter into the city, and you will be told what you must do."

⁷ The men who traveled with him stood speechless, hearing the sound, but seeing no one. ⁸ Saul arose from the ground, and when his eyes were opened, he saw no one. They led him by the hand, and brought him into Damascus. ⁹ He was without sight for three days, and neither ate nor drank.

¹⁰ Now there was a certain disciple at Damascus named Ananias. The Lord said to him in a vision, "Ananias!"

He said, "Behold, it's me, Lord."

¹¹ The Lord said to him, "Arise, and go to the street which is called Straight, and inquire in the house of Judah for one named Saul, a man of Tarsus. For behold, he is praying, ¹² and in a vision he has seen a man named Ananias coming in, and laying his hands on him, that he might receive his sight."

¹³ But Ananias answered, "Lord, I have heard from many about this man, how much evil he did to your saints at Jerusalem. ¹⁴ Here he has authority from the chief priests to bind all who call on your name."

¹⁵ But the Lord said to him, "Go your way, for he is my chosen vessel to bear my name before the nations and kings, and the children of Israel. ¹⁶ For I will show him how many things he must suffer for my name's sake."

¹⁷ Ananias departed, and entered into the house. Laying his hands on him, he said, "Brother Saul, the Lord, who appeared to you on the road by which you came, has sent me, that you may receive your sight, and be filled with the Holy Spirit." ¹⁸ Immediately something like scales fell from his eyes, and he received his sight. He arose and was baptized. ¹⁹ He took food and was strengthened.

Saul Preaches in Damascus

Saul stayed several days with the disciples who were at Damascus. ²⁰ Immediately in the synagogues he proclaimed the Christ, that he is the Son of God. ²¹ All who heard him were amazed, and said, "Isn't this he who in Jerusalem made havoc of those who called on this name? And he had come here intending to bring them bound before the chief priests!"

²² But Saul increased more in strength, and confounded the Jews who lived at Damascus, proving that this is the Christ. ²³ When many days were fulfilled, the Jews conspired together to kill him, ²⁴ but their plot became known to Saul. They watched the gates both day and night that they might kill him, ²⁵ but his disciples took him by night, and let him down through the wall, lowering him in a basket.

Saul Preaches in Jerusalem

²⁶ When Saul had come to Jerusalem, he tried to join himself to the disciples; but they were all afraid of him, not believing that he was a disciple. ²⁷ But Barnabas took him, and brought him to the apostles, and declared to them how he had seen the Lord on the way, and that he had spoken to him, and how at Damascus he had preached boldly in the name of Jesus. ²⁸ He was with them entering into Jerusalem, ²⁹ preaching boldly in the name of the Lord Jesus. He spoke and disputed against the Hellenists, but they were seeking to kill him. ³⁰ When the brothers knew it, they brought him down to Caesarea, and sent him off to Tarsus.

³¹ So the assemblies throughout all Judea and Galilee and Samaria had peace, and were built up. They were multiplied, walking in the fear of the Lord and in the comfort of the Holy Spirit.

Aeneas and Dorcas Healed

³² As Peter went throughout all those parts, he came down also to the saints who lived at Lydda. ³³ There he found a certain man named Aeneas, who had

been bedridden for eight years, because he was paralyzed. ³⁴ Peter said to him, "Aeneas, Jesus Christ heals you. Get up and make your bed!" Immediately he arose. ³⁵ All who lived at Lydda and in Sharon saw him, and they turned to the Lord.

³⁶ Now there was at Joppa a certain disciple named Tabitha, which when translated, means Dorcas. This woman was full of good works and acts of mercy which she did. ³⁷ In those days, she became sick, and died. When they had washed her, they laid her in an upper room. ³⁸ As Lydda was near Joppa, the disciples, hearing that Peter was there, sent two men to him, imploring him not to delay in coming to them. ³⁹ Peter got up and went with them. When he had come, they brought him into the upper room. All the widows stood by him weeping, and showing the coats and garments which Dorcas had made while she was with them. ⁴⁰ Peter sent them all out, and knelt down and prayed. Turning to the body, he said, "Tabitha, get up!" She opened her eyes, and when she saw Peter, she sat up. ⁴¹ He gave her his hand, and raised her up. Calling the saints and widows, he presented her alive. ⁴² And it became known throughout all Joppa, and many believed in the Lord. ⁴³ He stayed many days in Joppa with a tanner named Simon.

1. *Describe Saul's unique conversion experience.*

2. *What did the Lord say to Ananias about how He wanted to use Saul?*

3. *Name three things that Saul did to indicate that he had really become a believer.*

4. *Why did people in Lydda and Sharon and Joppa believe in the Lord?*

5. *Describe the condition of the Church at this time.*

115. NO LONGER UNCLEAN
Acts 10:1-48

Although the Church began with Jews who believed in Jesus, it was God's will that the Christian movement would come in contact with non-Jews. This would present a problem to the Jewish Christians. For centuries, the nation of Israel, the Jews, thought themselves to be the only people who could receive the blessings of God. All non-Jews were considered unclean and were called Gentiles by the Jewish people. For this reason, Peter, a Jew, was amazed by a vision showing him that nothing God had created was unclean. As Peter obeyed the voice of the Holy Spirit and went to preach to the Gentiles, the Holy Spirit was poured out on them. This convinced the Apostles that God did not show favoritism but accepted people from every race, nation and culture.

Great Bible Truths

Cornelius Calls for Peter

10 Now there was a certain man in Caesarea, Cornelius by name, a centurion of what was called the Italian Regiment, ² a devout man, and one who feared God with all his house, who gave gifts for the needy generously to the people, and always prayed to God. ³ At about the ninth hour of the day, he clearly saw in a vision an angel of God coming to him, and saying to him, "Cornelius!" ⁴ He, fastening his eyes on him, and being frightened, said, "What is it, Lord?" He said to him, "Your prayers and your gifts to the needy have gone up for a memorial before God. ⁵ Now send men to Joppa, and get Simon, who is also called Peter. ⁶ He lodges with a tanner named Simon, whose house is by the seaside."

⁷ When the angel who spoke to him had departed, Cornelius called two of his household servants and a devout soldier of those who waited on him continually. ⁸ Having explained everything to them, he sent them to Joppa.

Peter's Vision

⁹ Now on the next day as they were on their journey, and got close to the city, Peter went up on the housetop to pray at about noon. ¹⁰ He became hungry and desired to eat, but while they were preparing, he fell into a trance. ¹¹ He saw heaven opened and a certain container descending to him, like a great sheet let down by four corners on the earth, ¹² in which were all kinds of four-footed animals of the earth, wild animals, reptiles, and birds of the sky. ¹³ A voice came to him, "Rise, Peter, kill and eat!"

¹⁴ But Peter said, "Not so, Lord; for I have never eaten anything that is common or unclean."

¹⁵ A voice came to him again the second time, "What God has cleansed, you must not call unclean." ¹⁶ This was done three times, and immediately the vessel was received up into heaven. ¹⁷ Now while Peter was very perplexed in himself what the vision which he had seen might mean, behold, the men who were sent by Cornelius, having made inquiry for Simon's house, stood before the gate, ¹⁸ and called and asked whether Simon, who was also called Peter, was lodging there.

¹⁹ While Peter was pondering the vision, the Spirit said to him, "Behold, three men seek you. ²⁰ But arise, get down, and go with them, doubting nothing; for I have sent them."

²¹ Peter went down to the men, and said, "Behold, I am he whom you seek. Why have you come?"

²² They said, "Cornelius, a centurion, a righteous man and one who fears God, and well-spoken of by all the nation of the Jews, was directed by a holy angel to invite you to his house, and to listen to what you say." ²³ So he called them in and provided a place to stay.

Peter at Cornelius' House

On the next day Peter arose and went out with them, and some of the brothers from Joppa accompanied him. ²⁴ On the next day they entered into Caesarea.

Cornelius was waiting for them, having called together his relatives and his near friends. ²⁵ When Peter entered, Cornelius met him, fell down at his feet, and worshiped him.

²⁶ But Peter raised him up, saying, "Stand up! I myself am also a man." ²⁷ As he talked with him, he went in and found many gathered together. ²⁸ He said to them, "You yourselves know how it is an unlawful thing for a man who is a Jew to join himself or come to one of another nation, but God has shown me that I shouldn't call any man unholy or unclean.²⁹ Therefore also I came without complaint when I was sent for. I ask therefore, why did you send for me?"

³⁰ Cornelius said, "Four days ago, I was fasting until this hour, and at the ninth hour, I prayed in my house, and behold, a man stood before me in bright clothing, ³¹ and said, 'Cornelius, your prayer is heard, and your gifts to the needy are remembered in the sight of God. ³² Send therefore to Joppa, and summon Simon, who is also called Peter. He lodges in the house of a tanner named Simon, by the seaside. When he comes, he will speak to you.' ³³ Therefore I sent to you at once, and it was good of you to come. Now therefore we are all here present in the sight of God to hear all things that have been commanded you by God."

Peter's Acknowledges God's Ideal

³⁴ Peter opened his mouth and said, "Truly I perceive that God doesn't show favoritism;³⁵ but in every nation he who fears him and works righteousness is acceptable to him.³⁶ The word which he sent to the children of Israel, preaching good news of peace by Jesus Christ—he is Lord of all— ³⁷ you yourselves know what happened, which was proclaimed throughout all Judea, beginning from Galilee, after the baptism which John preached; ³⁸ even Jesus of Nazareth, how God anointed him with the Holy Spirit and with power, who went about doing good and healing all who were oppressed by the devil, for God was with him.

³⁹ We are witnesses of everything he did both in the country of the Jews, and in Jerusalem; whom they also killed, hanging him on a tree.⁴⁰ God raised him up the third day, and gave him to be revealed, ⁴¹ not to all the people, but to witnesses who were chosen before by God, to us, who ate and drank with him after he rose from the dead. ⁴² He commanded us to preach to the people and to testify that this is he who is appointed by God as the Judge of the living and the dead. ⁴³ All the prophets testify about him, that through his name everyone who believes in him will receive remission of sins."

⁴⁴ While Peter was still speaking these words, the Holy Spirit fell on all those who heard the word. ⁴⁵ They of the circumcision [the Jewish believers who came with Peter] were amazed, as many as came with Peter, because the gift of the Holy Spirit was also poured out on the Gentiles. ⁴⁶ For they heard them speaking in other languages and magnifying God.

Then Peter answered, ⁴⁷ "Can anyone forbid these people from being baptized with water? They have received the Holy Spirit just like us." ⁴⁸ He commanded them to be baptized in the name of Jesus Christ. Then they asked him to stay some days.

1. Describe Cornelius. Why did the angel appear to him?
2. What did God tell Peter through this vision?
3. What did Peter say that everyone who believed in Jesus received?
4. How did the disciples know that the Gentiles believed Peter's message and became believers? What was the proof? What did they do next?

B. THE EXPANSION OF CHRISTIANITY INTO THE WORLD

After only a few years, the Church had spread to all parts of Judea and Palestine; and it included people from all levels of society, rich and poor, educated and uneducated, Jew and Gentile. The time had come for the Church to expand beyond the borders of Palestine and fulfill Jesus' command to go into the entire world. In this section we read of the journeys of the first missionaries of the Church and how, through their preaching, people from all parts of the Roman world came to believe in Jesus Christ. As these believers gathered together for worship and teaching, they became the Church in the place where they lived, a part of the total body of believers around the world.

116. INTO ALL THE WORLD
Acts 13

The Church at Antioch obeyed the voice of the Holy Spirit and sent out Saul and Barnabas to preach the word of God to people of other nations. This was the beginning of the worldwide spread of the Christian movement, which continues even today. As they traveled from one place to another, they told all who would listen about forgiveness of sins through Jesus Christ. We will follow Saul, now called Paul, to various places in the Roman world and see how God used these first missionaries to make many disciples and establish them in new churches in every place Paul visited. Although many Jews and Gentiles alike came to believe, there was also opposition, which led to persecution against them.

Barnabas and Saul Sent Off

13 ¹Now in the assembly that was at Antioch there were some prophets and teachers: Barnabas, Simeon who was called Niger, Lucius of Cyrene, Manaen the foster brother of Herod the tetrarch, and Saul. ² As they served the Lord and fasted, the Holy Spirit said, "Separate Barnabas and Saul for me, for the work to which I have called them." ³ Then, when they had fasted and prayed and laid their hands on them, they sent them away.

To Cyprus

⁴ So, being sent out by the Holy Spirit, they went down to Seleucia. From there they sailed to Cyprus. ⁵ When they were at Salamis, they proclaimed the word of God in the Jewish synagogues. They had also John as their attendant. ⁶ When

they had gone through the island to Paphos, they found a certain sorcerer, a false prophet, a Jew, whose name was Bar Jesus, ⁷ who was with the proconsul, Sergius Paulus, a man of understanding. This man summoned Barnabas and Saul, and sought to hear the word of God. ⁸ But Elymas the sorcerer (for so is his name by interpretation) withstood them, seeking to turn aside the proconsul from the faith. ⁹ But Saul, who is also called Paul, filled with the Holy Spirit, fastened his eyes on him, ¹⁰ and said, "Full of all deceit and all cunning, you son of the devil, you enemy of all righteousness, will you not cease to pervert the right ways of the Lord? ¹¹ Now, behold, the hand of the Lord is on you, and you will be blind, not seeing the sun for a season!"

Immediately a mist and darkness fell on him. He went around seeking someone to lead him by the hand. ¹² Then the proconsul, when he saw what was done, believed, being astonished at the teaching of the Lord.

In Antioch of Pisidia

¹³ Now Paul and his company set sail from Paphos, and came to Perga in Pamphylia. John departed from them and returned to Jerusalem. ¹⁴ But they, passing on from Perga, came to Antioch of Pisidia. They went into the synagogue on the Sabbath day, and sat down. ¹⁵ After the reading of the law and the prophets, the rulers of the synagogue sent to them, saying, "Brothers, if you have any word of exhortation for the people, speak."

¹⁶ Paul stood up, and beckoning with his hand said, "Men of Israel, and you [Gentiles] who fear God, listen. ¹⁷ The God of this people chose our fathers, and exalted the people when they stayed as aliens in the land of Egypt, and with an uplifted arm, he led them out of it. ¹⁸ For a period of about forty years he put up with them in the wilderness. ¹⁹ When he had destroyed seven nations in the land of Canaan, he gave them their land for an inheritance, for about four hundred fifty years.

²⁰ After these things he gave them judges until Samuel the prophet. ²¹ Afterward they asked for a king, and God gave to them Saul the son of Kish, a man of the tribe of Benjamin, for forty years. ²² When he had removed him, he raised up David to be their king, to whom he also testified, 'I have found David the son of Jesse, a man after my heart, who will do all my will.' ²³ From this man's offspring, God has brought salvation to Israel according to his promise, ²⁴ before his coming, when John had first preached the baptism of repentance to Israel. ²⁵ As John was fulfilling his course, he said, 'What do you suppose that I am? I am not he. But behold, one comes after me the sandals of whose feet I am not worthy to untie.'

²⁶ Brothers, children of the stock of Abraham, and those among you who fear God, the word of this salvation is sent out to you. ²⁷ For those who dwell in Jerusalem, and their rulers, because they didn't know him, nor the voices of the

prophets which are read every Sabbath, fulfilled them by condemning him. ²⁸ Though they found no cause for death, they still asked Pilate to have him killed. ²⁹ When they had fulfilled all things that were written about him, they took him down from the tree, and laid him in a tomb. ³⁰ But God raised him from the dead, ³¹ and he was seen for many days by those who came up with him from Galilee to Jerusalem, who are his witnesses to the people.

³² We bring you good news of the promise made to the fathers, ³³that God has fulfilled the same to us, their children, in that he raised up Jesus. As it is also written in the second psalm,

> 'You are my Son.
> Today I have become your father.'

³⁴"Concerning that he raised him up from the dead, now no more to return to corruption, he has spoken thus:

> 'I will give you the holy and sure blessings of David.'

³⁵ Therefore he says also in another psalm,

> 'You will not allow your Holy One to see decay.'

³⁶ For David, after he had in his own generation served the counsel of God, fell asleep, and was laid with his fathers, and saw decay. ³⁷ But he whom God raised up saw no decay. ³⁸ Be it known to you therefore, brothers, that through this man is proclaimed to you remission of sins, ³⁹ and by him everyone who believes is justified from all things, from which you could not be justified by the law of Moses. ⁴⁰ Beware therefore, lest that come on you which is spoken in the prophets:

> ⁴¹'Behold, you scoffers, and wonder, and perish;
> for I work a work in your days,
> a work which you will in no way believe,
> even if one declares it to you.'"

⁴² So when the Jews went out of the synagogue, the Gentiles begged that these words might be preached to them the next Sabbath. ⁴³ Now when the synagogue broke up, many of the Jews and of the devout proselytes followed Paul and Barnabas; who, speaking to them, urged them to continue in the grace of God. ⁴⁴ The next Sabbath almost the whole city was gathered together to hear the word of God. ⁴⁵ But when the Jews saw the multitudes, they were filled with jealousy, and contradicted the things which were spoken by Paul, and blasphemed. ⁴⁶ Paul and Barnabas spoke out boldly, and said, "It was necessary that God's word should be spoken to you first. Since indeed you thrust it from you, and judge yourselves unworthy of eternal life, behold, we turn to the Gentiles. ⁴⁷ For so has the Lord commanded us, saying,

> 'I have set you as a light for the Gentiles,
> that you should bring salvation to the uttermost
> parts of the earth.'" (Isaiah 49:6)

⁴⁸ As the Gentiles heard this, they were glad, and glorified the word of God. As many as were appointed to eternal life believed. ⁴⁹ The Lord's word was spread abroad throughout all the region. ⁵⁰ But the Jews stirred up the devout and prominent women and the chief men of the city, and stirred up a persecution against Paul and Barnabas, and threw them out of their borders. ⁵¹ But they shook off the dust of their feet against them, and came to Iconium. ⁵² The disciples were filled with joy with the Holy Spirit.

1. What were the leaders of the Antioch Church doing when the Holy Spirit spoke to them?

2. Paul usually began his ministry in a new place by visiting and speaking in the local Jewish synagogue, if there were one. Why did he do this?

3. Why did the proconsul Sergius Paulus believe? Satan opposed Paul in every city. Why do you think this happened?

4. In Antioch of Pisidia, some Jews, although interested in Paul's message at first, later rejected the message if it meant including Gentiles in God's Kingdom. Did you notice that Paul implied that they also rejected God's ultimate plan for Israel "to be a light to the Gentiles, to bring salvation to the ends of the earth"? Did those Jews love God or just themselves? What lesson is there for us to see?

5. Why did the two apostles decide to take their message to the Gentiles? How did the Gentiles react? What lesson is there for us to see?

6. Using Paul's message, review the history of Israel and tie it into the coming of the Messiah, who is Jesus Christ.

Pause for Reflection: Did you see that some Jews, although at first interested in Paul's message, rejected the idea that Gentiles were to be part of the Kingdom of God? Paul said that by taking this attitude they are rejecting God's plan that Israel was to be a light to the Gentiles, bringing salvation to the world. What do you think of this heartbreaking attitude motivated by jealousy? Did the Jews love God or just themselves? What lesson may we learn from this?

117. OPEN DOORS
Acts 15:36-41 and 16:1-40

Paul and Barnabas prepared for a second missionary journey. Unfortunately, there was a disagreement between Paul and Barnabas as to whether they should take Mark along as before. They ended up going different ways, Barnabas back to Cyprus and Paul to what is now Turkey. Although Paul thought that he should be in that area and beyond in Asia, the Holy Spirit led him to Greece and to Europe. When Paul successfully confronted Satan in a compelling situation, this led to strong opposition in Philippi, a major Roman city of Macedonia. Although Paul and his companion Silas were beaten and jailed, the power of God again proved to be stronger than prison doors. God used a hopeless situation to bring about His purposes, as the jailer and his entire household came to believe in the Lord Jesus.

Paul and Barnabas Disagree

15 [36] After some days Paul said to Barnabas, "Let's return now and visit our brothers in every city in which we proclaimed the word of the Lord, to see how they are doing." [37] Barnabas planned to take John, who was called Mark, with them also. [38] But Paul didn't think that it was a good idea to take with them someone who had withdrawn from them in Pamphylia, and didn't go with them to do the work. [39] Then the contention grew so sharp that they separated from each other. Barnabas took Mark with him, and sailed away to Cyprus, [40] but Paul chose Silas, and went out, being commended by the brothers to the grace of God. [41] He went through Syria and Cilicia, strengthening the assemblies.

Timothy Joins Paul and Silas

16 [1] He came to Derbe and Lystra: and behold, a certain disciple was there, named Timothy, the son of a Jewess who believed; but his father was a Greek. [2] The brothers who were at Lystra and Iconium gave a good testimony about him. [3] Paul wanted to have him go out with him, and he took and circumcised him because of the Jews who were in those parts; for they all knew that his father was a Greek. [4] As they went on their way through the cities, they delivered the decrees to them to keep which had been ordained by the apostles and elders who were at Jerusalem. [5] So the assemblies were strengthened in the faith, and increased in number daily.

Paul's Call to Go to Macedonia (Europe)

[6] When they had gone through the region of Phrygia and Galatia, they were forbidden by the Holy Spirit to speak the word in Asia. [7] When they had come opposite Mysia, they tried to go into Bithynia, but the Spirit didn't allow them. [8] Passing by Mysia, they came down to Troas. [9] A vision appeared to Paul in the night. There was a man of Macedonia standing, begging him, and saying, "Come over into Macedonia and help us." [10] When he had seen the vision, immediately we sought to go out to Macedonia, concluding that the Lord had called us to preach the Good News to them. [11] Setting sail therefore from Troas, we made a straight course to Samothrace, and the day following to Neapolis; [12] and from there to Philippi, which is a city of Macedonia, the foremost of the district, a Roman colony. We were staying some days in this city.

Lydia's Conversion

[13] On the Sabbath day we went outside of the city by a riverside, where we supposed there was a place of prayer, and we sat down, and spoke to the women who had come together. [14] A certain woman named Lydia, a seller of purple, of the city of Thyatira, one who worshiped God, heard us; whose heart the Lord opened to listen to the things which were spoken by Paul. [15] When she and her household were baptized, she begged us, saying, "If you have judged me to be

faithful to the Lord, come into my house, and stay." So she persuaded us.

Paul and Silas Go to Jail

[16] As we were going to prayer, a certain girl having a spirit of divination met us, who brought her masters much gain by fortune telling. [17] Following Paul and us, she cried out, "These men are servants of the Most High God, who proclaim to us a way of salvation!" [18] She was doing this for many days. But Paul, becoming greatly annoyed, turned and said to the spirit, "I command you in the name of Jesus Christ to come out of her!" It came out that very hour.

[19] But when her masters saw that the hope of their gain was gone, they seized Paul and Silas, and dragged them into the marketplace before the rulers. [20] When they had brought them to the magistrates, they said, "These men, being Jews, are agitating our city, [21] and advocate customs which it is not lawful for us to accept or to observe, being Romans."

[22] The multitude rose up together against them, and the magistrates tore their clothes off of them, and commanded them to be beaten with rods. [23] When they had laid many stripes on them, they threw them into prison, charging the jailer to keep them safely, [24] who, having received such a command, threw them into the inner prison, and secured their feet in the stocks.

Opened Prison Doors

[25] But about midnight Paul and Silas were praying and singing hymns to God, and the prisoners were listening to them. [26] Suddenly there was a great earthquake, so that the foundations of the prison were shaken; and immediately all the doors were opened, and everyone's bonds were loosened.

[27] The jailer, being roused out of sleep and seeing the prison doors open, drew his sword and was about to kill himself, supposing that the prisoners had escaped. [28] But Paul cried with a loud voice, saying, "Don't harm yourself, for we are all here!"

[29] He called for lights, sprang in, fell down trembling before Paul and Silas, [30] brought them out, and said, "Sirs, what must I do to be saved?"

[31] They said, "Believe in the Lord Jesus Christ, and you will be saved, you and your household." [32] They spoke the word of the Lord to him, and to all who were in his house. [33] He took them the same hour of the night, and washed their stripes, and was immediately baptized, he and all his household. [34] He brought them up into his house, and set food before them, and rejoiced greatly, with all his household, having believed in God.

[35] But when it was day, the magistrates sent the sergeants, saying, "Let those men go." [36] The jailer reported these words to Paul, saying, "The magistrates have sent to let you go; now therefore come out, and go in peace."

[37] But Paul said to them, "They have beaten us publicly, without a trial, men who are Romans, and have cast us into prison! Do they now release us secretly? No, most certainly, but let them come themselves and bring us out!"

[38] The sergeants reported these words to the magistrates, and they were afraid when they heard that they were Romans, [39] and they came and begged them. When they had brought them out, they asked them to depart from the city.

⁴⁰ They went out of the prison, and entered into Lydia's house. When they had seen the brothers, they encouraged them, and departed.

1. Why did Paul want to go back and visit the churches? Was he successful?
2. What was the lasting significance of Paul's taking the Gospel to Europe instead of to Asia?
3. How did Paul know that Lydia was a believer?
4. What did Paul say to the evil spirit in the girl that caused it to leave her?
5. Why were Paul and Silas beaten and jailed?
6. How did God bring good out of a potentially bad situation?
7. What was Paul's answer to the jailer's question?

118. THE UNKNOWN GOD
Acts 17

Paul and Silas traveled through Greece, going toward Athens and taking the word of God to both Jews and Greeks. Many believed in Jesus. In Athens, Paul had an interesting situation when he shared the gospel with pagan philosophers. Greece was the center of learning at that time. The Athenian Greeks prided themselves on having a superior culture, which they felt reflected their great knowledge and varied philosophies. Although they were a religious people and had many beautiful temples filled with many idols and false gods, they were living in abject darkness. They had no idea of the true God's grandeur, that He created the universe, that He created men to live everywhere on earth, and that He even gave man a living Spirit with the idea that God and man could have a mutual relationship. However, these learned men suspected that there was more to life than their religion offered. One of their philosophers had once said that "men were offspring of god." If that were true, this god needed recognition, so they made an altar dedicated to the UNKNOWN GOD, whoever that might be. In this passage, we see how the Holy Spirit led Paul to build a bridge of faith. He identified the unknown God they worshiped in ignorance. In a wonderfully instructive discourse, Paul was able to enlighten their blind hope in the God whose existence they vaguely suspected through a rational explanation of who that God was. From there, he sought to build a response of faith in the only true God, the One who had been there all the time. What an awakening that must have been that day!

Paul in Thessalonica

17 Now when they had passed through Amphipolis and Apollonia, they came to Thessalonica, where there was a Jewish synagogue. ² Paul, as was his custom, went in to them, and for three Sabbath days reasoned with them from the Scriptures, ³ explaining and demonstrating that the Christ had to suffer and rise again from the dead, and saying, "This Jesus, whom I proclaim to you, is the Christ."

⁴ Some of them were persuaded, and joined Paul and Silas, of the devout Greeks a great multitude, and not a few of the chief women.

⁵ But the unpersuaded Jews took along some wicked men from the marketplace, and gathering a crowd, set the city in an uproar. Assaulting the house of Jason, they sought to bring them out to the people. ⁶ When they didn't find them, they dragged Jason and certain brothers before the rulers of the city, crying, "These who have turned the world upside down have come here also, ⁷ whom Jason has received. These all act contrary to the decrees of Caesar, saying that there is another king, Jesus!"

⁸ The multitude and the rulers of the city were troubled when they heard these things. ⁹ When they had taken security from Jason and the rest, they let them go.

Paul in Beroea

¹⁰ The brothers immediately sent Paul and Silas away by night to Beroea. When they arrived, they went into the Jewish synagogue. ¹¹ Now these [Jews] were more noble than those in Thessalonica, in that they received the word with all readiness of the mind, examining the Scriptures daily to see whether these things were so. ¹² Many of them therefore believed; also of the prominent Greek women, and not a few men.

¹³ But when the Jews of Thessalonica had knowledge that the word of God was proclaimed by Paul at Beroea also, they came there likewise, agitating the multitudes. ¹⁴ Then the brothers immediately sent out Paul to go as far as to the sea, and Silas and Timothy still stayed there. ¹⁵ But those who escorted Paul brought him as far as Athens. [After] receiving a commandment to Silas and Timothy that they should come to him very quickly, they departed.

Paul Preaches in Athens

¹⁶ Now while Paul waited for them at Athens, his spirit was provoked within him as he saw the city full of idols. ¹⁷ So he reasoned in the synagogue with the Jews and the devout persons, and in the marketplace every day with those who met him. ¹⁸ Some of the Epicurean and Stoic philosophers also were conversing with him. Some said, "What does this babbler want to say?" Others said, "He seems to be advocating foreign deities," because he preached Jesus and the resurrection. ¹⁹ They took hold of him, and brought him to the Areopagus, saying, "May we know what this new teaching is, which is spoken by you? ²⁰ For you bring certain strange things to our ears. We want to know therefore what these things mean."

²¹ Now all the Athenians and the strangers living there spent their time in nothing else, but either to tell or to hear some new thing. ²² Paul stood in the middle of the Areopagus, and said, "You men of Athens, I perceive that you are very religious in all things. ²³ For as I passed along, and observed the objects of your worship, I found also an altar with this inscription: 'TO AN UNKNOWN GOD.' What therefore you worship in ignorance, this I announce to you. ²⁴ The God who made the world and all things in it, he, being Lord of heaven and earth, doesn't dwell in temples made with hands, ²⁵ neither is he served by men's

hands, as though he needed anything, seeing he himself gives to all life and breath, and all things. ²⁶ He made from one blood every nation of men to dwell on all the surface of the earth, having determined appointed seasons, and the boundaries of their dwellings, ²⁷ that they should seek the Lord, if perhaps they might reach out for him and find him, though he is not far from each one of us.

²⁸ 'For in him we live, and move, and have our being.' As some of your own poets have said, 'For we are also his offspring.' ²⁹ Being then the offspring of God, we ought not to think that the Divine Nature is like gold, or silver, or stone, engraved by art and design of man. ³⁰ The times of ignorance therefore God overlooked. But now he commands that all people everywhere should repent, ³¹ because he has appointed a day in which he will judge the world in righteousness by the man whom he has ordained; of which he has given assurance to all men, in that he has raised him from the dead."

³² Now when they heard of the resurrection of the dead, some mocked; but others said, "We want to hear you again concerning this." ³³ Thus Paul went out from among them. ³⁴ But certain men joined with him, and believed, among whom also was Dionysius the Areopagite, and a woman named Damaris, and others with them.

1. Why was Paul greatly distressed in Athens?
2. Why did the Greeks want to hear Paul's teaching?
3. From Paul's message to the Greeks, describe the God who made the world.
4. What new, intriguing philosophical idea was Paul suggesting to the Athenians? Do you see how he built a bridge from the unknown to the known so they could more easily believe?
5. Why should we **not** think that the divine being is like an image made of gold, silver or stone?
6. Why should all men repent? v.31
7. Paul preached that Jesus rose from the dead. Why did some philosophers not believe that? Why is the resurrection of Jesus so important?

119. THE ONLY WAY
Acts 18:1-17 and 19:1-41 and 20:1

The Good News about Jesus Christ and those who believed in Him came to be known by people everywhere as "the Way." We know that Jesus himself said, "I am the way, the truth and the life," the only way to God. During his long stay in Ephesus, Paul told both Jews and Greeks about the Way. Many people believed. Those who already believed received the Holy Spirit, while others confessed their evil deeds of sorcery. However, there were some who refused to accept Jesus Christ as the only way to God. They caused a great disturbance, which resulted in Paul's having to leave the city.

Great Bible Truths

Paul in Corinth

18 After these things Paul departed from Athens, and came to Corinth. ² He found a certain Jew named Aquila, a man of Pontus by race, who had recently come from Italy, with his wife Priscilla, because Claudius had commanded all the Jews to depart from Rome. He came to them, ³ and because he practiced the same trade, he lived with them and worked, for by trade they were tent makers. ⁴ He reasoned in the synagogue every Sabbath, and persuaded Jews and Greeks.

⁵ But when Silas and Timothy came down from Macedonia, Paul was compelled by the Spirit, testifying to the Jews that Jesus was the Christ. ⁶ When they opposed him and blasphemed, he shook out his clothing and said to them, "Your blood be on your own heads! I am clean. From now on, I will go to the Gentiles!"

⁷ He departed there, and went into the house of a certain man named Justus, one who worshiped God, whose house was next door to the synagogue. ⁸ Crispus, the ruler of the synagogue, believed in the Lord with all his house. Many of the Corinthians, when they heard, believed and were baptized. ⁹ The Lord said to Paul in the night by a vision, "Don't be afraid, but speak and don't be silent; ¹⁰ for I am with you, and no one will attack you to harm you, for I have many people in this city."

¹¹ He lived there a year and six months, teaching the word of God among them. ¹² But when Gallio was proconsul of Achaia, the Jews with one accord rose up against Paul and brought him before the judgment seat, ¹³ saying, "This man persuades men to worship God contrary to the law."

¹⁴ But when Paul was about to open his mouth, Gallio said to the Jews, "If indeed it were a matter of wrong or of wicked crime, you Jews, it would be reasonable that I should bear with you; ¹⁵ but if they are questions about words and names and your own law, look to it yourselves. For I don't want to be a judge of these matters."

¹⁶ He drove them from the judgment seat. ¹⁷ Then all the Greeks laid hold on Sosthenes, the ruler of the synagogue, and beat him before the judgment seat. Gallio didn't care about any of these things.

Paul in Ephesus

19 ¹While Apollos was at Corinth, Paul, having passed through the upper country, came to Ephesus, and found certain disciples. ²He said to them, "Did you receive the Holy Spirit when you believed?"

They said to him, "No, we haven't even heard that there is a Holy Spirit." ³ He said, "Into what then were you baptized?"

They said, "Into John's baptism."

⁴ Paul said, "John indeed baptized with the baptism of repentance, saying to the people that they should believe in the one who would come after him, that is, in Jesus."

⁵ When they heard this, they were baptized in the name of the Lord Jesus. ⁶ When Paul had laid his hands on them, the Holy Spirit came on them, and they spoke with other languages and prophesied. ⁷ They were about twelve men in all. ⁸ He entered into the synagogue, and spoke boldly for a period of three months, reasoning and persuading about the things concerning God's Kingdom.

⁹ But when some were hardened and disobedient, speaking evil of the Way before the multitude, he departed from them, and separated the disciples, reasoning daily in the school of Tyrannus. ¹⁰ This continued for two years, so that all those who lived in Asia heard the word of the Lord Jesus, both Jews and Greeks. ¹¹ God worked special miracles by the hands of Paul, ¹² so that even handkerchiefs or aprons were carried away from his body to the sick, and the evil spirits went out.

¹³ But some of the itinerant Jews, exorcists, took on themselves to invoke over those who had the evil spirits the name of the Lord Jesus, saying, "We adjure you by Jesus whom Paul preaches." ¹⁴ There were seven sons of one Sceva, a Jewish chief priest, who did this. ¹⁵ The evil spirit answered, "Jesus I know, and Paul I know, but who are you?" ¹⁶ The man in whom the evil spirit was leaped on them, and overpowered them, and prevailed against them, so that they fled out of that house naked and wounded.

¹⁷ This became known to all, both Jews and Greeks, who lived at Ephesus. Fear fell on them all, and the name of the Lord Jesus was magnified. ¹⁸ Many also of those who had believed came, confessing, and declaring their deeds. ¹⁹ Many of those who practiced magical arts brought their books together and burned them in the sight of all. They counted their price, and found it to be fifty thousand pieces of silver. ²⁰ So the word of the Lord was growing and becoming mighty. ²¹ Now after these things had ended, Paul determined in the spirit, when he had passed through Macedonia and Achaia, to go to Jerusalem, saying, "After I have been there, I must also see Rome." ²² Having sent into Macedonia two of those who served him, Timothy and Erastus, he himself stayed in Asia for a while.

The Riot in Ephesus

²³ About that time there arose no small stir concerning the Way. ²⁴ For a certain man named Demetrius, a silversmith, who made silver shrines of Artemis, brought no little business to the craftsmen, ²⁵ whom he gathered together, with the workmen of like occupation, and said, "Sirs, you know that by this business we have our wealth. ²⁶ You see and hear, that not at Ephesus alone, but almost throughout all Asia, this Paul has persuaded and turned away many people, saying that they [there] are no gods that are made with hands. ²⁷ Not only is there danger that this our trade come into disrepute, but also that the temple of the great goddess Artemis will be counted as nothing, and her majesty destroyed, whom all Asia and the world worships."

²⁸ When they heard this they were filled with anger, and cried out, saying,

"Great is Artemis of the Ephesians!" ²⁹ The whole city was filled with confusion, and they rushed with one accord into the theater, having seized Gaius and Aristarchus, men of Macedonia, Paul's companions in travel. ³⁰ When Paul wanted to enter in to the people, the disciples didn't allow him. ³¹ Certain also of the Asiarchs, being his friends, sent to him and begged him not to venture into the theater. ³² Some therefore cried one thing, and some another, for the assembly was in confusion. Most of them didn't know why they had come together.

³³ They brought Alexander out of the multitude, the Jews putting him forward. Alexander beckoned with his hand, and would have made a defense to the people. ³⁴ But when they perceived that he was a Jew, all with one voice for a time of about two hours cried out, "Great is Artemis of the Ephesians!"

³⁵ When the town clerk had quieted the multitude, he said, "You men of Ephesus, what man is there who doesn't know that the city of the Ephesians is temple keeper of the great goddess Artemis, and of the image which fell down from Zeus? ³⁶ Seeing then that these things can't be denied, you ought to be quiet, and to do nothing rash. ³⁷ For you have brought these men here, who are neither robbers of temples nor blasphemers of your goddess. ³⁸ If therefore Demetrius and the craftsmen who are with him have a matter against anyone, the courts are open, and there are proconsuls. Let them press charges against one another. ³⁹ But if you seek anything about other matters, it will be settled in the regular assembly. ⁴⁰ For indeed we are in danger of being accused concerning today's riot, there being no cause. Concerning it, we wouldn't be able to give an account of this commotion.

⁴¹ When he had thus spoken, he dismissed the assembly.
20 After the uproar had ceased, Paul sent for the disciples, took leave of them, and departed to go into Macedonia.

> 1. When Paul was strongly opposed by the Jews in Corinth, how did he change his strategy in order to keep preaching the Gospel? How was he encouraged, knowing that he was doing the right thing?
>
> 2. In each new city, Paul began his ministry in the same place. Where was that and why?
>
> 3. Why did the twelve believers in Ephesus not receive the Holy Spirit?
>
> 4. What extraordinary miracles did God do through Paul?
>
> 5. Why did the evil spirit overpower the sons of Sceva? What effect did this have on the population?
>
> 6. What was the issue that provoked the riot against the Way in Ephesus?

120. SAD FAREWELLS
Acts 20:7-38 and 21:1-36 and 22:23-29

Paul set out to return to Jerusalem. He stopped along the way to visit the people of several different churches to bid them farewell. Although he knew that he would be arrested in Jerusalem, Paul continued his journey despite the sorrowful pleadings of his friends.

Eutychus Raised from the Dead at Troas

20 [7] On the first day of the week, when the disciples were gathered together to break bread, Paul talked with them, intending to depart on the next day, and continued his speech until midnight.

[8] There were many lights in the upper room where we were gathered together. [9] A certain young man named Eutychus sat in the window, weighed down with deep sleep. As Paul spoke still longer, being weighed down by his sleep, he fell down from the third floor, and was taken up dead. [10] Paul went down, and fell upon him, and embracing him said, "Don't be troubled, for his life is in him." [11] When he had gone up, and had broken bread, and eaten, and had talked with them a long while, even until break of day, he departed. [12] They brought the boy in alive, and were greatly comforted.

Paul's Farewell to Ephesian Elders

[13] But we who went ahead to the ship set sail for Assos, intending to take Paul aboard there, for he had so arranged, intending himself to go by land. [14] When he met us at Assos, we took him aboard, and came to Mitylene. [15] Sailing from there, we came the following day opposite Chios. The next day we touched at Samos and stayed at Trogyllium, and the day after we came to Miletus. [16] For Paul had determined to sail past Ephesus, that he might not have to spend time in Asia; for he was hastening, if it were possible for him, to be in Jerusalem on the day of Pentecost.

[17] From Miletus he sent to Ephesus, and called to himself the elders of the assembly. [18] When they had come to him, he said to them, "You yourselves know, from the first day that I set foot in Asia, how I was with you all the time, [19] serving the Lord with all humility, with many tears, and with trials which happened to me by the plots of the Jews; [20] how I didn't shrink from declaring to you anything that was profitable, teaching you publicly and from house to house, [21] testifying both to Jews and to Greeks repentance toward God, and faith toward our Lord Jesus.

[22] Now, behold, I go bound by the Spirit to Jerusalem, not knowing what will happen to me there; [23] except that the Holy Spirit testifies in every city, saying that bonds and afflictions wait for me. [24] But these things don't count; nor do I hold my life dear to myself, so that I may finish my race with joy, and the ministry which I received from the Lord Jesus, to fully testify to the Good News of the grace of God. [25] "Now, behold, I know that you all, among whom I went about preaching God's Kingdom, will see my face no more. [26] Therefore

I testify to you today that I am clean from the blood of all men, ²⁷ for I didn't shrink from declaring to you the whole counsel of God. ²⁸ Take heed, therefore, to yourselves, and to all the flock, in which the Holy Spirit has made you overseers, to shepherd the assembly of the Lord and God which he purchased with his own blood. ²⁹ For I know that after my departure, vicious wolves will enter in among you, not sparing the flock. ³⁰ Men will arise from among your own selves, speaking perverse things, to draw away the disciples after them. ³¹ Therefore watch, remembering that for a period of three years I didn't cease to admonish everyone night and day with tears.

³² Now, brothers, I entrust you to God, and to the word of his grace, which is able to build up, and to give you the inheritance among all those who are sanctified. ³³ I coveted no one's silver, or gold, or clothing. ³⁴ You yourselves know that these hands served my necessities, and those who were with me.³⁵ In all things I gave you an example, that so laboring you ought to help the weak, and to remember the words of the Lord Jesus, that he himself said, 'It is more blessed to give than to receive.'"

³⁶ When he had spoken these things, he knelt down and prayed with them all. ³⁷ They all wept a lot, and fell on Paul's neck and kissed him, ³⁸ sorrowing most of all because of the word which he had spoken, that they should see his face no more. And they accompanied him to the ship.

On to Jerusalem

21 ¹When we had departed from them and had set sail, we came with a straight course to Cos, and the next day to Rhodes, and from there to Patara. ² Having found a ship crossing over to Phoenicia, we went aboard, and set sail. ³ When we had come in sight of Cyprus, leaving it on the left hand, we sailed to Syria, and landed at Tyre, for there the ship was to unload her cargo. ⁴ Having found disciples, we stayed there seven days. These said to Paul through the Spirit, that he should not go up to Jerusalem. ⁵ When those days were over, we departed and went on our journey. They all, with wives and children, brought us on our way until we were out of the city. Kneeling down on the beach, we prayed. ⁶ After saying goodbye to each other, we went on board the ship, and they returned home again.

⁷ When we had finished the voyage from Tyre, we arrived at Ptolemais. We greeted the brothers, and stayed with them one day. ⁸ On the next day, we, who were Paul's companions, departed, and came to Caesarea. We entered into the house of Philip the evangelist, who was one of the seven, and stayed with him. ⁹ Now this man had four virgin daughters who prophesied.

¹⁰ As we stayed there some days, a certain prophet named Agabus came down from Judea. ¹¹ Coming to us, and taking Paul's belt, he bound his own feet and hands, and said, "Thus says the Holy Spirit: 'So will the Jews at Jerusalem bind the man who owns this belt, and will deliver him into the hands of the Gentiles.'"

¹² When we heard these things, both we and they of that place begged him

not to go up to Jerusalem. ¹³ Then Paul answered, "What are you doing, weeping and breaking my heart? For I am ready not only to be bound, but also to die at Jerusalem for the name of the Lord Jesus." ¹⁴ When he would not be persuaded, we ceased, saying, "The Lord's will be done." ¹⁵ After these days we took up our baggage and went up to Jerusalem. ¹⁶ Some of the disciples from Caesarea also went with us, bringing one Mnason of Cyprus, an early disciple, with whom we would stay.

Paul's Arrival in Jerusalem

¹⁷ When we had come to Jerusalem, the brothers received us gladly. ¹⁸ The day following, Paul went in with us to James; and all the elders were present. ¹⁹ When he had greeted them, he reported one by one the things which God had worked among the Gentiles through his ministry.

²⁰ They, when they heard it, glorified God. They said to him, "You see, brother, how many thousands there are among the Jews of those who have believed, and they are all zealous for the law. ²¹ They have been informed about you, that you teach all the Jews who are among the Gentiles to forsake Moses, telling them not to circumcise their children neither to walk after the customs. ²² What then? The assembly must certainly meet, for they will hear that you have come. ²³ Therefore do what we tell you. We have four men who have taken a vow. ²⁴ Take them, and purify yourself with them, and pay their expenses for them, that they may shave their heads. Then all will know that there is no truth in the things that they have been informed about you, but that you yourself also walk keeping the law. ²⁵ But concerning the Gentiles who believe, we have written our decision that they should observe no such thing, except that they should keep themselves from food offered to idols, from blood, from strangled things, and from sexual immorality."

²⁶ Then Paul took the men, and the next day, purified himself and went with them into the temple, declaring the fulfillment of the days of purification, until the offering was offered for every one of them.

Paul Arrested

²⁷ When the seven days were almost completed, the Jews from Asia, when they saw him in the temple, stirred up all the multitude and laid hands on him, ²⁸ crying out, "Men of Israel, help! This is the man who teaches all men everywhere against the people, and the law, and this place. Moreover, he also brought Greeks into the temple, and has defiled this holy place!" ²⁹ For they had seen Trophimus, the Ephesian, with him in the city, and they supposed that Paul had brought him into the temple.

³⁰ All the city was moved, and the people ran together. They seized Paul and dragged him out of the temple. Immediately the doors were shut. ³¹ As they were trying to kill him, news came up to the commanding officer of the regiment that all Jerusalem was in an uproar. ³² Immediately he took soldiers and centurions, and ran down to them. They, when they saw the chief captain

and the soldiers, stopped beating Paul.

³³ Then the commanding officer came near, arrested him, commanded him to be bound with two chains, and inquired who he was and what he had done. ³⁴ Some shouted one thing, and some another, among the crowd. When he couldn't find out the truth because of the noise, he commanded him to be brought into the barracks.³⁵ When he came to the stairs, he was carried by the soldiers because of the violence of the crowd; ³⁶ for the multitude of the people followed after, crying out, "Away with him!"

22 ²³As they cried out, and threw off their cloaks, and threw dust into the air, ²⁴ the commanding officer commanded him to be brought into the barracks, ordering him to be examined by scourging, that he might know for what crime they shouted against him like that. ²⁵ When they had tied him up with thongs, Paul asked the centurion who stood by, "Is it lawful for you to scourge a man who is a Roman, and not found guilty?"

²⁶ When the centurion heard it, he went to the commanding officer and told him, "Watch what you are about to do, for this man is a Roman!"

²⁷ The commanding officer came and asked him, "Tell me, are you a Roman?"

He said, "Yes." ²⁸ The commanding officer answered, "I bought my citizenship for a great price."

Paul said, "But I was born a Roman."

²⁹ Immediately those who were about to examine him departed from him, and the commanding officer also was afraid when he realized that he was a Roman, because he had bound him.

1. What task did the Lord Jesus give to Paul? (20:24)

2. What instructions did Paul give to the elders of the Church at Ephesus?

3. Why did the pleadings of the people not cause Paul to change his mind?

4. Why were the Jews in Jerusalem so angry with Paul?

5. Why did the commander not have Paul beaten?

121. BOUND BY LOVE
Acts 24:1-9, 22-27 and 25:1-22 and 26:1-32 and 27:1-2 and 28:14b-31

After his arrest, Paul was taken before Governor Felix and later Porcius Festus and then King Agrippa. Paul used every opportunity to tell these high ranking Roman officials about Jesus Christ and how Jesus changed his life. After being imprisoned for two years, Paul was finally sent to Rome to stand trial before the Emperor, Caesar. Although Paul was again kept under guard for another two years, he used his time to preach and teach about the Kingdom of God. It is during these times of imprisonment that Paul wrote many of his letters to the churches. Through the centuries, God has used these letters to preserve for all believers the teachings of Paul as revealed to him by the Holy Spirit.

The Trial Before Felix

24 [1] After five days, the high priest, Ananias, came down with certain elders and an orator, one Tertullus. They informed the governor against Paul. [2] When he was called, Tertullus began to accuse him, saying, "Seeing that by you we enjoy much peace, and that excellent measures are coming to this nation, [3] we accept it in all ways and in all places, most excellent Felix, with all thankfulness. [4] But, that I don't delay you, I entreat you to bear with us and hear a few words.

[5] For we have found this man to be a plague, an instigator of insurrections among all the Jews throughout the world, and a ringleader of the sect of the Nazarenes. [6] He even tried to profane the temple, and we arrested him and we wanted to judge him according to our law. [7] But the commanding officer, Lysias, came by and with great violence took him out of our hands, [8] commanding his accusers to come to you. By examining him yourself you may ascertain all these things of which we accuse him."

[9] The Jews also joined in the attack, affirming that these things were so.

[22] But Felix, having more exact knowledge concerning the Way, deferred them, saying, "When Lysias, the commanding officer, comes down, I will decide your case." [23] He ordered the centurion that Paul should be kept in custody, and should have some privileges, and not to forbid any of his friends to serve him or to visit him.

[24] But after some days, Felix came with Drusilla, his wife, who was a Jewess, and sent for Paul, and heard him concerning the faith in Christ Jesus. [25] As he reasoned about righteousness, self-control, and the judgment to come, Felix was terrified, and answered, "Go your way for this time, and when it is convenient for me, I will summon you." [26] Meanwhile, he also hoped that money would be given to him by Paul, that he might release him. Therefore also he sent for him more often, and talked with him.

[27] But when two years were fulfilled, Felix was succeeded by Porcius Festus, and desiring to gain favor with the Jews, Felix left Paul in bonds.

Paul Appeals to Caesar

25 [1] Festus therefore, having come into the province, after three days went up to Jerusalem from Caesarea. [2] Then the high priest and the principal men of the Jews informed him against Paul, and they begged him, [3] asking a favor against him, that he would summon him to Jerusalem; plotting to kill him on the way.

[4] However Festus answered that Paul should be kept in custody at Caesarea, and that he himself was about to depart shortly. [5] "Let them therefore", said he, "that are in power among you go down with me, and if there is anything wrong in the man, let them accuse him."

[6] When he had stayed among them more than ten days, he went down to

Caesarea, and on the next day he sat on the judgment seat, and commanded Paul to be brought.⁷ When he had come, the Jews who had come down from Jerusalem stood around him, bringing against him many and grievous charges which they could not prove, ⁸ while he said in his defense, "Neither against the law of the Jews, nor against the temple, nor against Caesar, have I sinned at all."

⁹ But Festus, desiring to gain favor with the Jews, answered Paul and said, "Are you willing to go up to Jerusalem, and be judged by me there concerning these things?" ¹⁰ But Paul said, "I am standing before Caesar's judgment seat, where I ought to be tried. I have done no wrong to the Jews, as you also know very well. ¹¹ For if I have done wrong, and have committed anything worthy of death, I don't refuse to die; but if none of those things is true that they accuse me of, no one can give me up to them. I appeal to Caesar!"

¹² Then Festus, when he had conferred with the council, answered, "You have appealed to Caesar. To Caesar you shall go."

Festus Consults King Agrippa
¹³ Now when some days had passed, King Agrippa and Bernice arrived at Caesarea, and greeted Festus. ¹⁴ As he stayed there many days, Festus laid Paul's case before the king, saying, "There is a certain man left a prisoner by Felix; ¹⁵ about whom, when I was at Jerusalem, the chief priests and the elders of the Jews informed me, asking for a sentence against him.

¹⁶ To whom I answered that it is not the custom of the Romans to give up any man to destruction, before the accused has met the accusers face to face, and has had opportunity to make his defense concerning the matter laid against him. ¹⁷ When therefore they had come together here, I didn't delay, but on the next day sat on the judgment seat, and commanded the man to be brought. ¹⁸ Concerning whom, when the accusers stood up, they brought no charge of such things as I supposed;¹⁹ but had certain questions against him about their own religion, and about one Jesus, who was dead, whom Paul affirmed to be alive. ²⁰ Being perplexed how to inquire concerning these things, I asked whether he was willing to go to Jerusalem and there be judged concerning these matters. ²¹ But when Paul had appealed to be kept for the decision of the emperor, I commanded him to be kept until I could send him to Caesar."

²² Agrippa said to Festus, "I also would like to hear the man myself."

"Tomorrow," he said, "you shall hear him."

Paul's Defense Before Agrippa
26 Agrippa said to Paul, "You may speak for yourself."

Then Paul stretched out his hand, and made his defense.

² "I think myself happy, King Agrippa, that I am to make my defense before you today concerning all the things that I am accused by the Jews, ³ especially because you are expert in all customs and questions which are among the Jews. Therefore I beg you to hear me patiently.

⁴ "Indeed, all the Jews know my way of life from my youth up, which was

from the beginning among my own nation and at Jerusalem; ⁵ having known me from the first, if they are willing to testify, that after the strictest sect of our religion I lived a Pharisee.⁶ Now I stand here to be judged for the hope of the promise made by God to our fathers, ⁷ which our twelve tribes, earnestly serving night and day, hope to attain. Concerning this hope I am accused by the Jews, King Agrippa!

⁸ Why is it judged incredible with you, if God does raise the dead? ⁹ "I myself most certainly thought that I ought to do many things contrary to the name of Jesus of Nazareth. ¹⁰ This I also did in Jerusalem. I both shut up many of the saints in prisons, having received authority from the chief priests, and when they were put to death I gave my vote against them. ¹¹ Punishing them often in all the synagogues, I tried to make them blaspheme. Being exceedingly enraged against them, I persecuted them even to foreign cities.

Paul Tells of His Conversion

¹² "Whereupon as I traveled to Damascus with the authority and commission from the chief priests, ¹³ at noon, O king, I saw on the way a light from the sky, brighter than the sun, shining around me and those who traveled with me. ¹⁴ When we had all fallen to the earth, I heard a voice saying to me in the Hebrew language, 'Saul, Saul, why are you persecuting me? It is hard for you to kick against the goads.'

¹⁵ "I said, 'Who are you, Lord?' "He said, 'I am Jesus, whom you are persecuting. ¹⁶ But arise, and stand on your feet, for I have appeared to you for this purpose: to appoint you a servant and a witness both of the things which you have seen, and of the things which I will reveal to you; ¹⁷ delivering you from the people, and from the Gentiles, to whom I send you, ¹⁸ to open their eyes, that they may turn from darkness to light and from the power of Satan to God, that they may receive remission of sins and an inheritance among those who are sanctified by faith in me.'

¹⁹ "Therefore, King Agrippa, I was not disobedient to the heavenly vision, ²⁰ but declared first to them of Damascus, at Jerusalem, and throughout all the country of Judea, and also to the Gentiles, that they should repent and turn to God, doing works worthy of repentance. ²¹ For this reason the Jews seized me in the temple, and tried to kill me. ²² Having therefore obtained the help that is from God, I stand to this day testifying both to small and great, saying nothing but what the prophets and Moses said would happen, ²³ how the Christ must suffer, and how, by the resurrection of the dead, he would be first to proclaim light both to these people and to the Gentiles."

²⁴ As he thus made his defense, Festus said with a loud voice, "Paul, you are crazy! Your great learning is driving you insane!"

²⁵ But he said, "I am not crazy, most excellent Festus, but boldly declare words of truth and reasonableness. ²⁶ For the king knows of these things, to whom also I speak freely. For I am persuaded that none of these things is hidden

from him, for this has not been done in a corner. ²⁷ King Agrippa, do you believe the prophets? I know that you believe."

²⁸ Agrippa said to Paul, "With a little persuasion are you trying to make me a Christian?"

²⁹ Paul said, "I pray to God, that whether with little or with much, not only you, but also all that hear me today, might become such as I am, except for these bonds."

³⁰The king rose up with the governor, and Bernice, and those who sat with them. ³¹ When they had withdrawn, they spoke to one another, saying, "This man does nothing worthy of death or of bonds." ³² Agrippa said to Festus, "This man might have been set free if he had not appealed to Caesar."

Paul Sails for Rome

27 ¹When it was determined that we should sail for Italy, they delivered Paul and certain other prisoners to a centurion named Julius, of the Augustan band. ² Embarking in a ship of Adramyttium, which was about to sail to places on the coast of Asia, we put to sea; Aristarchus, a Macedonian of Thessalonica, being with us.

28 ¹⁴So we came to Rome. ¹⁵ From there the brothers, when they heard of us, came to meet us as far as The Market of Appius and The Three Taverns. When Paul saw them, he thanked God, and took courage. ¹⁶ When we entered into Rome, the centurion delivered the prisoners to the captain of the guard, but Paul was allowed to stay by himself with the soldier who guarded him.

Paul Preaches at Rome Under Guard

¹⁷ After three days Paul called together those who were the leaders of the Jews. When they had come together, he said to them, "I, brothers, though I had done nothing against the people, or the customs of our fathers, still was delivered prisoner from Jerusalem into the hands of the Romans, ¹⁸ who, when they had examined me, desired to set me free, because there was no cause of death in me. ¹⁹ But when the Jews spoke against it, I was constrained to appeal to Caesar, not that I had anything about which to accuse my nation. ²⁰ For this cause therefore I asked to see you and to speak with you. For because of the hope of Israel I am bound with this chain." ²¹ They said to him, "We neither received letters from Judea concerning you, nor did any of the brothers come here and report or speak any evil of you. ²² But we desire to hear from you what you think. For, as concerning this sect, it is known to us that everywhere it is spoken against." ²³ When they had appointed him a day, many people came to him at his lodging. He explained to them, testifying about God's Kingdom, and persuading them concerning Jesus, both from the law of Moses and from the prophets, from morning until evening.²⁴ Some believed the things which were spoken, and some disbelieved.

²⁵ When they didn't agree among themselves, they departed after Paul had

spoken one word, "The Holy Spirit spoke rightly through Isaiah, the prophet, to our fathers, ²⁶ saying,

> 'Go to this people, and say,
> in hearing, you will hear,
> but will in no way understand.
> In seeing, you will see, but will in no way perceive.
> ²⁷For this people's heart has grown callous.
> Their ears are dull of hearing.
> Their eyes they have closed.
> Lest they should see with their eyes,
> hear with their ears,
> understand with their heart,
> and would turn again,
> and I would heal them.' (Isaiah 6:9-10)

²⁸ "Be it known therefore to you, that the salvation of God is sent to the nations. They will also listen."

²⁹ When he had said these words, the Jews departed, having a great dispute among themselves.³⁰ Paul stayed two whole years in his own rented house, and received all who were coming to him, ³¹ preaching God's Kingdom, and teaching the things concerning the Lord Jesus Christ with all boldness, without hindrance.

1. What accusations did the Jews make against Paul? Were they true?

2. Why did Paul appeal his case to Caesar?

3. What did Paul speak about that caused Felix to be afraid? Why?

4. What did Paul say that caused Festus to interrupt him?

5. Why did King Agrippa put Paul off? All three of these rulers plainly heard the Gospel but hesitated to believe. Why?

6. In his divine encounter with Jesus on the way to Damascus, Jesus told Paul what he was to do and what the outcome would be. Please read vv17-18 again and review the process: God planned to use Paul's message to Gentile pagans to bring light into their darkness, which will cause them to turn from Satan to God, receive forgiveness of sin, and be given a place (the church) to be with other forgiven sinners. Have you seen any part of this process taking part in your life?

7. Who are those who hear but never understand and see but never perceive? What does God want to do for those who **DO** hear and see the truth?

8. Paul ended his message to the Jewish leaders in Rome with a very important announcement (v 28). What was that all-important news? Why would this observation cause a dispute among the Jews?

VI. CHRIST TEACHES HIS CHURCH

Before Jesus returned to heaven, he told His disciples to go to all the nations and teach them to obey everything He had commanded them. Because He would not be with them in bodily form, Christ told His disciples that the Holy Spirit would teach them all things and remind them of everything He had said to them. Although the disciples preached the commands of Christ, they also found it necessary to write letters of instruction to the believers. Written to the people of the churches in cities throughout the world of the first century, these letters contained the basic and essential teachings of Christ.

Having been with Jesus during His life on earth, Peter, James and John, under the anointing of the Holy Spirit, gave deep insight into the teachings of Christ and how believers were to obey His commands. Because of Paul's love and concern for the welfare and growth of the believers in the churches, he wrote many letters, especially during his times of imprisonment. Although God used ordinary men to write these letters, they were inspired by the Holy Spirit. This made these writings the same as if Christ Himself were speaking to His Church, giving all believers everywhere His personal instructions for their lives.

A. NEW LIFE IN CHRIST

Because the new believers of the first century came from varied cultures and religions, the disciples wrote to them, explaining God's purpose in sending Jesus. They made it very clear that it was the evil and wickedness of man that caused God's anger with mankind. However, it was the love of God that caused Him to send His only Son as the sacrifice for the sins of all peoples. Anyone who accepts God's sacrifice of His Son as payment for their sins is forgiven and becomes a new person. Those who have this new life in Christ are then free from the bondages of sin and religion and able to live lives that are pleasing to God.

122. THE WORD OF GOD
Psalms 119: 105, 129-130, 160, 162-163, 165; Psalms 119: 9-11; Romans 15:4; Matthew 4:4; Psalms 19: 7-11; Proverbs 30:5; Isaiah 34:16; Isaiah 40:8; 2 Timothy 3:16-17; 2 Peter 1:16-21; 1 Corinthians 2:6-16; Isaiah 55:10-11; and Hebrews 4:12-13

The Bible is no ordinary book. God recorded His thoughts over many years, using ordinary men who were inspired by the Holy Spirit to write truth that God wanted everyone to know. For that reason we call the Bible the "written word of God." The Holy Spirit's presence in God's word makes it living and active, giving it divine power to speak to our hearts. The Bible is God's love letter to men, explaining everything that men need to know to have faith in God and to live a godly life.

God's Word Gives Light and Truth

119 ^{105}Your word is a lamp to my feet,
    and a light for my path.
      ^{129}Your testimonies are wonderful,

Great Bible Truths

therefore my soul keeps them.
¹³⁰The entrance of your words gives light.
It gives understanding to the simple.
¹⁶⁰ All of your words are truth.
Every one of your righteous ordinances endures forever.
¹⁶² I rejoice at your word,
as one who finds great plunder.
¹⁶³ I hate and abhor falsehood.
I love your law
¹⁶⁵ Those who love your law have great peace.
Nothing causes them to stumble.

The Word of God Instructs Us

119 ⁹How can a young man keep his way pure?
By living according to your word.
¹⁰ With my whole heart, I have sought you.
Don't let me wander from your commandments.
¹¹ I have hidden your word in my heart,
that I might not sin against you.

15 ⁴For whatever things were written before were written for our learning, that through patience and through encouragement of the Scriptures we might have hope.

4 ⁴ But he [Jesus] answered, "It is written, 'Man shall not live by bread alone, but by every word that proceeds out of the mouth of God.'"

God's Word Is Perfect, Pure, True and Eternal

19 ⁷Yahweh's law is perfect, restoring the soul.
Yahweh's testimony is sure, making wise the simple.
⁸ Yahweh's precepts are right, rejoicing the heart.
Yahweh's commandment is pure, enlightening the eyes.
⁹ The fear of Yahweh is clean, enduring forever.
Yahweh's ordinances are true, and righteous altogether.
¹⁰ More to be desired are they than gold, yes, than much fine gold;
sweeter also than honey and the extract of the honeycomb.
¹¹ Moreover by them is your servant warned.
In keeping them there is great reward.

30 ⁵"Every word of God is flawless.
He is a shield to those who take refuge in him.

34 ¹⁶ Search in the book of Yahweh, and read:

40 ⁸The grass withers,
the flower fades;
but the word of our God stands forever."

Great Bible Truths

Scripture Is the Divine Word of God

3 [16]Every Scripture is God-breathed and profitable for teaching, for reproof, for correction, and for instruction in righteousness, [17] that the man of God may be complete, thoroughly equipped for every good work.

1 [16]For we did not follow cunningly devised fables, when we made known to you the power and coming of our Lord Jesus Christ, but we were eyewitnesses of his majesty.[17] For he received from God the Father honor and glory, when the voice came to him from the Majestic Glory, "This is my beloved Son, in whom I am well pleased." [18] We heard this voice come out of heaven when we were with him on the holy mountain. [19] We have the more sure word of prophecy; and you do well that you heed it, as to a lamp shining in a dark place, until the day dawns, and the morning star arises in your hearts: [20] knowing this first, that no prophecy of Scripture is of private interpretation.[21] For no prophecy ever came by the will of man: but holy men of God spoke, being moved by the Holy Spirit.

God's Word Reveals His Thoughts and Plans

2 [6]We speak wisdom, however, among those who are full grown; yet a wisdom not of this world, nor of the rulers of this world, who are coming to nothing. [7] But we speak God's wisdom in a mystery, the wisdom that has been hidden, which God foreordained before the worlds for our glory, [8] which none of the rulers of this world has known. For had they known it, they wouldn't have crucified the Lord of glory. [9] But as it is written,

> "Things which an eye didn't see,
> and an ear didn't hear,
> which didn't enter into the heart of man,
> these God has prepared for those who love him."

[10] But to us, God revealed them through the Spirit. For the Spirit searches all things, yes, the deep things of God. [11] For who among men knows the things of a man, except the spirit of the man, which is in him? Even so, no one knows the things of God, except God's Spirit. [12] But we received, not the spirit of the world, but the Spirit which is from God, that we might know the things that were freely given to us by God. [13] Which things also we speak, not in words which man's wisdom teaches, but which the Holy Spirit teaches, comparing spiritual things with spiritual things. [14] Now the natural man doesn't receive the things of God's Spirit, for they are foolishness to him, and he can't know them, because they are spiritually discerned. [15] But he who is spiritual discerns all things, and he himself is judged by no one. [16] "For who has known the mind of the Lord, that he should instruct him?" But we have Christ's mind.

God's Word Accomplishes Its Purpose

55 [10] For as the rain comes down and the snow from the sky,
and doesn't return there, but waters the earth,

and makes it grow and bud,
and gives seed to the sower and bread to the eater;
¹¹ so is my word that goes out of my mouth:
it will not return to me void,
but it will accomplish that which I please,
and it will prosper in the thing I sent it to do.

God's Word Is Powerful

4 ¹²For the word of God is living and active, and sharper than any two-edged sword, piercing even to the dividing of soul and spirit, of both joints and marrow, and is able to discern the thoughts and intentions of the heart. ¹³ There is no creature that is hidden from his sight, but all things are naked and laid open before the eyes of him to whom we must give an account.

> 1. Describe the characteristics of the Bible.
>
> 2. What will the Word of God (the Bible) do for us? Will God's Word change your thinking and acting?
>
> 3. Where did Peter get his information about the power and coming of Jesus Christ?
>
> 4. How (the method) did the prophets speak and write?
>
> 5. Can we trust the Bible to be true? Why?

123. GOD CONFRONTS SIN AND EVIL
Romans 1

Paul's letter to the believers at Rome gave basic instruction about the new life in Jesus. Rome was the capital of the Roman Empire. Most Romans were pagans, believing in many false gods. However, there were Jews and Christians too. Those believers had questions about salvation and growing in Jesus. Paul's answers lay out a complete plan of salvation and righteous living for all mankind. In the first part we learned that ignorance and rejection of the true God leads to a downward process that ultimately ends in a degraded life of evil and wickedness. For this reason, the righteous anger and judgment of God must come upon all those who refuse to come to knowledge of the Truth.

Paul's Greetings

1 Paul, a servant of Jesus Christ, called to be an apostle, set apart for the Good News of God, ² which he promised before through his prophets in the holy Scriptures, ³ concerning his Son, who was born of the offspring of David according to the flesh, ⁴ who was declared to be the Son of God with power, according to the Spirit of holiness, by the resurrection from the dead, Jesus Christ our Lord, ⁵ through whom we received grace and apostleship, for obedience of faith among all the nations, for his name's sake; ⁶ among whom you are also called to belong to Jesus Christ; ⁷ to all who are in Rome, beloved of God, called to be saints: Grace to you and peace from God our Father and the Lord Jesus Christ.

A Prayer of Thanksgiving

[8] First, I thank my God through Jesus Christ for all of you, that your faith is proclaimed throughout the whole world. [9] For God is my witness, whom I serve in my spirit in the Good News of his Son, how unceasingly I make mention of you always in my prayers, [10] requesting, if by any means now at last I may be prospered by the will of God to come to you. [11] For I long to see you, that I may impart to you some spiritual gift, to the end that you may be established; [12] that is, that I with you may be encouraged in you, each of us by the other's faith, both yours and mine.

[13] Now I don't desire to have you unaware, brothers, that I often planned to come to you, and was hindered so far, that I might have some fruit among you also, even as among the rest of the Gentiles. [14] I am debtor both to Greeks and to foreigners, both to the wise and to the foolish. [15] So, as much as is in me, I am eager to preach the Good News to you also who are in Rome.

The Power of the Gospel for Salvation

[16] For I am not ashamed of the Good News of Christ, for it is the power of God for salvation for everyone who believes; for the Jew first, and also for the Greek. [17] For in it is revealed God's righteousness from faith to faith. As it is written, "But the righteous shall live by faith."

All People Have Done Wrong

[18] For the wrath of God is revealed from heaven against all ungodliness and unrighteousness of men, who suppress the truth in unrighteousness, [19] because that which is known of God is revealed in them, for God revealed it to them. [20] For the invisible things of him since the creation of the world are clearly seen, being perceived through the things that are made, even his everlasting power and divinity; that they may be without excuse. [21] Because, knowing God, they didn't glorify him as God, neither gave thanks, but became vain in their reasoning, and their senseless heart was darkened.

[22] Professing themselves to be wise, they became fools, [23] and traded the glory of the incorruptible God for the likeness of an image of corruptible man, and of birds, and four-footed animals, and creeping things. [24] Therefore God also gave them up in the lusts of their hearts to uncleanness, that their bodies should be dishonored among themselves, [25] who exchanged the truth of God for a lie, and worshiped and served the creature rather than the Creator, who is blessed forever. Amen.

[26] For this reason, God gave them up to vile passions. For their women changed the natural function into that which is against nature. [27] Likewise also the men, leaving the natural function of the woman, burned in their lust toward one another, men doing what is inappropriate with men, and receiving in themselves the due penalty of their error. [28] Even as they refused to have God in their knowledge, God gave them up to a reprobate mind, to do those things which are not fitting; [29] being filled with all unrighteousness, sexual immorality,

wickedness, covetousness, malice; full of envy, murder, strife, deceit, evil habits, secret slanderers, [30] backbiters, hateful to God, insolent, haughty, boastful, inventors of evil things, disobedient to parents, [31] without understanding, covenant breakers, without natural affection, unforgiving, unmerciful; [32] who, knowing the ordinance of God, that those who practice such things are worthy of death, not only do the same, but also approve of those who practice them.

1. Review vv 16-17. This is the theme and outline of this letter and the Good News (Gospel) of Jesus Christ. What is the Gospel?

2. Why are people without excuse for not knowing the truth about God? What are the two things that they did not do that sent them on the wrong track?

3. Can you see how people who do not follow God soon develop futile thinking and become fools? Do you know someone like this?

4. Describe those who have a depraved mind. Why did God give them over to do evil?

5. Can you see how important it is to have a thankful heart? (v.21)

124. EVERYMAN'S NEED FOR SALVATION
Romans 2:1-11 and 3:9-31 and 4:13-25

In this selection, we read about how Paul turned his attention to the Jews, who prided themselves as being the only God-fearing people alive. They believed that God saved, blessed and kept them because of their faithful obedience to the rules and practices established by their leaders over the years. In effect, they believed that they earned their relationship with God by the things they did. Paul showed that this was wrong thinking. Although God used the Israelite nation to accomplish His plan of sending the Savior, Paul, himself a Jew, explained that they, too, needed salvation through Jesus Christ. Using the example of Abraham, Paul showed that they needed to have faith and trust in God's provision of Jesus Christ's sacrificial atonement. No longer could they depend upon their good works and religious deeds to save them from God's judgment or make them right (justified) before God. From now on, to be saved, they, too, needed to have faith in Jesus, just like the Gentiles. All the world's religions, with the exception of Christianity, even errant groups of Christianity (commonly called cults), hold the major tenet that mankind is saved to heaven and eternal life according to how he lived on earth. Thus, he thinks that he earns his salvation apart from a total reliance upon the undeserved gift of salvation that comes through Jesus Christ's sacrificial death on the cross. Christianity is absolutely unique in that it maintains that man is saved only through faith in Jesus Christ, not by anything he is or that he himself can do.

Great Bible Truths

No Excuse for Sin

2 Therefore you are without excuse, O man, whoever you are who judge. For in that which you judge another, you condemn yourself. For you who judge practice the same things. ² We know that the judgment of God is according to truth against those who practice such things. ³ Do you think this, O man who judges those who practice such things, and do the same, that you will escape the judgment of God? ⁴ Or do you despise the riches of his goodness, forbearance, and patience, not knowing that the goodness of God leads you to repentance?

God's Righteous Judgment

⁵ But according to your hardness and unrepentant heart you are treasuring up for yourself wrath in the day of wrath, revelation, and of the righteous judgment of God; ⁶ who "will pay back to everyone according to their works:" ⁷ to those who by patience in well-doing seek for glory, honor, and incorruptibility, eternal life; ⁸ but to those who are self-seeking, and don't obey the truth, but obey unrighteousness, will be wrath and indignation, ⁹ oppression and anguish, on every soul of man who does evil, to the Jew first, and also to the Greek. ¹⁰ But glory, honor, and peace go to every man who does good, to the Jew first, and also to the Greek. ¹¹ For there is no partiality with God.

No-One Is Righteous

3 ⁹What then? Are we better than they? No, in no way. For we previously warned both Jews and Greeks, that they are all under sin. ¹⁰ As it is written,

> "There is no one righteous;
> No, not one.
> ¹¹ There is no one who understands.
> There is no one who seeks after God.
> ¹²They have all turned aside.
> They have together become unprofitable.
> There is no one who does good,
> no, not so much as one."
> ¹³ "Their throat is an open tomb.
> With their tongues they have used deceit."
> "The poison of vipers is under their lips";
> ¹⁴ "whose mouth is full of cursing and bitterness."
> ¹⁵ "Their feet are swift to shed blood.
> ¹⁶ Destruction and misery are in their ways.
> ¹⁷ The way of peace, they haven't known."
> ¹⁸ "There is no fear of God before their eyes."

¹⁹ Now we know that whatever things the law says, it speaks to those who are under the law, that every mouth may be closed, and all the world may be brought under the judgment of God. ²⁰ Because by the works of the law, no flesh will be justified in his sight. For through the law comes the knowledge of sin.

How God Makes People Right – Through Faith

[21] But now apart from the law, a righteousness of God has been revealed, being testified by the law and the prophets; [22] even the righteousness of God through faith in Jesus Christ to all and on all those who believe. For there is no distinction, [23] for all have sinned, and fall short of the glory of God; [24] being justified freely by his grace through the redemption that is in Christ Jesus; [25] whom God sent to be an atoning sacrifice, through faith in his blood, for a demonstration of his righteousness through the passing over of prior sins, in God's forbearance; [26] to demonstrate his righteousness at this present time; that he might himself be just, and the justifier of him who has faith in Jesus.

[27] Where then is the boasting? It is excluded. By what kind of law? Of works? No, but by a law of faith. [28] We maintain therefore that a man is justified by faith apart from the works of the law. [29] Or is God the God of Jews only? Isn't he the God of Gentiles also? Yes, of Gentiles also, [30] since indeed there is one God who will justify the circumcised by faith, and the uncircumcised through faith. [31] Do we then nullify the law through faith? May it never be! No, we establish the law.

Abraham's Example of Faith

4 [13] For the promise to Abraham and to his offspring that he should be heir of the world wasn't through the law, but through the righteousness of faith. [14] For if those who are of the law are heirs, faith is made void, and the promise is made of no effect. [15] For the law produces wrath, for where there is no law, neither is there disobedience.

[16] For this cause it is of faith, that it may be according to grace, to the end that the promise may be sure to all the offspring, not to that only which is of the law, but to that also which is of the faith of Abraham, who is the father of us all. [17] As it is written, "I have made you a father of many nations." (Gen.17:5) This is in the presence of him whom he believed: God, who gives life to the dead, and calls the things that are not, as though they were.

[18] Besides hope, Abraham in hope believed, to the end that he might become a father of many nations, according to that which had been spoken, "So will your offspring be." [19] Without being weakened in faith, he didn't consider his own body, already having been worn out, (he being about a hundred years old), and the deadness of Sarah's womb. [20] Yet, looking to the promise of God, he didn't waver through unbelief, but grew strong through faith, giving glory to God, [21] and being fully assured that what he had promised, he was also able to perform. [22] Therefore it also was "credited to him for righteousness." [23] Now it was not written that it was accounted to him for his sake alone, [24] but for our sake also, to whom it will be accounted, who believe in him who raised Jesus, our Lord, from the dead, [25] who was delivered up for our trespasses, and was raised for our justification.

1. Is every living person a sinner who deserves God's judgment? Is everyone without excuse? Why?

2. Does living a good life and doing good things make up for sin?

3. Who gives us righteousness, and how did He do it?

4. How do we, as sinners, receive righteousness i.e., (sins forgiven, salvation, promise of eternal life) in the eyes of God?

5. Paul said that Abraham "is the father of us all." Do you understand why after reading Paul's explanation?

Pause for Reflection: We have covered Christianity's basic doctrine – that mankind is saved only by faith in Jesus Christ. This is often referred to as "justification by faith." Do you understand it completely, and realize that there is nothing at all that you can do to earn salvation?

125. PEACE WITH GOD
Romans 5:1-14 and Hebrews 9:22-28 and 10:1-18

As sinners we are all separated from God and deserve the penalty of death that came first to Adam. However, the sacrifice of Christ's life on the cross did away with sin once and for all. Now all those who believe by faith in Jesus Christ can be forgiven of their sin and find peace with God.

Peace and Joy

5 Being therefore justified by faith, we have peace with God through our Lord Jesus Christ; ² through whom we also have our access by faith into this grace in which we stand. We rejoice in hope of the glory of God. ³ Not only this, but we also rejoice in our sufferings, knowing that suffering produces perseverance; ⁴ and perseverance, proven character; and proven character, hope: ⁵ and hope doesn't disappoint us, because God's love has been poured out into our hearts through the Holy Spirit who was given to us.

⁶ For while we were yet weak, at the right time Christ died for the ungodly. ⁷ For one will hardly die for a righteous man. Yet perhaps for a righteous person someone would even dare to die. ⁸ But God commends his own love toward us, in that while we were yet sinners, Christ died for us.

⁹ Much more then, being now justified by his blood, we will be saved from God's wrath through him. ¹⁰ For if, while we were enemies, we were reconciled to God through the death of his Son, much more, being reconciled, we will be saved by his life. ¹¹ Not only so, but we also rejoice in God through our Lord Jesus Christ, through whom we have now received the reconciliation.

Death Through Adam, Life Through Christ

¹² Therefore as sin entered into the world through one man, and death through sin; and so death passed to all men, because all sinned. ¹³ For until the law, sin was in the world; but sin is not charged when there is no law. ¹⁴ Nevertheless

death reigned from Adam until Moses, even over those whose sins weren't like Adam's disobedience, who is a foreshadowing of him who was to come.

Christ's Death Takes Away Our Sins

9 [22] According to the law, nearly everything is cleansed with blood, and apart from shedding of blood there is no remission. [23] It was necessary therefore that the copies of the things in the heavens should be cleansed with these; but the heavenly things themselves with better sacrifices than these. [24] For Christ hasn't entered into holy places made with hands, which are representations of the true, but into heaven itself, now to appear in the presence of God for us; [25] nor yet that he should offer himself often, as the high priest enters into the holy place year by year with blood not his own, [26] or else he must have suffered often since the foundation of the world. But now once at the end of the ages, he has been revealed to put away sin by the sacrifice of himself. [27] Inasmuch as it is appointed for men to die once, and after this, judgment, [28] so Christ also, having been offered once to bear the sins of many, will appear a second time, without sin, to those who are eagerly waiting for him for salvation.

Christ's Sacrifice Once for All

10 [1] For the law, having a shadow of the good to come, not the very image of the things, can never with the same sacrifices year by year, which they offer continually, make perfect those who draw near. [2] Or else wouldn't they have ceased to be offered, because the worshipers, having been once cleansed, would have had no more consciousness of sins? [3] But in those sacrifices there is a yearly reminder of sins. [4] For it is impossible that the blood of bulls and goats should take away sins.

[5] Therefore when he comes into the world, he says,
"Sacrifice and offering you didn't desire,
but you prepared a body for me.
[6] You had no pleasure in whole burnt offerings and sacrifices for sin.
[7] Then I said, 'Behold, I have come
(in the scroll of the book it is written of me)
to do your will, O God.'"

[8] previously saying, "Sacrifices and offerings and whole burnt offerings and sacrifices for sin you didn't desire, neither had pleasure in them" (those which are offered according to the law), [9] then he has said, "Behold, I have come to do your will." He takes away the first, that he may establish the second, [10] by which will we have been sanctified through the offering of the body of Jesus Christ once for all.

[11] Every priest indeed stands day by day serving and often offering the same sacrifices, which can never take away sins, [12] but he, when he had offered one sacrifice for sins forever, sat down on the right hand of God; [13] from that time waiting until his enemies are made the footstool of his feet. [14] For by one offering he has perfected forever those who are being sanctified.

Great Bible Truths

God's New Covenant with Man

[15] The Holy Spirit also testifies to us, for after saying,

> [16]"This is the covenant that I will make with them:
> After those days,' says the Lord,
> 'I will put my laws on their heart,
> I will also write them on their mind;'"
> Then he says,
> [17]"I will remember their sins
> and their iniquities no more."

[18] Now where remission [forgiveness] of these is, there is no more offering for sin.

1. *How do we have peace with God?*

2. *How does God demonstrate His love for us?*

3. *How did Jesus Christ do away with sin?*

4. *Why are the old Jewish sacrifices for sin not necessary anymore?*

5. *Describe the New Covenant that the Holy Spirit makes with each believer. (Do you remember that this plan to profoundly change men's lives was promised in the Old Testament? See selection 64, p.135.)*

126. A NEW LIFE WITH GOD
Galatians 2:19-20; Romans 6:1-23 and 2 Corinthians 5:14-21

Once we accept the sacrifice of Christ's death on the cross, our old self becomes dead to the power of sin. We are given a new life that is free from the slavery to sin, and we become able to do what is good and pleasing to God. As a new creation in Christ, we can experience a life of holiness now as well as in heaven with God, in life that will never end.

Jesus Lives in Me

2 [19] For I, through the law, died to the law, that I might live to God. [20] I have been crucified with Christ, and it is no longer I who live, but Christ lives in me. That life which I now live in the flesh, I live by the faith of the Son of God, who loved me, and gave himself up for me.

Dead to Sin, Alive in Christ

6 What shall we say then? Shall we continue in sin, that grace may abound? [2] May it never be! We who died to sin, how could we live in it any longer? [3] Or don't you know that all we who were baptized into Christ Jesus were baptized into his death? [4] We were buried therefore with him through baptism to death, that just as Christ was raised from the dead through the glory of the Father, so we also might walk in newness of life.

[5] For if we have become united with him in the likeness of his death, we will also be part of his resurrection; [6] knowing this, that our old man [our sinful selves controlled by sin] was crucified with him, that the body of sin might be done away with, so that we would no longer be in bondage to sin. [7] For he who has died has been freed from sin.

⁸ But if we died with Christ, we believe that we will also live with him; ⁹ knowing that Christ, being raised from the dead, dies no more. Death no more has dominion over him! ¹⁰ For the death that he died, he died to sin one time; but the life that he lives, he lives to God.

Say No to Sin; Yes to God
¹¹ Thus consider yourselves also to be dead to sin, but alive to God in Christ Jesus our Lord. ¹² Therefore don't let sin reign in your mortal body, that you should obey it in its lusts.¹³Also, do not present your members to sin as instruments of unrighteousness, but present yourselves to God, as alive from the dead, and your members as instruments of righteousness to God. ¹⁴ For sin will not have dominion over you. For you are not under law, but under grace.

Slaves to Righteousness
¹⁵ What then? Shall we sin, because we are not under law, but under grace? May it never be! ¹⁶ Don't you know that when you present yourselves as servants and obey someone, you are the servants of whomever you obey; whether of sin to death, or of obedience to righteousness? ¹⁷ But thanks be to God, that, whereas you were bondservants of sin, you became obedient from the heart to that form of teaching to which you were delivered. ¹⁸ Being made free from sin, you became bondservants of righteousness.

¹⁹ I speak in human terms because of the weakness of your flesh, for as you presented your members as servants to uncleanness and to wickedness upon wickedness, even so now present your members as servants to righteousness for sanctification. ²⁰ For when you were servants of sin, you were free in regard to righteousness. ²¹ What fruit then did you have at that time in the things of which you are now ashamed? For the end of those things is death. ²² But now, being made free from sin, and having become servants of God, you have your fruit of sanctification, and the result of eternal life.²³ For the wages of sin is death, but the free gift of God is eternal life in Christ Jesus our Lord.

5 ¹⁴For the love of Christ constrains us; because we judge thus, that one died for all, therefore all died. ¹⁵ He died for all, that those who live should no longer live to themselves, but to him who for their sakes died and rose again.

A New Creation in Christ
¹⁶ Therefore we know no one after the flesh from now on. Even though we have known Christ after the flesh, yet now we know him so no more. ¹⁷ Therefore if anyone is in Christ, he is a new creation. The old things have passed away. Behold, all things have become new.¹⁸ But all things are of God, who reconciled us to himself through Jesus Christ, and gave to us the ministry of reconciliation; ¹⁹ namely, that God was in Christ reconciling the world to himself, not reckoning to them their trespasses, and having committed to us the word of reconciliation.

²⁰ We are therefore ambassadors on behalf of Christ, as though God were entreating by us: we beg you on behalf of Christ, be reconciled to God. ²¹ For him who knew no sin he made to be sin on our behalf; so that in him we might become the righteousness of God.

1. How can we too live a new life? What happened to our old self? What two things are we told not to do?
2. Paul said that when the believer is in Christ he dies to sin and is alive to God. The believer lives a new life and though God's help can say NO to temptation and sin, and YES to God and right living. Do you believe that this could happen in your life?
3. How do we become slaves to righteousness?
4. What benefit (fruit) do we have when we become slaves to God? What is the important result of that benefit?
5. What happens to anyone who is in Christ? (v.17)

127. ALIVE IN CHRIST
Ephesians 2:1-22 and Titus 3:1-8

Before we come to Christ, we are all spiritually dead because of our sin. Only God's grace and mercy provide for our salvation, because all our sins are forgiven through Jesus' sacrifice on the cross. Now we are alive in Jesus, experiencing a new life in Him. We have direct access to God the Father through the Holy Spirit. As His forever-loved children, we become God's agents to do good things for others, as God directs us. We do these not to earn our salvation, but out of gratitude for His having saved us from a certain death.

Made Alive in Christ
2 You were made alive when you were dead in transgressions and sins, ² in which you once walked according to the course of this world, according to the prince of the power of the air, the spirit who now works in the children of disobedience; ³ among whom we also all once lived in the lust of our flesh, doing the desires of the flesh and of the mind, and were by nature children of wrath, even as the rest. ⁴ But God, being rich in mercy, for his great love with which he loved us, ⁵ even when we were dead through our trespasses, made us alive together with Christ (by grace you have been saved), ⁶ and raised us up with him, and made us to sit with him in the heavenly places in Christ Jesus, ⁷ that in the ages to come he might show the exceeding riches of his grace in kindness toward us in Christ Jesus; ⁸ for by grace you have been saved through faith, and that not of yourselves; it is the gift of God, ⁹ not of works, that no one would boast.

Living a Life of Good Works
¹⁰ For we are his workmanship, created in Christ Jesus for good works, which God prepared before that we would walk in them.

Believers Are One in Christ
¹¹ Therefore remember that once you, the Gentiles in the flesh, who are called "uncircumcision" by that which is called "circumcision", (in the flesh, made by hands); ¹² that you were at that time separate from Christ, alienated from the commonwealth of Israel, and strangers from the covenants of the promise, having no hope and without God in the world. ¹³ But now in Christ Jesus you who once were far off are made near in the blood of Christ.

¹⁴ For he is our peace, who made both one, and broke down the middle wall of partition, ¹⁵ having abolished in the flesh the hostility, the law of commandments contained in ordinances, that he might create in himself one new man of the two, making peace; ¹⁶ and might reconcile them both in one body to God through the cross, having killed the hostility thereby. ¹⁷ He came and preached peace to you who were far off and to those who were near. ¹⁸ For through him we both have our access in one Spirit to the Father.

The Family of God

¹⁹ So then you are no longer strangers and foreigners, but you are fellow citizens with the saints, and of the household of God, ²⁰ being built on the foundation of the apostles and prophets, Christ Jesus himself being the chief cornerstone; ²¹ in whom the whole building, fitted together, grows into a holy temple in the Lord; ²² in whom you also are built together for a habitation of God in the Spirit.

Doing What Is Good

3 Remind them to be in subjection to rulers and to authorities, to be obedient, to be ready for every good work, ² to speak evil of no one, not to be contentious, to be gentle, showing all humility toward all men. ³ For we were also once foolish, disobedient, deceived, serving various lusts and pleasures, living in malice and envy, hateful, and hating one another. ⁴ But when the kindness of God our Savior and his love toward mankind appeared, ⁵ not by works of righteousness, which we did ourselves, but according to his mercy, he saved us, through the washing of regeneration and renewing by the Holy Spirit, ⁶ whom he poured out on us richly, through Jesus Christ our Savior;⁷ that, being justified by his grace, we might be made heirs according to the hope of eternal life. ⁸ This saying is faithful, and concerning these things I desire that you affirm confidently, so that those who have believed God may be careful to maintain good works. These things are good and profitable to men.

1. What caused us to be the objects of God's anger?

2. Why did God make us alive with Christ? (Eph.2:4)

3. How are we saved? Can we work for our salvation or earn it in any way?

4. How are we brought near to God? How do we have access to the Father?

5. What are we being built together to become?

6. Read 2:8-10 again. We cannot earn our salvation because it is a gift of God; yet, once we are saved through Jesus' sacrifice, we are "to do good works which God prepared for us to do."
    a. Why are these good works important?
    b. Why should we do them?
    c. What is the benefit of these good works?

7. Can you see how a true understanding of the verses in the final selection promotes humility? Gratitude? A life of service?

128. THE STRUGGLE WITHIN US
Romans 7:14-25 and 1 John 1:5-10 and 2:1-11

After we have experienced new life in Christ, we still have the tendency to sin. Even Paul struggled with his sinful nature and sought to be free from his evil deeds. The good news is that if we do commit sin, we can be cleansed through the blood of Jesus Christ by confessing the wrong we have done.

Struggling with Sin

7 ¹⁴For we know that the law is spiritual, but I am fleshly, sold under sin. ¹⁵ For I don't know what I am doing. For I don't practice what I desire to do; but what I hate, that I do. ¹⁶ But if what I don't desire, that I do, I consent to the law that it is good. ¹⁷ So now it is no more I that do it, but sin which dwells in me.

¹⁸ For I know that in me, that is, in my flesh, dwells no good thing. For desire is present with me, but I don't find it doing that which is good. ¹⁹ For the good which I desire, I don't do; but the evil which I don't desire, that I practice. ²⁰ But if what I don't desire, that I do, it is no more I that do it, but sin which dwells in me. ²¹ I find then the law, that, to me, while I desire to do good, evil is present. ²² For I delight in God's law after the inward man, ²³ but I see a different law in my members, warring against the law of my mind, and bringing me into captivity under the law of sin which is in my members. ²⁴ What a wretched man I am! Who will deliver me out of the body of this death?

²⁵ I thank God through Jesus Christ, our Lord! So then with the mind, I myself serve God's law, but with the flesh, the sin's law.

Walking in the Light

1 ⁵This is the message which we have heard from him and announce to you, that God is light, and in him is no darkness at all. ⁶ If we say that we have fellowship with him and walk in the darkness, we lie, and don't tell the truth. ⁷ But if we walk in the light, as he is in the light, we have fellowship with one another, and the blood of Jesus Christ, his Son, cleanses us from all sin. ⁸ If we say that we have no sin, we deceive ourselves, and the truth is not in us.

Assurance of Forgiveness of Sins

⁹ If we confess our sins, he is faithful and righteous to forgive us the sins, and to cleanse us from all unrighteousness. ¹⁰ If we say that we haven't sinned, we make him a liar, and his word is not in us.

Assurance of Salvation Through Jesus

2 ¹My little children, I write these things to you so that you may not sin. If anyone sins, we have a Counselor with the Father, Jesus Christ, the righteous. ² And he is the atoning sacrifice for our sins, and not for ours only, but also for the whole world. ³ This is how we know that we know him: if we keep his commandments. ⁴ One who says, "I know him," and doesn't keep his commandments, is a liar, and the truth isn't in him. ⁵ But whoever keeps his word, God's love has most certainly been perfected in him. This is how we know that we are in him: ⁶ he who says he remains in him ought himself also to walk just like he walked.

⁷ Brothers, I write no new commandment to you, but an old commandment which you had from the beginning. The old commandment is the word which you have had from the beginning.

The Command to Love Others

⁸ Again, I write a new commandment to you, which is true in him and in you; because the darkness is passing away, and the true light already shines. ⁹ He who says he is in the light and hates his brother, is in the darkness even until now.

¹⁰ He who loves his brother remains in the light, and there is no occasion for stumbling in him. ¹¹ But he who hates his brother is in the darkness, and walks in the darkness, and doesn't know where he is going, because the darkness has blinded his eyes.

1. What causes the struggle within us between good and evil?
2. What must we do in order for God to forgive us of our sins?
3. Who is our defense when we struggle against sin?
4. How do we walk in the light? Why do we walk in the light?
5. How do we know that we are in Christ?
6. Can you hate your brother and still be in the light?

129. ETERNAL LIFE IN THE SON
1 John 5:1-21

We end this section, Your New Life in Christ, with the assurance of salvation taken from the Bible. We can be assured of God's promise to us that all who believe in Jesus Christ have eternal life, because this life is found only in Jesus. As believers, we express our love for God by obeying His commandments. We can be successful because God's divine power, the Holy Spirit, helps us have victory by overcoming the world and its temptations for evil. The next section of Bible readings will explain this more completely.

Love God and Obey Him

5 ¹Whoever believes that Jesus is the Christ has been born of God. Whoever loves the Father also loves the child who is born of him. ² By this we know that we love the children of God, when we love God and keep his commandments. ³ For this is the love of God, that we keep his commandments. His commandments are not grievous. ⁴ For whatever is born of God overcomes the world. This is the victory that has overcome the world: your faith. ⁵ Who is he who overcomes the world, but he who believes that Jesus is the Son of God?

⁶ This is he who came by water and blood, Jesus Christ; not with the water only, but with the water and the blood. It is the Spirit who testifies, because the

Spirit is the truth. [7] For there are three who testify: [8] the Spirit, the water, and the blood; and the three agree as one. [9] If we receive the witness of men, the witness of God is greater; for this is God's testimony which he has testified concerning his Son. [10] He who believes in the Son of God has the testimony in himself. He who doesn't believe God has made him a liar, because he has not believed in the testimony that God has given concerning his Son. [11] The testimony is this, that God gave to us eternal life, and this life is in his Son. [12] He who has the Son has the life. He who doesn't have God's Son doesn't have the life.

[13] These things I have written to you who believe in the name of the Son of God, that you may know that you have eternal life, and that you may continue to believe in the name of the Son of God.

God's Help Comes Through Prayer

[14] This is the boldness which we have toward him, that, if we ask anything according to his will, he listens to us. [15] And if we know that he listens to us, whatever we ask, we know that we have the petitions which we have asked of him.

[16] If anyone sees his brother sinning a sin not leading to death, he shall ask, and God will give him life for those who sin not leading to death. There is a sin leading to death. I don't say that he should make a request concerning this. [17] All unrighteousness is sin, and there is a sin not leading to death. [18] We know that whoever is born of God doesn't sin, but he who was born of God keeps himself, and the evil one doesn't touch him. [19] We know that we are of God, and the whole world lies in the power of the evil one. [20] We know that the Son of God has come, and has given us an understanding, that we know him who is true, and we are in him who is true, in his Son Jesus Christ. This is the true God, and eternal life. [21] Little children, keep yourselves from idols.

1. *How do we know that we love the children of God?*
2. *How do we demonstrate our love for God? Are His commandments burdensome?*
3. *What is the testimony of the believer?*
4. *Do you understand that God hears and answers our prayers when we pray according to His will?*
5. *Who is the true God and source of eternal life?*

B. LIFE THROUGH THE HOLY SPIRIT

Once a person has experienced new life in Christ, he is given the Spirit of God (the Holy Spirit) to live within him and help him live a holy and fruitful Christian life. As long as we obey the Holy Spirit in our lives, we will continue to bear the fruit of the Spirit. The Holy Spirit also gives us power over trials and temptations as well as joy in the midst of pain and suffering. Life through the Spirit is a life of faith as we trust God for the needs of the present as well as the future.

130. THE SPIRIT OF SONSHIP
Romans 8:1-17

It is the Spirit of God (the Holy Spirit) within a believer who gives him the power to live in a way that is pleasing to God. Remember, Jesus broke the curse of sin enabling us to break the cycle of sin. All those who belong to Christ need no longer be controlled by their sinful natures, but instead are made spiritually alive to God, through the Holy Spirit that lives within them. The Holy Spirit of God within us tells us that we are God's children and heirs of all His blessings and promises through His Son.

Life Through the Spirit

8 ¹There is therefore now no condemnation to those who are in Christ Jesus, who don't walk according to the flesh, but according to the Spirit. ² For the law of the Spirit of life in Christ Jesus made me free from the law of sin and of death. ³ For what the law couldn't do, in that it was weak through the flesh, God did, sending his own Son in the likeness of sinful flesh and for sin, he condemned sin in the flesh; ⁴ that the ordinance of the law might be fulfilled in us, who walk not after the flesh, but after the Spirit.

⁵ For those who live according to the flesh set their minds on the things of the flesh, but those who live according to the Spirit, the things of the Spirit. ⁶ For the mind of the flesh is death, but the mind of the Spirit is life and peace; ⁷ because the mind of the flesh is hostile towards God; for it is not subject to God's law, neither indeed can it be.⁸ Those who are in the flesh can't please God.

⁹ But you are not in the flesh but in the Spirit, if it is so that the Spirit of God dwells in you. But if any man doesn't have the Spirit of Christ, he is not his. ¹⁰ If Christ is in you, the body is dead because of sin, but the spirit is alive because of righteousness. ¹¹ But if the Spirit of him who raised up Jesus from the dead dwells in you, he who raised up Christ Jesus from the dead will also give life to your mortal bodies through his Spirit who dwells in you.

¹² So then, brothers, we are debtors, not to the flesh, to live after the flesh. ¹³ For if you live after the flesh, you must die; but if by the Spirit you put to death the deeds of the body, you will live. ¹⁴ For as many as are led by the Spirit of God, these are children of God. ¹⁵ For you didn't receive the spirit of bondage again to fear, but you received the Spirit of adoption, by whom we cry, "Abba! Father!" ¹⁶ The Spirit himself testifies with our spirit that we are children of God; ¹⁷ and if children, then heirs; heirs of God, and joint heirs with Christ; if indeed we suffer with him, that we may also be glorified with him.

> 1. Why is there no longer any condemnation for those who are in Christ Jesus?
>
> 2. Who sets their minds on what their sinful nature desires? What is the result?

3. Who sets their minds on what the Spirit desires? What is the result? How do we please God?

4. Who gives life to our mortal bodies? How does this happen? What difference does it make?

5. What is the believer's response to the truth? Paul calls us "debtors," an obligation to not live after fleshly desires. Does this make sense to you?

6. Who are the sons of God? How do we know? Will knowing this make a difference in our lives?

131. LIFE BY THE SPIRIT
Galatians 2:20 and Romans 12:1-2 and Galatians 5:13-26 and 6:1-10

God has given us the power to live according to His perfect will by living His life through us. However, as free beings, we can make choices. It is the responsibility of each individual believer to exercise his own will and obey God's law of love. We must offer ourselves to be under the control of the Holy Spirit so that we show the fruit of the Spirit in our lives. The way we act toward other people is evidence as to whether we are living by the Spirit or according to our sinful natures.

Christ Living in Me
2 [20] I have been crucified with Christ and it is no longer I that live, but Christ living in me. That life which I now live in the flesh, I live by the faith of the Son of God, who loved me, and gave himself up for me.

Living Sacrifices
12 [1] Therefore I urge you, brothers, by the mercies of God, to present your bodies a living sacrifice, holy, acceptable to God, which is your spiritual service. [2] Don't be conformed to this world, but be transformed by the renewing of your mind, so that you may prove what is the good, well-pleasing, and perfect will of God.

Life by the Spirit
5 [13] For you, brothers, were called for freedom. Only don't use your freedom for gain to the flesh, but through love be servants to one another. [14] For the whole law is fulfilled in one word, in this: "You shall love your neighbor as yourself." [15] But if you bite and devour one another, be careful that you don't consume one another.

[16] But I say, walk by the Spirit, and you won't fulfill the lust of the flesh. [17] For the flesh lusts against the Spirit, and the Spirit against the flesh; and these are contrary to one another, that you may not do the things that you desire. [18] But if you are led by the Spirit, you are not under the law.

Living a Sinful Nature vs Spirit Filled Life
[19] Now the deeds of the flesh are obvious, which are: adultery, sexual immorality, uncleanness, lustfulness, [20] idolatry, sorcery, hatred, strife, jealousies and

outbursts of anger, rivalries, divisions, heresies, ²¹ envy, murders, drunkenness, orgies, and things like these; of which I forewarn you, even as I also forewarned you, that those who practice such things will not inherit God's Kingdom.

²² But the fruit of the Spirit is love, joy, peace, patience, kindness, goodness, faith, ²³ gentleness, and self-control. Against such things there is no law. ²⁴ Those who belong to Christ have crucified the flesh with its passions and lusts. ²⁵ If we live by the Spirit, let's also walk by the Spirit. ²⁶ Let's not become conceited, provoking one another, and envying one another.

Doing Good to All

6 Brothers, even if a man is caught in some fault, you who are spiritual must restore such a one in a spirit of gentleness; looking to yourself so that you also aren't tempted. ² Bear one another's burdens, and so fulfill the law of Christ. ³ For if a man thinks himself to be something when he is nothing, he deceives himself. ⁴ But let each man test his own work, and then he will take pride in himself and not in his neighbor.⁵ For each man will bear his own burden. ⁶ But let him who is taught in the word share all good things with him who teaches. ⁷ Don't be deceived. God is not mocked, for whatever a man sows, that he will also reap. ⁸ For he who sows to his own flesh will from the flesh reap corruption. But he who sows to the Spirit will from the Spirit reap eternal life. ⁹ Let us not be weary in doing good, for we will reap in due season, if we don't give up. ¹⁰ So then, as we have opportunity, let's do what is good toward all men, and especially toward those who are of the household of the faith.

1. *If Jesus lives in me, how do I conduct my life so that all I do becomes a spiritual worship to God?*

2. *Sum up the entire law in one commandment.*

3. *What are the acts of the sinful nature? Will those who do these things inherit the kingdom of God?*

4. *What is the fruit of the Spirit? How should we live by the Spirit? Can you memorize the nine good fruits and make them part of your daily living?*

5. *How does a person reap what he sows?*

132. FILLED WITH THE SPIRIT
Ephesians 1:1-23 and 4:17-32 and 5:1-21

In the next few passages, Paul made it clear that the Christian life was a life set apart from the former life of sin. In his letter to the believers in Ephesus, Paul referred to the Gentiles as those who were still living in darkness, indulging in every kind of sin. The new believers used to live this kind of life themselves, but they had to change. They could change because all believers had the special presence of God, the Holy Spirit, to help them. Paul said that God gave believers every spiritual

Great Bible Truths

blessing needed so that they could live a life dedicated to serving God. Using some specific examples, Paul instructed the believers to not live as before but, instead, to live holy lives as imitators of God. Believers should live as children of the light and be filled with the empowering Holy Spirit, singing and praising God with thankful hearts.

Spiritual Blessings in Christ

1 ¹Paul, an apostle of Christ Jesus through the will of God, to the saints who are at Ephesus, and the faithful in Christ Jesus: ² Grace to you and peace from God our Father and the Lord Jesus Christ.

³ Blessed be the God and Father of our Lord Jesus Christ, who has blessed us with every spiritual blessing in the heavenly places in Christ; ⁴ even as he chose us in him before the foundation of the world, that we would be holy and without defect before him in love; ⁵ having predestined us for adoption as children through Jesus Christ to himself, according to the good pleasure of his desire, ⁶ to the praise of the glory of his grace, by which he freely gave us favor in the Beloved, ⁷ in whom we have our redemption through his blood, the forgiveness of our trespasses, according to the riches of his grace, ⁸ which he made to abound toward us in all wisdom and prudence, ⁹ making known to us the mystery of his will, according to his good pleasure which he purposed in him ¹⁰ to an administration of the fullness of the times, to sum up all things in Christ, the things in the heavens, and the things on the earth, in him; ¹¹ in whom also we were assigned an inheritance, having been foreordained according to the purpose of him who does all things after the counsel of his will;

Believers Sealed by the Holy Spirit

¹² to the end that we should be to the praise of his glory, we who had before hoped in Christ: ¹³ in whom you[Gentiles]also, having heard the word of the truth, the Good News of your salvation—in whom, having also believed, you were sealed with the promised Holy Spirit, ¹⁴ who is a pledge of our inheritance, to the redemption of God's own possession, to the praise of his glory.

Paul Prays for the Ephesian Believers

¹⁵ For this cause I also, having heard of the faith in the Lord Jesus which is among you, and the love which you have toward all the saints, ¹⁶ don't cease to give thanks for you, making mention of you in my prayers, ¹⁷ that the God of our Lord Jesus Christ, the Father of glory, may give to you a spirit of wisdom and revelation in the knowledge of him; ¹⁸ having the eyes of your hearts enlightened [that your minds might have understanding], that you may know what is the hope of his calling, and what are the riches of the glory of his inheritance in the saints, ¹⁹ and what is the exceeding greatness of his power toward us who believe, according to that working of the strength of his might ²⁰ which he worked in Christ, when he raised him from the dead, and made him to sit at his right hand in the heavenly places, ²¹ far above all rule, and authority, and power,

and dominion, and every name that is named, not only in this age, but also in that which is to come. ²² He put all things in subjection under his feet, and gave him to be head over all things for the assembly, ²³ which is his body, the fullness of him who fills all in all.

Living a Changed Lifestyle

4 ¹⁷This I say therefore, and testify in the Lord, that you no longer walk as the rest of the Gentiles also walk, in the futility of their mind, ¹⁸ being darkened in their understanding, alienated from the life of God, because of the ignorance that is in them, because of the hardening of their hearts; ¹⁹ who having become callous gave themselves up to lust, to work all uncleanness with greediness. ²⁰ But you did not learn Christ that way; ²¹ if indeed you heard him, and were taught in him, even as truth is in Jesus: ²² that you put away, as concerning your former way of life, the old man, that grows corrupt after the lusts of deceit; ²³ and that you be renewed in the spirit of your mind, ²⁴ and put on the new man, who in the likeness of God has been created in righteousness and holiness of truth.

²⁵ Therefore putting away falsehood speak truth each one with his neighbor. For we are members of one another. ²⁶ "Be angry, and don't sin." Don't let the sun go down on your wrath, ²⁷ and don't give place to the devil. ²⁸ Let him who stole steal no more; but rather let him labor, producing with his hands something that is good, that he may have something to give to him who has need. ²⁹ Let no corrupt speech proceed out of your mouth, but only what is good for building others up as the need may be, that it may give grace to those who hear. ³⁰ Don't grieve the Holy Spirit of God, in whom you were sealed for the day of redemption. ³¹ Let all bitterness, wrath, anger, outcry, and slander, be put away from you, with all malice. ³² And be kind to one another, tender hearted, forgiving each other, just as God also in Christ forgave you.

Be Imitators of God

5 Be therefore imitators of God, as beloved children. ² Walk in love, even as Christ also loved you, and gave himself up for us, an offering and a sacrifice to God for a sweet-smelling fragrance. ³ But sexual immorality, and all uncleanness, or covetousness, let it not even be mentioned among you, as becomes saints; ⁴ nor filthiness, nor foolish talking, nor jesting, which are not appropriate; but rather giving of thanks.

⁵ Know this for sure, that no sexually immoral person, nor unclean person, nor covetous man, who is an idolater, has any inheritance in the Kingdom of Christ and God. ⁶ Let no one deceive you with empty words. For because of these things, the wrath of God comes on the children of disobedience. ⁷ Therefore don't be partakers with them.

Living as Children of the Light

⁸ For you were once darkness, but are now light in the Lord. Walk as children of light,⁹ for the fruit of the Spirit is in all goodness and righteousness

and truth, [10] proving what is well pleasing to the Lord. [11] Have no fellowship with the unfruitful deeds of darkness, but rather even reprove them. [12] For the things which are done by them in secret, it is a shame even to speak of. [13] But all things, when they are reproved, are revealed by the light, for everything that reveals is light. [14] Therefore he says, "Awake, you who sleep, and arise from the dead, and Christ will shine on you."

[15] Therefore watch carefully how you walk, not as unwise, but as wise; [16] redeeming the time, because the days are evil. [17] Therefore don't be foolish, but understand what the will of the Lord is. [18] Don't be drunken with wine, in which is dissipation, but be filled with the Spirit, [19] speaking to one another in psalms, hymns, and spiritual songs; singing, and making melody in your heart to the Lord; [20] giving thanks always concerning all things in the name of our Lord Jesus Christ, to God, even the Father;[21] subjecting yourselves to one another in the fear of Christ.

1. *How did the Gentiles or unbelievers live?*

2. *What were the believers taught?*

3. *Paul said that believers were to "imitate God;" to be pure in word and deed. In line with this, what specific instructions for righteousness and holiness did Paul give to all believers?*

4. *How should children of the light live? Name specific things we should do. Name things we should **NOT** do.*

5. *Can you see that a life based upon sensuality goes no-where, whereas believers, who live lives based upon Jesus' Spirit living within them, have a fulfilled life, pleasing to God, and a future reward of eternal life with God?*

133. PRESSING ON
Philippians 3:7-21 and 4:1 and Ephesians 3:14-21 and 2 Peter 1:3-11

This selection of Bible passages deals with how the new believer matures in his faith. Christian faith is not static. Rather, it is an ongoing process whereby we mature spiritually as we live our lives in an imitation of Christ. Reminding us that his past religious practices and rituals were of no value to him because they were powerless, Paul emphasizes that to be an imitator of Christ we must reject our previous way of living and keep pressing on to be like Jesus to reach the final goal and reward in heaven which is eternal life. This is possible because we inherited Christ's resurrection power when we were saved. In Paul's prayer for the Ephesian Christians, we are made aware of our need for the inner strength of the Holy Spirit in order to understand the love of Christ and to imitate His holy life. Peter also refers to the resurrection power of the Holy Spirit that each believer possesses. With the aid of this power we can be joined with Christ through His divine nature to live godly lives. This kind of living, Peter says, gives rise to godly character traits that enable us to be productive and effective in God's kingdom.

Knowing the Power of Christ's Resurrection

3 [7]However, I consider those things that were gain to me as a loss for Christ. [8] Yes most certainly, and I count all things to be a loss for the excellency of the knowledge of Christ Jesus, my Lord, for whom I suffered the loss of all things, and count them nothing but refuse, that I may gain Christ [9] and be found in him, not having a righteousness of my own, that which is of the law, but that which is through faith in Christ, the righteousness which is from God by faith; [10] that I may know him, and the power of his resurrection, and the fellowship of his sufferings, becoming conformed to his death; [11] if by any means I may attain to the resurrection from the dead.

Pressing on Towards the Goal

[12] Not that I have already obtained, or am already made perfect; but I press on, if it is so that I may take hold of that for which also I was taken hold of by Christ Jesus. [13] Brothers, I don't regard myself as yet having taken hold, but one thing I do. Forgetting the things which are behind, and stretching forward to the things which are before, [14] I press on toward the goal for the prize of the high calling of God in Christ Jesus. [15] Let us therefore, as many as are perfect, think this way. If in anything you think otherwise, God will also reveal that to you.

[16] Nevertheless, to the extent that we have already attained, let us walk by the same rule. Let us be of the same mind. [17] Brothers, be imitators together of me, and note those who walk this way, even as you have us for an example. [18] For many walk, of whom I told you often, and now tell you even weeping, as the enemies of the cross of Christ, [19] whose end is destruction, whose god is the belly, and whose glory is in their shame, who think about earthly things.

[20] For our citizenship is in heaven, from where we also wait for a Savior, the Lord Jesus Christ; [21] who will change the body of our humiliation to be conformed to the body of his glory, according to the working by which he is able even to subject all things to himself.

4 Therefore, my brothers, beloved and longed for, my joy and crown, so stand firm in the Lord, my beloved.

A Prayer for the Ephesians

3 [14]For this cause, I bow my knees to the Father of our Lord Jesus Christ, [15] from whom every family in heaven and on earth is named, [16] that he would grant you, according to the riches of his glory, that you may be strengthened with power through his Spirit in the inward man; [17] that Christ may dwell in your hearts through faith; to the end that you, being rooted and grounded in love, [18] may be strengthened to comprehend with all the saints what is the width and length and height and depth, [19] and to know Christ's love which surpasses knowledge, that you may be filled with all the fullness of God.

[20] Now to him who is able to do exceedingly abundantly above all that we ask or think, according to the power that works in us, [21] to him be the glory in the assembly and in Christ Jesus to all generations forever and ever. Amen.

Power to Be Useful in God's Kingdom

1 [3]Seeing that his divine power has granted to us all things that pertain to life and godliness, through the knowledge of he has granted to us his precious and exceedingly great promises; that through these you may become partakers of the divine nature, having escaped from the corruption that is in the world by lust.

Steps to Spiritual Growth

[5] Yes, and for this very cause adding on your part all diligence, in your faith supply moral excellence; and in moral excellence, knowledge; [6]and in knowledge, self-control; and in self-control patience; and in patience godliness; [7]and in godliness brotherly affection; and in brotherly affection, love.

[8] For if these things are yours and abound, they make you to be not idle nor unfruitful to the knowledge of our Lord Jesus Christ. [9] For he who lacks these things is blind, seeing only what is near, having forgotten the cleansing from his old sins. [10] Therefore, brothers, be more diligent to make your calling and election sure. For if you do these things, you will never stumble. [11] For thus you will be richly supplied with the entrance into the eternal Kingdom of our Lord and Savior, Jesus Christ.

1. Why did Paul consider that all his past religious practices were loss and rubbish?

2. What one thing occupied Paul's desires?

3. Name four things for which Paul prayed for the Ephesian Christians. Can that prayer be yours also?

4. According to Peter, what has God's power given us?

5. What qualities must we possess in order to be effective and productive in our knowledge of Jesus Christ?

134. TRIALS AND TEMPTATIONS
1 Peter 5:6-11 and James 1:2-18 and
1 John 2:18-27, Ephesians 6:10-18 and Philippians 4:4-8

We have seen that in the Christian life, the goal for a believer in God is to always look forward. A person who has found God and rejected the former sinful life finds that living the God-centered life is an ever developing process. Happily the believer anticipates a better life through growing spiritually. However we still live in an imperfect world which is full of temptations to evil, many of which lead to trials which test our ability to stand firm in our new life with God. Of course, we do this with the support of the Holy Spirit. Not to grow spiritually is to be stagnant. As we press on in our Christian lives with the help of the Holy Spirit, we face many trials and temptations from the enemy of our souls, the devil (or Satan). Although it is not God who tempts us, He does use our trials to strengthen us and teach us. It is through righteousness, faith, the Word of God and prayer that we are able to stand against the forces of evil and experience what Paul called the peace that passes all understanding.

Advice to Stand Firm Under Pressure

5 ⁶ Humble yourselves therefore under the mighty hand of God, that he may exalt you in due time; ⁷casting all your worries on him, because he cares for you. ⁸ Be sober and self-controlled. Be watchful. Your adversary, the devil, walks around like a roaring lion, seeking whom he may devour. ⁹ Withstand him steadfast in your faith, knowing that your brothers who are in the world are undergoing the same sufferings.

¹⁰ But may the God of all grace, who called you to his eternal glory by Christ Jesus, after you have suffered a little while, perfect, establish, strengthen, and settle you. ¹¹ To him be the glory and the power forever and ever. Amen.

Trials and Temptations

1 ²Count it all joy, my brothers, when you fall into various temptations, ³ knowing that the testing of your faith produces endurance. ⁴ Let endurance have its perfect work that you may be perfect and complete, lacking in nothing. ⁵ But if any of you lacks wisdom, let him ask of God, who gives to all liberally and without reproach; and it will be given to him. ⁶ But let him ask in faith, without any doubting, for he who doubts is like a wave of the sea, driven by the wind and tossed. ⁷ For let that man not think that he will receive anything from the Lord. ⁸ He is a double-minded man, unstable in all his ways.

⁹ But let the brother in humble circumstances glory in his high position; ¹⁰ and the rich, in that he is made humble, because like the flower in the grass, he will pass away. ¹¹ For the sun arises with the scorching wind, and withers the grass, and the flower in it falls, and the beauty of its appearance perishes. So also will the rich man fade away in his pursuits.

¹² Blessed is the man who endures temptation, for when he has been approved, he will receive the crown of life, which the Lord promised to those who love him.

¹³ Let no man say when he is tempted, "I am tempted by God," for God can't be tempted by evil, and he himself tempts no one. ¹⁴ But each one is tempted when he is drawn away by his own lust, and enticed. ¹⁵ Then the lust, when it has conceived, bears sin; and the sin, when it is full grown, produces death. ¹⁶ Don't be deceived, my beloved brothers.¹⁷ Every good gift and every perfect gift is from above, coming down from the Father of lights, with whom can be no variation, nor turning shadow. ¹⁸ Of his own will he gave birth to us by the word of truth, that we should be a kind of first fruits of his creatures.

The Test of True Belief

2 ¹⁸ Little children, these are the end times, and as you heard that the Antichrist is coming, even now many antichrists have arisen. By this we know that it is the final hour. ¹⁹ They went out from us, but they didn't belong to us; for if they had belonged to us, they would have continued with us. But they left, that they might be revealed that none of them belong to us. ²⁰ You have an anointing from the Holy One, and you all have knowledge. ²¹ I have not written to you because you don't know the truth, but because you know it, and because no lie is of the truth. ²² Who is the liar but he who denies that Jesus is the Christ? This is the Antichrist, he who denies the Father and the Son. ²³ Whoever denies the Son doesn't have the Father. He who confesses the Son has the Father also. ²⁴Therefore, as for you, let that remain in you which you heard from the beginning. If that which you heard from the beginning remains in you, you also will remain in the Son, and in the Father. ²⁵ This is the promise which he promised us, the eternal life. ²⁶ These things I have written to you concerning those who would lead you astray. ²⁷ As for you, the anointing which you received from him remains in you, and you don't need for anyone to teach you. But as his anointing teaches you concerning all things, and is true, and is no lie, and even as it taught you, you will remain in him.

Wear the Armor of God

6 ¹⁰Finally, be strong in the Lord, and in the strength of his might. ¹¹ Put on the whole armor of God, that you may be able to stand against the wiles of the devil. ¹² For our wrestling is not against flesh and blood, but against the principalities, against the powers, against the world's rulers of the darkness of this age, and against the spiritual forces of wickedness in the heavenly places. ¹³ Therefore put on the whole armor of God, that you may be able to withstand in the evil day, and, having done all, to stand. ¹⁴ Stand therefore, having the utility belt of truth buckled around your waist, and having put on the breastplate of righteousness, ¹⁵ and having fitted your feet with the preparation of the Good News of peace; ¹⁶ above all, taking up the shield of faith, with which you will be able to quench all the fiery darts of the evil one. ¹⁷ And take the helmet of salvation, and the sword of the Spirit, which is the [spoken] word of God; ¹⁸ with all prayer and requests, praying at all times in the Spirit, and being watchful to this end in all perseverance and requests for all the saints.

Always Be Thankful

4 ⁴Rejoice in the Lord always! Again I will say, "Rejoice!" ⁵ Let your gentleness be known to all men. The Lord is at hand. ⁶ In nothing be anxious, but in everything, by prayer and petition with thanksgiving, let your requests be made known to God. ⁷ And the peace of God, which surpasses all understanding, will guard your hearts and your thoughts in Christ Jesus.

Concentrate on the Good

⁸ Finally, brothers, whatever things are true, whatever things are honorable, whatever things are just, whatever things are pure, whatever things are lovely, whatever things are of good report; if there is any virtue, and if there is any praise, think about these things.

> 1. *How should we resist the devil?*
> 2. *Why should we be joyful during trials? What is the result of perseverance?*

3. What should we do when we lack wisdom? Why should we not doubt when we pray?
4. How is each person tempted?
5. God promised his believing and obedient children that they would received a new heart and new spirit so that they would inwardly know the truth. (see selection 64 p.135) Can you see how the apostle John reminds of this truth in verses? (2:27) Will you believe it and live by it?
6. Against what is our struggle? Name the various parts of the "armor of God."
7. With what attitude should we present our requests to God in prayer?
8. Why must we be thankful (rejoice) in all circumstances? What is the result of a thankful heart to God?
9. What things should occupy our thoughts?

135. THE BENEFITS OF SUFFERING
1 Peter 4:1-19 and Romans 8:18-39

The life of joy that we live through the Holy Spirit is one that may require suffering. Remember, we are in a spiritual war, and our mortal enemy, the devil, will do all that he can to tempt us to sin and to put false ideas in our mind, thereby blunting the effectiveness of our faith. God sometimes uses difficult circumstances, which we see as suffering, as a means to discipline us. Suffering is sometimes our best teacher. People who do not understand the reason for the Christian's new life style may bring abuse and insults against believers, trying to make them ashamed of their faith in Jesus Christ. If we suffer for the name of Jesus, we are blessed and should rejoice because of the future glory we will receive. God never promised that suffering would never come; but in spite of the problems and sufferings of this life, His promise is to never separate us from His love. God has made us more than conquerors over these things because we have Jesus to defend us and keep us in His perfect love and peace.

Living for God
4 Therefore, since Christ suffered for us in the flesh, arm yourselves also with the same mind; for he who has suffered in the flesh has ceased from sin; ² that you no longer should live the rest of your time in the flesh for the lusts of men, but for the will of God.³ For we have spent enough of our past time doing the desire of the Gentiles, and having walked in lewdness, lusts, drunken binges, orgies, carousings, and abominable idolatries.⁴ They think it is strange that you don't run with them into the same excess of riot, blaspheming: ⁵ who will give account to him who is ready to judge the living and the dead. ⁶ For to this end the Good News [salvation in Jesus Christ] was preached even to the dead [believers who have died, some murdered for believing in Jesus], that they might be judged indeed as men in the flesh [that though they died and will be resurrected as all people must], however, they continue to live [for] God in the [domain of the] Spirit.

Great Bible Truths

A Call for Christian Discipline

⁷ But the end of all things is near. Therefore be of sound mind, self-controlled, and sober in prayer. ⁸ And above all things be earnest in your love among yourselves, for love covers a multitude of sins. ⁹ Be hospitable to one another without grumbling. ¹⁰ As each has received a gift, employ it in serving one another, as good managers of the grace of God in its various forms. ¹¹ If anyone speaks, let it be as if it were the very words of God. If anyone serves, let it be as of the strength which God supplies, that in all things God may be glorified through Jesus Christ, to whom belong the glory and the dominion forever and ever. Amen.

Suffering for Being a Christian

¹² Beloved, don't be astonished at the fiery trial which has come upon you, to test you, as though a strange thing happened to you. ¹³ But because you are partakers of Christ's sufferings, rejoice; that at the revelation of his glory you also may rejoice with exceeding joy. ¹⁴ If you are insulted for the name of Christ, you are blessed; because the Spirit of glory and of God rests on you. On their part he is blasphemed, but on your part he is glorified. ¹⁵ For let none of you suffer as a murderer, or a thief, or an evil doer, or a meddler in other men's matters. ¹⁶ But if one of you suffers for being a Christian, let him not be ashamed; but let him glorify God in this matter.

¹⁷ For the time has come for judgment to begin with the household of God. If it begins first with us, what will happen to those who don't obey the Good News of God? ¹⁸"If it is hard for the righteous to be saved, what will happen to the ungodly and the sinner?" ¹⁹ Therefore let them also who suffer according to the will of God in doing good entrust their souls to him, as to a faithful Creator.

Our Future Glory

8 ¹⁸For I consider that the sufferings of this present time are not worthy to be compared with the glory which will be revealed toward us. ¹⁹ For the creation waits with eager expectation for the children of God to be revealed. ²⁰ For the creation was subjected to vanity, not of its own will, but because of him who subjected it, in hope ²¹ that the creation itself also will be delivered from the bondage of decay into the liberty of the glory of the children of God.

²² For we know that the whole creation groans and travails in pain together until now. ²³ Not only so, but ourselves also, who have the first fruits of the Spirit, even we ourselves groan within ourselves, waiting for adoption, the redemption of our body. ²⁴ For we were saved in hope, but hope that is seen is not hope. For who hopes for that which he sees? ²⁵ But if we hope for that which we don't see, we wait for it with patience. ²⁶ In the same way, the Spirit also helps our weaknesses, for we don't know how to pray as we ought. But the Spirit himself makes intercession for us with groanings which can't be uttered. ²⁷ He who searches the hearts knows what is on the Spirit's mind, because he makes intercession for the saints according to God.

More Than Conquerors

²⁸ We know that all things work together for good for those who love God, to those who are called according to his purpose. ²⁸ For whom he foreknew, he also predestined to be conformed to the image of his Son, that he might be

the firstborn among many brothers. ³⁰ Whom he predestined, those he also called. Whom he called, those he also justified. Whom he justified, those he also glorified.

³¹ What then shall we say about these things? If God is for us, who can be against us? ³² He who didn't spare his own Son, but delivered him up for us all, how would he not also with him freely give us all things? ³³ Who could bring a charge against God's chosen ones? It is God who justifies. ³⁴ Who is he who condemns? It is Christ who died, yes rather, who was raised from the dead, who is at the right hand of God, who also makes intercession for us.

³⁵ Who shall separate us from the love of Christ? Could oppression, or anguish, or persecution, or famine, or nakedness, or peril, or sword? ³⁶ Even as it is written, "For your sake we are killed all day long. We were accounted as sheep for the slaughter." ³⁷ No, in all these things, we are more than conquerors through him who loved us. ³⁸ For I am persuaded, that neither death, nor life, nor angels, nor principalities, nor things present, nor things to come, nor powers, ³⁹ nor height, nor depth, nor any other created thing, will be able to separate us from the love of God, which is in Christ Jesus our Lord.

1. How should Christians live when the end of all things is near? Name specific things we should do.
2. Why should we rejoice when we suffer for loving Jesus? Why are we blessed for this? What should you continue to do?
3. How does the Holy Spirit help us when we don't know how to pray?
4. Did you notice that even creation is under sin's curse? This explains why everything in nature eventually decays and dies.
5. For those who love God, what promise do we have when we face adversity? Can you memorize Romans 8:28?
6. Can anyone bring a charge against us or condemn us? Why not?
7. Can anyone or anything separate us from the love of God? Why not?

136. FAITH IN GOD
Hebrews 11 and 12:1-3 and James 5:13-18

Faith is taking God at His word and acting on it. The life of a Christian through the Holy Spirit is a life of faith and trust in God. Jesus Christ is God's only antidote for sin and must be received by faith. Even when we cannot see evidence of God's promises, we must continue to believe that He will fulfill His Word to us. We read how people in the past trusted God even though they did not understand His purposes or see the results immediately. God is pleased with men and women who will trust Him and look to Him in prayer to meet their needs.

What Is Faith?
11 ¹Now faith is assurance of things hoped for, proof of things not seen. ² For by this, the elders obtained testimony. ³ By faith, we understand that the universe has been framed by the word of God, so that what is seen has not been made out of things which are visible.

Heroes of Faith

[4] By faith, Abel offered to God a more excellent sacrifice than Cain, through which he had testimony given to him that he was righteous, God testifying with respect to his gifts; and through it he, being dead, still speaks. [5] By faith, Enoch was taken away, so that he wouldn't see death, and he was not found, because God translated him. For he has had testimony given to him that before his translation he had been well pleasing to God. [6] Without faith it is impossible to be well pleasing to him, for he who comes to God must believe that he exists, and that he is a rewarder of those who seek him. [7] By faith, Noah, being warned about things not yet seen, moved with godly fear, prepared a ship for the saving of his house, through which he condemned the world, and became heir of the righteousness which is according to faith.

[8] By faith, Abraham, when he was called, obeyed to go out to the place which he was to receive for an inheritance. He went out, not knowing where he went.

[9] By faith, he lived as an alien in the land of promise, as in a land not his own, dwelling in tents, with Isaac and Jacob, the heirs with him of the same promise. [10] For he looked for the city which has the foundations, whose builder and maker is God.

[11] By faith, even Sarah herself received power to conceive, and she bore a child when she was past age, since she counted him faithful who had promised. [12] Therefore as many as the stars of the sky in multitude, and as innumerable as the sand which is by the sea shore, were fathered by one man, and him as good as dead.

[13] These all died in faith, not having received the promises, but having seen them and embraced them from afar, and having confessed that they were strangers and pilgrims on the earth. [14] For those who say such things make it clear that they are seeking a country of their own. [15] If indeed they had been thinking of that country from which they went out, they would have had enough time to return. [16] But now they desire a better country, that is, a heavenly one. Therefore God is not ashamed of them, to be called their God, for he has prepared a city for them.

[17] By faith, Abraham, being tested, offered up Isaac. Yes, he who had gladly received the promises was offering up his one and only son; [18] even he to whom it was said, "your offspring will be accounted as from Isaac"; [19] concluding that God is able to raise up even from the dead. Figuratively speaking, he also did receive him back from the dead.

[20] By faith, Isaac blessed Jacob and Esau, even concerning things to come. [21] By faith, Jacob, when he was dying, blessed each of the sons of Joseph, and worshiped, leaning on the top of his staff. [22] By faith, Joseph, when his end was near, made mention of the departure of the children of Israel; and gave instructions concerning his bones.

[23] By faith, Moses, when he was born, was hidden for three months by his parents, because they saw that he was a beautiful child, and they were not afraid of the king's commandment. [24] By faith, Moses, when he had grown up, refused to be called the son of Pharaoh's daughter,[25] choosing rather to share ill treatment with God's people, than to enjoy the pleasures of sin for a time; [26] accounting the

reproach of Christ greater riches than the treasures of Egypt; for he looked to the reward.

[27] By faith, he left Egypt, not fearing the wrath of the king; for he endured, as seeing him who is invisible. [28] By faith, he kept the Passover, and the sprinkling of the blood, that the destroyer of the firstborn should not touch them. [29] By faith, they passed through the Red Sea as on dry land. When the Egyptians tried to do so, they were swallowed up.

[30] By faith, the walls of Jericho fell down, after they had been encircled for seven days. [31] By faith, Rahab the prostitute, didn't perish with those who were disobedient, having received the spies in peace.

[32] What more shall I say? For the time would fail me if I told of Gideon, Barak, Samson, Jephthah, David, Samuel, and the prophets; [33] who, through faith subdued kingdoms, worked out righteousness, obtained promises, stopped the mouths of lions, [34] quenched the power of fire, escaped the edge of the sword, from weakness were made strong, grew mighty in war, and caused foreign armies to flee. [35] Women received their dead by resurrection. Others were tortured, not accepting their deliverance, that they might obtain a better resurrection. [36] Others were tried by mocking and scourging, yes, moreover by bonds and imprisonment. [37] They were stoned. They were sawn apart. They were tempted. They were slain with the sword. They went around in sheep skins and in goat skins; being destitute, afflicted, ill-treated [38] (of whom the world was not worthy), wandering in deserts, mountains, caves, and the holes of the earth.

[39] These all, having had testimony given to them through their faith, didn't receive the promise, [40] God having provided some better thing concerning us, so that apart from us they should not be made perfect [we and the ancient saints will share perfection together].

Follow Jesus' Example

12 Therefore let us also, seeing we are surrounded by so great a cloud of witnesses, lay aside every weight and the sin which so easily entangles us, and let us run with patience the race that is set before us, [2] looking to Jesus, the author and perfecter of faith, who for the joy that was set before him endured the cross, despising its shame, and has sat down at the right hand of the throne of God. [3] For consider him who has endured such contradiction of sinners [personal attacks and hostility] against himself, that you don't grow weary, fainting in your souls.

The Power of Prayer

5 [13] Is any among you suffering? Let him pray. Is any cheerful? Let him sing praises. [14] Is any among you sick? Let him call for the elders of the assembly, and let them pray over him, anointing him with oil in the name of the Lord, [15] and the prayer of faith will heal him who is sick, and the Lord will raise him up. If he has committed sins, he will be forgiven. [16] Confess your offenses to one another, and pray for one another, that you may be healed. The insistent prayer of a righteous person is powerfully effective. [17] Elijah was a man with a nature like ours, and he prayed earnestly that it might not rain, and it didn't rain on the earth for three years and six months. [18] He prayed again, and the sky gave rain, and the earth produced its fruit [crops].

1. What is faith? What do we understand by faith?
2. Why is it impossible to please God without faith? v.6
3. How did Noah demonstrate that he had faith in God?
4. Describe three incidents in Abraham's life that showed he had faith in God.
5. Describe three incidents in Moses' life that showed that he had faith in God.
6. On whom should we fix our eyes? Why did Jesus endure the cross?
7. Biblical examples show us that faith allows God to participate in believer's lives. Why not pray when we are sick or have other troubles? What kind of prayer is powerful and effective?

137. LIFE AFTER DEATH
Hebrews 9:27-28; John 14:1-4;
1 Corinthians 15:1-26, 35-58 and 2 Corinthians 4:7-18 and 5:1-10
1 Thessalonians 4:13-18 and 5:1-11; 2 Peter 3:1-14

The most critical event in our lifetime is our personal death. Since everyone will eventually die, an important Bible truth is knowledge of the afterlife. What comes next? Is there life after death? There have always been lots of false teaching and folk tales about this subject, all of them distortions of the truth. The concept of eternal life that all cultures embrace is rooted in the fact that man, who is made in God's image, was originally destined to live forever. (Yes, the Bible teaches that there IS life after death.) However, our physical death, which we must all experience, where the soul is torn away from the body, is an unwelcome, unwanted abhorrent distortion of God's original plan. It came about because of sin.

Only the Bible provides us with the truth. According to the Scriptures, Christ died for our sins, was buried, and was raised on the third day after His death. The fact of Jesus' resurrection is the fundamental cornerstone of the Christian message because without proof of His bodily resurrection, it would be futile to believe and trust in Jesus. Jesus predicted his own resurrection. He comforted His disciples about His impending death with His promise of preparing a place for them in heaven where they will live eternally. The promise of eternal life after our earthly death is our guarantee that we will live forever. This truth should be a comfort to all believers, and an admonition to those who think that they can live without receiving Jesus Christ as their savior.

When believers die, they experience a condition described by Paul as "sleep," which helps us understand the death experience. Our physical bodies are buried, but our souls go immediately, in a conscious state, to be with Jesus in heaven and reign with Him in absolute love. When non-believers die, those who have not believed in Jesus but rejected His offer of salvation before they died, their souls go to a place referred to in the Bible as Sheol/Hades, the place of the dead. The location of Hades is thought to be somewhere in the bowels of the earth. This is a temporary intermediate holding place for the lost souls until the final judgement. However, in heaven everything anticipates what Jesus called the "very end of the age," or the Day of the Lord.

Jesus predicted and taught about the Day of the Lord (See selection 100). The Day of the Lord is the end of all earthly existence, a time of judgment for everyone who has ever lived, and a beginning of eternal life in either heaven or hell. At that time, everyone who has ever lived will be resurrected from the dead. Each person's eternal destiny will be determined, based upon that individual's spiritual state. Every believer will be given a new spiritually transformed body, similar in form to his old body and recognizable, yet with new capacities seen in Jesus' resurrected body. It will be a body not limited as before to natural laws, but instead infused by the power and quickened by the life of the Holy Spirit. We will keep our unique identities, living eternally in an unlimited, powerful, incorruptible body, gloriously adaptable to the new heaven and earth. Our souls and new bodies will be reunited for all eternity in perfection - no evil, no aging, no pain, no tears and no goodbyes. We believers need no longer fear death or judgment because our sins have been forgiven, and we will not suffer the wrath of God when we die. Instead, a glorious home awaits us in the presence of Jesus. In contrast, non-believers have no hope for heaven. They rejected Jesus' offer of salvation and their destiny is eternal torment in hell's lake of fire.

Death Comes to Everyone
9 [27] Inasmuch as it is appointed for men to die once, and after this, judgment, [28] so Christ also, having been offered once to bear the sins of many, will appear a second time, without sin, to those who are eagerly waiting for him for salvation.

Jesus Comforts His Disciples
14 "Don't let your heart be troubled. Believe in God. Believe also in me. [2] In my Father's house are many homes. If it weren't so, I would have told you. I am going to prepare a place for you. [3] If I go and prepare a place for you, I will come again, and will receive you to myself; that where I am, you may be there also. [4] Where I go, you know, and you know the way."

The Resurrection of Jesus Christ
15 [1] Now I [Paul] declare to you, brothers, the Good News which I preached to you, which also you received, in which you also stand, [2] by which also you are saved, if you hold firmly the word which I preached to you—unless you believed in vain. [3] For I delivered to you first of all that which I also received: that Christ died for our sins according to the Scriptures, [4] that he was buried, that he was raised on the third day according to the Scriptures, [5] and that he appeared to Cephas [Peter], then to the twelve.

[6] Then he appeared to over five hundred brothers at once, most of whom remain until now, but some have also fallen asleep. [7] Then he appeared to James, then to all the apostles, [8] and last of all, as to the child born at the wrong time, he appeared to me also. [9] For I am the least of the apostles, who is not worthy to be called an apostle, because I persecuted the assembly of God. [10] But by the grace of God I am what I am. His grace which was given to me was not futile, but I

worked more than all of them; yet not I, but the grace of God which was with me. ¹¹ Whether then it is I or they, so we preach, and so you believed.

The Resurrection of the Dead

¹² Now if Christ is preached, that he has been raised from the dead, how do some among you say that there is no resurrection of the dead? ¹³ But if there is no resurrection of the dead, neither has Christ been raised. ¹⁴ If Christ has not been raised, then our preaching is in vain, and your faith also is in vain. ¹⁵ Yes, we are found false witnesses of God, because we testified about God that he raised up Christ, whom he didn't raise up, if it is so that the dead are not raised. ¹⁶ For if the dead aren't raised, neither has Christ been raised. ¹⁷ If Christ has not been raised, your faith is vain; you are still in your sins. ¹⁸ Then they also who are fallen asleep [have died] in Christ have perished. ¹⁹ If we have only hoped in Christ in this life, we are of all men most pitiable.

²⁰ But now Christ has been raised from the dead. He became the first fruits of those who are asleep. ²¹ For since death came by man, the resurrection of the dead also came by man. ²² For as in Adam all die, so also in Christ all will be made alive. ²³ But each in his own order: Christ the first fruits, then those who are Christ's, at his coming. ²⁴ Then the end comes, when he will deliver up the Kingdom to God, even the Father; when he will have abolished all rule and all authority and power. ²⁵ For he must reign until he has put all his enemies under his feet. ²⁶ The last enemy that will be abolished is death.

The Nature of the Resurrection Body

³⁵ But someone will say, "How are the dead raised?" and, "With what kind of body do they come?" ³⁶ You foolish one, that which you yourself sow is not made alive unless it dies. ³⁷ That which you sow, you don't sow the body that will be, but a bare grain, maybe of wheat, or of some other kind. ³⁸ But God gives it a body even as it pleased him, and to each seed a body of its own. ³⁹ All flesh is not the same flesh, but there is one flesh of men, another flesh of animals, another of fish, and another of birds. ⁴⁰ There are also celestial bodies, and terrestrial bodies; but the glory of the celestial differs from that of the terrestrial. ⁴¹ There is one glory of the sun, another glory of the moon, and another glory of the stars; for one star differs from another star in glory.

⁴²So also is the resurrection of the dead. The body is sown perishable; it is raised imperishable. ⁴³ It is sown in dishonor; it is raised in glory. It is sown in weakness; it is raised in power. ⁴⁴ It is sown a natural body; it is raised a spiritual body. There is a natural body and there is also a spiritual body.

⁴⁵ So also it is written, "The first man, Adam, became a living soul." The last Adam became a life-giving spirit. ⁴⁶ However that which is spiritual isn't first, but that which is natural, then that which is spiritual. ⁴⁷ The first man is of the earth, made of dust. The second man is the Lord from heaven. ⁴⁸ As is the one made of dust, such are those who are also made of dust; and as is the heavenly, such are they also that are heavenly. ⁴⁹ As we have borne the image of those made of

dust, let's also bear the image of the heavenly. ⁵⁰ Now I say this, brothers, that flesh and blood can't inherit God's Kingdom; neither does the perishable inherit imperishable.

The Christian's Confidence

⁵¹ Behold, I tell you a mystery. We will not all sleep [die], but we [who are still alive] will all be changed, ⁵² in a moment, in the twinkling of an eye, at the last trumpet. For the trumpet will sound, and the dead will be raised incorruptible, and we will be changed. ⁵³ For this perishable body must become imperishable, and this mortal must put on immortality. ⁵⁴ But when this perishable body will have become imperishable, and this mortal will have put on immortality, then what is written will happen:

"Death is swallowed up in victory."
⁵⁵ "Death, where is your sting?
Hades, where is your victory?"

⁵⁶ The sting of death is sin, and the power of sin is the law. ⁵⁷ But thanks be to God, who gives us the victory through our Lord Jesus Christ. ⁵⁸ Therefore, my beloved brothers, be steadfast, immovable, always abounding in the Lord's work, because you know that your labor is not in vain in the Lord.

We Will Live Forever

4 ⁷We have this treasure in clay vessels, that the exceeding greatness of the power may be of God, and not from ourselves. ⁸ We are pressed on every side, yet not crushed; perplexed, yet not to despair; ⁹ pursued, yet not forsaken; struck down, yet not destroyed; ¹⁰ always carrying in the body the putting to death of the Lord Jesus, that the life of Jesus may also be revealed in our body. ¹¹ For we who live are always delivered to death for Jesus' sake, that the life also of Jesus may be revealed in our mortal flesh.

¹² So then death works in us, but life in you. ¹³ But having the same spirit of faith, according to that which is written, "I believed, and therefore I spoke." We also believe, and therefore also we speak; ¹⁴ knowing that he who raised the Lord Jesus will raise us also with Jesus, and will present us with you. ¹⁵ For all things are for your sakes, that the grace, being multiplied through the many, may cause the thanksgiving to abound to the glory of God.

¹⁶ Therefore we don't faint, but though our outward man is decaying, yet our inward man is renewed day by day. ¹⁷ For our light affliction, which is for the moment, works for us more and more exceedingly an eternal weight of glory; ¹⁸ while we don't look at the things which are seen, but at the things which are not seen. For the things which are seen are temporal, but the things which are not seen are eternal.

Away from Our Body, at Home with the Lord

5 For we know that if the earthly house of our tent [body] is dissolved, we have a building from God, a house not made with hands, eternal, in the heavens. ² For most certainly in this we groan, longing to be clothed with our habitation which is from heaven; ³ if so be that being clothed we will not be found naked. ⁴ For indeed we who are in this tent do groan, being burdened; not that we desire to be unclothed, but that we desire to be clothed, that what is mortal may be swallowed up by life. ⁵ Now he who made us for this very thing is God, who also gave to us the down payment of the Spirit.

⁶ Therefore we are always confident and know that while we are at home in the body, we are absent from the Lord; ⁷ for we walk by faith, not by sight. ⁸ We are courageous, I say, and are willing rather to be absent from the body, and to be at home with the Lord. ⁹ Therefore also we make it our aim, whether at home or absent, to be well pleasing to him. ¹⁰ For we must all be revealed before the judgment seat of Christ; that each one may receive the things in the body, according to what he has done, whether good or bad.

The Coming of the Lord

4 ¹³But we don't want you to be ignorant, brothers, concerning those who have fallen asleep[have died], so that you don't grieve like the rest, who have no hope. ¹⁴ For if we believe that Jesus died and rose again, even so God will bring with him those who have fallen asleep in Jesus. ¹⁵ For this we tell you by the word of the Lord, that we who are alive, who are left to the coming of the Lord, will in no way precede those who have fallen asleep. ¹⁶ For the Lord himself will descend from heaven with a shout, with the voice of the archangel, and with God's trumpet. The dead in Christ will rise first, ¹⁷ then we who are alive, who are left, will be caught up together with them in the clouds, to meet the Lord in the air. So we will be with the Lord forever. ¹⁸Therefore comfort one another with these words.

Be Ready for the Lord's Coming

5 But concerning the times and the seasons, brothers, you have no need that anything be written to you. ² For you yourselves know well that the day of the Lord comes like a thief in the night. ³ For when they are saying, "Peace and safety," then sudden destruction will come on them, like birth pains on a pregnant woman; and they will in no way escape.⁴ But you, brothers, aren't in darkness, that the day should overtake you like a thief. ⁵ You are all children of light, and children of the day. We don't belong to the night, nor to darkness, ⁶ so then let's not sleep, as the rest do, but let's watch and be sober. ⁷ For those who sleep, sleep in the night, and those who are drunk are drunk in the night. ⁸ But let us, since we belong to the day, be sober, putting on the breastplate of faith and love, and, for a helmet, the hope of salvation. ⁹ For God didn't appoint us to wrath, but to the obtaining of salvation through our Lord Jesus Christ, ¹⁰ who died for us, that, whether we wake or sleep, we should live together with him. ¹¹ Therefore exhort one another, and build each other up, even as you also do.

The Day of the Lord

3 ¹ This is now, beloved, the second letter that I [Peter] have written to you; and in both of them I stir up your sincere mind by reminding you; ² that you should remember the words which were spoken before by the holy prophets, and the commandments of us, the apostles of the Lord and Savior: ³ knowing this first, that in the last days mockers will come, walking after their own lusts, ⁴ and saying, "Where is the promise of his coming? For, from the day that the fathers fell asleep, all things continue as they were from the beginning of the creation." ⁵ For this they willfully forget, that there were heavens from of old, and an earth formed out of water and amid water, by the word of God; ⁶ by which means the world that then was, being overflowed with water, perished. ⁷ But the heavens that now are, and the earth, by the same word have been stored up for fire, being reserved against the day of judgment and destruction of ungodly men.

⁸ But don't forget this one thing, beloved, that one day is with the Lord as a thousand years, and a thousand years as one day. ⁹ The Lord is not slow concerning his promise, as some count slowness; but is patient with us, not wishing that any should perish, but that all should come to repentance. ¹⁰ But the day of the Lord will come as a thief in the night; in which the heavens will pass away with a great noise, and the elements will be dissolved with fervent heat, and the earth and the works that are in it will be burned up. ¹¹ Therefore since all these things will be destroyed like this, what kind of people ought you to be in holy living and godliness, ¹² looking for and earnestly desiring the coming of the day of God, which will cause the burning heavens to be dissolved, and the elements will melt with fervent heat? ¹³ But, according to his promise, we look for new heavens and a new earth, in which righteousness dwells.
¹⁴ Therefore, beloved, seeing that you look for these things, be diligent to be found in peace, without defect and blameless in his sight.

1. What did Paul say was the last enemy of God to be destroyed?
2. How important is the Christ's resurrection to the Christian faith?
3. What is the sting of death? Who has given us victory over it?
4. When a Christian believer dies, what happens to his body? What happens to his soul?
5. Describe what will happen when the Lord Jesus returns. When will that be?
6. Meanwhile, while we await the return of Jesus Christ, how should we live as children of the light?

Pause for Reflection: *All Christianity is based upon the foundation of the resurrection. Paul makes it clear, no resurrection, no Christian faith. The hundreds of eyewitnesses provide irrefutable proof of Jesus' bodily resurrection. His resurrection broke the power of death. It was the best thing that could ever happen to mankind because it answers his question: Is this life on earth all that there is or is there life after death? The resurrection demonstrates the immense power and sovereignty of God over life and death. It gives us hope and a new perspective about our being. Since life is permanent it has infinite meaning, promising a marvelous adventure that will never end. The resurrection proves that not only does God expect you to live forever but you will have an important part in that "forever" - and for that reason you will need your new body to do His will in eternity. Because of our future resurrection into eternal life we can endure earthly trials, using this life as a training ground, living in anticipation for the glorious life in heaven to follow.*

138. PROCLAIMING THE TRUTH
Romans 10:8-15 and Colossians 2:6-10 and 16-23 and 1 Timothy 4:1-16 and 2 Timothy 3:10-17 and 4:1-5

As believers in Jesus Christ and those who are living in the Spirit, we are responsible before God to tell others about the way to salvation. We must not allow ourselves to be deceived by false teachers, who use human philosophies and regulations to try to lead us away from Jesus. If we heed Paul's instructions to Timothy and follow only the teachings of the Word of God in Scripture, we will be equipped to proclaim the truth to those who have never heard.

The Believers Confession

10 [8]But what does it say? "The word is near you, in your mouth, and in your heart"; that is, the word of faith, which we preach: [9] that if you will confess with your mouth that Jesus is Lord, and believe in your heart that God raised him from the dead, you will be saved. [10] For with the heart, one believes unto righteousness; and with the mouth confession is made unto salvation. [11] For the Scripture says, "Whoever believes in him will not be disappointed."
[12] For there is no distinction between Jew and Greek; for the same Lord is Lord of all, and is rich to all who call on him. [13] For, "Whoever will call on the name of the Lord will be saved." [14] How then will they call on him in whom they have not believed? How will they believe in him whom they have not heard? How will they hear without a preacher? [15] And how will they preach unless they are sent? As it is written:

"How beautiful are the feet
of those who preach the Good News of peace,
who bring glad tidings of good things!"

Freedom from Human Regulations Through Life with Christ

2 [6]As therefore you received Christ Jesus, the Lord, walk in him, [7] rooted and built up in him, and established in the faith, even as you were taught, abounding in it in thanksgiving. [8] Be careful that you don't let anyone rob you through his philosophy and vain deceit, after the tradition of men, after the elements of the world, and not after Christ. [9] For in him all the fullness of the Godhead dwells bodily, [10] and in him you are made full, who is the head of all principality and power;

[16] Let no one therefore judge you in eating, or in drinking, or with respect to a feast day or a new moon or a Sabbath day, [17] which are a shadow of the things to come; but the body is Christ's. [18] Let no one rob you of your prize by a voluntary humility and worshiping of the angels, dwelling in the things which he has not seen, vainly puffed up by his fleshly mind, [19] and not holding firmly to the Head, from whom all the body, being supplied and knit together through the joints and ligaments, grows with God's growth.[20] If you died with Christ from the elements of the world, why, as though living in the world, do you subject yourselves to ordinances, [21] "Don't handle, nor taste, nor touch"[22] (all of which

perish with use), according to the precepts and doctrines of men? ²³ Which things indeed appear like wisdom in self-imposed worship, and humility, and severity to the body; but aren't of any value against the indulgence of the flesh.

Instructions to Timothy
4 The Spirit says expressly that in later times some will fall away from the faith, paying attention to seducing spirits and doctrines of demons, ² through the hypocrisy of men who speak lies, branded in their own conscience as with a hot iron; ³ forbidding marriage and commanding to abstain from foods which God created to be received with thanksgiving by those who believe and know the truth. ⁴ For every creature of God is good, and nothing is to be rejected, if it is received with thanksgiving. ⁵ For it is sanctified through the word of God and prayer. ⁶ If you instruct the brothers of these things, you will be a good servant of Christ Jesus, nourished in the words of the faith, and of the good doctrine which you have followed. ⁷ But refuse profane and old wives' fables. Exercise yourself toward godliness. ⁸ For bodily exercise has some value, but godliness has value in all things, having the promise of the life which is now, and of that [life] which is to come. ⁹ This saying is faithful and worthy of all acceptance. ¹⁰ For to this end we both labor and suffer reproach, because we have set our trust in the living God, who is the Savior of all men, especially of those who believe. ¹¹ Command and teach these things.

¹² Let no man despise your youth; but be an example to those who believe, in word, in your way of life, in love, in spirit, in faith, and in purity. ¹³ Until I come, pay attention to reading, to exhortation, and to teaching. ¹⁴ Don't neglect the gift that is in you, which was given to you by prophecy, with the laying on of the hands of the elders. ¹⁵ Be diligent in these things. Give yourself wholly to them, that your progress may be revealed to all.¹⁶ Pay attention to yourself, and to your teaching. Continue in these things, for in doing this you will save both yourself and those who hear you.

Paul's Charge to Timothy
3 ¹⁰But you did follow my teaching, conduct, purpose, faith, patience, love, steadfastness, ¹¹ persecutions, and sufferings: those things that happened to me at Antioch, Iconium, and Lystra. I endured those persecutions. The Lord delivered me out of them all. ¹² Yes, and all who desire to live godly in Christ Jesus will suffer persecution. ¹³ But evil men and impostors will grow worse and worse, deceiving and being deceived. ¹⁴ But you remain in the things which you have learned and have been assured of, knowing from whom you have learned them. ¹⁵ From infancy, you have known the holy Scriptures which are able to make you wise for salvation through faith, which is in Christ Jesus.

All Scripture Inspired by God
¹⁶ Every Scripture is God-breathed and profitable for teaching, for reproof, for correction, and for instruction in righteousness, ¹⁷ that the man of God may be complete, thoroughly equipped for every good work.

Preach the Good News

4 ¹I command you therefore before God and the Lord Jesus Christ, who will judge the living and the dead at his appearing and his Kingdom: ² preach the word; be urgent in season and out of season; reprove, rebuke, and exhort with all patience and teaching. ³For the time will come when they will not listen to the sound doctrine, but, having itching ears, will heap up for themselves teachers after their own lusts; ⁴ and will turn away their ears from the truth, and turn aside to fables. ⁵ But you be sober in all things, suffer hardship, do the work of an evangelist, and fulfill your ministry.

> 1. *Paul described a two-step process that results when a person hears the Good News about Jesus and is saved. What are those steps?*
>
> 2. *Who will be saved? (see Romans 10:13) Can you believe this?*
>
> 3. *Although everyone everywhere should hear the Gospel of Jesus Christ, what is necessary for this to happen?*
>
> 4. *Who is head over every power and authority? Why?*
>
> 5. *Why do human rules and regulations not have any spiritual value for the believer?*
>
> 6. *Paul warned Timothy that many things block or blunt the basic Gospel message.*
>   *a. What are they?*
>   *b. Where do they originate?*
>   *c. Have you had any experience with odd teachings?*
>
> 7. *In what ways is Scripture (the Bible) useful to us?*
>
> 8. *What charge did Paul give to Timothy? Does this commission apply to all believers even today?*

Pause for Reflection: *Did you realize that any believer can be a witness to Jesus' love and share it with someone who does not know about Jesus?*

C. THE CHRISTIAN LIFE OF LOVE

Christianity is unique among the world's religions because it is based upon love. Love is the primary motivation for all that we do because God Himself is the source of all love. God chose to create mankind in his image for the purpose of having a personal relationship with his creation based upon love. Because we serve God, who is love, our lives must be ruled by love, reflecting God's character and attitudes in all aspects of our dealings with other people. Love is the key to all our relationships: family, society, church and business and government. The following passages are Scripture's teachings about the nature of love and how love affects our lives on all levels of existence and interaction with others.

139. GOD IS LOVE
1 John 4:7-21; Mark 12:28-34 and Philippians 2:1-11

One of the greatest truths in the Bible is the marvelous fact that God is love. God demonstrated his love for us when He gave us His Son, Jesus, as a sacrifice for our sins. His purpose was to reestablish the loving creator-creature relationship that was lost in Eden when Adam and Eve disobeyed God and broke that special bond. God loves us beyond what we could possibly imagine. Because of His love, we can be confident that our God, who knows us intimately, cares for us, providing for all our needs in every situation. This is a great comfort to every believer because we never need to worry or live fearfully in a world cursed by sin and its consequences.

Because God is love, He expects His followers to love one another, serving with the same attitude of humility as Jesus. We see that although He was one with God, Jesus Christ took the form of a man to become a humble servant, willing to die on the cross. Let us ask God to give us the same mind and attitude that Jesus has.

Love Comes from God

4 [7] Beloved, let us love one another, for love is of God; and everyone who loves has been born of God, and knows God. [8] He who doesn't love doesn't know God, for God is love. [9] By this God's love was revealed in us, that God has sent his one and only Son into the world that we might live through him. [10] In this is love, not that we loved God, but that he loved us, and sent his Son as the atoning sacrifice for our sins. [11] Beloved, if God loved us in this way, we also ought to love one another.

[12] No one has seen God at any time. If we love one another, God remains in us, and his love has been perfected in us. [13] By this we know that we remain in him and he in us, because he has given us of his Spirit. [14] We have seen and testify that the Father has sent the Son as the Savior of the world. [15] Whoever confesses that Jesus is the Son of God, God remains in him, and he in God. [16] We know and have believed the love which God has for us. God is love, and he who remains in love remains in God, and God remains in him.

[17] In this love has been made perfect among us, that we may have boldness in the Day of Judgment, because as he is, even so are we in this world. [18] There is no fear in love; but perfect love casts out fear, because fear has punishment. He who fears is not made perfect in love. [19] We love him, because he first loved us. [20] If a man says, "I love God," and hates his brother, he is a liar; for he who doesn't love his brother whom he has seen, how can he love God whom he has not seen? [21] This commandment we have from him, that he who loves God should also love his brother.

The Great Commandment

12 [28] One of the scribes came, and heard them questioning together, and knowing that he had answered them well, asked him, "Which commandment is the greatest of all?"

[29] Jesus answered, "The greatest is, 'Hear, Israel, the Lord our God, the Lord is one: [30] you shall love the Lord your God with all your heart, and with all your soul, and with all your mind, and with all your strength.' This is the first commandment. [31] The second is like this, 'You shall love your neighbor as yourself.' There is no other commandment greater than these."

³² The scribe said to him, "Truly, teacher, you have said well that he is one, and there is none other but he, ³³ and to love him with all the heart, and with all the understanding, with all the soul, and with all the strength, and to love his neighbor as himself, is more important than all whole burnt offerings and sacrifices." ³⁴ When Jesus saw that he answered wisely, he said to him, "You are not far from God's Kingdom."

Imitating Christ's Humility

2 ¹If there is therefore any exhortation [encouragement by belonging to Christ, any comfort from His love], if any fellowship of the Spirit, if any tender mercies and compassion, ² make my joy full, by being likeminded, having the same love, being of one accord, of one mind; ³ doing nothing through rivalry or through conceit, but in humility, each counting others better than himself; ⁴ each of you not just looking to his own things, but each of you also to the things of others. ⁵ Have this in your mind, which was also in Christ Jesus,

⁶Who, existing in the form of God,
   didn't consider equality with God
   a thing to be grasped,
⁷but emptied himself,
   taking the form of a servant,
   being made in the likeness of men.
⁸And being found in human form,
   he humbled himself,
   becoming obedient to death,
   yes, the death of the cross.
⁹Therefore God also highly exalted him,
   and gave to him the name which is above every name;
¹⁰that at the name of Jesus every knee should bow,
   of those in heaven, those on earth, and those under the earth,
¹¹and that every tongue should confess that Jesus Christ is Lord,
   to the glory of God the Father.

1. *Where does love come from? What is love?*
2. *How is God's love made complete in us? Why?*
3. *How do we know that we live in God and He lives in us?*
4. *Can you see how God demonstrated, through Jesus, that He truly loves us?*
5. *Why is there no fear in love? Why should we never be fearful?*
6. *If you imitated Christ's attitude, describe the kind of person you would be.*

140. LOVE ONE ANOTHER
Galatians 5:13-15: Colossians 3:12-17: Romans 12:9-21 and 1 John 3:11-24

Love is more than just saying, "I love you" with words. Sincere love must be expressed in our actions and deeds toward one another, our brothers and sisters in Christ as well as our enemies. Only those who obey God's command to love one another can expect Him to answer their prayers and have His active presence live within them.

Love Is Service Above Self

5 [13] For you, brothers, were called for freedom. Only don't use your freedom for gain to the flesh, but through love be servants to one another. [14] For the whole law is fulfilled in one word, in this: "You shall love your neighbor as yourself." [15] But if you bite and devour one another, be careful that you don't consume one another.

Walking in Love Creates Unity

3 [12] Put on therefore, as God's chosen ones, holy and beloved, a heart of compassion, kindness, lowliness, humility, and perseverance; [13] bearing with one another, and forgiving each other, if any man has a complaint against any; even as Christ forgave you, so you also do. [14] Above all these things, walk in love, which is the bond of perfection. [15] And let the peace of God rule in your hearts, to which also you were called in one body; and be thankful. [16] Let the word of Christ dwell in you richly; in all wisdom teaching and admonishing one another with psalms, hymns, and spiritual songs, singing with grace in your heart to the Lord.

[17] Whatever you do, in word or in deed, do all in the name of the Lord Jesus, giving thanks to God the Father, through him.

Love

12 [9] Let love be without hypocrisy. Abhor that which is evil. Cling to that which is good. [10] In love of the brothers be tenderly affectionate to one another; in honor preferring one another; [11] not lagging in diligence; fervent in spirit; serving the Lord; [12] rejoicing in hope; enduring in troubles; continuing steadfastly in prayer; [13] contributing to the needs of the saints; given to hospitality. [14] Bless those who persecute you; bless, and don't curse. [15] Rejoice with those who rejoice. Weep with those who weep. [16] Be of the same mind one toward another. Don't set your mind on high things, but associate with the humble. Don't be wise in your own conceits. [17] Repay no one evil for evil. Respect what is honorable in the sight of all men. [18] If it is possible, as much as it is up to you, be at peace with all men. [19] Don't seek revenge yourselves, beloved, but give place to God's wrath. For it is written, "Vengeance belongs to me; I will repay, says the Lord." [20] Therefore "If your enemy is hungry, feed him. If he is thirsty, give him a drink; for in doing so, you will heap coals of fire on his head."

[21] Don't be overcome by evil, but overcome evil with good.

Love One Another

3 [11] For this is the message which you heard from the beginning, that we should love one another; [12] unlike Cain, who was of the evil one, and killed his brother. Why did he kill him? Because his deeds were evil, and his brother's righteous. [13] Don't be surprised, my brothers, if the world hates you. [14] We know that we have passed out of death into life, because we love the brothers. He who doesn't love his brother remains in death.

[15] Whoever hates his brother is a murderer, and you know that no murderer has eternal life remaining in him. [16] By this we know love, because he laid down his life for us. And we ought to lay down our lives for the brothers. [17] But whoever

has the world's goods, and sees his brother in need, and closes his heart of compassion against him, how does the love of God remain in him?

[18] My little children, let's not love in word only, or with the tongue only, but in deed and truth. [19] And by this we know that we are of the truth, and persuade our hearts before him, [20] because if our heart condemns us, God is greater than our heart, and knows all things.

[21] Beloved, if our hearts don't condemn us, we have boldness toward God; [22] and whatever we ask, we receive from him, because we keep his commandments and do the things that are pleasing in his sight. [23] This is his commandment, that we should believe in the name of his Son, Jesus Christ, and love one another, even as he commanded. [24] He who keeps his commandments remains in him, and he in him. By this we know that he remains in us, by the Spirit which he gave us.

1. What should rule in our hearts? What should dwell in us richly?
2. In what specific ways does Paul say that love can be expressed to others in our daily lives?
3. Why should we love our enemies and not take revenge? Who is our advocate when we are wronged?
4. Why did Cain murder his brother Abel? Do you see how hate is connected with murder?
5. What is God's simple command found in v.23? In whom does Christ's Spirit live? How do we know it?

141. THE BODY OF CHRIST
Romans 12:3-8 and 1 Corinthians 12:1-31a and 1 Peter 4:7-11

The Church is made up of believers who are members of the Body of Christ, of whom Jesus is the Head. Within the Body of Christ, different gifts are given by the Holy Spirit to each member. Just as parts of our human bodies have different functions, each member of the church, using his particular gift, works with others for the good of the whole Body, doing cheerfully that which God has assigned him to do without jealousy or complaint.

Different Strokes for Different Folks

12 [3] For I say, through the grace that was given me, to every man who is among you, not to think of himself more highly than he ought to think; but to think reasonably, as God has apportioned to each person a measure of faith. [4] For even as we have many members in one body, and all the members don't have the same function, [5] so we, who are many, are one body in Christ, and individually members one of another.

[6] Having gifts differing according to the grace that was given to us, if prophecy, let us prophesy according to the proportion of our faith; [7] or service, let us give ourselves to service; or he who teaches, to his teaching; [8] or he who exhorts, to his exhorting: he who gives, let him do it with liberality; he who rules,

with diligence; he who shows mercy, with cheerfulness.

Spiritual Gifts

12 ¹Now concerning spiritual things, brothers, I don't want you to be ignorant. ² You know that when you were heathen, you were led away to those mute idols, however you might be led. ³ Therefore I make known to you that no man speaking by God's Spirit says, "Jesus is accursed." No one can say, "Jesus is Lord," but by the Holy Spirit.

⁴ Now there are various kinds of gifts, but the same Spirit. ⁵ There are various kinds of service, and the same Lord. ⁶ There are various kinds of workings, but the same God, who works all things in all. ⁷ But to each one is given the manifestation of the Spirit for the profit of all. ⁸ For to one is given through the Spirit the word of wisdom, and to another the word of knowledge, according to the same Spirit; ⁹ to another faith, by the same Spirit; and to another gifts of healings, by the same Spirit; ¹⁰ and to another workings of miracles; and to another prophecy; and to another discerning of spirits; to another different kinds of languages; and to another the interpretation of languages. ¹¹ But the one and the same Spirit produces all of these, distributing to each one separately as he desires.

One Body, Many Parts

¹² For as the body is one, and has many members, and all the members of the body, being many, are one body; so also is Christ. ¹³ For in one Spirit we were all baptized into one body, whether Jews or Greeks, whether bond or free; and were all given to drink into one Spirit. ¹⁴ For the body is not one member, but many. ¹⁵ If the foot would say, "Because I'm not the hand, I'm not part of the body," it is not therefore not part of the body. ¹⁶ If the ear would say, "Because I'm not the eye, I'm not part of the body," it's not therefore not part of the body. ¹⁷ If the whole body were an eye, where would the hearing be? If the whole were hearing, where would the smelling be?

¹⁸ But now God has set the members, each one of them, in the body, just as he desired. ¹⁹ If they were all one member, where would the body be? ²⁰ But now they are many members, but one body. ²¹ The eye can't tell the hand, "I have no need for you," or again the head to the feet, "I have no need for you." ²² No, much rather, those members of the body which seem to be weaker are necessary.

²³ Those parts of the body which we think to be less honorable, on those we bestow more abundant honor; and our unpresentable parts have more abundant propriety; ²⁴ whereas our presentable parts have no such need. But God composed the body together, giving more abundant honor to the inferior part, ²⁵ that there should be no division in the body, but that the members should have the same care for one another. ²⁶ When one member suffers, all the members suffer with it. Or when one member is honored, all the members rejoice with it.

²⁷ Now you are the body of Christ, and members individually. ²⁸ God has set some in the assembly: first apostles, second prophets, third teachers, then miracle workers, then gifts of healings, helps, governments, and various kinds of languages. ²⁹ Are all apostles? Are all prophets? Are all teachers? Are all miracle

workers? ³⁰ Do all have gifts of healings? Do all speak with various languages? Do all interpret? ³¹ But earnestly desire the best gifts.

Use God's Gifts Wisely

4 ⁷But the end of all things is near. Therefore be of sound mind, self-controlled, and sober in prayer. ⁸ And above all things be earnest in your love among yourselves, for love covers a multitude of sins. ⁹ Be hospitable to one another without grumbling. ¹⁰ As each has received a gift, employ it in serving one another, as good managers of the grace of God in its various forms.

¹¹ If anyone speaks, let it be as if it were the very words of God. If anyone serves, let it be as of the strength which God supplies, that in all things God may be glorified through Jesus Christ, to whom belong the glory and the dominion forever and ever. Amen.

1. How should we think of ourselves?

2. How does the Christian Church resemble a human body?

3. Name the different gifts that are given by grace from God.

4. What manifestations of the Holy Spirit are given for the common good of the believers?

5. What different ministry functions of the body of Christ has God appointed in the Church?

6. Do you see your spiritual gift in these passages?

142. THE GIFT OF UNITY AND LOVE
Romans 13:8-10; Ephesians 4:1-16 and 1 Corinthians 12:31b and 13:1-13

It is love that causes the Body of Christ to grow and be built up, not religious deeds and practices done to impress others. Even the gifts and manifestations of the Holy Spirit must be done with an attitude of love, or they are of no value. The characteristics of love are described here in detail so that we can compare our own lives with the standard of love that God requires. The greatest and most excellent gift we can give to the Body of Christ is a life of love.

The Call to Love

13⁸ Owe no one anything, except to love one another; for he who loves his neighbor has fulfilled the law. ⁹ For the commandments, "You shall not commit adultery," "You shall not murder," "You shall not steal," "You shall not covet," and whatever other commandments there are, are all summed up in this saying, namely, "You shall love your neighbor as yourself." ¹⁰ Love doesn't harm a neighbor. Love therefore is the fulfillment of the law.

Unity in the Body of Christ

4 ¹I therefore, the prisoner in the Lord, beg you to walk worthily of the calling with which you were called,² with all lowliness and humility, with patience, bearing with one another in love; ³ being eager to keep the unity of the Spirit in the bond of peace.⁴ There is one body, and one Spirit, even as you also were called in one hope of your calling; [5] one Lord, one faith, one baptism, [6] one God and Father of all, who is over all, and through all, and in us all.

[7] But to each one of us was the grace given according to the measure of the gift of Christ. [8] Therefore he says, "When he ascended on high, he led captivity captive, and gave gifts to men." [9] Now this, "He ascended", what is it but that he also first descended into the lower parts of the earth? [10] He who descended is the one who also ascended far above all the heavens, that he might fill all things.

Ministry Gifts for Building the Body of Christ

[11] He gave some to be apostles; and some, prophets; and some, evangelists; and some, shepherds and teachers; [12] for the perfecting of the saints, to the work of serving, to the building up of the body of Christ; [13] until we all attain to the unity of the faith, and of the knowledge of the Son of God, to a full grown man, to the measure of the stature of the fullness of Christ; [14] that we may no longer be children, tossed back and forth and carried about with every wind of doctrine, by the trickery of men, in craftiness, after the wiles of error; [15] but speaking truth in love, we may grow up in all things into him, who is the head, Christ; [16] from whom all the body, being fitted and knit together through that which every joint supplies, according to the working in measure of each individual part, makes the body increase to the building up of itself in love.

Love Is the Greatest Gift

12 [31] Moreover, I show a most excellent way to you.

13 [1] If I speak with the languages of men and of angels, but don't have love, I have become sounding brass, or a clanging cymbal. [2] If I have the gift of prophecy, and know all mysteries and all knowledge; and if I have all faith, so as to remove mountains, but don't have love, I am nothing. [3] If I dole out all my goods to feed the poor, and if I give my body to be burned, but don't have love, it profits me nothing.

[4] Love is patient and is kind; love doesn't envy. Love doesn't brag, is not proud, [5] doesn't behave itself inappropriately, doesn't seek its own way, is not provoked, takes no account of evil; [6] doesn't rejoice in unrighteousness, but rejoices with the truth; [7] bears all things, believes all things, hopes all things, endures all things. [8] Love never fails. But where there are prophecies, they will be done away with. Where there are various languages, they will cease. Where there is knowledge, it will be done away with.

[9] For we know in part, and we prophesy in part; [10] but when that which is complete has come, then that which is partial will be done away with. [11] When I was a child, I spoke as a child, I felt as a child, I thought as a child. Now that I have become a man, I have put away childish things. [12] For now we see in a mirror, dimly, but then face to face. Now I know in part, but then I will know fully, even as I was also fully known.

[13] But now faith, hope, and love remain—these three. The greatest of these is love.

1. How do you keep the unity of the Holy Spirit among a group of believers? Who is the Head of the Church?
2. Since love creates unity, can you see how "unity depends on me"?
3. Did you notice five additional ministry gifts of the Holy Spirit? Why are these given to the body? What is their purpose?
4. Why are religious practices and even good deeds of no value if we don't do them out of love?
5. Describe love. Compare your own life to the description you gave.
6. What is the greatest and most excellent way?

143. CARE OF THE CHURCH
James 2:1-19 and 1 Timothy 3:1-13 and 1 Peter 5:1-5

Within the body of believers, the values of the world tend to creep in, causing us to judge other people by their outward appearance and position in society. Scripture tells us to be very careful to treat all people the same, whether rich or poor, not showing partiality to anyone. It is not enough to just have faith; we should put our faith into action by doing deeds of love and kindness for others. Because the leaders of the Church must care for the believers, there are specific requirements that must be met by anyone desiring a place of leadership.

Favoritism Forbidden

2 [1] My brothers, don't hold the faith of our Lord Jesus Christ of glory with partiality. [2] For if a man with a gold ring, in fine clothing, comes into your synagogue, and a poor man in filthy clothing also comes in; [3] and you pay special attention to him who wears the fine clothing, and say, "Sit here in a good place"; and you tell the poor man, "Stand there," or "Sit by my footstool"; [4] haven't you shown partiality among yourselves, and become judges with evil thoughts?

[5] Listen, my beloved brothers. Didn't God choose those who are poor in this world to be rich in faith, and heirs of the Kingdom which he promised to those who love him? [6] But you have dishonored the poor man. Don't the rich oppress you, and personally drag you before the courts? [7] Don't they blaspheme the honorable name by which you are called?

[8] However, if you fulfill the royal law, according to the Scripture, "You shall love your neighbor as yourself," you do well. [9] But if you show partiality, you commit sin, being convicted by the law as transgressors. [10] For whoever keeps the whole law, and yet stumbles in one point, he has become guilty of all. [11] For he who said, "Do not commit adultery," also said, "Do not commit murder." Now if you do not commit adultery, but murder, you have become a transgressor of the law. [12] So speak, and so do, as men who are to be judged by a law of freedom. [13] For judgment is without mercy to him who has shown no mercy. Mercy triumphs over judgment.

Faith and Deeds

¹⁴ What good is it, my brothers, if a man says he has faith, but has no works? Can faith save him? ¹⁵ And if a brother or sister is naked and in lack of daily food, ¹⁶ and one of you tells them, "Go in peace, be warmed and filled"; and yet you didn't give them the things the body needs, what good is it? ¹⁷ Even so faith, if it has no works, is dead in itself. ¹⁸ Yes, a man will say, "You have faith, and I have works." Show me your faith without works, and I by my works will show you my faith. ¹⁹ You believe that God is one. You do well. The demons also believe, and shudder.

Overseers and Deacons

3 ¹This is a faithful saying: if a man seeks the office of an overseer, he desires a good work. ² The overseer therefore must be without reproach, the husband of one wife, temperate, sensible, modest, hospitable, good at teaching; ³ not a drinker, not violent, not greedy for money, but gentle, not quarrelsome, not covetous; ⁴ one who rules his own house well, having children in subjection with all reverence; ⁵ (but if a man doesn't know how to rule his own house, how will he take care of the assembly of God?) ⁶ not a new convert, lest being puffed up he fall into the same condemnation as the devil. ⁷ Moreover he must have good testimony from those who are outside, to avoid falling into reproach and the snare of the devil.

⁸ Servants, in the same way, must be reverent, not double-tongued, not addicted to much wine, not greedy for money; ⁹ holding the mystery of the faith in a pure conscience. ¹⁰ Let them also first be tested; then let them serve if they are blameless. ¹¹ Their wives in the same way must be reverent, not slanderers, temperate, faithful in all things. ¹² Let servants be husbands of one wife, ruling their children and their own houses well. ¹³ For those who have served well gain for themselves a good standing, and great boldness in the faith which is in Christ Jesus.

To Elders and Young Men

5 ¹I exhort the elders among you, as a fellow elder, and a witness of the sufferings of Christ, and who will also share in the glory that will be revealed. ² Shepherd the flock of God which is among you, exercising the oversight, not under compulsion, but voluntarily, not for dishonest gain, but willingly; ³ neither as lording it over those entrusted to you, but making yourselves examples to the flock.

⁴ When the chief Shepherd is revealed, you will receive the crown of glory that doesn't fade away. ⁵ Likewise, you younger ones, be subject to the elder. Yes, all of you clothe yourselves with humility, to subject yourselves to one another; for "God resists the proud, but gives grace to the humble."

1. Who is rich in faith and will therefore inherit the Kingdom?
2. Why should we not show favoritism among believers?
3. How should our faith and deeds work together?
4. Describe the kind of man an overseer or leader of the Church should be. Describe the kind of man a deacon in the Church should be.
5. If an overseer or elder is to be like a shepherd, how should he act?

144. THE SECRET OF GIVING
2 Corinthians 9:6-15 and 1 Timothy 5:17-18
and 6:3-10, 17-19 and Philippians 4:10-20

One of the secrets of the Christian life that we can learn is to give generously and cheerfully to others. Giving is an expression of love in a good deed. We have seen that God loves us so much that He has given us everything that we would ever need for life here on earth and for eternity. The believer, in turn, spontaneously expresses God's love by giving of himself to others. The secret is that giving brings blessing, not only to those who receive the gift, but also to the giver. Because the love of money leads to all kinds of evil, we should learn to be content with the simple necessities of life in order to avoid temptation. Paul expressed his gratitude to those who had given so generously to him and promised that God would meet all their needs because of their sacrifices of love. Paul discovered that you cannot outgive God.

Sowing Gifts Generously

9 ⁶Remember this: he who sows sparingly will also reap sparingly. He who sows bountifully will also reap bountifully. ⁷ Let each man give according as he has determined in his heart; not grudgingly, or under compulsion; for God loves a cheerful giver. ⁸ And God is able to make all grace abound to you, that you, always having all sufficiency in everything, may abound to every good work. ⁹ As it is written,

"He has scattered abroad, he has given to the poor.
His righteousness remains forever."

¹⁰ Now may he who supplies seed to the sower and bread for food, supply and multiply your seed for sowing, and increase the fruits of your righteousness; ¹¹ you being enriched in everything to all liberality, which produces through us thanksgiving to God. ¹² For this service of giving that you perform not only makes up for lack among the saints, but abounds also through many givings of thanks to God; ¹³ seeing that through the proof given by this service, they glorify God for the obedience of your confession to the Good News of Christ, and for the liberality of your contribution to them and to all; ¹⁴ while they themselves also, with supplication on your behalf, yearn for you by reason of the exceeding grace of God in you. ¹⁵ Now thanks be to God for his unspeakable gift!

5 ¹⁷Let the elders who rule well be counted worthy of double honor, especially those who labor in the word and in teaching. ¹⁸ For the Scripture says, "You shall not muzzle the ox when it treads out the grain." And, "The laborer is worthy of his wages."

The Love of Money

6 ³If anyone teaches a different doctrine, and doesn't consent to sound words, the words of our Lord Jesus Christ, and to the doctrine which is according to godliness, ⁴ he is conceited, knowing nothing, but obsessed with arguments, disputes, and word battles, from which come envy, strife, insulting, evil suspicions, [5] constant friction of people of corrupt minds and destitute of the truth, who suppose that godliness is a means of gain. Withdraw yourself from such.

[6] But godliness with contentment is great gain. [7] For we brought nothing into the world, and we certainly can't carry anything out. [8] But having food and clothing, we will be content with that. [9] But those who are determined to be rich fall into a temptation and a snare and many foolish and harmful lusts, such as drown men in ruin and destruction. [10] For the love of money is a root of all kinds of evil. Some have been led astray from the faith in their greed, and have pierced themselves through with many sorrows.

[17] Charge those who are rich in this present world that they not be haughty, nor have their hope set on the uncertainty of riches, but on the living God, who richly provides us with everything to enjoy; [18] that they do good, that they be rich in good works, that they be ready to distribute, willing to communicate; [19] laying up in store for themselves a good foundation against the time to come, that they may lay hold of eternal life.

Thanks for Their Gifts

4 [10]But I rejoice in the Lord greatly, that now at length you have revived your thought for me; in which you did indeed take thought, but you lacked opportunity. [11] Not that I speak in respect to lack, for I have learned in whatever state I am, to be content in it. [12] I know how to be humbled, and I know also how to abound. In everything and in all things I have learned the secret both to be filled and to be hungry, both to abound and to be in need. [13] I can do all things through Christ, who strengthens me. [14] However you did well that you shared in my affliction. [15] You yourselves also know, you Philippians, that in the beginning of the Good News, when I departed from Macedonia, no assembly shared with me in the matter of giving and receiving but you only. [16] For even in Thessalonica you sent once and again to my need. [17] Not that I seek for the gift, but I seek for the fruit that increases to your account. [18] But I have all things, and abound. I am filled, having received from Epaphroditus the things that came from you, a sweet-smelling fragrance, an acceptable and well-pleasing sacrifice to God. [19] My God will supply every need of yours according to his riches in glory in Christ Jesus. [20] Now to our God and Father be the glory forever and ever! Amen.

> 1. What should be our attitude toward giving? Do we worship God through giving?
> 2. Describe the person who teaches false doctrines.
> 3. With what should we be content? Why? What is the root of all kinds of evil?
> 4. In whom should we put our hope? Why? How do we lay up treasures for eternity?

Great Bible Truths

   5. What was Paul's secret to contentment in any circumstance? Could you live that way?
   6. Please memorize vv. 13 and 19, great promises from God. Can we outgive God?
   7. Have you discovered the secret of giving?

145. THE CHRISTIAN FAMILY
Ephesians 5:22-33 and 1 Peter 3:1-7
and Ephesians 6:1-9 and Colossians 3:18-25 and 4:1

The Christian life of love includes not only our relationships with fellow believers but also a commitment of ourselves to those closest to us, our families. The relationship of unity between a husband and wife is compared to the unity and love of Christ for His Church. Specific instructions are given for husbands and wives, children and fathers, servants and masters. As in all our relationships, the basis for the Christian family is to be the love of Jesus Christ.

Wives and Husbands

5 ^{22}Wives, be subject to your own husbands, as to the Lord. ^{23} For the husband is the head of the wife, and Christ also is the head of the assembly, being himself the savior of the body. ^{24} But as the assembly is subject to Christ, so let the wives also be to their own husbands in everything.

^{25} Husbands, love your wives, even as Christ also loved the assembly, and gave himself up for it; ^{26} that he might sanctify it, having cleansed it by the washing of water with the word, ^{27} that he might present the assembly to himself gloriously, not having spot or wrinkle or any such thing; but that it should be holy and without defect. ^{28} Even so husbands also ought to love their own wives as their own bodies. He who loves his own wife loves himself. ^{29} For no man ever hated his own flesh; but nourishes and cherishes it, even as the Lord also does the assembly; ^{30} because we are members of his body, of his flesh and bones.

^{31} "For this cause a man will leave his father and mother, and will be joined to his wife. The two will become one flesh." ^{32} This mystery is great, but I speak concerning Christ and of the assembly. ^{33} Nevertheless each of you must also love his own wife even as himself; and let the wife see that she respects her husband. **3** In the same way, wives, be in subjection to your own husbands; so that, even if any don't obey the Word, they may be won by the behavior of their wives without a word; ^{2} seeing your pure behavior in fear [your respect for God]. ^{3} Let your beauty be not just the outward adorning of braiding the hair, and of wearing jewels of gold, or of putting on fine clothing; ^{4} but in the hidden person of the heart, in the incorruptible adornment of a gentle and quiet spirit, which is in the sight of God very precious. ^{5} For this is how the holy women before, who hoped in God also adorned themselves, being in subjection to their own husbands: ^{6} as Sarah obeyed Abraham, calling him lord, whose children [daughters] you now are, if you do well, and are not put in fear by any terror. and you may live long on the earth."

⁷ You husbands, in the same way, live with your wives according to knowledge [sensitive understanding], giving honor to the woman, as to the weaker vessel, as being also joint heirs of the grace of life; that your prayers may not be hindered.

Children and Parents
6 Children, obey your parents in the Lord, for this is right. ² "Honor your father and mother," which is the first commandment with a promise: ³ "that it may be well with you, and you may live long on the earth."

⁴ You fathers, don't provoke your children to wrath, but nurture them in the discipline and instruction of the Lord.

Slaves and Masters
⁵ Servants, be obedient to those who according to the flesh [world's system] are your masters, with fear and trembling, in singleness of your heart, as to Christ; ⁶ not in the way of service only when eyes are on you, as men pleasers; but as servants of Christ, doing the will of God from the heart; ⁷ with good will doing service, as to the Lord, and not to men; ⁸ knowing that whatever good thing each one does, he will receive the same again from the Lord, whether he is bound or free.

⁹ You masters, do the same things to them, and give up threatening, knowing that he who is both their Master and yours is in heaven, and there is no partiality with him.

Rules for Christian Households
3 ¹⁸Wives, be in subjection to your husbands, as is fitting in the Lord.

¹⁹Husbands, love your wives, and don't be bitter against them.

²⁰Children, obey your parents in all things, for this pleases the Lord.

²¹Fathers, don't provoke your children, so that they won't be discouraged.

²²Servants, obey in all things those who are your masters according to the flesh, not just when they are looking, as men pleasers, but in singleness of heart, fearing God. ²³ And whatever you do, work heartily, as for the Lord, and not for men, ²⁴ knowing that from the Lord you will receive the reward of the inheritance; for you serve the Lord Christ.²⁵ But he who does wrong will receive again for the wrong that he has done, and there is no partiality.

4 ¹Masters, give to your servants that which is just and equal, knowing that you also have a Master in heaven.

> 1. How is the relationship between husband and wife like the relationship between Jesus Christ and His Church?
>
> 2. How should wives behave toward their husbands? What kind of beauty is of great worth in God's sight?

3. How should husbands treat their wives?

4. What instructions are given for children? For fathers?

5. What instructions are given for slaves and masters? How can these instructions be applied to today's work environment?

6. What is the believer's goal in everything that he does? vv. 23-24

146. CHRISTIAN CONDUCT
1 Corinthians 6:1-20 and 2 Thessalonians 3:6-13 and 2 Corinthians 6:14-18 and 7:1; and 1 Corinthians 10:23-24

Because the life of the Christian is based upon love, there is no place for lawsuits, disputes, immorality or idleness. Our love for God and gratitude for our salvation should control our business relationships, social contacts and our work. We must no longer live as we did in the past, since our lives have been bought with the price of the precious blood of Jesus Christ, our Savior.

Lawsuits Among Believers

6 Dare any of you, having a matter against his neighbor, go to law before the unrighteous, and not before the saints? [2] Don't you know that the saints will judge the world? And if the world is judged by you, are you unworthy to judge the smallest matters? [3] Don't you know that we will judge angels? How much more, things that pertain to this life? [4] If then, you have to judge things pertaining to this life, do you set them to judge who are of no account in the assembly? [5] I say this to move you to shame. Isn't there even one wise man among you who would be able to decide between his brothers? [6] But brother goes to law with brother, and that before unbelievers!

[7] Therefore it is already altogether a defect in you, that you have lawsuits one with another. Why not rather be wronged? Why not rather be defrauded? [8] No, but you yourselves do wrong, and defraud, and that against your brothers. [9] Or don't you know that the unrighteous will not inherit God's Kingdom? Don't be deceived. Neither the sexually immoral, nor idolaters, nor adulterers, nor male prostitutes, nor homosexuals, [10] nor thieves, nor covetous, nor drunkards, nor slanderers, nor extortionists, will inherit God's Kingdom. [11] Such were some of you, but you were washed. But you were sanctified. But you were justified in the name of the Lord Jesus, and in the Spirit of our God.

Sexual Immorality

[12] "All things are lawful for me," but not all things are expedient [worthwhile]. "All things are lawful for me," but I will not be brought under the power of anything. [13] "Foods for the belly, and the belly for foods," but God will bring to nothing both it and them. But the body is not for sexual immorality, but for the Lord; and the

Lord for the body. ¹⁴ Now God raised up the Lord, and will also raise us up by his power.

¹⁵ Don't you know that your bodies are members of Christ? Shall I then take the members of Christ, and make them members of a prostitute? May it never be! ¹⁶ Or don't you know that he who is joined to a prostitute is one body? For, "The two", he says, "will become one flesh." ¹⁷ But he who is joined to the Lord is one spirit.

¹⁸ Flee sexual immorality! "Every sin that a man does is outside the body," but he who commits sexual immorality sins against his own body. ¹⁹ Or don't you know that your body is a temple of the Holy Spirit which is in you, which you have from God? You are not your own, ²⁰ for you were bought with a price. Therefore glorify God in your body and in your spirit, which are God's.

Warning Against Idleness
3 ⁶Now we command you, brothers, in the name of our Lord Jesus Christ, that you withdraw yourselves from every brother who walks in rebellion [unwilling to work], and not after the tradition which they received from us. ⁷ For you know how you ought to imitate us. For we didn't behave ourselves rebelliously among you, ⁸ neither did we eat bread from anyone's hand without paying for it, but in labor and travail worked night and day, that we might not burden any of you; ⁹ not because we don't have the right, but to make ourselves an example to you, that you should imitate us. ¹⁰ For even when we were with you, we commanded you this: "If anyone will not work, don't let him eat."

¹¹ For we hear of some who walk among you in rebellion, who don't work at all, but are busybodies. ¹² Now those who are that way, we command and exhort in the Lord Jesus Christ, that with quietness they work, and eat their own bread. ¹³ But you, brothers, don't be weary in doing well.

Do Not Be Yoked with Unbelievers
6 ¹⁴Don't be unequally yoked with unbelievers, for what fellowship [commonality] have righteousness and iniquity? Or what fellowship [harmony] has light with darkness? ¹⁵ What agreement has Christ with Belial? Or what portion has a believer with an unbeliever? ¹⁶ What agreement has a temple of God with idols? For you are a temple of the living God. Even as God said, "I will dwell in them, and walk in them; and I will be their God, and they will be my people."

¹⁷Therefore
> "'Come out from among them,
> and be separate,' says the Lord.
> 'Touch no unclean thing.
> I will receive you.

ⁱ⁸ I will be to you a Father.
You will be to me sons and daughters,'
says the Lord Almighty."

7 ¹Having therefore these promises, beloved, let us cleanse ourselves from all defilement of flesh and spirit, perfecting holiness in the fear of God.

How to Use Christian Freedom
10 ²³"All things are lawful for me," but not all things are profitable. "All things are lawful for me," but not all things build up. ²⁴ Let no one seek his own, but each one his neighbor's good.

1. *Should believers bring lawsuits against one another and settle their disputes in government courts? Why not?*

2. *Who will **NOT** inherit the Kingdom of God?*

3. *Why should we flee sexual immorality? Who owns our bodies and why?*

4. *What was Paul's rule concerning laziness and work?*

5. *Why should we not be yoked together with unbelievers?*

6. *Who is the temple of the living God? Why should we be separate from unbelievers?*

7. *Do you understand the believer's freedom? Read it again (10:23).*

147. THE CHRISTIAN AND GOVERNMENT
1 Peter 2:13-17 and Romans 13:1-10 and 1 Timothy 2:1-6

Because we live in a country controlled by government officials, we are under their rule and authority. As Christians, we are also under a Higher Authority (God), who establishes all governments and uses them for our good and protection. The rule of love, then, will cause us to pray for our government leaders and submit to those who have authority over us.

Submission to Rulers
2 ¹³Therefore subject yourselves to every ordinance of man for the Lord's sake: whether to the king, as supreme; ¹⁴ or to governors, as sent by him for vengeance on evildoers and for praise to those who do well. ¹⁵ For this is the will of God, that by well-doing you should put to silence the ignorance of foolish men: ¹⁶ as free, and not using your freedom for a cloak of wickedness, but as bondservants of God. ¹⁷ Honor all men. Love the brotherhood. Fear God. Honor the king.

Great Bible Truths

Submission to Authorities

13 Let every soul be in subjection to the higher authorities, for there is no authority except from God, and those who exist are ordained by God. ² Therefore he who resists the authority, withstands the ordinance of God; and those who withstand will receive to themselves judgment. ³ For rulers are not a terror to the good work, but to the evil. Do you desire to have no fear of the authority? Do that which is good, and you will have praise from the same, ⁴ for he is a servant of God to you for good. But if you do that which is evil, be afraid, for he doesn't bear the sword in vain; for he is a servant of God, an avenger for wrath [anger and punishment] to him who does evil. ⁵ Therefore you need to be in subjection, not only because of the wrath, but also for conscience' sake.

⁶ For this reason you also pay taxes, for they are servants of God's service, attending continually on this very thing.⁷ Therefore give everyone what you owe: if you owe taxes, pay taxes; if customs, then customs; if respect, then respect; if honor, then honor. ⁸ Owe no one anything, except to love one another; for he who loves his neighbor has fulfilled the law.

⁹ For the commandments, "You shall not commit adultery," "You shall not murder," "You shall not steal," "You shall not covet," and whatever other commandments there are, are all summed up in this saying, namely, "You shall love your neighbor as yourself." ¹⁰ Love doesn't harm a neighbor. Love therefore is the fulfillment of the law.

Pray for Your Government Leaders

2 ¹I exhort therefore, first of all, that petitions, prayers, intercessions, and givings of thanks, be made for all men: ² for kings and all who are in high places; that we may lead a tranquil and quiet life in all godliness and reverence. ³ For this is good and acceptable in the sight of God our Savior; ⁴ who desires all people to be saved and come to full knowledge of the truth. ⁵ For there is one God, and one mediator between God and men, the man Christ Jesus, ⁶ who gave himself as a ransom for all; the testimony in its own times.

1. *How should we live? To whom should we show respect? How?*

2. *Who established the existing authorities? Against whom do we rebel when we rebel against authority?*

3. *Should we be honest when making out our income tax forms? Why? Should we pay our debts?*

4. *One rule sums up all the commandments. How does this fulfill all the other commandments?*

5. *Why should we pray for all those in authority?*

Pause for Reflection: *Think about 2:4. Do you feel drawn to be part of God's awesome goal?"*

D. ETERNAL LIFE TO COME

This world, as we know it, will not continue forever, but will come to an end. Jesus spoke of this future event while He was on earth. (See selections 99 and 100.) The last book of the New Testament records the visions and revelations given by God to Jesus' disciple John. While these revelations give us a picture of things to come in the future, they also encourage us to live pure and holy lives while we are on earth. This life on earth is a training ground for eternity. Since no one knows when the end will come, we need to be prepared for the moment when Jesus returns. The best way to be prepared for eternal life with God is to live a fruitful life now. We should be investing ourselves and our resources today for the life to come by serving God and others. The final hope of every Christian is to know we will spend eternity in heaven with Jesus Christ. Through John's revelations, we are given a descriptive account of that future hope, a world without sin filled with the light and love of God. All those who have believed in Jesus Christ as their Savior are assured of eternal life in heaven.

148. THE LIVING ONE
Revelation 1:1-20

Many years after Jesus Christ returned to heaven, the disciple John was exiled to the island of Patmos as punishment for preaching about the Savior Jesus Christ. While he was there, John, the last living disciple, was given a vision of Jesus, who came to him and spoke to him of the present situation and of future end-time events. Coming to bring a message to the churches, Jesus Christ revealed Himself in all His beauty and glorious splendor as the Living One, the First and the Last.

Introduction

1 This is the Revelation of Jesus Christ, which God gave him to show to his servants the things which must happen soon, which he sent and made known by his angel to his servant, John, ² who testified to God's word, and of the testimony of Jesus Christ, about everything that he saw. ³Blessed is he who reads and those who hear the words of the prophecy, and keep the things that are written in it, for the time is at hand.

Greetings to the Churches

⁴John, to the seven assemblies that are in Asia:

Grace to you and peace, from God, who is and who was and who is to come; and from the seven Spirits who are before his throne; ⁵ and from Jesus Christ, the faithful witness, the firstborn of the dead, and the ruler of the kings of the earth.

To him who loves us, and washed us from our sins by his blood; ⁶ and he made us to be a Kingdom, priests to his God and Father; to him be the glory and the dominion forever and ever. Amen.

⁷ Behold he is coming with the clouds,
and every eye will see him,
including those who pierced him.
All the tribes of the earth will mourn over him.
Even so, Amen.

⁸ "I am the Alpha and the Omega," says the Lord God, "who is and who was and who is to come, the Almighty."

John Tells of His Vision with Jesus

⁹ I, John, your brother and partner with you in oppression, Kingdom, and perseverance in Christ Jesus, was on the isle that is called Patmos because of God's Word and the testimony of Jesus Christ. ¹⁰ I was in the Spirit on the Lord's day, and I heard behind me a loud voice, like a trumpet ¹¹ saying, "What you see, write in a book and send to the seven assemblies: to Ephesus, Smyrna, Pergamum, Thyatira, Sardis, Philadelphia, and to Laodicea."

John Describes Jesus

¹² I turned to see the voice that spoke with me. Having turned, I saw seven golden lamp stands. ¹³ And among the lamp stands was one like a son of man clothed with a robe reaching down to his feet, and with a golden sash around his chest. ¹⁴ His head and his hair were white as white wool, like snow. His eyes were like a flame of fire. ¹⁵ His feet were like burnished brass, as if it had been refined in a furnace. His voice was like the voice of many waters. ¹⁶ He had seven stars in his right hand. Out of his mouth proceeded a sharp two-edged sword. His face was like the sun shining at its brightest.

¹⁷ When I saw him, I fell at his feet like a dead man. He laid his right hand on me, saying, "Don't be afraid. I am the first and the last, ¹⁸ and the Living one. I was dead, and behold, I am alive forever more. Amen. I have the keys of Death and of Hades.

¹⁹ Write therefore the things which you have seen, and the things which are, and the things which will happen hereafter; ²⁰ the mystery of the seven stars which you saw in my right hand, and the seven golden lamp stands. The seven stars are the angels of the seven assemblies. The seven lamp stands are seven assemblies.

1. *Why did God give this revelation?*

2. *Who is Jesus Christ, and what has He done for us?*

3. *Whose was the voice speaking to John? Describe the person he saw.*

4. *The Bible describes God and Jesus Christ in many ways and in many times. In this passage we see a beautiful example of Jesus' glory and majesty. (Review vv. 6-7, 12-18.)*

5. *What did Jesus say about himself? Do you believe that Jesus is God?*

6. *What are the seven stars? What are the seven lampstands?*

149. THE CHURCHES IN ASIA
Revelation 2:1-29 and 3:1-22

Although Jesus was speaking to the seven churches in Asia (present day Turkey), His messages were recorded by John for all believers. Just as He knew everything about the people of these churches, He also knows all about us, our good deeds as well as our sins. These passages remind us of the ongoing spiritual war between God and Satan. There are always temptations to veer from the faith and to follow false teaching, to relax vigilance and to fall into sin, or to live without the love of God evident in our lives. Jesus encourages all believers to repent of their sins and remain faithful to Him, no matter what the cost. Many blessings and rewards await those who overcome evil and do His will to the end.

To the Church in Ephesus

2 "To the angel of the assembly in Ephesus write: "He who holds the seven stars in his right hand, he who walks among the seven golden lamp stands says these things: ² "I know your works, and your toil and perseverance, and that you can't tolerate evil men, and have tested those who call themselves apostles, and they are not, and found them false. ³ You have perseverance and have endured for my name's sake, and have not grown weary.

⁴ But I have this against you, that you left your first love. ⁵ Remember therefore from where you have fallen, and repent and do the first works; or else I am coming to you swiftly, and will move your lamp stand out of its place, unless you repent.⁶ But this you have, that you hate the works of the Nicolaitans, which I also hate.

⁷ He who has an ear, let him hear what the Spirit says to the assemblies. To him who overcomes I will give to eat from the tree of life, which is in the Paradise of my God.

To the Church in Smyrna

⁸"To the angel of the assembly in Smyrna write:

"The first and the last, who was dead, and has come to life says these things: ⁹"I know your works, oppression, and your poverty (but you are rich), and the blasphemy of those who say they are Jews, and they are not, but are a synagogue of Satan. ¹⁰ Don't be afraid of the things which you are about to suffer. Behold, the devil is about to throw some of you into prison, that you may be tested; and you will have oppression for ten days. Be faithful to death, and I will give you the crown of life.

¹¹ He who has an ear, let him hear what the Spirit says to the assemblies. He who overcomes won't be harmed by the second death.

To the Church in Pergamum

¹² "To the angel of the assembly in Pergamum write:

"He who has the sharp two-edged sword says these things:

¹³"I know your works and where you dwell, where Satan's throne is. You hold firmly to my name, and didn't deny my faith in the days of Antipas my witness,

my faithful one, who was killed among you, where Satan dwells.

¹⁴ But I have a few things against you, because you have there some who hold the teaching of Balaam, who taught Balak to throw a stumbling block before the children of Israel, to eat things sacrificed to idols, and to commit sexual immorality. ¹⁵ So you also have some who hold to the teaching of the Nicolaitans likewise. ¹⁶ Repent therefore, or else I am coming to you quickly, and I will make war against them with the sword of my mouth.

¹⁷ He who has an ear, let him hear what the Spirit says to the assemblies. To him who overcomes, to him I will give of the hidden manna, and I will give him a white stone, and on the stone a new name written, which no one knows but he who receives it.

To the Church in Thyatira

¹⁸"To the angel of the assembly in Thyatira write:

"The Son of God, who has his eyes like a flame of fire, and his feet are like burnished brass, says these things: ¹⁹"I know your works, your love, faith, service, patient endurance, and that your last works are more than the first.

²⁰ But I have this against you, that you tolerate your woman, Jezebel, who calls herself a prophetess. She teaches and seduces my servants to commit sexual immorality, and to eat things sacrificed to idols. ²¹ I gave her time to repent, but she refuses to repent of her sexual immorality. ²² Behold, I will throw her into a bed, and those who commit adultery with her into great oppression, unless they repent of her works. ²³ I will kill her children with Death, and all the assemblies will know that I am he who searches the minds and hearts. I will give to each one of you according to your deeds.

²⁴But to you I say, to the rest who are in Thyatira, as many as don't have this teaching, who don't know what some call 'the deep things of Satan,' to you I say, I am not putting any other burden on you. ²⁵ Nevertheless, hold that which you have firmly until I come.

²⁶ He who overcomes, and he who keeps my works to the end, to him I will give authority over the nations.

²⁷ He will rule them with a rod of iron, shattering them like clay pots; as I also have received of my Father: ²⁸ and I will give him the morning star.

²⁹ He who has an ear, let him hear what the Spirit says to the assemblies.

To the Church in Sardis

3 "And to the angel of the assembly in Sardis write:

"He who has the seven Spirits of God, and the seven stars says these things:

"I know your works, that you have a reputation of being alive, but you are dead. ² Wake up, and keep the things that remain, which you were about to throw away, for I have found no works of yours perfected before my God. ³ Remember therefore how you have received and heard. Keep it, and repent. If therefore you won't watch, I will come as a thief, and you won't know what hour I will come upon you.

⁴ Nevertheless you have a few names in Sardis that did not defile their garments. They will walk with me in white, for they are worthy. ⁵ He who overcomes will be arrayed in white garments, and I will in no way blot his name out of the book of life, and I will confess his name before my Father, and before his angels. ⁶ He who has an ear, let him hear what the Spirit says to the assemblies.

To the Church in Philadelphia

⁷"To the angel of the assembly in Philadelphia write:

"He who is holy, he who is true, he who has the key of David, he who opens and no one can shut, and who shuts and no one opens, says these things:

⁸"I know your works (behold, I have set before you an open door, which no one can shut), that you have a little power, and kept my word, and didn't deny my name.⁹ Behold, I give some of the synagogue of Satan, of those who say they are Jews, and they are not, but lie. Behold, I will make them to come and worship before your feet, and to know that I have loved you. ¹⁰ Because you kept my command to endure, I also will keep you from the hour of testing, which is to come on the whole world, to test those who dwell on the earth.

¹¹ I am coming quickly! Hold firmly that which you have, so that no one takes your crown. ¹² He who overcomes, I will make him a pillar in the temple of my God, and he will go out from there no more. I will write on him the name of my God, and the name of the city of my God, the new Jerusalem, which comes down out of heaven from my God, and my own new name. ¹³ He who has an ear, let him hear what the Spirit says to the assemblies.

To the Church in Laodicea

¹⁴ "To the angel of the assembly in Laodicea write:

"The Amen, the Faithful and True Witness, the Head of God's creation [Jesus], says these things:

¹⁵"I know your works, that you are neither cold nor hot. I wish you were cold or hot.¹⁶ So, because you are lukewarm, and neither hot nor cold, I will vomit you out of my mouth. ¹⁷Because you say, 'I am rich, and have gotten riches, and have need of nothing;' and don't know that you are the wretched one, miserable, poor, blind, and naked; ¹⁸ I counsel you to buy from me gold refined by fire, that you may become rich; and white garments, that you may clothe yourself, and that the shame of your nakedness may not be revealed; and eye salve to anoint your eyes, that you may see.

¹⁹ As many as I love, I reprove and chasten. Be zealous therefore, and repent. ²⁰ Behold, I stand at the door and knock. If anyone hears my voice and opens the door, then I will come in to him, and will dine with him, and he with me.

²¹ He who overcomes, I will give to him to sit down with me on my throne,

as I also overcame, and sat down with my Father on his throne. ²² He who has an ear, let him hear what the Spirit says to the assemblies."

1. What good things did Jesus have to say about the Church at Ephesus? What things did Jesus hold against it? What is given to him who overcomes?

2. What did Jesus say would happen to some in the Church in Smyrna? Who would receive the crown of life?

3. What good things did Jesus have to say about the Church in Pergamum? What did Jesus hold against it? What is given to him who overcomes?

4. What good things did Jesus have to say about the Church at Thyatira? What did Jesus have against it? What is given to him who overcomes?

5. What did not please Jesus about the Church in Sardis? What did he say about a few people? What would be the rewards for those who overcome?

6. What good things had the Church in Philadelphia done? What promises did Jesus make to those who kept his command?

7. What did Jesus have to say about the Church in Laodicea? What counsel did He give it? Explain what you think He meant? What is given to him who overcomes?

8. Jesus stands and knocks at the door of every person's heart (v.20). What does that person have to do to let Him in?

150. THE THRONE OF GOD
Revelation 4:1-11 and 5:1-14 and 7:9-17

As John's vision continued, he was given a glimpse into heaven, where he saw the throne of God. Around and before the throne were those worshiping God and Jesus Christ, praising the Lamb who was slain for the sins of mankind. The great multitude of people before the throne was all those believers in Jesus Christ who had passed from death into their eternal reward, life in heaven forever with God.

Amazing Scene at the Throne in Heaven

4 ¹After these things I looked and saw a door opened in heaven, and the first voice that I heard, like a trumpet speaking with me, was one saying, "Come up here, and I will show you the things which must happen after this."
² Immediately I was in the Spirit. Behold, there was a throne set in heaven, and one sitting on the throne ³ that looked like a jasper stone and a sardius. There was a rainbow around the throne, like an emerald to look at. ⁴ Around the throne

were twenty-four thrones. On the thrones were twenty-four elders sitting, dressed in white garments, with crowns of gold on their heads. [5] Out of the throne proceed lightnings, sounds, and thunders. There were seven lamps of fire burning before his throne, which are the seven Spirits of God. [6] Before the throne was something like a sea of glass, similar to crystal.

In the middle of the throne, and around the throne were four living creatures full of eyes before and behind. [7] The first creature was like a lion, and the second creature like a calf, and the third creature had a face like a man, and the fourth was like a flying eagle. [8] The four living creatures, each one of them having six wings, are full of eyes around and within. They have no rest day and night, saying,

> "Holy, holy, holy
> is the Lord God, the Almighty,
> who was and who is and who is to come!"

[9] When the living creatures give glory, honor, and thanks to him who sits on the throne, to him who lives forever and ever, [10] the twenty-four elders fall down before him who sits on the throne, and worship him who lives forever and ever, and throw their crowns before the throne, saying,

> [11] "Worthy are you, our Lord and God, the Holy One,
> to receive the glory, the honor, and the power,
> for you created all things,
> and because of your desire they existed, and were created!"

The Scroll and the Lamb

5 I saw, in the right hand of him who sat on the throne, a book written inside and outside, sealed shut with seven seals. [2] I saw a mighty angel proclaiming with a loud voice, "Who is worthy to open the book, and to break its seals?"[3] No one in heaven above, or on the earth, or under the earth, was able to open the book, or to look in it.[4] And I wept much, because no one was found worthy to open the book, or to look in it.[5] One of the elders said to me, "Don't weep. Behold, the Lion who is of the tribe of Judah, the Root of David, has overcome; he who opens the book and its seven seals."

[6] I saw in the middle of the throne and of the four living creatures, and in the middle of the elders, a Lamb standing, as though it had been slain, having seven horns, and seven eyes, which are the seven Spirits of God, sent out into all the earth. [7] Then he came, and he took it out of the right hand of him who sat on the throne. [8] Now when he had taken the book, the four living creatures and the twenty-four elders fell down before the Lamb, each one having a harp, and golden bowls full of incense, which are the prayers of the saints.[9] They sang a new song, saying,

> "You are worthy to take the book,
> and to open its seals:
> for you were killed,

and bought us for God with your blood,
out of every tribe, language, people, and nation,
[10] and made us kings and priests to our God,
and we will reign on earth."

[11] I saw, and I heard something like a voice of many angels around the throne, the living creatures, and the elders; and the number of them was ten thousands of ten thousands, and thousands of thousands;
[12] saying with a loud voice,
"Worthy is the Lamb who has been killed
to receive the power, wealth,
wisdom, strength, honor, glory, and blessing!"

[13] I heard every created thing which is in heaven, on the earth, under the earth, on the sea, and everything in them, saying,
"To him who sits on the throne,
and to the Lamb be the blessing,
the honor, the glory, and the dominion,
forever and ever! Amen!"

[14] The four living creatures said, "Amen!" The elders fell down and worshiped.

The Great Multitude in White Robes

7 [9] After these things I looked, and behold, a great multitude, which no man could number, out of every nation and of all tribes, peoples, and languages, standing before the throne and before the Lamb, dressed in white robes, with palm branches in their hands. [10] They cried with a loud voice, saying,
"Salvation be to our God,
who sits on the throne,
and to the Lamb!"

[11] All the angels were standing around the throne, the elders, and the four living creatures; and they fell on their faces before his throne, and worshiped God, [12] saying,
"Amen!
Blessing, glory,
wisdom, thanksgiving, honor,
power, and might,
be to our God forever and ever!
Amen."

[13] One of the elders answered, saying to me, "These who are arrayed in white robes, who are they, and from where did they come?"
[14] I told him, "My lord, you know."
He said to me, "These are those who came out of the great tribulation. They washed their robes, and made them white in the Lamb's blood. [15] Therefore
they are before the throne of God,
they serve him day and night in his temple.

He who sits on the throne will spread his tabernacle [will protect them with His presence] over them.
¹⁶ They will never be hungry, neither thirsty anymore;
neither will the sun beat on them, nor any heat;
¹⁷ for the Lamb who is in the middle of the throne shepherds them,
and leads them to springs of waters of life.
And God will wipe away every tear from their eyes."

1. Describe the throne of God in heaven.

2. How did the twenty-four elders worship the Lord almighty?

3. Who was the Lion of Judah, the Root of David and the Lamb?

4. What song of praise did the elders sing before the Lamb? What song did the angels sing? What song did every creature sing?

5. Who was the great multitude? What song did they sing?

6. How did God reward those who came out of the great tribulation?

151. THE BOOK OF LIFE
Revelation 19:1-16 and 20:11-15

As John continued to look into heaven he saw the great multitude of believers, worshiping God and rejoicing over the wedding of the Lamb and His bride, the Church of Jesus Christ. All people who have ever lived must stand before the throne of God to be judged according to what they have done during their lives on earth. Only those who have had their sins washed in the blood of the Lamb will have their names written in the Book of Life.

Hallelujah!
19 After these things I heard something like a loud voice of a great multitude in heaven, saying,
"Hallelujah!
Salvation, power, and glory belong to our God:
² for true and righteous are his judgments.
For he has judged the great prostitute,
who corrupted the earth with her sexual immorality,
and he has avenged the blood of his servants at her hand."
³ A second said
"Hallelujah!
Her smoke goes up forever and ever."
⁴ The twenty-four elders and the four living creatures fell down and worshiped God who sits on the throne, saying,
"Amen! Hallelujah!"
⁵ A voice came from the throne, saying,

"Give praise to our God, all you his servants,
you who fear him, the small and the great!"

⁶ I heard something like the voice of a great multitude, and like the voice of many waters, and like the voice of mighty thunders, saying,

"Hallelujah!
For the Lord our God, the Almighty, reigns!
⁷ Let us rejoice and be exceedingly glad, and let us give the glory to him.
For the marriage of the Lamb has come,
and his wife has made herself ready."
⁸ It was given to her that she would array herself
in bright, pure, fine linen.

(the fine linen stands for the righteous acts of the saints.)

⁹ He said to me, "Write, 'Blessed are those who are invited to the marriage supper of the Lamb.'" He said to me, "These are true words of God."

¹⁰ I fell down before his feet to worship him. He said to me, "Look! Don't do it! I am a fellow bondservant with you and with your brothers who hold the testimony of Jesus. Worship God, for the testimony of Jesus is the Spirit of Prophecy."

The Rider on the White Horse

¹¹ I saw the heaven opened, and behold, a white horse, and he who sat on it is called Faithful and True. In righteousness he judges and makes war. ¹² His eyes are a flame of fire, and on his head are many crowns. He has names written and a name written which no one knows but he himself. ¹³ He is clothed in a garment sprinkled with blood. His name is called "The Word of God." ¹⁴ The armies which are in heaven followed him on white horses, clothed in white, pure, fine linen. ¹⁵ Out of his mouth proceeds a sharp, double-edged sword, that with it he should strike the nations. He will rule them with an iron rod. He treads the wine press of the fierceness of the wrath of God, the Almighty. ¹⁶ He has on his garment and on his thigh a name written,

"KING OF KINGS, AND LORD OF LORDS."

The Dead Are Judged

20 ¹¹I saw a great white throne, and him who sat on it, from whose face the earth and the heaven fled away [vanished]. There was found no place for them. ¹² I saw the dead, the great and the small, standing before the throne, and they opened books. Another book was opened, which is the book of life. The dead were judged out of the things which were written in the books, according to their works. ¹³ The sea gave up the dead who were in it. Death and Hades gave up the dead who were in them. They were judged, each one according to his works. ¹⁴ Death and Hades were thrown into the lake of fire. This is the second death, the lake of fire. ¹⁵ If anyone was not found written in the book of life, he was cast into the lake of fire.

1. What did the multitude say about God's judgment?
2. Who was the bride?
3. Who was the rider on the white horse? Describe Him.
4. Who stood before the throne? How are the dead judged?
5. Who was thrown into the lake of fire?
6. What is the book of life? Whose names are in it? Why?

152. THE NEW HEAVEN AND EARTH
Revelation 21:1-14, 22-27 and 22:1-21

The final revelation given to John was a beautiful vision of the Holy City, the New Jerusalem, the City of God coming down from heaven. All was new. John described this glorious city and the river of life that flowed out from it. God's new creation was totally perfect. Creation had come full circle, as man's broken relationship with God was healed. Heaven was not an afterthought but the intent of all creation. Nothing impure can be there, no tears, death or sadness, only pure joy. It is the happiest of all endings. However, only those who have had their sins forgiven, whose names are written in the Book of Life, can enter the city. May all those who have been washed in the blood of the Lamb eagerly look forward to the time of His coming, and say with John, "Come, Lord Jesus!"

The New Jerusalem
21 ¹I saw a new heaven and a new earth: for the first heaven and the first earth have passed away, and the sea is no more.² I saw the holy city, New Jerusalem, coming down out of heaven from God, prepared like a bride adorned for her husband.³ I heard a loud voice out of heaven saying, "Behold, God's dwelling is with people, and he will dwell with them, and they will be his people, and God himself will be with them as their God. ⁴ He will wipe away from them every tear from their eyes. Death will be no more; neither will there be mourning, nor crying, nor pain, any more. The first things have passed away."

⁵ He who sits on the throne said, "Behold, I am making all things new." He said, "Write, for these words of God are faithful and true."

⁶ He said to me, "It is done! I am the Alpha and the Omega, the Beginning and the End. I will give freely to him who is thirsty from the spring of the water of life. ⁷ He who overcomes, I will give him these things. I will be his God, and he will be my son. ⁸ But for the cowardly, unbelieving, sinners, abominable, murderers, sexually immoral, sorcerers, idolaters, and all liars, their part is in the lake that burns with fire and sulfur, which is the second death."

⁹ One of the seven angels who had the seven bowls, who were loaded with the seven last plagues came, and he spoke with me, saying, "Come here. I will show you the wife, the Lamb's bride." ¹⁰ He carried me away in the Spirit to a great and high mountain, and showed me the holy city, Jerusalem, coming down

out of heaven from God, ¹¹ having the glory of God. Her light was like a most precious stone, as if it were a jasper stone, clear as crystal; ¹² having a great and high wall; having twelve gates, and at the gates twelve angels; and names written on them, which are the names of the twelve tribes of the children of Israel. ¹³ On the east were three gates; and on the north three gates; and on the south three gates; and on the west three gates. ¹⁴ The wall of the city had twelve foundations, and on them twelve names of the twelve Apostles of the Lamb.

²² I saw no temple in it, for the Lord God, the Almighty, and the Lamb, are its temple. ²³ The city has no need for the sun, neither of the moon, to shine, for the very glory of God illuminated it, and its lamp is the Lamb. ²⁴ The nations will walk in its light. The kings of the earth bring the glory and honor of the nations into it. ²⁵ Its gates will in no way be shut by day (for there will be no night there), ²⁶and they shall bring the glory and the honor of the nations into it so that they may enter.²⁷ There will in no way enter into it anything profane, or one who causes an abomination or a lie, but only those who are written in the Lamb's book of life.

The River of Life

22 ¹He showed me a river of water of life, clear as crystal, proceeding out of the throne of God and of the Lamb, ² in the middle of its street. On this side of the river and on that was the tree of life, bearing twelve kinds of fruits, yielding its fruit every month. The leaves of the tree were for the healing of the nations. ³ There will be no curse any more. The throne of God and of the Lamb will be in it, and his servants serve him. ⁴ They will see his face, and his name will be on their foreheads. ⁵ There will be no night, and they need no lamp light; for the Lord God will illuminate them. They will reign forever and ever.

⁶ He said to me, "These words are faithful and true. The Lord God of the spirits of the prophets sent his angel to show to his bondservants the things which must happen soon."

Jesus Is Coming

⁷"Behold, I come quickly. Blessed is he who keeps the words of the prophecy of this book."

⁸ Now I, John, am the one who heard and saw these things. When I heard and saw, I fell down to worship before the feet of the angel who had shown me these things. ⁹ He said to me, "See you don't do it! I am a fellow bondservant with you and with your brothers, the prophets, and with those who keep the words of this book. Worship God!"

¹⁰ He said to me, "Don't seal up the words of the prophecy of this book, for the time is at hand. ¹¹ He who acts unjustly, let him act unjustly still. He who is filthy, let him be filthy still. He who is righteous, let him do righteousness still. He who is holy, let him be holy still."

¹² "Behold, I come quickly. My reward is with me, to repay to each man according to his work. ¹³ I am the Alpha and the Omega, the First and the Last, the Beginning and the End.

¹⁴ Blessed are those who do his commandments, that they may have the right to the tree of life, and may enter in by the gates into the city. ¹⁵ Outside are the dogs, the sorcerers, the sexually immoral, the murderers, the idolaters, and everyone who loves and practices falsehood.

¹⁶ I, Jesus, have sent my angel to testify [declare] these things to you for the assemblies. I am the root and the offspring of David; the Bright and Morning Star."

¹⁷ The Spirit and the bride say, "Come!" He who hears, let him say, "Come!" He who is thirsty, let him come. He who desires, let him take the water of life freely.

¹⁸ I testify [declare] to everyone who hears the words of the prophecy of this book, if anyone adds to them, may God add to him the plagues which are written in this book. ¹⁹ If anyone takes away from the words of the book of this prophecy, may God take away his part from the tree of life, and out of the holy city, which are written in this book.

²⁰ He who testifies [declares] these things says, "Yes, I come quickly." Amen! Yes, come, Lord Jesus.

²¹ The grace of the Lord Jesus Christ be with all the saints. Amen.

1. What will happen when the Lord Jesus comes again?

2. What happened to the first heaven and earth? What was coming down out of heaven?

3. What did the voice from the throne say? Who will be in the lake of burning sulfur?

4. Describe the Holy City. Why was there no temple in the city? Why was there no sun or moon? Who will enter the city?

5. Describe the river of life. The tree of life lines the river. Do you remember the tree of life mentioned in the Garden of Eden? What are the leaves of the tree for?

6. Who may enter the city? Who is left outside?

7. Who is coming soon, just as He promised?

8. Are you prepared to meet Him when he comes?

9. Is your name written in the Book of Life?

THE END

A Note From the Publishers

We hope that you have enjoyed your journey through Great Bible Truths. Our goal has been that through these many Bible selections you have met God and His Truth in some way. It is our hope that the reading of Great Bible Truths will have been a meaningful part of your life. For a complete understanding of the Scriptures, we encourage you to obtain a copy of the Bible or New Testament so that the Holy Spirit may continue to teach you from the Word of God.

May God bless you and lead you into all the truth.

Ephesians 3:20 Publishing Co.
Reaching America Ministries
4180 44th Street
Grand Rapids, MI 49512

Acknowledgments

The editors are grateful to the united efforts of many who contributed to this project. To Rev. John De Vries who devised the basic format and much of the material for this book. To Jan Underhill for a beautiful cover and excellent book design.

To Judy Arnett, Marion Van Den Heuvel who oversaw the manuscript for correct grammar and style for clarity. To my pastor friends whose input was invaluable.

To those donors who in faith provided funds for this initial printing.

To God, to Whom be the glory as His love for mankind is being known throughout the Americas.

The world can be a scary place!

We live in a world of increasing anxiety and loneliness. A world of increasing violence and economic hardship. A world of pandemics and natural disasters.

The Bible doesn't ignore the real world. It addresses every one of these topics. And many more. It tells us what to expect in life, what to expect in our lifetimes, and what to expect in our personal lives.

The Bible teaches how to face the world and live in confidence and peace!

We can help you apply the Bible to your life situations.

This QR Code links to an encrypted and safe web page designed for people who receive a copy of this book. On this page are several absolutely free resources. There is nothing to buy, no request for a donation, and no one will contact you unless you specifically ask. If you:

- are struggling and want to live with peace and confidence;
- are concerned about your spiritual life;
- need to talk to someone about something in your life;
- would like more free reading material about the Bible,
- would like to have a personal relationship with Jesus Christ;

Scan this code now!